While nothing can substitute for the expertise of your own doctor, no prescription is more valuable than knowledge.

*That is why I'm proud of the **Self-Care Advisor**. It's a quick and reliable resource that will help you find out more about your health concerns. And it will help you decide when you should call your doctor to seek medical attention.*

I have dedicated my life to ensuring that information about health is readily available, understandable, and accurate. This book is an example of that resolve. It was written by leading health journalists and educators with the purpose of providing helpful, easy-to-understand information of the highest quality.

*Keep the **Self-Care Advisor** in a place where you can find it easily. Each time you use it, I know you will benefit by learning how to take better care of yourself and your family.*

*Watch for our revised and updated editions. We are committed to keeping the **Self-Care Advisor** current and inclusive of the latest changes in medicine. Please remember always to consult your doctor whenever you need help making a health care decision.*

Taking an interest in and being committed to good health will pay dividends in better health. On behalf of TIME LIFE MEDICAL, I wish you well.

Sincerely,

C. Everett Koop, M.D.
Medical Director
TIME LIFE MEDICAL

Dr. Koop's Self-Care Advisor

THE ESSENTIAL HOME HEALTH GUIDE FOR YOU AND YOUR FAMILY

By the editors of Time Inc Health
and the staff of Time Life Medical

This book is not intended to replace common sense or a doctor's advice.
Given the differences of age, gender, and medical history, only your doctor can
render a definitive diagnosis and recommend treatment for you and your family.
The *Self-Care Advisor* is as accurate as its publisher, authors, and medical
consultants can make it; nevertheless, they disclaim all liability and cannot
be held responsible for any problems that may arise from its use.

First edition, second printing: May 1996

ISBN: 0-9644119-1-1

Medical Advisors

········◆········

C. Everett Koop, M.D.
Former United States Surgeon General
Medical Director, Time Life Medical

Florence Comite, M.D.
Founder, Women's Health at Yale
Associate Professor, Internal Medicine,
Pediatrics, Obstetrics and Gynecology
Yale University School of Medicine
Deputy Medical Director, Time Life Medical

Chairmen of the Advisory Board

David Chernof, M.D., F.A.C.P.
Associate Clinical Professor of Medicine
(Hematology/Oncology), University of
California Los Angeles Medical Center; former
Senior Medical Director, Blue Cross of California

Ronald J. Pion, M.D.
Clinical Professor (Obstetrics and
Gynecology), University of California
Los Angeles Medical Center; Chairman
and CEO, Lynx Worldwide, Inc.

Ernie Chaney, M.D.
Professor of Family and Community Medicine, University of Kansas School of Medicine–Wichita

Gregory Gray, M.D., Ph.D.
Associate Professor of Clinical Psychiatry and the Behavioral Sciences, University of Southern California School of Medicine; Chief of Psychiatry, Los Angeles County–University of Southern California Medical Center

Margaret Hammerschlag, M.D.
Professor of Pediatrics and Medicine, State University of New York, Health Sciences Center, Brooklyn

Stephen Hanauer, M.D.
Professor of Medicine and Clinical Pharmacology, University of Chicago Medical Center

John Heckenlively, M.D.
Professor of Ophthalmology, Jules Stein Eye Institute, University of California Los Angeles Medical Center

Ron Kaufman, M.D., F.A.C.P., F.A.C.R.
Associate Professor of Medicine (Rheumatology), University of Southern California School of Medicine; Chief of Staff, Los Angeles County–University of Southern California Medical Center

Denis Kollar, M.D.
Chief of Staff, Queen of the Valley Hospital, West Covina, California

John M. Luce, M.D.
Professor of Medicine and Anesthesiology, University of California San Francisco

Stephen N. Rous, M.D., F.A.C.S., F.A.A.P.
Professor of Surgery, Dartmouth Medical School; Chief of Urology, Veterans Affairs Medical Center, White River Junction, Vermont

Rowena Sobczyk, M.D.
Director, After Hours, Southeastern Health Services (Prucare), Atlanta, Georgia

Michael A. Weber, M.D.
Chairman, Department of Medicine, The Brookdale University Hospital and Medical Center; Professor of Medicine, State University of New York, Health Sciences Center, Brooklyn

Barry W. Wolcott, M.D.
Associate Professor of Military and Emergency Medicine, Uniformed Services University of the Health Sciences, Bethesda, Maryland

Gayle E. Woodson, M.D.
Professor of Otolaryngology, University of Tennessee, Memphis College of Medicine

♦

If you don't take care of
your body, where will you live?

~Aaron Goode, age 10

Contents

If you don't find what you're looking for here, turn to the index, which begins on page 310.

If you don't find what you're looking for here, turn to the index, which begins on page 310.

If you don't find what you're looking for here, turn to the index, which begins on page 310.

How This Book Can Help

◆

Of all the rules for taking care of your health, the most valuable may be one you seldom hear: Remember who's in charge. The important day-to-day decisions about your own health and vitality are made by one person—you.

Many people go to the doctor when they don't need to. Many do the opposite and wait too long. The *Self-Care Advisor* steers you clear of both extremes, showing what you can do to take care of yourself and your family and when it's time to call your doctor.

Covering more than 300 of the most common health concerns in the United States, the book is organized according to the parts of the body: If you know where you hurt, you can turn to that section in the table of contents. If you miss what you're looking for there, you'll find it in the extensive index beginning on page 310.

Most sections open with quick-reference charts. A chart may provide an immediate answer to your question about a symptom; it may direct you to an entry elsewhere in the book; or it may suggest calling your doctor.

If the book directs you to a doctor, you may need to call just for advice or for both advice and an appointment. And there will be times when you need to see the doctor right away. If so, the book will say so: "Call for an immediate appointment."

When you need emergency help, you'll see, "Call 911 or go to an emergency facility **immediately.**" (Some areas of the country don't have 911 service. If yours doesn't, be sure to write the local emergency number in the front of your phone book—or, better yet, on a label right on the telephone.) Use 911 only when you're fairly certain you need it; your health insurance probably doesn't cover an ambulance trip for a nonemergency situation. Use the same guideline for going to an emergency facility; otherwise, you may find yourself facing a longer wait than you would in a doctor's office.

Thanks to our board of medical advisors and to the hundreds of other doctors who helped with the *Self-Care Advisor,* you can trust the information it contains. Of course, if your doctor's advice conflicts with advice you find in the book, listen to your doctor; he or she should know your medical history and specific needs. In the end, though, it is *your* health, and there's no substitute for your full, informed participation in the decisions that you and your family will be making. We hope that this book becomes a trusted companion along the way and that it helps you enjoy a long and healthy life.

Emergency & First Aid

◆

I n this section, you'll find situations that can be life-threatening and that call for fast action. Some of the procedures require a bit of careful reading, especially those on pages 14 to 19, but it's well worth going over those pages now. You don't need to memorize them—but if you're at least familiar with the techniques and actions they describe, you may be the one who saves a life. Start with the ABCs, CPR, the Recovery Position, and Shock, because they're important parts of many emergency treatments.

From page 19 on, emergencies are arranged in alphabetical order. Emergency procedures are continually updated; check with your local chapter of the American Heart Association or American Red Cross every year or so to make sure the information is still current.

It's easy to set yourself up with the basic tools for first aid. They're listed in the box on page 16.

At many points in this chapter, you will be advised to call 911. If your area does not have 911 service, write your local emergency number below, and dial it whenever the instructions say to call 911. Better yet, put the number right beside your phone.

My local emergency number: _____

CPR

Cardiopulmonary Resuscitation

SIGNS AND SYMPTOMS

Signs of cardiac or respiratory arrest:
■ Pale or bluish face.
■ Chest doesn't rise or fall; no breath.
■ No heartbeat or pulse.
■ Loss of consciousness.

CHECKING THE ABCs

Airway, Breathing, Circulation

A

Airway—open it. Gently tilt back the person's head and lift the chin. This will enable the lungs to get air through the nose and mouth. **Caution:** If you suspect a head, neck, or back injury, do not tilt the head; moving it could cause further injury. (See page 37.)

B

Breathing—look, listen, and feel for it. Look for the person's chest to rise. Put your ear to the mouth to listen and feel for exhaled air, since chest movement alone might not mean breathing.

C

Circulation—check for a pulse. Gently press two fingers—but not your thumb—on the person's neck between the Adam's apple, or voice box, and the muscle on the side of the neck, and feel for a pulse. If you're checking for an **infant's pulse** (up to age one): Gently press two fingers—not your thumb—on the inside of the infant's arm, between the elbow and armpit. If you still do not feel a pulse, put your ear to the chest and listen for a heartbeat.

When the heart and lungs stop working, the treatment is cardiopulmonary resuscitation (CPR), a combination of rescue breathing and chest compressions. The goals are to open the airway, breathe for the victim until he or she can breathe independently, reestablish circulation, and keep oxygen going to the brain until help arrives.

For practice, have someone read the instructions below aloud as you follow them.

Cautions:
➤ CPR can cause serious injury. If you have no CPR training, ask if anyone nearby has been trained before you begin.
➤ Do not perform chest compressions unless both breathing and heartbeat have stopped. Use only rescue breathing if the person still has a pulse.

WHAT TO DO

For an adult or a child over eight (for an **infant,** see page 16; for a **child one to eight,** see page 17):
➤ Check for breathing. Look for the victim's chest to rise, and put your ear to his or her mouth, listening and feeling for air.
➤ If the victim is not breathing, call 911 and begin treatment. **Caution:** If you suspect **choking,** see page 25. If you suspect a **head, neck, or back injury,** see page 37; moving may cause further injury.
➤ Lay the person flat on his or her back. Kneel beside the person, halfway between the head and chest, facing the head.
➤ Turn the head to one side. Looking into the mouth, slide your index finger inside

each cheek to the base of the tongue and back out to sweep out loose objects.

➤ Gently tilt back the head, and lift the chin to open the airway.

Rescue breathing:

➤ If the person is still not breathing, begin rescue breathing. Pinch his or her nose shut, put your mouth over his or her mouth, and seal your lips tightly against the skin. Breathe into the mouth for 1½ to 2 seconds, watching for the person's chest to rise. Remove your mouth, and let the chest fall. Repeat with another breath. **Caution:** Breathe only hard enough and long enough to make the chest rise. If air gets into the stomach, it can cause vomiting.

➤ If the chest does not rise, gently tilt the head farther back. Again, give 2 breaths.

➤ Now check for a pulse. Gently press two fingers—not your thumb—on the neck between the Adam's apple, or voice box, and the muscle on the side of the neck.

➤ If the person has a pulse but is still not breathing, continue rescue breathing. Give 1 breath every 5 seconds, and check the pulse every 12 breaths. Continue until medical help arrives.

Chest compressions:

➤ If you feel no pulse, prepare to give chest compressions. **Caution:** Be certain the victim has no pulse before starting.

➤ Kneeling right next to the person, position yourself so that your hands are on his or her breastbone and your shoulders are directly over your hands.

➤ Using the index and middle fingers of one hand, touch the notch where the ribs meet the bottom of the breastbone.

➤ Place the heel of your second hand beside your fingers, closer to the victim's head, on the midline of the breastbone.

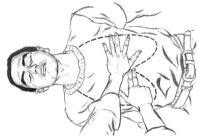

➤ Now that your second hand is in place on the person's breastbone, lift your first

hand and place it on top of the second hand. Interlace the fingers of both hands, and raise them up so that you leave only the heel of your second hand on the person's chest. Keep your arms straight and elbows locked.

➤ Press down forcefully to depress the breastbone 1½ to 2 inches. Release the pressure, but don't lift your hands off the person's chest. Give 15 compressions, at the count of "one and two and three and four...," pressing down each time you say a number. **Caution:** Use short thrusts, straight down. Do not rock your body back and forth.

➤ Repeat rescue breathing—2 breaths of 1½ to 2 seconds each.

➤ Repeat the cycle of 2 breaths and 15 chest compressions four times. Then recheck for a pulse.

➤ If the person still has no pulse and is not breathing, repeat the series of breaths, chest compressions, and pulse checking. Continue until the victim has a pulse and begins to breathe on his or her own, or until help arrives.

(CPR for infants and children, next page)

CPR FOR INFANTS
UP TO AGE ONE

Sweeping the mouth: Turn the infant's head to one side. Looking into the mouth, slide your little finger down the inside of the cheek to the base of the tongue and back out to sweep out any loose objects. Gently lift the chin to open the airway.

Rescue breathing: If the infant is not breathing, keep the chin lifted with one hand and tightly seal your lips over the mouth and nose. Breathe into the child's mouth and nose for 1 to 1½ seconds, watching for the chest to rise. Remove your mouth, and let the chest fall. Repeat with another breath. Breathe forcefully but not so hard that air goes into the stomach. If the infant still does not breathe, give 1 breath every 3 seconds and check for a pulse or heartbeat every 20 breaths.

Checking for a pulse: Gently press two fingers—not your thumb—on the inside of the infant's arm, between the elbow and armpit. If you do not feel a pulse, listen for a heartbeat.

Preparing for chest compressions: If the infant has no pulse, prepare to give chest compressions. **Caution:** Be certain the infant has no pulse before starting. Place the index finger of the hand nearest the head on the breastbone, in the center of an imaginary line between the nipples. Place two or three fingers of the other hand next to and below the index finger, then remove the index finger. Use your free hand to help keep the infant's head tilted backward.

Chest compressions: Bend your elbow slightly, and press straight down with your fingers, depressing the infant's breastbone ½ to 1 inch. Release the pressure, but don't remove your fingers. Give 5 chest compressions, at the count of "one, two, three...," pressing down each time you say a number.

Do not rock back and forth. Repeat a 1-breath, 5-compression cycle 20 times; then recheck for a pulse. Continue until the infant has a pulse and begins to breathe on his or her own, or until medical help arrives.

A BASIC FIRST-AID KIT

Every house should have at least one well-equipped first-aid kit, including an emergency handbook, and every member of the household should know where it is. Keep another kit in the trunk of your car, especially if you travel frequently. You can buy a first-aid kit at a drugstore or make one yourself. Either way, be sure that your kit includes the following items:

Gauze pads and rolls of gauze
(assorted sizes)
Adhesive tape
Adhesive bandages
Triangular bandage
Cold pack ("chemical ice")
Plastic bags
Disposable gloves
Antiseptic towelettes
Small flashlight and extra batteries
Scissors and tweezers
Emergency thermal blanket
Syrup of ipecac
Antiseptic ointment
Activated charcoal
Personal medications and
emergency phone numbers

Source: American Red Cross

RECOVERY POSITION

Place an unconscious but breathing person in the recovery position to keep the airway open. **Caution:** Do not place someone in this position if you suspect a **head, neck, or back injury** (see page 37). Moving the victim could cause further injury.

❶ Kneeling beside the victim, turn his or her head toward you. Tuck the arm closest to you under the person's body, keeping it straight. Put the other arm across the chest. Place the far ankle over the near ankle.
❷ Then, while supporting the head with one hand, grip the person's clothes at the far hip with the other hand and pull him or her gently over onto the stomach. Support the person's body with your knees as it rolls.
❸ Carefully tilt the person's chin back to open the airway. Then bend the near arm and knee to prop up the body and make breathing easier. Make sure the other arm is out from under the body, lying straight beside it.

Check frequently to be sure the person is still breathing.

CPR FOR CHILDREN AGES ONE TO EIGHT

Sweeping the mouth: Turn the child's head to one side. Looking into the mouth, slide your index finger inside the cheek to the base of the tongue and back out, to sweep out loose objects. Gently tilt the head back, and lift the chin to open the airway.

Rescue breathing: If the child is not breathing, pinch the nose shut and seal your lips tightly around the child's mouth. Breathe into the mouth for 1 to 1½ seconds, watching for the chest to rise. Remove your mouth, and let the chest fall. Repeat with another breath. If the child is still not breathing, give 1 breath every 3 seconds, and check for a pulse every 20 breaths.

Checking for a pulse: Gently press two fingers between the voice box and the muscle on the side of the neck. Feel for a pulse.

Preparing for chest compressions: If you are certain the child has no pulse, prepare to give chest compressions. Position yourself next to the child so your shoulders are directly over the chest. Using the hand nearest the child's head, touch your middle and index fingers to the notch where the ribs meet the bottom of the breastbone. Place the heel of your other hand beside and above your fingers, toward the child's head, on the midline of the breastbone. (You will cross your hands.) Take away your first hand and use it to keep the head tilted back. Only the heel of the other hand should now be touching the child's chest. Keep your arm straight and elbow locked.

Chest compressions: Press down forcefully with the heel of your hand to depress the child's breastbone 1 to 1½ inches. Release the pressure after a moment, but don't remove your hand. Give 5 chest compressions, counting "one and two and…," pressing down each time you say a number. Do not rock back and forth. Repeat a cycle of 1 breath and 5 compressions 20 times, then recheck for a pulse. Continue until the child has a pulse and begins to breathe on his or her own, or until medical help arrives.

Shock results when vital organs are deprived of blood, usually by sudden, serious injury or illness. The symptoms are the body's way of responding to blood loss. Shock can be fatal if untreated and requires immediate emergency care.

Signs and Symptoms

- Weak, rapid, or irregular pulse.
- Cold, clammy, pale, or bluish skin.
- Rapid, shallow breathing.
- Confusion, anxiety, and/or loss of consciousness.

What to Do

Caution: If you think the victim might have a fractured pelvis or a **head, neck, or back injury** (see page 37), do not move him or her unless you absolutely must. Moving may cause further injury.

➤ Call 911 **immediately.**

➤ Check the victim's **ABCs** (see box on page 14): Lift the chin to open the airway, and check for breathing and pulse.

If the person is not breathing or does not have a pulse or heartbeat:

➤ Begin **CPR** (see page 14).

If the person is breathing and has a pulse:

➤ Lay the victim on his or her back, with the feet elevated 12 inches, so that blood can flow toward the brain.

➤ Recheck the person's airway. If he or she begins to choke or vomit, turn the head to one side so that vomit will not block the airway.

➤ Try to determine the cause of shock, and perform first aid for the appropriate emergency. If the victim is bleeding externally, apply pressure to the wound. Watch for signs of **internal bleeding** (see opposite page).

➤ Reassure the person, and make him or her warm and as comfortable as possible. Loosen any tight clothing, and cover the person with a blanket, sheet, or additional clothing.

Cautions:

➤ Do not use an electric blanket or any other form of direct heat.

➤ Do not place a pillow under the head, since a bend in the neck might block the airway.

➤ Do not give anything to eat or drink.

SHOCK FROM AN ALLERGIC REACTION

Anaphylactic shock is a severe, often immediate, and sometimes fatal allergic reaction to a bee sting or to certain foods or drugs.

Signs and Symptoms

- Itching or hives.
- Flushed face or warm skin.
- Dizziness.
- Swollen face or tongue.
- Nausea, vomiting, or abdominal cramps.
- Wheezing or difficulty breathing.
- Increased heart rate.
- Loss of consciousness.

What to Do

➤ Call 911 **immediately,** and treat the victim as you would for **shock** (see **what to do,** left).

➤ Try to keep the person calm.

➤ Determine if the person was stung by an insect (see page 20). If it was a bee sting, carefully scrape the stinger (if there is one) off the skin, using a knife blade, the edge of a credit card, or a fingernail. Do not use tweezers or push down on the stinger; this may force more venom into the skin.

➤ Some people know they have severe allergic reactions and may have emergency supplies on hand. If so, help the person take the medicine, which may be a shot of epinephrine. Follow the instructions included with the medication.

SHOCK FROM INTERNAL BLEEDING

Internal bleeding is a frequent cause of shock.

Signs and Symptoms
- Coughing up or vomiting blood.
- Rectal or vaginal bleeding, abnormally heavy menstrual bleeding, or blood in the urine.
- Bruises, swelling, hardness, or tenderness in the abdomen or other areas.
- Skull, chest, or abdominal wounds.
- Weak, rapid pulse.
- Shortness of breath or shallow breathing.
- Dilated pupils.
- Cool, clammy, pale, or bluish skin.
- Intense thirst.
- Dizziness, confusion, or loss of consciousness.

What to Do
Caution: If you suspect a **head, neck, or back injury,** see page 37. Moving the victim could cause further injury.
- Call 911 **immediately.**
- Check the person's **ABCs** (see box on page 14): Lift the chin to open the airway, then check for breathing and a pulse. If the person is not breathing or does not have a pulse or a heartbeat, begin **CPR** (see page 14). While you wait for medical help, periodically recheck the ABCs.
- Keep the person calm and still. Do not give him or her anything to eat or drink.
- If the victim's arm or leg is swollen or misshapen, immobilize it (see **fractures and dislocations,** page 35).
- Watch for signs of **shock** (see **signs and symptoms,** far left) while you wait for medical help. If necessary, begin first aid for shock.

Animal Bites

- Control any bleeding by applying direct pressure to the wound until the bleeding stops, using a clean cloth (or, if necessary, your hand). Hold the edges of the flesh together. (See **cuts, scrapes, and wounds,** page 27.)
- If the wound is minor, clean it thoroughly with soap and water, then apply antibiotic ointment and a bandage.
- If the bite is deep, do not attempt to clean the wound after controlling the bleeding. Call your doctor for an immediate appointment. If it's a deep bite, it may require stitches and could become infected; a tetanus shot or rabies treatment may be necessary.
- Report any wild animal bites to your doctor and local health department or animal control center.
- If possible (whether the animal is wild or domestic), have the animal confined by authorities and checked for rabies. Unvaccinated pets—along with stray cats and dogs, and wild animals such as raccoons, bats, foxes, and skunks—may carry rabies. Infection from rabies is rare but can be fatal if untreated.

Cautions:
- If an animal is foaming or drooling from the mouth, acting strangely, or biting without provocation, it may be rabid. Contact your doctor and local health department for advice.
- Do not touch, feed, or try to capture wild animals.
- Watch for signs of infection in a bite wound: redness, pain, swelling, tenderness, pus, hot skin, fever. Call your doctor for advice if they develop.

Appendicitis

- Abdominal tenderness and pain that usually starts in the upper stomach and moves to the lower-right abdomen within hours. The pain often increases until it becomes sharp and severe.
- Vomiting, nausea, or loss of appetite.
- Constipation or, less frequently, diarrhea.
- Low fever.

If untreated, an inflamed and infected appendix (a condition known as appendicitis) often ruptures after 24 hours and spreads infection to other abdominal organs. To prevent this, surgery is required to remove the appendix before it ruptures.

Pain in the abdomen may also signal other disorders, such as **food poisoning** (see page 35), **gallstones** (see page 119), **kidney stones** (see page 132), urinary tract infections (see **painful urination,** page 134), and intestinal obstruction (see **abdominal pain** chart, page 113).

WHAT TO DO

- ➤ If abdominal pain persists for more than four hours, call a doctor for emergency advice. If a doctor isn't available, call 911 or go to an emergency facility.
- ➤ Keep the person quiet and as comfortable as possible.
- ➤ Monitor the symptoms for 4 to 12 hours, being alert to severe pain in the lower-right abdomen. Some symptoms of appendicitis may resemble those of severe indigestion or stomach flu, so the type and location of the abdominal pain are important signals to watch for. (In some cases, however, the pain never moves to the lower-right abdomen.)

Cautions:
- ➤ If the person is constipated, do not give him or her laxatives, which can indirectly cause the appendix to rupture.
- ➤ Do not use an electric blanket or apply direct heat to the abdomen.
- ➤ Be aware that taking painkillers or antibiotics can mask appendicitis symptoms.

Bee and Wasp Stings

SIGNS AND SYMPTOMS

Minor stings:
- Pain at the sting site that may persist for several hours.
- Swelling, redness, and itching or burning at the sting site.

Insect sting allergies:
- Rapid swelling of the tongue, throat, eyes, or lips.
- Difficulty breathing.
- Severe itching or hives.
- Cramping.
- Numbness.
- Reddish rash.
- Dizziness or loss of consciousness.

Multiple stings:
- Swelling, redness, and pain.
- Headache.
- Muscle cramps.
- Fever.
- Drowsiness or loss of consciousness.

WHAT TO DO

Minor stings:
- ➤ Remove any stinger, scraping it out with a knife, the edge of a credit card, or a fingernail. But do not use tweezers or push on the stinger; this may squeeze more poison into the skin.
- ➤ Wash the area with soap and water.
- ➤ Apply a cold compress.

Allergic reactions to a sting or stings:
- ➤ Call 911 or go to an emergency facility **immediately.**
- ➤ If waiting for medical help to arrive, watch for the symptoms of **anaphylactic shock** (see page 18), such as itching, flushed or swollen face, dizziness, nausea,

or loss of consciousness. If necessary, begin **CPR** (see page 14).

➤ If an emergency kit containing epinephrine to counter allergic reactions is available, administer the drug. **Caution:** Do not give epinephrine if the person is elderly or has a heart condition.

➤ If the stinger is still in the skin, scrape it out with a knife, the edge of a credit card, or a fingernail. Do not use tweezers or push on the stinger; this may squeeze more poison into the skin.

Blow to the Abdomen

SIGNS AND SYMPTOMS

- Hard or tender abdomen.
- Vomiting, nausea, and/or loss of appetite.
- Bleeding from the rectum or vagina, or blood in the urine.
- Cold, clammy skin.
- Rapid, weak pulse.
- Uneven (rapid or slow) breathing.
- Confusion or memory loss.

Watch for signs of abdominal injuries following any accident, especially an automobile, skiing, or bicycling accident. A blow to the abdomen may lead to **internal bleeding** (see page 19) and **shock** (see page 18), a life-threatening condition.

WHAT TO DO

➤ Call 911 or go to an emergency facility **immediately.**

➤ Check the victim's **ABCs** (see box on page 14): Lift the chin to open the airway, then check for breathing and pulse.

➤ If the person is not breathing or does not have a pulse, begin **CPR** (see page 14).

➤ Look for signs of **shock** (see page 18), such as weak, rapid pulse; cold, clammy skin; rapid, shallow breathing; and confusion or anxiety. If symptoms are present, begin first aid for shock.

➤ If awaiting medical help, lay the victim down with the feet elevated above the heart. Keep him or her warm with a blanket, and loosen any tight clothing. **Caution:** Do not give the person anything to eat or drink.

Bruises

SIGNS AND SYMPTOMS

- Red or black-and-blue discoloring of skin.
- Swelling.
- Pain.

Falling or being hit can lead to bruises—a black eye is one common type—which indicate bleeding and damage to the tissues below the skin. Most bruises heal on their own, but first aid can speed up the process.

WHAT TO DO

➤ To reduce pain and swelling, apply a cold compress—a plastic bag of ice cubes wrapped in a damp cloth, a package of frozen vegetables, or simply a cold, damp cloth—to the bruised area within 15 minutes of injury, if possible. Leave it on for 10 to 30 minutes at a time, and leave it off for 30 to 45 minutes between applications. Repeat several times over the next three days. Apply only moderate pressure.

➤ If the bruise is on an arm or a leg, rest the limb for one to three days. If you can, elevate the bruised area to reduce fluid build-up and swelling.

Call your doctor for advice:

➤ If the bruise doesn't fade or go away after 14 days.

➤ If signs of infection (increased pain, swelling, redness, pus, or unexplained fever) appear.

➤ If vision problems accompany a black eye; this may indicate eye damage.

➤ If a bruise shows up for no apparent reason; this could signal another medical condition.

Burns

the nerve endings. **Fourth-degree burns** go through all the layers of skin to the tissues and organs below.

SIGNS AND SYMPTOMS

- Redness, charring, or a dry, white mark.
- Pain.
- Blisters.
- Swelling.

Depending on their depth (not the area they cover or their painfulness), burns are ranked as first-, second-, third-, or fourth-degree. **First-degree burns** sear only the outer layer of the skin, but can be very painful. **Second-degree burns** injure both the outer and inner layers of skin and often produce blisters, swelling, and severe pain. **Third-degree burns**—typified by charred or white skin—are painless because they burn through all the layers of the skin, including

WHAT TO DO

➤ Remove the victim from the source of the burns. If the person's clothing is on fire, lay him or her on the ground so the burning clothing is on top. Smother the flames with a blanket, coat, or any other cloth that is handy, or tell the person to roll over slowly. **Caution:** If you suspect a **head, neck, or back injury** (see page 37), do not move the person unless absolutely necessary. Moving him or her may cause further injury.

➤ Call 911 or go to an emergency facility **immediately** if the burns cover more than a small area; involve the face, hands, feet, or genital area; or appear to be third- or fourth-degree.

➤ If the person appears to be unconscious, check his or her **ABCs** (see box on page

CHEMICAL BURNS

Signs and Symptoms
- Burn marks or blisters.
- Headache or abdominal pain.
- Difficulty breathing.
- Seizures.
- Dizziness or loss of consciousness.

What to Do
➤ Move the victim so he or she is away from the chemical.

➤ If it is a dry chemical, such as lime, brush off any particles. Protect your hands when doing so.

➤ Place the burned area under running water for at least 15 minutes to dilute the chemical. **Caution:** When mixed with water, certain chemicals cause worse burns. If you know you have spilled metal compounds on yourself, flush the area with oil. For carbolic acid, use alcohol.

➤ If the burn is in the eye, pour water

over the open eye from the inside corner to the outside. (See **eye injuries,** page 32.)

➤ As you flush the burn, remove any of the person's jewelry or clothing that may have come in contact with the chemical.

➤ Cover the burn with a sterile, dry bandage.

➤ If the person is unconscious, check his or her **ABCs** (see box on page 14): Lift the chin to open the airway, then check for breathing and pulse.

➤ If the person is not breathing or does not have a pulse or heartbeat, call 911 and begin **CPR** (see page 14).

➤ A person who has an eye burn should go to an emergency facility **immediately.** For any other chemical burn, call a doctor for an emergency appointment. If a doctor isn't available, call 911 or go to an emergency facility.

14): Lift the chin to open the airway, then check for breathing and pulse. If the person is not breathing or has no pulse, begin **CPR** (see page 14).

➤ Remove any clothing or jewelry from the burned area before swelling begins. **Cautions:** Do not remove any clothing that is stuck to the burned skin. Do not breathe or cough on the burned skin.

➤ If the burned area is smaller than the size of the victim's chest, loosely cover it with a sheet or towel that has been soaked in cool water and wrung out, or hold the burned skin under cool running water or in a bowl of cool water for about 10 minutes, or until the pain stops or decreases.

➤ For burns larger than the size of the victim's chest, loosely cover the burned skin with a clean, dry cloth. If fluid oozes through the cloth, place another cloth over it.

➤ To reduce swelling, elevate a burned arm or leg so that it's higher than the level of the person's heart.

➤ Unless the victim is vomiting or has lost consciousness, you may give him or her small sips of water.

➤ If the person has lost consciousness but is still breathing, support the head and roll him or her onto the stomach, into the **recovery position** (see box on page 17).

Cautions:

➤ Do not put the person into the recovery position if you suspect a **head, neck, or back injury** (see page 37), or if the burn is on the chest or elsewhere on the front of the body.

➤ Do not apply any ointments, lotions, butter, baking soda, or ice to the burn.

➤ Do not break any blisters.

➤ If the burned area is larger than the size of the victim's chest, do not apply water (this could lead to hypothermia).

➤ Do not use adhesive bandages or cotton balls, which stick to the skin.

Chest Pain

SIGNS AND SYMPTOMS

■ Dull, sharp, crushing, stabbing, or severe burning pain, or pressure or tightness in the chest. Pain may spread to the jaw, neck, back, or arms, especially the left arm.

Depending on the type of pain and the accompanying symptoms, chest pain may indicate a variety of ailments, including **heart attack** (see page 38), angina, a collapsed lung, pleurisy (inflammation of the sac around the lungs), an injured rib or a pulled chest muscle, an **ulcer** (see page 130), **heartburn** (see page 121), or **anxiety** (see page 202). Chest pain that lasts longer than a few minutes should never be ignored.

WHAT TO DO

➤ If you suspect a **heart attack** (see page 38), call 911 or go to an emergency facility **immediately.**

➤ For more information, see **chest pain** chart, page 103.

Childbirth

Emergency

SIGNS AND SYMPTOMS

■ Uterine contractions less than three minutes apart.
■ An overwhelming need to push.
■ Feeling or seeing the head of the baby between the legs.

WHAT TO DO

Since childbirth is a natural process, it's best not to interfere unless necessary. Do not try to delay delivery; do not let the woman cross her legs; and do not try to push the baby back into her vagina.

Before delivery:

➤ If there is a liquid discharge from the woman's vagina, call a doctor for emergency advice. If a doctor isn't available, call 911 or go to an emergency facility **immediately.**

➤ If uterine contractions are regular and occurring three to five minutes apart, call 911 or go to an emergency facility **immediately.**

➤ If there is no time to get to the hospital and medical help has not yet arrived, keep the woman warm and as comfortable as possible. On a large, flat area, put down a plastic sheet (if available), then a clean sheet (or newspapers, if a sheet isn't available) and pillows or other supporting materials for her to lie on. Gather some clean, dry towels.

➤ Help the woman remove any clothing below her belly.

➤ Keep her calm. If she is in pain, reassure her and tell her to take deep, slow breaths.

➤ Wash your hands with soap and water. Scrub under your fingernails, and remove all of your jewelry.

➤ If possible, boil some string and a pair of scissors to sterilize them.

During delivery:

➤ Don't be alarmed if you see bloody fluid (this is normal). But if the woman bleeds more than one to two cups before, during, or after delivery, call 911 **immediately,** if you have not already done so.

➤ Watch for the baby's head to appear in the vagina. This means birth is about to happen.

➤ Support the baby's head as it and the shoulders emerge, but do not pull. The baby's body should naturally turn to one side and slide out. Since the baby will be slippery, use a clean, dry towel to catch hold of him or her.

➤ If the baby's shoulders seem stuck during delivery, gently press on the area just above the woman's pubic hair.

➤ When the head emerges, make sure the umbilical cord is not wrapped around the neck. If it is, hook your finger underneath it and gently slip it over the baby's head.

➤ If the baby does not emerge headfirst, gently press on the area just above the pubic hair to hasten delivery. Support the baby's body as it emerges. **Caution:** If the baby's head does not emerge, gently lift the baby's body upward. Do not pull the baby out.

After delivery:

➤ If the baby is still enclosed in the amniotic sac, tear the sac open with your fingers.

➤ To drain fluids from the baby's mouth and nose, hold him or her so that the head is lower than the feet, with the head turned to the side.

➤ Wipe the baby's mouth and nose with a clean, dry towel.

➤ If the baby is not breathing, hold him or her so that the head is lower than the feet, then tap the soles of the feet. Immediately rub the baby's back. If the baby does not start to breathe after one minute, begin **infant CPR** (see page 16).

➤ If the baby is breathing, wipe him or her off with a clean, dry towel. Do not wash off any white material that covers the body.

➤ Wrap the baby in a clean, dry towel, making sure not to cover the face.

➤ If medical help is on the way, and if the baby is breathing and is close to full term, do not cut the umbilical cord. Otherwise, when the umbilical cord is no longer moving, use sterilized string to tightly tie off the cord, about 4 inches from the baby's navel. Use sterilized scissors to cut off the umbilical cord an inch or so beyond the knot, toward the mother.

➤ Save the placenta after it slides out (usually about 10 to 20 minutes after delivery). Place it in a container to give to medical personnel. **Caution:** Do not pull on the umbilical cord or otherwise try to get the placenta out.

➤ After the placenta slides out, massage the mother's lower abdomen to help control any bleeding.

➤ Keep both mother and baby warm until medical help arrives.

Choking

SIGNS AND SYMPTOMS

- Gagging.
- Coughing, or difficulty breathing or speaking.
- Clutching the neck with the hands.
- Bluish skin or bulging eyes.
- Seizures or loss of consciousness.

WHAT TO DO

➤ Call 911 **immediately.**

➤ Looking into the person's mouth, slide your index finger down the inside of the cheek to the base of the tongue and back out, to sweep out any loose objects that you can see and retrieve easily. **Cautions:** Do not try to retrieve an object you can't see that may be lodged in the person's throat. This might force the object farther down the airway. If you suspect a **head, neck, or back injury,** see page 37. It may be dangerous to move the victim.

➤ Give abdominal thrusts (the Heimlich maneuver): Standing behind the victim, place your arms around the waist. Make a fist with one hand, and place it in the middle of the abdomen, just above the navel and below the ribs. Hold your fist with your other hand.

Give five quick, repeated thrusts, pushing inward and upward. Pause. Continue with five thrusts, a pause, and five more thrusts until the object is dislodged or until the victim loses consciousness. **Cautions:** Do not use the Heimlich maneuver if the person can talk, cough, or make noise. If the person is pregnant or obese, place your fist on the middle of the breastbone.

➤ If the person loses consciousness, lay him or her flat on the back.

➤ Check the victim's mouth: Hold the tongue and lift the chin. Looking into the mouth, slide your index finger down the inside of the cheek to the base of the tongue and back out, to sweep out any loose objects. Remember, do not try to retrieve an object lodged in the throat unless you can see it and grasp it.

➤ Open the airway by gently tilting back the head and lifting the chin.

➤ Look, listen, and feel for breathing. Be sure to put your ear to the person's mouth; chest movement alone might not mean breathing.

➤ If the person is breathing, give first aid for **loss of consciousness** (see page 34).

➤ If the person is not breathing, begin rescue breathing: Pinch the victim's nose shut, and seal your lips tightly over the person's mouth. Watching the person's chest, breathe into his or her mouth hard enough and long enough to make the chest rise. Remove your mouth, and watch for the chest to fall. Repeat with another breath. If the person's chest does not rise with each breath, gently tilt the head farther back and again give two full breaths.

➤ If the chest still does not rise, give five abdominal thrusts: With the person still lying on his or her back, position the heel of

WHAT TO DO FOR A CHOKING INFANT (UP TO AGE ONE)

❶ Call 911 **immediately.**
❷ Then give five back blows: Lay the infant face down on your lower arm, supporting your arm with your leg. Hold the baby's chin between your index finger and thumb, keeping the head lower than the body. Forcefully strike the back five times between the shoulder blades with the heel of your other hand.

❸ If the object is not dislodged by the back blows, give chest thrusts: Turn the infant onto his or her back, with the head lower than the rest of the body. Place your index and middle fingers on the infant's breastbone (in the center of the chest), just below the nipples. Give five quick thrusts.

❹ Repeat sets of five back blows and five chest thrusts until the object is dislodged or the infant loses consciousness.

If the infant loses consciousness, look into his or her mouth and sweep the inside of the mouth with your little finger. Then gently tilt the head back and lift the chin. If you see an object and believe that you can easily remove it, slide your finger down the inside of the cheek to the base of the tongue, and sweep it out. **Caution:** Do not try to retrieve an object you can't see that is lodged in the infant's throat. You may push it farther down.
❺ If the infant isn't breathing, begin rescue breathing: Keep the infant's head tilted with one hand and the chin lifted with the other.

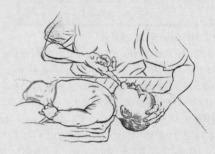

Tightly seal your lips around the infant's mouth and nose, then give two breaths, removing your mouth between breaths. Breathe forcefully, but only long enough and hard enough to make the chest rise. If the infant's chest does not rise with each breath, gently tilt the head farther back and try again to give two breaths.

❻ If the infant's chest does not rise with the additional breaths, continue giving breaths, back blows, and chest thrusts, and sweeping the mouth. Repeat a sequence of two breaths, five back blows, five chest thrusts, and a sweep of the mouth until the object is dislodged or medical help arrives.

one of your hands against the middle of the abdomen, just above the navel and below the ribs. Place your other hand on top of the first. Give quick thrusts, pressing your hands inward and upward, aiming toward the spine. **Caution:** Do not press to either side as you thrust.

➤ Check the mouth again (see above), make sure the airway is open, and breathe twice again into the person's mouth.

➤ If the chest does not rise, repeat the sequence of five abdominal thrusts, a sweep of the mouth, and two full breaths. Continue until the object is dislodged or medical help arrives.

➤ If the object is dislodged from the throat but the victim is not breathing, begin **CPR** (see page 14).

WHAT TO DO IF YOU ARE CHOKING AND ALONE

➤ If you can get to a phone and can talk, call 911 **immediately.**

➤ If you can't, make a fist with one hand and place it in the middle of your abdomen, just above the navel and below the ribs. Hold your fist with your other hand. Keeping your elbows out, press your fist with a quick thrust into your abdomen and upward, aiming toward your spine. Give yourself abdominal thrusts until the object is dislodged.

➤ Alternatively, bend over the back of a tall chair, countertop, or some other firm, hard object, and press forcefully.

➤ If you see an object lodged in your throat and can sweep it out with your finger, do so. But do not try to retrieve an object you can't see. You may force it farther down your airway.

➤ If you're successful in dislodging the object, call your doctor for advice. If he or she isn't available, go to an emergency facility; there may be complications from either the choking episode or the first aid.

Cuts, Scrapes, and Wounds

Almost no one goes through life without a few scrapes, cuts, and punctures. Scrapes can be painful but generally cause only minor bleeding. Cuts—usually from knives, broken glass, or other sharp-edged objects—often lead to heavy bleeding. Puncture wounds do not usually bleed severely, unless they rupture major blood vessels or organs, but they are prone to infection.

WHAT TO DO

➤ Call a doctor for emergency advice if a wound is deeper than ¼ inch and longer than 1 inch; if it has jagged edges; if it's located on the face, hand, foot, knee, or elbow; or if it doesn't stop bleeding after five minutes of applying direct pressure. If a doctor isn't available, go to an emergency facility.

Severe bleeding:

➤ Call 911 or go to an emergency facility **immediately.**

➤ Lay the victim flat on his or her back. **Cautions:** If you suspect a **head, neck, or back injury,** see page 37; moving the person may cause further injury. If the person is bleeding around a broken bone, see **fractures and dislocations,** page 35.

➤ If possible, position the person so that the wound is higher than the heart, to reduce blood flow.

➤ If the victim is unconscious, check the **ABCs** (see box on page 14): Lift the chin to open the airway, then check for breathing and pulse. Also watch for symptoms of

shock (see page 18): weak, rapid pulse; rapid, shallow breathing; cold, clammy skin; confusion or loss of consciousness.

➤ If the victim is not breathing or does not have a pulse or heartbeat, begin **CPR** (see page 14).

➤ Remove any visible objects from the wound, if this can be done easily. **Caution:** Do not remove any objects that are stuck or embedded in the wound, especially in the chest or back. Do not probe the wound.

➤ Apply direct pressure to the wound, using a clean cloth (or, if necessary, your hand). Hold the edges of the flesh together. Maintain pressure until the bleeding stops. **Cautions:** If there is an embedded object, use a clean cloth or your hands to

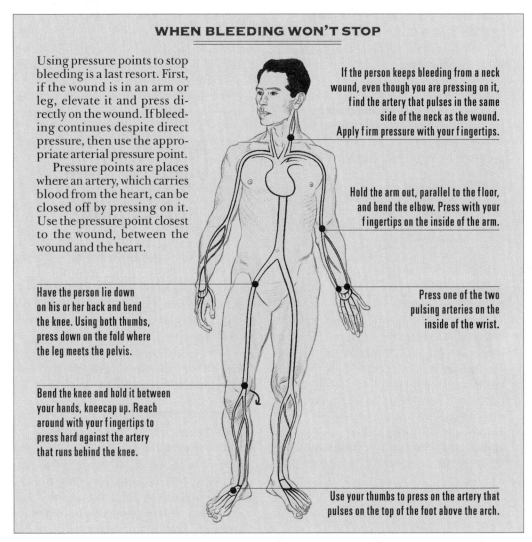

WHEN BLEEDING WON'T STOP

Using pressure points to stop bleeding is a last resort. First, if the wound is in an arm or leg, elevate it and press directly on the wound. If bleeding continues despite direct pressure, then use the appropriate arterial pressure point.

Pressure points are places where an artery, which carries blood from the heart, can be closed off by pressing on it. Use the pressure point closest to the wound, between the wound and the heart.

If the person keeps bleeding from a neck wound, even though you are pressing on it, find the artery that pulses in the same side of the neck as the wound. Apply firm pressure with your fingertips.

Hold the arm out, parallel to the floor, and bend the elbow. Press with your fingertips on the inside of the arm.

Have the person lie down on his or her back and bend the knee. Using both thumbs, press down on the fold where the leg meets the pelvis.

Press one of the two pulsing arteries on the inside of the wrist.

Bend the knee and hold it between your hands, kneecap up. Reach around with your fingertips to press hard against the artery that runs behind the knee.

Use your thumbs to press on the artery that pulses on the top of the foot above the arch.

put pressure around the wound. Do not put pressure on the object itself. Also, do not put direct pressure on an open **fracture** (see page 35) or an **eye injury** (see page 32).

➤ If blood seeps through the cloth, do not remove the cloth. Place another piece of cloth on top of the first, and continue to apply pressure.

➤ If the bleeding does not stop after five minutes, apply pressure to the major artery closest to the wound, between the wound and the heart (see illustration, opposite page).

➤ When the bleeding stops, wrap a bandage or a clean cloth around the wound. **Cautions:** Do not remove any cloths placed on the wound to help stop the bleeding. Place a clean cloth over the previous ones. If an object is embedded in the wound, bandage around it to support it.

➤ Keep the victim calm and still until medical help arrives.

Head wound:

➤ If the injury is more than a minor bump or a surface cut, call 911 **immediately.**

➤ Do not move the person unless you absolutely must; this can cause further injury (see **head, neck, and back injuries,** page 37).

➤ If a head wound is bleeding but not deep, cover the wound with a clean bandage or cloth and apply direct pressure. If the cloth becomes soaked with blood, do not remove it; place additional cloths on top of the first.

➤ Apply a cold compress to ease pain and swelling.

➤ Keep the victim calm and still until medical help arrives.

➤ Watch the person for 24 hours for signs of serious injury; signs may include confusion, unusual drowsiness, bleeding from the ears or nose, or loss of movement on one side of the body.

Cut of the eye and/or eyelid:

➤ Cover both eyes lightly with bandages. **Caution:** Do not apply direct pressure to a bleeding eye.

➤ Call a doctor for an emergency appointment. If he or she isn't available, call 911 or go to an emergency facility.

BLOOD POISONING

Blood poisoning (septicemia) is the term for a bacterial infection in the blood, which can result from a contaminated wound (or from appendicitis, a burn, a urinary tract infection, or dental work). The bloodstream then carries the infection to other parts of the body.

Signs and Symptoms

■ Fever and chills.
■ Headache.
■ Fatigue or confusion.
■ Loss of appetite, nausea, or diarrhea.
■ Warm, flushed skin.
■ Increased heart rate.

What to Do

➤ Call a doctor for emergency advice. If a doctor isn't available, call 911 or go to an emergency facility. Antibiotics may be required.

➤ Watch for signs of septic shock (a common side effect of blood poisoning): rapid pulse and breathing, fainting, and possibly confusion or coma. If symptoms appear, call 911 or go to an emergency facility **immediately.** If you are waiting for medical help to arrive, see **shock,** page 18.

Minor bleeding, a puncture wound, or a scrape:

➤ Clean the wound with soap and water.

➤ Cover the wound with a sterile bandage to stop the bleeding and prevent infection. If you are using an elastic bandage, be careful not to apply it so tightly that it restricts internal blood flow. Make sure that you can slip a finger between the bandage and the skin.

➤ For deep puncture wounds, call your doctor for emergency advice.

➤ Watch for signs of infection: redness, swelling, pain, pus, and fever. If the wound becomes infected, call a doctor for advice and an appointment.

➤ Make sure that the person is vaccinated against tetanus.

Drowning

Drowning occurs when water enters the airway, blocking the air supply to the lungs. Besides happening in lakes, oceans, rivers, and public swimming pools, drownings occur at home—in bathtubs, backyard pools, whirlpool baths, and, with toddlers, in pails and toilets. Knowledge of rescue breathing and CPR procedures can be vital.

WHAT TO DO

➤ If a person is floating facedown in the water or is having difficulty swimming, alert any nearby lifeguard or emergency personnel and call 911 **immediately.**

➤ If you are in the water with a drowning person who has stopped breathing, begin the rescue breathing phase of **CPR** (see page 14), if possible. Looking into the person's mouth, sweep it out with your index finger. Tilt the head back, pinch the nostrils closed, and breathe into the mouth (if the victim is an infant or a child, see pages 16 or 17). As you pause between breaths, move toward land. **Caution:** Don't attempt rescue breathing in the water unless you can safely stand up in it, or unless you are a very strong swimmer.

➤ If a person has been pulled from the water and is unconscious, check his or her **ABCs** (see box on page 14): Lift the chin to open the airway, then check for breathing and pulse. If the person is not breathing or does not have a pulse or heartbeat, begin **CPR** (see page 14). If the victim is a child or an infant, see page 16 or 17.

➤ Since water and food are often coughed up by the victim during rescue breathing, turn the head to the side periodically and sweep out the mouth with your finger.

➤ If the person is on land and unconscious but breathing, support the head and roll him or her onto the stomach into the **recovery position** (see box on page 17), to keep the airway open. **Caution:** Do not place the person in the recovery position if you suspect a **head, neck, or back injury** (see page 37)—for example, one caused by a diving accident.

➤ Remove any wet clothing, and cover the victim with a coat, blanket, or dry clothes.

➤ Keep the person still and quiet while waiting for medical help to arrive.

Caution: In cold water or in icy conditions, especially, watch for symptoms of **hypothermia** (shivering, uncoordinated movements, drowsiness, loss of consciousness). See page 39 for emergency treatment.

Ear Emergencies

While an earache may signal an ear emergency, it is also associated with many conditions that aren't emergencies, ranging from an **ear infection** (see page 71) to a blockage from **earwax** (see page 73). If you have a persistent earache, call your doctor's office for advice.

WHAT TO DO

If blood or fluids are draining from the ear:

➤ If you know or suspect that the victim has a head injury, call 911 or go to an emergency facility **immediately.**

➤ Loosely cover the ear with a clean cloth, and tape the cloth in place. Do not try to stop the drainage, and do not try to clean the ear.

➤ Lay the person flat on his or her back if awaiting medical help. **Caution:** If you suspect a **head, neck, or back injury,** see page 37. Moving the person could cause permanent injury.

If an eardrum has burst:

➤ If a person suddenly experiences earache; pain, ringing, or buzzing in the ear; hearing difficulty; or discharge (including pus or blood), he or she may have a ruptured eardrum. Call a doctor for an immediate appointment.

➤ To prevent infection, cover the ear with a dry, sterile pad.

➤ Give an over-the-counter pain reliever such as acetaminophen or aspirin. Never give aspirin to a child under 12 who has chicken pox, flu, or any other illness you suspect of being caused by a virus, such as a bad respiratory infection. (See box on **Reye's syndrome,** page 92.)

If a foreign object is in the ear:

➤ Shake the object out: Tilt the person's head so that the affected ear is nearest the ground. Ask the person to shake his or her head, or shake it for the person. You may be able to help dislodge the object by straightening the ear canal; do so by gently pulling the top of the ear up and toward the back of the head.

➤ Pick the object out: If the object does not fall out, look into the person's ear. If you can see the object and if it is flexible—but is not a live insect—carefully try to remove it with a pair of tweezers.

➤ If the object is embedded so deeply that you can't see it or the tip of the tweezers when you touch it, do not try to remove it yourself. Go to an emergency facility.

If a live insect is inside the ear:

➤ Kill the insect by pouring a small amount of oil, vinegar, or alcohol into the ear. This will also help alleviate pain.

➤ Tilt the victim's head so that the affected ear is nearest the sky. Gently pull the victim's earlobe backward and upward, and pour in warm—not hot—mineral oil, olive oil, or baby oil. The insect should float out of the ear.

Cautions:

➤ Do not push or poke at any object that is in the ear.

➤ Do not try to pick out a hard object such as a bean or a bead.

➤ Do not try to remove an object from the ear of a child (or anyone) who will not keep still.

➤ Do not hit the victim's head to try to dislodge an object.

Electric Shock

SIGNS AND SYMPTOMS

■ Burn marks (which may be small, or deep and charred) on the mouth or other skin.
■ Tingling sensation.
■ Sudden headache or dizziness.
■ Muscle pains.
■ Loss of consciousness, which may include loss of breathing as well as heartbeat.

WHAT TO DO

➤ Stop the flow of electricity as quickly and safely as possible: Unplug the electrical appliance (don't use the appliance switch, which may be faulty), or turn off the building's main power switch.

➤ If you are unable to do either, separate the victim from the live current: Insulate yourself by standing on a pile of clothes, a book, newspapers, a rubber mat, or a piece of wood. Then using a dry, nonconductive object, such as a wooden broomstick, a wooden chair, or a rope, separate the victim from the current. **Caution:** Do not use your hands, or anything wet or metal.

➤ Check the person's **ABCs** (see box on page 14): Lift the chin to open the airway, then check for breathing and pulse. If the person is not breathing or does not have a pulse or heartbeat, call 911 and begin **CPR** (see page 14). If the person is unconscious but is still breathing, support the head and roll him or her onto the stomach, into the **recovery position** (see box on page 17).

- Check for and treat any other serious injuries. Treat **burns** (see page 22); there may be burns at both the entry and exit sites of the electrical current. If there are serious injuries or burns, call 911 or go to an emergency facility **immediately. Caution:** Keep in mind that electrical burns are often deeper and more serious than they appear.
- Make the person as comfortable as possible, covering him or her with a coat or blanket. Make sure the airway is open. Do not place a pillow under the head, since bending the neck might block the airway.
- If you suspect the person has been struck by lightning, call 911 or go to an emergency facility **immediately.** You may touch a lightning victim right away (his or her body will not conduct electricity) and begin first aid for electric shock.
- For other electric shocks, call a doctor for emergency advice. If a doctor isn't available, call 911 or go to an emergency facility, even if the person seems unharmed.

If someone has been shocked by a downed electrical wire:
- If the person is near a high-voltage current, stay at least 20 feet away.
- Call the power company to have the power turned off, then call 911.
- If the person is conscious and inside a car, tell him or her to stay there unless the car is on fire (in that case, the victim should jump out and away from the car).
- Once the power is turned off, begin first aid for electric shock.

Cautions:
- Do not touch a person who is still touching a live current.
- Do not touch the electrical wire.

Eye Injuries

SIGNS AND SYMPTOMS

- Cut or bruise visible on the surface of the eye.
- Pain in or around the eye.
- Bloodshot, dry feeling, itching, or teary eye.
- Rapid blinking, or inability to keep the eye open.
- Sensitivity to light.
- Impaired vision.
- Headache.
- Pupils of different sizes.

WHAT TO DO

- If there is bleeding from inside the eye, elevate the person's head above the heart, cover both eyes with a clean cloth, and call 911 or go to an emergency facility **immediately. Caution:** If you suspect a **head, neck, or back injury** (see page 37), do not reposition or move the person. You may cause further injury.

Foreign objects embedded in the eye:
- Call 911 or go to an emergency facility **immediately.**

Cautions:
- If an object is embedded in the eye, do not try to remove it.
- Do not touch or press the object, and do not let the victim rub the eye.
- If the object is large, such as a stick or a pencil, place a paper cup or paper cone over the eye so that the cup supports the object; you may need to punch a hole in the bottom of the cup. Tape the cup into place. Cover the victim's other eye with a clean cloth. This will help prevent movement of the injured eye.
- If the object is small, cover both eyes with a clean cloth and loosely tie it into place for the trip to the emergency facility.

Foreign objects not embedded in the eye:
- If the person is wearing contact lenses and

can safely remove them, he or she should do so. The object may come out with the contact lens.

➤ If the object does not come out, wash your hands with soap and water. Ask the person to sit in good light and to look up as you gently pull down the lower eyelid. Look inside the eye and the lower eyelid. If you see the object there, release the lower lid and gently pull the upper eyelid down over the lower eyelid. This will produce tears, which may wash the object out of the eye.

➤ If the object does not wash out with tears, flush it out with running water—either from a cup or from the tap. The person can also try opening his or her eyes underwater in a bowl of fresh tap water.

➤ If you do not see the object in the eye or inside the lower eyelid, tell the person to look down as you place a cotton swab or firm matchstick lengthwise across his or her upper eyelid. Hold the person's upper lashes and eyelid, and pull gently upward and fold the upper eyelid over the swab or matchstick.

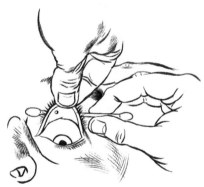

If you see the object on the inside of the upper eyelid, flush it out with water or lift it off with the corner of a soft, clean, damp cloth or dampened cotton swab.

➤ Wash the eye gently with cool water or saline solution.

➤ If you cannot find or remove the object, or if the person is in pain or has difficulty seeing after you've removed the object, cover both eyes with a clean cloth and tie it in place. Go to an emergency facility.

Cautions:

➤ Do not use a tissue, cotton swab, or tweezers to lift off an object that is on the colored part of the eye or on the pupil.

➤ Do not let the person rub the eye, since this may scratch the eye's surface.

Chemical in the eye:

➤ If the person is wearing contact lenses, ask him or her to remove them.

➤ Flush the eye with water: Hold the injured eye open (separating the eyelids) under gently running water, from either a faucet or a cup, for 15 to 20 minutes. Tilt the head so that the injured eye is lowest, to make sure the chemical doesn't splash into the other eye. The water should run from the inside corner of the eye to the outside corner.

➤ If both eyes are affected, let the water run over both eyes to their outside corners. Make sure the water gets underneath both eyelids. **Cautions:** Do not put anything other than water in the eye. Do not let the person rub the eye.

➤ Cover the eye with a clean cloth. Then tie a bandage over both eyes to help prevent movement of the affected eye.

➤ Call 911 or go to an emergency facility **immediately.** Give as much information as you can to emergency personnel, especially if you can identify the chemical.

Scratched eyeball:

➤ Wash your hands. A scratched eyeball can become infected.

➤ Rinse the eye with cool, clean water for 5 to 15 minutes. The water should run from the inside corner of the eye to the outside. Hold the eyelid open to make sure the water gets underneath.

➤ Cover both eyes with a clean cloth, and tie it in place.

➤ Go to an emergency facility.

Fainting and Loss of Consciousness

Just before fainting:
- Yawning, light-headedness, dizziness, or weakness.
- Pale skin or cold, clammy skin.
- Sweat on the face, neck, or hands.

Extended loss of consciousness:
- Lack of awareness or response for several minutes.

An episode of **fainting**—partial or brief loss of consciousness usually caused by a short-term drop in blood flow to the brain—is generally not harmful. **Loss of consciousness** for more than a minute or two, however, may indicate a more serious condition: concussion, stroke, or other brain damage; abnormal heart rhythm or heart attack; significant blood loss; a lack of oxygen in the blood; diabetic coma; epilepsy; or drug reaction. To determine whether someone is unconscious, tap the person on the shoulder and ask, "Are you okay?" If the person doesn't respond, he or she has probably lost consciousness.

WHAT TO DO

Cautions:
- Do not attempt to revive someone by slapping, shaking, or throwing cold water.
- Do not place a pillow under the head. Bending the neck might block the airway.
- Do not give the person anything to eat or drink (including alcohol) until he or she has fully regained consciousness. If you know the person is diabetic, however, try giving sips of soda or juice.

Someone about to faint:
- Keep the person from falling, then help him or her to lie down.
- Elevate the legs 8 to 12 inches, so that blood can flow to the brain.
- Loosen any tight clothing, especially at the neck or waist.
- Wipe the forehead with a cool, wet cloth.

Someone who has already fainted:
- Lay the person down on his or her back. Elevate the legs about 8 to 12 inches. **Caution:** If you suspect a **head, neck, or back injury,** see page 37. Moving the person may cause further injury.
- Loosen any tight clothing, especially at the neck or waist.
- Check the victim's **ABCs** (see box on page 14): Lift the chin to open the airway, then check for breathing and pulse. If the person is not breathing or does not have a pulse or heartbeat, call 911 and begin **CPR** (see page 14).
- If the victim has fallen, check for injuries. Look especially for head wounds. If any are present, call a doctor for emergency advice or, if a doctor isn't available, call 911 or go to an emergency facility.
- If vomiting begins, place the person on his or her side so that the airway isn't blocked.

Extended loss of consciousness:
- If the victim has been injured, remove him or her to a safe spot. **Caution:** If you suspect the person has a **head, neck, or back injury,** see page 37. Moving him or her may cause further injury.
- Call 911.
- Check the victim's **ABCs** (see box on page 14): Lift the chin to open the airway, then check for breathing and pulse. If the person is not breathing, or he or she does not have a pulse or heartbeat, begin **CPR** (see page 14).
- To keep the airway open, support the victim's head and roll him or her onto the stomach, into the **recovery position** (see box on page 17). **Caution:** Do not place a person in the recovery position if you suspect a head, neck, or back injury.
- Check for any medical identification that indicates whether the victim has diabetes, epilepsy, or drug allergies. Relay this information to medical personnel. (See page 42 for treatment of epileptic **seizures.** See **anaphylactic shock,** page 18, for emergency treatment of allergic drug reactions.)

➤ Keep the victim warm with a blanket or coat until medical help arrives.

➤ Wipe the forehead with a cool, wet cloth.

Food Poisoning

SIGNS AND SYMPTOMS

Bacterial:
■ Fever.
■ Many stools or diarrhea (often severe or explosive), which may be bloody.
■ Severe abdominal pain and cramps.
■ Vomiting.

Botulism:
■ Nausea, vomiting, diarrhea.
■ Blurred vision or drooping eyelids.
■ Dry mouth, difficulty swallowing.
■ Difficulty breathing.
■ Muscle weakness or paralysis.

Viral:
■ Vomiting, diarrhea, and abdominal cramps.

Chemical:
■ Vomiting and diarrhea.
■ Sweating.
■ Dizziness and mental confusion.
■ Tearing of the eyes.
■ Excess saliva.
■ Stomach pain.

Spoiled or contaminated food—which has often been undercooked or left unrefrigerated—can lead to food poisoning. The most common type is **bacterial,** usually caused by salmonella or staphylococcal bacteria passed along by human hands during the preparation of food. **Botulism,** typically caused by bacterial toxins that form when foods such as vegetables or fruits are incorrectly preserved or canned at home, is a rare but severe form. **Viruses** that contaminate food and **chemical toxins** found in certain foods, such as some mushrooms, moldy peanuts, and potato sprouts, can also cause food poisoning.

WHAT TO DO

➤ If symptoms of botulism (muscle weakness, difficulty swallowing and breathing, blurred vision) or severe chemical food poisoning (vomiting, diarrhea, mental confusion, stomach pain) occur, call 911 or go to an emergency facility **immediately.** These are life-threatening conditions.

➤ Call your doctor for an immediate appointment if vomiting and diarrhea are severe. Treatment for dehydration may be needed.

➤ If mild symptoms of food poisoning occur, allow vomiting and diarrhea to flush the toxins out of the system. Do not eat solid food during periods of vomiting and diarrhea.

➤ Once fluids can be kept in the stomach, replace lost fluids by drinking clear liquids (such as water, sports drinks, or noncaffeinated tea) for about 12 hours, then eat bland foods such as rice, cooked cereals, bread, crackers, or broth for the next 24 hours or so.

Fractures and Dislocations

SIGNS AND SYMPTOMS

■ Pain.
■ Misshapen body part.
■ Bruising or discolored skin.
■ Swelling.
■ Visible bone.
■ Numbness in limb.
■ Loss of function of injured area.

Fractures are breaks, cracks, or chips in a bone. When the skin is not broken, it's called a closed fracture. When a fractured bone breaks through the skin, it's called an open fracture. Open fractures are less common and more dangerous, because they may lead to severe blood loss or infection. **Dislocations** occur when bones are moved from their normal place at a joint, causing the joint to stop functioning. Dislocated joints often appear deformed.

WHAT TO DO

If you suspect the victim has a broken neck or back, or any kind of **head, neck, or back injury,** see page 37. Moving the person may cause further injury.

➤ Call 911 or go to an emergency facility **immediately** if the person shows symptoms of **shock** or of **internal bleeding** (see page 19). Call 911 if he or she is unconscious or can't be moved.

➤ If the victim is unconscious, check the **ABCs** (see box on page 14). If the victim is not breathing or does not have a pulse or heartbeat, begin **CPR** (see page 14).

➤ Keep the person still. Unless absolutely necessary, do not move a person who has an injured pelvis, which can also indicate a lower spine injury.

➤ Check for and treat any other serious injuries. If the victim is bleeding around or near a broken bone, do not wash or probe the wound. Stop the bleeding by placing a clean cloth over the wound and tying a bandage over it. (See **cuts, scrapes, and wounds,** page 27.)

➤ If the person is mobile and conscious, no matter whether you think a bone is broken or simply dislocated, call a doctor for an emergency appointment. If not available, go to the nearest emergency facility.

Cautions:

➤ If you aren't sure whether a bone is broken, treat it as though it is.

➤ Do not attempt to straighten or change the position of a misshapen bone or joint.

To immobilize an injured finger or toe:

➤ Elevate the finger or toe above the level of the victim's heart, while applying a cold compress for 10 to 15 minutes at a time. Place a small cloth or cotton ball between the injured finger or toe and an uninjured one, then tape them together.

To immobilize the arm, wrist, or hand:

➤ For an injured forearm: Support the injured area with your hands, and place the lower arm at a right angle over the person's stomach. Place the arm or wrist on a newspaper or magazine padded with a towel or pillow; then, using cloth folded into bandages, tie the newspaper or magazine around the arm or wrist to make a splint. The ties should be on either side of the injured area. The splint should extend beyond the joints surrounding the injury.

➤ Use a large piece of cloth (or towel or shirt) as a sling: Fold the cloth so that it forms a triangle. Slide the wide part of the triangle under the injured arm and tie the loose ends around the neck. Fold over any extra material near the elbow and pin it in place. **Caution:** Make sure that the sling is snug but not so tight that it cuts off blood circulation to the injured limb.

➤ For other arm, wrist, or hand injuries, immobilize the arm with a sling, as above.

To immobilize the lower leg:

➤ Make a splint using boards or—if boards aren't available—a blanket.

➤ To make a board splint, find two long boards (or broomsticks). One board should be the length of the victim's leg from hip to heel, and the second should stretch from the groin to the heel. Pad the boards with blankets or pillows; then place the boards on either side of the injured leg, so that the padded sides touch the leg. Tie the boards in place at the groin, thigh, knee, and ankle.

➤ To make a blanket splint, roll up the blanket and place it between the victim's legs. Then tie the victim's legs together at the groin, thighs, knees, and ankles.

To immobilize the upper leg or hip:

Hip fractures are marked by unbearable pain when trying to walk, and bruising, swelling, tenderness, or deformity in the hip.

Caution: Do not splint an upper leg or hip unless you have to move the victim. Do not tie the splint in place over the break.

➤ If it's necessary to splint an upper leg or hip, locate two long boards. One should extend from under the victim's armpit to the heel. The second should extend from the groin to the heel. Pad the boards with blankets or pillows, then place the boards on either side of the injured leg so that the padded sides touch the leg. Tie the boards in place at the chest, waist, groin, thigh, knee, and ankle.

Head, Neck, and Back Injuries

SIGNS AND SYMPTOMS

Head injury:
■ Head wound, which may bleed heavily or show up as a bruise or lump on the scalp, or as a bruise behind the ear.
■ Blood or fluid draining from the ear, nose, or mouth that is not caused by obvious direct injury to that area.
■ Bruising around the eyes.
■ Headache, nausea, vomiting.
■ Vision changes, slurred speech, or difficulty breathing.
■ Dizziness, confusion, seizures, loss of balance, or loss of consciousness.

Neck or back injuries:
■ Severe pain in the back or neck.
■ Tingling sensation or loss of movement in the arms or legs.
■ Loss of bladder or bowel control.
■ Abnormal position of the head, neck, or back.
■ Loss of consciousness.

Be especially alert for head, neck, and back injuries following vehicle accidents; jumping, falling, or diving accidents; and gunshot wounds to the head or chest.

Multiple wounds, a broken helmet, or loss of consciousness after physical trauma are other likely indicators. Since victims of head, neck, and back injuries require special care—in order to avoid possible permanent paralysis—it's important to determine the kind of injury.

WHAT TO DO

Do not move a victim unless it's absolutely necessary, as in the case of a fire, explosion, or other life-and-death situation. Moving someone with a head, neck, or back injury could cause permanent spinal cord damage and even paralysis. If you must transport someone, make sure the head, neck, and back are aligned and well supported. Do not, however, turn the head sharply to straighten it.

➤ Call 911 **immediately.**
➤ Keep the person calm and completely still.
➤ If the person is unconscious, check the **ABCs** (see box on page 14): If the victim is not breathing or does not have a pulse or heartbeat, begin **CPR** (see page 14). Do not move the neck unless absolutely essential to keep the airway open. If you need to place the victim on his or her back for CPR, support the head, neck, and back together, and carefully roll the person onto the back. Make sure you keep the head, neck, and back lined up. It's best to have someone help you do this.
➤ Treat any obvious injuries, such as **cuts, scrapes, and wounds** (see page 27) or **fractures and dislocations** (see page 35).
➤ Keep the victim warm, using a blanket or coat, and as comfortable as possible, until medical help arrives. Do not give anything to eat or drink.
➤ To make sure the victim's head and spine remain still, you may gently place your hands on either side of the head to hold it in line with the body. Do not turn the head to straighten it; do not move it at all if the person resists or indicates pain. Do not put a pillow under the head, as bending the neck might cause the airway to become blocked.
➤ Keep the airway open. If the victim begins to choke or vomit, or loses consciousness, look into his or her mouth as you clear the

airway with your fingers. If it's necessary to turn the victim on his or her side, support the head, neck, and back together while carefully rolling the victim over. (It's best to have someone help you do this.) Gently cradle the victim's head and neck to hold them in place.

Cautions:

➤ Make sure the victim's head and neck stay in line with the body.

➤ Do not place the victim in the recovery position described early in this chapter.

Heart Attack

SIGNS AND SYMPTOMS

■ Crushing or squeezing chest pain or tightness that lasts 10 minutes or more. It often starts in the center of the chest, then spreads to the jaw, neck, back, or arms (especially the left arm).

■ Irregular or stopped heartbeat.

■ Shortness of breath.

■ Fear, anxiety, or dizziness.

■ Heavy sweating.

■ Nausea or vomiting.

■ Pale or bluish skin, lips, or finger-nails.

■ Loss of consciousness.

WHAT TO DO

➤ Call 911 **immediately.**

➤ If the person is unconscious, check the **ABCs** (see box on page 14): Lift the chin to open the airway, then check for breathing and pulse. If the victim is not breathing or does not have a pulse or heartbeat, begin **CPR** (see page 14). **Caution:** If you suspect a **head, neck, or back injury,** see page 37. Moving the victim may cause further injury.

➤ Loosen any tight clothing, especially around the neck, chest, or waist.

➤ Keep the person warm and as comfortable as possible. If necessary, cover him or her with a blanket or additional clothing.

➤ If the victim is unconscious but is breathing and has a heartbeat, support the head and roll him or her onto the stomach, into the **recovery position** (see page 17). **Caution:** Do not try to revive an unconscious person by slapping, shaking, or throwing cold water on him or her.

➤ If the person is conscious, a sitting or partially sitting position may make breathing easier. Offer reassurance. Ask if the person has prescription heart medication, and, if so, help him or her take it, following label instructions. Give him or her an aspirin to chew. **Caution:** Do not give anything to eat or drink.

➤ Continue to monitor breathing and pulse until medical help arrives. If breathing or pulse stops, begin CPR.

Heat Stroke and Heat Exhaustion

SIGNS AND SYMPTOMS

Heat stroke:

■ Body temperature higher than 104 degrees.

■ Dry, hot skin.

■ Rapid pulse and breathing.

■ Confusion, seizures, or loss of consciousness.

Heat exhaustion:

■ Cool, clammy skin.

■ Excessive perspiration.

■ Rapid pulse.

■ Headache.

■ Nausea and/or vomiting.

■ Abdominal or limb cramps.

■ Dizziness.

Heat stroke, which requires emergency treatment, occurs when the body is exposed to very hot conditions for a prolonged period of time. During heat stroke, the body's temperature rises to dangerous levels because its normal cooling mechanisms become overloaded and stop functioning.

Heat exhaustion, which typically occurs while exercising or working in hot weather without sufficient fluid intake, results when the body cannot produce enough sweat to cool itself off. Heat exhaustion is less serious than heat stroke but may lead to it. Both conditions are more common in the very young and the elderly.

WHAT TO DO

Heat stroke:
➤ Call 911 or go to an emergency facility **immediately.**
➤ Quickly move the victim to a cooler site.
➤ Remove any clothing; then place cool, wet cloths on the forehead and torso, or wrap the victim in wet towels or sheets, or sponge or splash cool water onto the skin.
➤ Fan the person with an electric fan, a hair dryer set on cool, or your hand.

Cautions:
➤ Do not give anything to eat or drink.
➤ Don't use an alcohol rubdown to cool off the victim.

Heat exhaustion:
➤ Move the victim to a cooler site.
➤ If the person is conscious, have him or her lie or sit down, and elevate the feet. Loosen any tight clothing, and remove any sweat-soaked clothing.
➤ Place cool, wet cloths on the forehead and torso, wrap the person in wet towels or sheets, or sponge or splash cool water onto the skin.
➤ Fan the person with an electric fan, a hair dryer set on cool, or your hand.
➤ If the victim is conscious and is able to swallow and breathe without difficulty, give him or her salt water (1 teaspoon salt mixed with 1 quart water) or plain water.
➤ If the victim's condition does not improve, call 911 or go to an emergency facility **immediately.**

Cautions:
➤ Do not use an alcohol rubdown to cool off the victim.
➤ Do not force the person to drink. Never give alcoholic or caffeinated beverages.

Hypothermia and Frostbite

SIGNS AND SYMPTOMS

Hypothermia:
■ Shivering.
■ Uncoordinated movements.
■ Drowsiness, weakness, or loss of consciousness.

Frostbite:
■ Numb, cold skin.
■ Skin that turns blue, white, or looks blackened and becomes hard, waxy, and frozen.
■ Loss of function in frozen area.

Hypothermia, a condition produced by a below-normal body temperature, can lead to loss of consciousness, cardiac arrest, and death, if left untreated. (Hypothermia can occur in mild temperatures if someone becomes wet and exhausted.) **Frostbite,** which is caused by long exposure to cold, freezes the skin and damages its underlying tissues.

WHAT TO DO

➤ Call 911 or go to an emergency facility **immediately.**
➤ If awaiting medical help and if symptoms of both hypothermia and frostbite are present, treat for hypothermia first.

Hypothermia:
➤ Check the person's **ABCs** (see box on page 14): Lift the chin to open the airway, then check for breathing and pulse. If the person is not breathing or does not have a pulse or heartbeat, begin **CPR** (see page 14). **Note:** Hypothermia victims often have very weak, slow pulses, so take extra time and care to check for the pulse.
➤ Gently carry or lead the victim to shelter.

- If the person's clothes are wet, change him or her into dry clothing.
- Slowly warm the victim. Cover the head and neck. Use your own body heat, blankets, or aluminum foil. Place warm compresses (cloths soaked in warm water) on the neck, chest, and groin. **Caution:** Do not use any form of direct heat, such as an electric blanket, to warm the person; the warming must be gradual.
- If the victim is conscious and can swallow, give sips of a warm, sweetened, nonalcoholic beverage.

Frostbite:
- Move the victim to a nearby shelter.
- Remove any tight clothing or jewelry.
- Place frostbitten hands or feet in a bowl of water no hotter than 105 degrees (it should be comfortable to normal skin) for 20 minutes. Gently stir the water, and add warm water as it cools. Otherwise, soak a cloth (preferably cotton) in warm water and place it on the frostbitten area for at least 30 minutes. Resoak the cloth in warm water to keep it warm.
- If warm water is not available, use your own body, blankets, or newspapers to warm the skin.
- Once the damaged skin is soft and warm, and the feeling and color return, dry it. Place a clean, dry cloth over the skin; place clean, dry cloths between frostbitten fingers. Wrap more dry cloths over the area to keep it warm.

Cautions:
- Do not use any form of direct heat, such as an electric blanket or a campfire, to warm frostbitten skin.
- Do not massage frostbitten skin.
- Do not let the victim smoke or drink alcoholic beverages while waiting for medical help to arrive.
- Do not thaw frostbitten skin if there is a chance of its becoming frozen again before you reach help; refreezing can cause further damage.

Nose Emergencies

SIGNS AND SYMPTOMS

Severe nosebleeds:
- Bleeding from a nostril or down the back of the throat.
- Gagging or choking.

Foreign objects in the nose:
- Irritation or itching in the nose.
- Difficulty breathing through one or both nostrils.
- Bleeding or foul-smelling discharge from a nostril.

WHAT TO DO

Severe nosebleeds:
- Call a doctor for emergency advice if you suspect a **head, neck, or back injury** (see page 37), if clear or bloody fluid is draining from the nose after an injury, if blood is streaming down the back of the throat, or if a nosebleed does not stop after 30 minutes. If not available, call 911 or go to an emergency facility.
- Have the person sit down.
- Try to stop the bleeding by pinching the person's nose shut while he or she bends the head forward. This helps keep blood from running down the throat, which can cause vomiting. Hold both nostrils—below the bridge—between the thumb and index finger, for 5 to 10 minutes. The person should breathe through the mouth.
- If the nose is still bleeding after 10 minutes, ask the person to gently blow out any clots and excess blood; this should be done only once.
- Pinch the victim's nose shut for 5 more minutes. If the bleeding still does not stop, roll up a small, clean cloth or tissue and place it in the bleeding nostril. Hold both nostrils between the thumb and index finger. Be careful not to push the cloth or tissue too far into the nose; make sure you can pull it out.
- Once the bleeding stops, place a cold cloth over the victim's nose and face for

about 10 minutes. The person should remain seated.

➤ Remove the cloth packing in the nostril after 30 to 60 minutes.

➤ Rub petroleum jelly inside the nostril to help prevent further bleeding or drying.

Cautions:

➤ The person should not blow or pick his or her nose, or bend over, for 12 hours.

➤ If the nose is misshapen or misaligned, or if there is swelling, pain, or bruising around the eyes, the nose may be broken. Have the victim sit down and press a cold cloth or ice pack against the nose. Go to an emergency facility.

Foreign objects in the nose:

➤ Ask the person to blow out the object. Press the unaffected nostril with a finger while blowing. Do not use tweezers or other tools to remove the object.

➤ If the object is still there, sniffing some pepper might help the person sneeze and blow it out. Warn the person not to inhale sharply.

➤ If the object is still there, go to an emergency facility.

Poisoning

SIGNS AND SYMPTOMS

- Headache or abdominal pain.
- Dizziness or seizures.
- Fever and chills.
- Vision problems.
- Unusual breath odor.
- Pale or bluish skin, or burn marks on the skin.
- Nausea and/or vomiting.
- Difficulty breathing.
- Drowsiness or loss of consciousness.

WHAT TO DO

Caution: Since a poisoning victim may have few symptoms, or symptoms not listed here, it's important to examine the scene for clues.

➤ If the victim has inhaled poisonous gases or toxic fumes—such as chlorine or carbon monoxide from car exhaust, faulty heating, or cooking equipment—take him or her to fresh air. **Caution:** Make sure to avoid the toxic fumes yourself. Get help, if necessary, in moving the victim.

➤ If the person is unconscious, call 911 and check his or her **ABCs** (see box on page 14): Lift the chin to open the airway, then check breathing and pulse. If the victim is not breathing or does not have a pulse or heartbeat, begin **CPR** (see page 14). **Caution:** If you suspect a **head, neck, or**

POISONOUS HOUSEHOLD SUBSTANCES

In addition to the items on the following list, many household cleansers, detergents, deodorizers, and disinfectants are poisonous if swallowed or inhaled. Drugs, medications, herbal remedies, and vitamins—whether prescription or over-the-counter—may be poisonous if combined, if mixed with alcohol, or if taken in large quantities. The following are common poisonous household items:

Antifreeze	Paint remover
Fuels	Paint thinner
Herbicides	Pesticides
Insecticides	Solvents
Mothballs	Tobacco
Oven cleaner	Turpentine

POISONOUS PLANTS

Hundreds of potentially poisonous plants—including houseplants—exist in the United States. Many plant parts, including seeds, berries, nuts, and bulbs, may be poisonous if swallowed. If you have a concern or question about a plant or plant part, call your local Poison Control Center for advice. Some of the most poisonous include:

Castor bean	Oleander
Foxglove	Poison hemlock
Jimsonweed	Water hemlock

back injury, see page 37; it may be dangerous to move the victim.

➤ Try to identify the poison. If the person is conscious, ask what he or she swallowed or inhaled. Look around for any open or nearby containers of chemicals, or for any plants or household products that the victim may have swallowed. Sniff for unusual odors. Look for cooking equipment or heaters that may have been left on.

➤ Call your local Poison Control Center. Tell center personnel, if you know, what chemical, plant, or household product has poisoned the victim. Wait for instructions on how to proceed. Do not try to induce vomiting unless told to do so.

➤ If the victim is unconscious but breathing, support the head and roll him or her onto the stomach, into the **recovery position** (see box on page 17).

Cautions:

➤ If you suspect the person has a **head, neck, or back injury** (see page 37), do not use the recovery position. Moving him or her could cause further injury.

➤ Do not give the victim anything to eat or drink unless you're told to do so.

➤ Do not rely on poisoning instructions given on container labels.

Seizures

SIGNS AND SYMPTOMS

■ Tingling sensation, twitching, muscle spasms or convulsions, or stiffening of the body.

■ Fixed stare or eyes rolling back.

■ Drooling.

■ Loss of bladder or bowel control.

■ Interrupted breathing.

■ Confusion, sleepiness, or loss of consciousness.

Seizures, while frightening, are usually not life-threatening. Causes include epilepsy, diabetes, heat stroke, fever (in children), electric shock, poisoning, brain injury, and drug or alcohol abuse.

WHAT TO DO

➤ Call 911 if this is the first time the person has had a seizure, if there is more than one seizure within a short time, if the seizure lasts more than five minutes, if the person is pregnant or diabetic, if the person has been seriously injured, or if the person does not regain consciousness.

➤ If someone looks as if he or she is going to have a seizure or begins to lose balance, help him or her to the ground. Check to see if the person is wearing a medical alert tag or is suffering from an injury. **Caution:** If you suspect a **head, neck, or back injury,** see page 37. Moving the victim may cause further injury.

➤ Protect the victim from self-injury: Remove eyeglasses. Push away any hard or sharp objects or furniture that the person might hit. Do not try to restrict movement, unless the victim is going to hurt himor herself.

➤ Lay the person on his or her side to prevent any vomit from entering the lungs. Put something soft under the head to protect it from injury.

➤ Do not put your hands in or near the victim's mouth during a seizure. Do not try to hold the person's tongue.

➤ Loosen any tight clothing.

➤ When the seizure has ended, help the person into a comfortable position on his or her side. Offer reassurance. He or she is likely to be tired and confused, and may fall asleep.

➤ If the person is unconscious, check the **ABCs** (see box on page 14): Lift the chin to open the airway, then check for breathing and pulse. If the victim is not breathing or does not have a pulse, call 911 and begin **CPR** (see page 14).

➤ Stay with the person until he or she is fully conscious and out of danger.

Shortness of Breath

SIGNS AND SYMPTOMS

- Feeling of breathlessness or labored breathing, even with little or no physical activity.
- Dizziness or light-headedness.

WHAT TO DO

➤ Help the person rest comfortably. A sitting position usually aids breathing.

➤ Offer reassurance. Shortness of breath can lead to panic, which can make breathing even more difficult.

➤ If the person can answer questions (even with gestures), try to determine the cause of the breathing difficulty.

➤ If symptoms occur along with chest pain (which may be crushing, burning, tightness, or pressure, and may spread to the jaw, neck, shoulder, or left arm), nausea, and dizziness, the person may be having a **heart attack** (see page 38). Call 911 or go to an emergency facility **immediately.**

➤ If symptoms occur with wheezing, chest tightness, or coughing, the victim may be having an asthma attack. Help him or her take any prescribed asthma medication. If this is the first attack or if it is more serious than previous attacks, call 911 or go to an emergency facility **immediately.**

➤ If symptoms are accompanied by a fever over 100 degrees or coughing, the person may have acute **bronchitis** (see page 82) or **pneumonia** (see page 94). Call a doctor for advice and an appointment. Give aspirin or another pain reliever for fever, and a cough medicine. But never give aspirin to a child under 12 who has chicken pox, flu, or any other illness you suspect of being caused by a virus, such as a bad respiratory infection; see box on **Reye's syndrome,** page 92.

➤ If symptoms occur during periods of anxiety, they may be related to **stress** (see page 212). Call your doctor for advice.

Snakebites

SIGNS AND SYMPTOMS

Rattlesnake, copperhead, and cottonmouth bites:
- Increasing pain at the bite site.
- Rapid swelling and skin discoloration at the bite site.
- Twitching skin.
- Dizziness, nausea, or sweating.
- Shock or convulsions.

Coral snake bites:
- Pain at the bite site.
- Drowsiness.
- Slurred speech or double vision.
- Delirium, tremors, or seizures.

Four types of poisonous snakes are found in the United States: rattlesnakes, copperheads, cottonmouths (also called water moccasins), and coral snakes (also called harlequin or bead snakes). Rattlesnakes, copperheads, and cottonmouths have triangular heads, slitlike eyes, and long fangs, and they leave similar bite marks (one small puncture wound, or two, about ⅛ inch apart). Rattlesnakes and copperheads shake their tails when disturbed, but only rattlesnakes have rattles at the ends of their tails. Cottonmouths open their mouths when angry, revealing the white lining for which they are named. Coral snakes have a black snout and red, black, and yellow or white rings along their bodies. Only a very small percentage of snakebites in the United States cause death, most from rattlesnakes (coral snakes are the most poisonous, but their bites are rare).

WHAT TO DO

If you aren't sure that the bite was from a poisonous snake, assume that it was, and begin first aid:

➤ Keep the victim calm and still. If possible, lay the person on his or her back so that the bite is below the level of the heart and the blood from the bite area runs more slowly to the heart.

- Identify the kind of snake, if you can. If you have to kill the snake, try not to damage the head, so that it can be identified. Stay as far from the snake as possible.
- Call 911 or go to an emergency facility. Tell emergency personnel what kind of snake bit the person, if you know.
- If the person is unconscious, check the **ABCs** (see box on page 14): Lift the chin to open the airway, then check for breathing and pulse. If the victim is not breathing or does not have a pulse or heartbeat, begin **CPR** (see page 14).
- Remove any constricting jewelry or clothing near the bite.
- If you are sure that the snake was poisonous, and it will take more than a half hour to get medical help, and if the bite is on a limb, apply a lightly tied tourniquet above the bite.

Cautions:
- Do not make an incision. Do not attempt to suck out venom with your mouth, or use a snakebite kit. These measures do not help.
- Do not apply ice or a cold compress to a snakebite.
- Do not let the person walk. If the person has to be moved, carry him or her.

Spider Bites and Scorpion Stings

SIGNS AND SYMPTOMS

- Bite mark, sting mark, swelling, or blister at the bite site.
- Pain in the bite or sting area, or in the stomach.
- Nausea, vomiting, chills, or fever.
- Difficulty breathing or swallowing.
- Severe sweating and excess saliva.

Two types of poisonous spiders are found in the United States—black widows and brown recluse (fiddleback) spiders—whose bites especially endanger children, seniors, and anyone who is ill. Black widows have a red spot on the abdomen and leave only a faint red bite mark. The brown recluse has a brown, violin-shaped marking on its back; watch for a blister, swelling, and bull's-eye-shaped bite. Scorpions have poisonous stingers in their long, upturned "tails," but only a few of the species found in the United States inflict fatal stings.

WHAT TO DO

- Wash the wound with soap and water.
- Apply an ice pack or cold compress.
- Call your doctor for emergency advice. If not available, call 911 or go to an emergency facility.
- If possible, bring the spider or scorpion to the doctor's office or emergency facility.

Caution: Watch for signs of **anaphylactic shock** (see page 18). If they appear, call 911 or go to an emergency facility **immediately.**

Sprains and Strains

SIGNS AND SYMPTOMS

- Pain.
- Swelling.
- Bruising.

A sprain is a tear or stretch in a ligament, the tissue band that connects the bones of a joint. Sprains are common in the ankles, knees, wrists, and fingers. A strain (often called a "pulled muscle") is a tear or stretch in a muscle or tendon. Strains often occur in the neck, back, thigh, and calf.

WHAT TO DO

- Treat a severe sprain (marked by swelling and intense pain) as though it were a **fracture** (see page 35), and call a doctor for an immediate appointment. Also call a doctor for a severe strain.
- If the sprain or strain feels mild, apply a cold pack—a plastic bag of ice cubes wrapped in a damp cloth or a package of frozen vegetables—several times a day for

up to three days. Leave it on for no more than 10 to 30 minutes at a time, and leave it off for 30 to 45 minutes between applications. Use only moderate pressure. This should reduce the pain and swelling by helping to control internal bleeding.

➤ While applying the ice, keep the injured area elevated above the heart, if possible, to reduce fluid buildup and swelling.

➤ Apply an elastic bandage to immobilize and support the sprained or strained area. Wrap the bandage in an upward spiral, starting several inches below the injured area. You may wrap the bandage over the ice pack temporarily. **Caution:** Do not wrap the bandage too tightly.

➤ If a sling is necessary, see **fractures and dislocations,** page 35.

➤ Do not put any weight on the strain or sprain for one to three days.

Stroke

SIGNS AND SYMPTOMS

■ Abrupt weakness or numbness of the face, arm, or leg (usually on just one side of the body).

■ Sudden difficulty seeing or loss of vision (often in only one eye).

■ Loss of speech, or difficulty speaking or understanding speech.

■ Sudden, severe headache.

■ Dizziness, unsteadiness, or sudden loss of consciousness.

A stroke occurs when blood flow to the brain is interrupted, usually because of a blocked artery. Though a stroke can be fatal or result in permanent disability, prompt medical attention may be able to reduce some of its most harmful effects.

WHAT TO DO

➤ Call 911 or go to an emergency facility **immediately.**

➤ If you're waiting for medical help to arrive, check the **ABCs** (see box on page 14):

Lift the chin to open the airway, then check for breathing and pulse. If the victim is not breathing or does not have a pulse, begin **CPR** (see page 14).

➤ If the victim is unconscious but breathing, support the head and roll him or her onto the stomach, into the **recovery position** (see box on page 17). **Caution:** Do not place the person in the recovery position if you suspect a **head, neck, or back injury** (see page 37). Moving him or her could cause further injury.

➤ If the victim is conscious, offer reassurance and comfort. Lay him or her down, with head and shoulders slightly elevated by pillows. Loosen any tight clothing.

➤ If vomit or fluid is draining from the victim's mouth, or if the victim is having difficulty swallowing, turn him or her onto the side so that the airway does not become blocked. **Caution:** Do not give anything to eat or drink.

Sunburn

SIGNS AND SYMPTOMS

■ Redness (even in dark-skinned people), burning sensation, painfulness and (sometimes) blistering of the skin.

■ Mild fever.

■ Headache.

WHAT TO DO

➤ Especially if the sunburned person is a child, watch for signs of dehydration or heat exhaustion, such as excessive sweating, clammy skin, and rapid pulse (see **heat stroke and heat exhaustion,** page 38). Give the person water to drink.

➤ If signs of **heat stroke** develop, such as high fever; dry, hot skin; and confusion (see page 38), call 911 or go to an emergency facility **immediately. Caution:** Do not give anything to drink if you suspect heat stroke.

- Soothe the burn with a cool bath or a cold compress.
- Take aspirin or acetaminophen for pain.
- If the skin blisters, do not cover the blisters. Call a doctor for advice.
- If the skin peels, apply a moisturizing lotion to relieve itching.
- To help prevent sunburn or to keep it from getting worse, use a sunscreen with a protection factor (SPF) of at least 15 if you're planning to be in the sun for more than a few minutes. Apply the sunscreen 30 minutes before going out, and reapply it every two hours. Most clothing provides insufficient sun protection; you may need to apply sunscreen all over.

Tick Bites

SIGNS AND SYMPTOMS

Lyme disease:
- A bull's-eye rash, often with a pale center, that may spread to several inches across. The rash begins to develop two days to a month after the bite, and may last two to four weeks or longer.
- Flulike symptoms—such as headache, fatigue, fever, chills, and aching muscles and joints—developing within a month of the bite.

Rocky Mountain spotted fever:
- Two to 14 days after a tick bite, a pink rash that starts near the wrists and ankles, then spreads to the face, torso, and other areas of the body. The rash turns deep red, then looks like red pinpricks.
- Fever, chills, and severe headache.

The bite of the tiny deer tick may result in **Lyme disease** (see page 276), which can cause arthritis, heart problems, and vision and hearing difficulties, among other ailments. Bites of some other ticks can cause **Rocky Mountain spotted fever,** an infection that can be life-threatening if untreated.

WHAT TO DO

- If you can see the tick embedded in the skin, grasp it with tweezers as close to the skin as possible, then pull it out gently and steadily. If tweezers aren't available, use a glove, a piece of paper, or plastic wrap. (If you have to use bare fingers, wash your hands immediately afterward.) Save the tick in a jar; rubbing alcohol will help preserve it. Avoid squeezing or twisting the tick's body, which could spread bacteria into your skin or blood. Do not attempt to burn a tick off the skin. If you cannot get all of the tick out, call a doctor for advice and an appointment.
- Wash the area with soap and water.
- Apply an antiseptic ointment or alcohol to prevent infection. An ice pack can help relieve pain, and calamine lotion will relieve itching.
- Watch for signs of Lyme disease or Rocky Mountain spotted fever.
- If symptoms develop, call a doctor for an immediate appointment. Bring the tick with you, if you saved it.

Tooth Knocked Out

WHAT TO DO

- Call a dentist **immediately** or go to an emergency facility. Teeth replanted within an hour or two can survive. Pick the tooth up by the crown, not the root, using sterile gauze. The tooth must be kept as sterile as possible.
- Wash the tooth quickly, either under running water or in saliva, and immediately put it back in the socket. Bite down gently on the tooth or hold it in place with a sterile gauze pad for the trip to the dentist.
- If the tooth can't be put in the socket, hold it in the side of the mouth or wrap it in sterile gauze (or paper towels) and place it in a closed container of cool milk for the trip to the dentist.
- If the socket is bleeding, cover it with a sterile gauze pad, then bite down to hold it there until you get to the dentist.

Problems & Solutions

I n the normal course of life, the human body requires surprisingly little maintenance beyond some fairly regular feeding, rest, and exercise. But at some times, in some ways, things go wrong for each of us. Fortunately, you can do a lot to set your body right again—beginning with learning what's really going on and when it's time to call a doctor.

On the following 230 pages, in entries covering a sweeping variety of health problems, you'll find the information you need. Each entry guides you through these logical steps: ➤ **Signs and Symptoms** ➤ **What You Can Do Now** ➤ **When to Call the Doctor** ➤ **How to Prevent It** ➤ **For More Help.**

You'll find a concise description of what your symptoms could mean, followed by clear suggestions for your best course of action. Each entry concludes with information on how to locate hotlines, organizations, books, and videos for more help.

Wherever you see the name of a condition emphasized—for example, **asthma**—you'll see the number of a page to turn to for further information about it. You'll also find quick-reference charts that allow you to sort out, at a glance, the connections between symptoms that may seem confusingly similar, their possible causes, and what you can do.

In addition, the color illustrations on pages 161 to 176 give you a revealing new look at what can happen inside the body.

We trust that you will find helpful advice here on practically any problem your family is likely to encounter or worry about.

Head & Nervous System

♦

Alzheimer's Disease

■ Memory problems that become progressively worse, eventually disrupting normal activities. A person with Alzheimer's often forgets what happened in the last half hour or asks the same question over and over.

■ Confusion, faulty judgment and reasoning, and an inability to complete simple tasks such as shopping or dialing new phone numbers.

■ An increasing tendency to lose things and to wander and get lost.

■ Neglect of personal hygiene and appearance.

■ Depression, paranoia, agitation, and anxiety—either as direct symptoms or as reflections of the distress people feel over the baffling loss of their abilities.

■ In later stages, failure to recognize familiar places and people.

■ In advanced stages, people suffer a near-total loss of memory, speech, and physical ability, and require full-time care and supervision.

An estimated 4 million Americans suffer from Alzheimer's disease, a deterioration of the brain that leads to severe memory loss, confused thinking, and personality changes. The condition is progressive and eventually fatal, although people with Alzheimer's can live ten years or more after symptoms first appear.

The exact cause of the disease is still unknown. It's most likely to appear in people over 65 and seems to run in families. A genetic link has also been found in some cases of early-onset Alzheimer's, a rare form that usually strikes people in their late forties or in their fifties.

Although no current treatment cures the disease, several new drugs that may slow its progress are being tested.

WHAT YOU CAN DO NOW

If you or a family member show signs of Alzheimer's:

➤ Get examined. Memory loss and disorientation are not necessarily indications of Alzheimer's (see box on **forgetfulness,** page 53). If someone close to you shows signs of short-term memory loss, make sure that this person sees his or her primary care physician to check for disorders with similar symptoms. These include depression, hypoglycemia, brain tumor, drug interactions or side effects, vitamin shortages, stroke, and other conditions in which memory problems may be reversible.

➤ If memory problems get worse over a period of months, see a neurologist or geriatrician for further tests.

If you're taking care of someone who has Alzheimer's:

➤ Keep the home environment as calm and

Headaches

Most people are familiar with occasional, pounding headaches, but many Americans—an estimated 50 million—have chronic, intense headaches. Symptoms vary from person to person; you may have all or only some of those associated with a particular type of headache. Headaches can also be a sign of a more serious condition.

SYMPTOMS	WHAT IT MIGHT BE	WHAT YOU CAN DO
Sudden, severe headache, paralysis on one side of body, nausea, vomiting, delirium, often seizures or loss of consciousness; possibly fever.	Brain hemorrhage.	Call 911 or go to emergency facility **immediately.**
Sudden, intense headache; weakness, paralysis, or numbness in one area of body; speech and visual disturbances; dizziness and confusion.	Stroke (see page 45).	Call 911 or go to emergency facility **immediately.**
Fever, headache, nausea and vomiting, stiff neck, aversion to light, red rash (sometimes), confusion.	Meningitis (see page 56).	Call doctor for emergency advice. If not available, call 911 or go to emergency facility.
Headache on waking that gets worse when you lie down, nausea and vomiting, double vision, dizziness, loss of memory, personality changes. Head pain comes on gradually but persists and grows worse over time (often months).	Brain tumor.	Call doctor for immediate appointment.
Intense eye pain, headache, nausea and vomiting, visual disturbances.	Glaucoma (see page 65).	Call doctor for immediate appointment.
Sudden, intense headache, dry mouth, sticky saliva, fatigue, thirst (sometimes).	Dehydration—particularly if headache follows nausea and vomiting (see page 127) or diarrhea (see page 116).	Call doctor for immediate appointment if symptoms are severe. Drink small amounts of liquids frequently, including sports drinks.

(continued)

Headaches *(continued)*

SYMPTOMS	WHAT IT MIGHT BE	WHAT YOU CAN DO
Extreme throbbing pain, often starting on one side of head; nausea, vomiting; visual disturbances; sensitivity to light and noise; dizziness.	Migraine headache.	Use over-the-counter painkillers. Rest in dark room. Apply ice packs. See doctor about stronger medication or other help if pain persists or recurs.
Severe, nonthrobbing pain, usually located around one eye; red, watery, bloodshot eye; nasal congestion; flushed face.	Cluster headache.	Apply ice packs and take hot showers. See doctor after first attack (symptoms could be caused by other, more serious problems). Doctor may prescribe medicine or pure oxygen (to be inhaled).
Steady pain that can be dull or intense and often feels like a band tightening around head; stiffness and tightness in neck, shoulders.	Tension headache.	Try over-the-counter painkillers. Get a deep muscle massage. Learn techniques of stress reduction, such as meditation. Apply ice packs and take hot showers. See doctor if pain persists.
Fever, pain behind forehead and eyes, accompanied by sinus congestion.	Sinus headache (see sinusitis, page 95).	Call doctor for advice and appointment. Infections can be treated with antibiotics. Use nasal decongestants, but for no more than two days.
Pain focused in front of and behind ear, sometimes spreading to face, neck, and shoulders; discomfort or clicking sound when opening mouth.	Temporomandibular disorder (see page 193).	Try over-the-counter painkillers. Try heat and massage. Call doctor for advice and appointment if symptoms persist.
Pounding headache and fatigue in coffee drinkers who skip their morning cup or quit abruptly.	Caffeine withdrawal.	Have cup of coffee for immediate relief. Cut back gradually if you're trying to break caffeine habit.

organized as possible. Particularly in the early stages, routines and visual aids such as checklists for daily tasks can help a person who has Alzheimer's maintain some self-sufficiency.

➤ Be patient. Forgetfulness, sudden mood changes, and difficult behavior are symptoms of the disease, not ill will.

➤ Help people who have Alzheimer's remain active and maintain their family and social ties as long as possible. If you take care of someone with the disease, consider contacting an Alzheimer's support group, which can help both of you.

➤ If the person with Alzheimer's tends to wander, have him or her wear a medical ID bracelet that says "Memory Impaired" and shows your phone number.

➤ Restrict driving. A person with Alzheimer's should not drive because the disease impairs judgment and coordination.

➤ Contact your doctor about ways to control symptoms like insomnia, agitated behavior, and depression.

A LITTLE FORGETFUL? DON'T FRET.

Everyone forgets things once in a while. Most middle-aged and older people find that their memory slows down a bit as they age. They may become more forgetful, and, more commonly, they may take a little longer to remember things than they used to. This does not mean that they have Alzheimer's disease.

Older people may sometimes become confused or forgetful because of emotional problems as they deal with major life changes—retirement, the death of a loved one, and other upheavals. In people of any age, high fever, poor nutrition, head injuries, and reactions to medication can cause temporary forgetfulness. That's normal. But if memory problems persist and become increasingly bothersome, call your doctor for advice and an appointment.

➤ Arrange for someone to take over for you now and then to relieve some of the stress.

HOW TO PREVENT IT

There is currently no known way to prevent Alzheimer's disease.

WHEN TO CALL THE DOCTOR

➤ If someone shows consistent symptoms of Alzheimer's. Because the individual may not be aware of the condition, it is often up to others to help. It's sometimes hard for people to recognize and acknowledge their own symptoms.

➤ If someone is in the later stages of Alzheimer's, at the first sign of an infection or other illness. The disease can undermine resistance.

➤ If the person with Alzheimer's endangers him- or herself or others.

➤ If you take care of a person with Alzheimer's and feel that you are approaching a breaking point.

FOR MORE HELP

Information line: Alzheimer's Disease Education and Referral Center, 800-438-4380, M–F 8:30–5 EST. Specialists answer questions and provide information and referrals to other organizations.

Information line: Alzheimer's Association, 919 N. Michigan Ave., #1000, Chicago, IL 60611-1676. 800-272-3900, 24-hour line. More than 200 chapters nationwide provide literature, referrals, and information on support groups.

Book: *Alzheimer's: A Caregiver's Guide and Sourcebook,* by Howard Gruetzner. A comprehensive resource for anyone coping with this disease. John Wiley & Sons, 1992, $14.95.

Video: *Alzheimer's Disease at Time of Diagnosis.* Clear, useful overview of causes and treatments, consisting of four reports—Understanding the Diagnosis, What Happens Next?, Treatment and Management, and Issues and Answers. Time Life Medical, 1996, $19.95.

Dizziness

SYMPTOMS	WHAT IT MIGHT BE	WHAT YOU CAN DO
After blow to head: dizziness and momentary loss of consciousness; headache, nausea, and vomiting.	Concussion (see head, neck, and back injuries, page 37).	Call 911 or go to emergency facility **immediately** after any blow to head that results in loss of consciousness.
Dizziness and fever over 104; no sweating; rapid pulse; confusion; hot, dry skin; loss of consciousness. Occurs after several hours in hot environment.	Heat stroke (see page 38).	Call 911 or go to emergency facility **immediately.** If waiting for medical help to arrive, cool person with cold, wet cloths and fan.
Dizziness, palpitations, shortness of breath, occasionally chest pressure or discomfort.	Irregular heartbeat (see page 108). ● Heart attack (see page 38).	Call 911 or go to emergency facility **immediately.**
Sudden dizziness and headache, weakness or numbness in face, arm, or leg; blurred vision or difficulty speaking; confusion.	Stroke (see page 45).	Call 911 or go to emergency facility **immediately.**
After head injury (often days or weeks later): dizziness and fatigue, weakness or numbness on one side of body.	Subdural hemorrhage and hematoma—bleeding and swelling in brain.	Call 911 or go to emergency facility **immediately.**
Dizziness; vomiting; sudden high fever; confusion; diarrhea; headache; red rash, often on palms of hands and soles of feet.	Toxic shock syndrome (see page 236). ● Other bacterial infection in blood.	Call 911 or go to emergency facility **immediately.**
Dizziness, nausea, vomiting, and headache; cramps in arms, legs, or abdomen; cool, clammy skin; excessive sweating; rapid pulse. Usually occurs while working or exercising in hot weather without drinking enough fluids.	Heat exhaustion (see page 38).	Call doctor for emergency advice. Watch for symptoms of heat stroke. Cool person with cold, wet cloths and fan. Give water or salt water.

Dizziness

SYMPTOMS	WHAT IT MIGHT BE	WHAT YOU CAN DO
Dizziness, frequent headaches, nausea and vomiting, double vision, seizures, confusion, memory loss.	Brain tumor.	Call doctor for immediate appointment.
Dizziness and headache, intense hunger, shaking, irritability, confusion, anxiety.	Hypoglycemia—low blood sugar, usually in people who take insulin.	Diabetics should eat or drink something containing sugar; for others, nonsugared foods. If symptoms persist, call doctor for advice and appointment. If person has seizure or loses consciousness, call 911 or go to emergency facility **immediately.**
Dizziness, weakness and fatigue, pale skin, shortness of breath.	Anemia (see page 264).	Call doctor for immediate appointment.
Earache, fever, chills, stuffy nose, blocked or full feeling in ear, muffled hearing, discharge from ear. In infants: tugging at ear, irritability, restlessness, lack of appetite.	Middle ear infection (see page 71).	Call doctor for immediate appointment.
Sudden, severe dizziness, nausea, and vomiting; loss of balance or hearing.	Ménière's syndrome. • Labyrynthitis.	See ear and hearing problems chart, page 69.
Within 24 hours after head or neck injury: pain and stiffness in neck, dizziness, headache, nausea and vomiting, difficulty walking (sometimes).	Whiplash, often caused by car collision.	Call doctor for immediate appointment if neck is injured. Apply ice packs and take pain relievers. Sleep with thin pillow under head and thin rolled-up towel under neck.
Dizziness, especially when moving head; nausea and vomiting.	Benign paroxysmal positional vertigo—dizziness related to inner ear.	Call doctor for advice and appointment.

Meningitis and Encephalitis

If you or someone close to you experience the following, call your doctor for emergency advice. If not available, call 911 or go to an emergency facility.

Meningitis in children:

- Fever of 100 degrees or higher, combined with:
- Headache or stiff neck. In a lying position, the head cannot be bent toward the chest (except in infants less than one month old) because of shooting pain in the neck and back.
- Irritability or listlessness.
- Loss of appetite.
- Turning away from bright lights.
- Possibly nausea and vomiting.
- In infants, a bulging of the soft spot of the skull.
- Possibly seizures.
- Rarely, a bumpy red or purple rash anywhere on the body.

Meningitis or encephalitis in adults:

- Fever, other flulike symptoms, and headache combined with:
- Eyes sensitive to light.
- Mental confusion, drowsiness, lethargy, or irritability.
- Delirium, seizures, or coma.
- Possibly, in encephalitis cases only, paralysis.
- Stiff neck, shoulders, or back. In meningitis cases only, shooting pain in the neck and back when head is bent forward.
- Rarely, in meningitis cases only, a bumpy red or purplish rash anywhere on the body.

Encephalitis in children:

- Same symptoms as in adults.
- In infants, a bulging of the soft spot of the skull.

Meningitis and encephalitis are brain diseases with similar symptoms, and both demand immediate medical attention.

Meningitis is an inflammation of the delicate membranes that cover the spinal cord and brain. Bacteria, viruses, and fungi can cause it. Bacterial meningitis can follow an illness such as pneumonia or an infection of the sinuses or the ears. A skull fracture or other head injury also raises the risk. Some forms of viral meningitis can spread from person to person through the air.

Bacterial meningitis can lead to death within hours if it goes untreated, but early care usually results in complete recovery. Treatment includes hospitalization and intravenous antibiotics.

Viral meningitis is usually a milder form of the illness that goes away on its own. It is treated with bed rest and plenty of liquids.

Encephalitis is an inflammation of the brain that is almost always caused by a virus. In the United States, it is most commonly caused by herpes simplex, the virus that causes cold sores. The illness can also be brought on by the chicken pox, mumps, or measles viruses. Another form is spread by mosquitoes and ticks.

Severe encephalitis, which is rare, can lead to brain damage or death. People with a mild case of encephalitis usually recover in two to three weeks.

➤ If a child or an adult shows the symptoms listed, call your doctor for emergency advice. If not available, call 911 or go to an emergency facility.

➤ Get early treatment for any serious infection or high fever.
➤ Ask your doctor about immunizing your child against meningitis.
➤ If you or your child have had close contact with a person who has bacterial meningitis, call your doctor for advice. You may be advised to take antibiotics (even if you show no symptoms) to ward off possible infection.

RED FLAG FOR CHILDREN

The bacterial form of meningitis, which strikes infants and young children more than adults, can lead to death within hours—or to permanent brain damage—if it goes untreated. Very young children are in particular danger, because they cannot describe their symptoms. Call 911 or go to an emergency facility **immediately** if a child has the symptoms listed. Early treatment usually results in full recovery.

➤ Avoid ticks by wearing long pants and long-sleeved shirts in grassy or wooded areas (see **tick bites,** page 46).
➤ Prevent insect bites by applying repellent.

FOR MORE HELP

Organization: National Institute of Neurological Disorders and Stroke, 31 Center Drive, MSC 2540, Bethesda, MD 20892-2540. 301-496-5751, M–F 9–5 EST. Ask for the information packet on meningitis and encephalitis.

Parkinson's Disease

SIGNS AND SYMPTOMS

Early symptoms:
■ Weakness.
■ Slight tremor of the head or hands.
■ Depression (sometimes).
■ Masklike appearance of the face and infrequent blinking.
■ Muscle stiffness.
■ Slowed movement.

Later symptoms:
■ Loss of balance.
■ Tremors in the hands and/or head when at rest.
■ Confusion and memory loss (in severe cases).

Parkinson's disease, which usually shows up in people who are over 60, results when nerve cells in the area of the brain that controls body movement begin to deteriorate. Genes, brain injury, and environmental toxins may trigger the disease in some people, but in most cases its causes are unknown.

There is no cure for Parkinson's disease, but many people find that medication—most commonly levodopa, in combination with other drugs—controls their symptoms. Current research suggests that some medications, such as selegiline, may even slow the progress of the disease.

WHAT YOU CAN DO NOW

➤ Since a small number of prescription drugs can cause symptoms similar to those of Parkinson's disease—particularly some used to treat psychiatric illnesses—check with your doctor to find out whether your symptoms could be drug-induced. If so, changing the drug or drugs might eliminate the symptoms.

After diagnosis:
➤ While experts agree that it is good for people who have Parkinson's to remain active and to exercise, do not tire yourself out. Find ways to relax, since stress and fatigue can make symptoms worse. As with any illness, it is important to eat well and take good care of yourself.
➤ Physical therapy, deep muscle massage, and yoga may help you move more easily, but consult your doctor before beginning any new program.
➤ Consider joining a support group. Many people with Parkinson's find that comradeship eases the depression that can accompany the disease.

WHEN TO CALL THE DOCTOR

➤ If you or someone close to you have symptoms of Parkinson's disease.
➤ If you have any new symptoms during treatment. They may be side effects of the medication you're taking or may indicate a worsening of the condition.

HOW TO PREVENT IT

There is no known way to prevent Parkinson's disease.

FOR MORE HELP

Organization: American Parkinson's Disease Association, 1250 Hylan Blvd., Staten Island, NY 10305. 800-223-2732, M–F 9–5 EST. Ask for referrals to one of the 500 support groups and 95 chapters nationwide. Also provides education, information on diet and exercise, counseling, and referrals to health professionals.

Organization: Parkinson's Disease Foundation, William Black Medical Research Bldg., 650 W. 168th St., New York, NY 10032-9982. 800-457-6676, M–F 9–8 EST. Ask for information on patient care, rehabilitation, and referrals to clinics across the country.

Organization: Parkinson Support Groups of America, 11376 Cherry Hill Rd., #204, Beltsville, MD 20705. 301-937-1545, 24-hour line. Connects people with Parkinson's disease and their families with others who are dealing with the condition.

Seizures and Epilepsy

SIGNS AND SYMPTOMS

- Many people with epilepsy experience a warning sign, known as an aura, that lasts a few seconds and is generally characterized by nausea, feelings of dread, distinctive smells and tastes, or distorted vision. Auras vary widely, but individuals usually have the same aura before each seizure.

Petit mal, or absence, seizure:
- An abrupt end to a person's activity as he or she simply stares blankly for several seconds, sometimes blinking or making chewing motions.

Grand mal, or tonic-clonic, seizure:
- Convulsions, jerking motions, and loss of consciousness, often accompanied by loss of bladder control and sometimes of bowel control. Should stop after one to two minutes; followed by confusion and sleepiness.

Other epileptic seizures:
- Seeing or hearing things that aren't there.
- Incoherent talk or out-of-character behavior and speech—sometimes mistaken for drug abuse.

Two and a half million Americans have epilepsy, a condition that results in recurring seizures—brief episodes in which the brain's electrical system is overloaded and malfunctions.

If a person has a single seizure, he or she probably does not have epilepsy. It's not uncommon, for example, for a very young child with a high fever to have a seizure. This needs medical attention, but does not necessarily mean the child has epilepsy (see **fevers in children,** page 248). In adults and children, other conditions that can trigger seizures include diabetes, meningitis, and encephalitis. Pregnancy, poisoning, heat stroke, and alcohol or drug abuse can also bring them on.

Epilepsy can start at any age, even over 65, but it usually appears first in childhood or early adulthood. Children who have petit mal seizures often outgrow them. In just over half the cases of epilepsy, the cause is unknown. In the rest, possible causes include severe head injury, brain tumor, stroke, poisoning, infection, and congenital brain damage. Experts believe that heredity can also play a role.

Up to 85 percent of people with epilepsy can control it with antiseizure medications. For those who cannot control their seizures any other way, brain surgery may help.

WHAT YOU CAN DO NOW

If you have epilepsy, take steps to avoid seizures or to minimize their effects:
➤ Take your medication regularly and in the

right dosage. (Missing doses can trigger a seizure.) Consult a doctor before switching to a generic brand, since your body may absorb it differently than it does your regular brand.

➤ If you experience a seizure warning sign, or aura, avoid a possible fall by lying down or moving away from any hazards.

➤ Be aware that stress, fatigue, and alcohol or drug abuse can bring on seizures.

➤ Keep a seizure diary, noting the kind of seizure, the time, and possible triggers. This can help you keep medication to a minimum and gain a measure of control over your condition.

➤ Wear an engraved medical identification bracelet to help others quickly understand the problem and lend assistance.

➤ Get regular exercise and practice relaxation techniques to help reduce stress and tension.

➤ Ask your doctor if it is safe for you to drive.

If you are with someone who has a seizure:

➤ See **seizures,** page 42, for emergency procedures.

WHEN TO CALL THE DOCTOR

Call 911 or go to an emergency facility **immediately:**

➤ If the seizure lasts more than five minutes, if a second seizure begins shortly after the first, or if the person does not seem to regain consciousness after the seizure.

➤ If the person is pregnant or diabetic.

Call your doctor for emergency advice. If not available, call 911 or go to an emergency facility:

➤ If your child has a high fever and has a seizure or what you suspect to be one.

Call for advice and an appointment:

➤ If someone you know, particularly a child, goes through periods of blank staring, loss of consciousness, confused memory, fainting spells or falls, or inappropriate blinking or chewing motions.

➤ If your doctor has prescribed antiseizure medication and you have side effects such as drowsiness, hyperactivity, disorientation, or sleep problems.

HOW TO PREVENT IT

There is no known way to prevent most kinds of epilepsy. Good prenatal care, avoiding substance abuse, and protecting yourself and your children from head injuries by using seat belts and bicycle helmets are commonsense ways to guard against the illness.

FOR MORE HELP

Organization: Epilepsy Foundation of America, 4351 Garden City Dr., Landover, MD 20785. 800-332-1000, in English and Spanish, M–F 9–5 EST. Staffers send information, answer questions, and refer callers to other resources. Offers recreational and educational programs for children with epilepsy, and information on local chapters and support groups.

Eyes

Cataracts

SIGNS AND SYMPTOMS

- Blurred or hazy vision.
- Discomfort or impaired vision that's caused by bright lights.
- A feeling of having a film over the eyes or of looking through fog.
- Double or triple vision occurring in one eye only.
- "Second sight"—a temporary improvement in near vision, so you may not need your reading glasses for a brief time.
- Opaque or white area visible when you look into the pupil of the eye (when a cataract is advanced).

A cataract is a clouding of the normally clear lens of the eye (see color illustration, page 161). It can obscure vision just as steam fogs a window. Cataracts usually develop slowly, over a period of years, and many people don't notice them at first, though vision loss may begin to interfere with the tasks of daily living, including safe driving.

Most cataracts are caused by the deterioration of the lens with age. Cataracts also result from certain diseases, such as diabetes, or from eye injuries, long-term exposure to bright sunlight, or the prolonged use of drugs such as corticosteroids (prescribed for illnesses such as arthritis). Cigarette smok-

ing may also increase the risk. Some babies are born with cataracts in one or both eyes, after developing them in the womb when the mother contracted German measles (rubella) during pregnancy.

The only accepted treatment today for cataracts is surgery. The entire lens of the eye or the interior of the lens is removed through a small incision. Usually it is replaced by a clear plastic lens. Less often, instead of inserting a new lens, the doctor prescribes special eyeglasses or contact lenses after surgery. You can usually have the surgery in the doctor's office and go home the same day. More than 95 percent of people who have cataract surgery report improved vision.

WHAT YOU CAN DO NOW

➤ If you suspect you have cataracts, call your doctor for advice on whether you should see an ophthalmologist (a medical doctor licensed to treat all eye conditions). He or she can tell you if you'll need surgery.

WHEN TO CALL THE DOCTOR

➤ If you have several of the symptoms, especially blurred vision or discomfort from bright lights.

HOW TO PREVENT IT

➤ Buy sunglasses that shield your eyes from the ultraviolet A (UVA) and ultraviolet B (UVB) rays in sunlight. Sunglasses that block out UVA and UVB light are labeled

Eye and Vision Problems

SYMPTOMS	WHAT IT MIGHT BE	WHAT YOU CAN DO
Sudden vision changes, such as blindness, double vision, blurring, flashes of light, floating dark shapes, loss of peripheral vision; acute, sustained pain.	Stroke (see page 45). • Transient ischemic attack—temporary blockage of artery, with symptoms like stroke. • Acute glaucoma (see page 65). • Macular degeneration—deterioration of center of retina. • Retinal detachment—hole in retina. • Optic neuritis—inflammation of optic nerve.	Call 911 or go to emergency facility **immediately** if you experience sudden blindness, loss of part of visual field, or double vision; you may be having a stroke. Call doctor for immediate appointment if you have any other sudden vision changes.
Redness, watering, pain, or a feeling of having something in the eye.	Foreign body in eye (see eye injuries, page 32).	Call doctor for immediate appointment if something is in colored part of eye or if you can't get particle out of white of eye.
Blurred vision; slow loss of peripheral (side) vision; sudden, severe eye pain; halos around lights; teary, aching eyes; headache; nausea; vomiting.	Glaucoma (see page 65).	Call doctor for immediate appointment.
Blurred vision, sensitivity to light, ache or pain in eye, headache, redness (no discharge).	Iritis/uveitis—inflammation inside eye.	Call doctor for immediate appointment; prescription drugs may help.
Either rapid, severe vision loss or gradual vision loss; dim or distorted vision, especially when reading; dark, empty area in center of visual field; straight lines look wavy.	Macular degeneration—the macula, a tiny spot at center of retina, begins to deteriorate or scar. Symptoms usually appear after age 55.	Call doctor for immediate appointment. Some forms can be slowed with laser treatment. **For more help:** Association for Macular Diseases, 210 E. 64th St., New York, NY 10021. 212-605-3719, M–F 10–1 EST.
Flashes of light, floating dark shapes, loss of peripheral vision.	Retinal detachment—hole in retina. Risk increases with age or after cataract surgery.	Call doctor for immediate appointment. In early stages, vision can be restored with surgery.

(continued)

Eye and Vision Problems *(continued)*

SYMPTOMS	WHAT IT MIGHT BE	WHAT YOU CAN DO
Small, red, painful bump at base of eyelash.	Stye.	See styes, page 66.
Red and itchy eyelids.	Blepharitis—inflammation and scaling of eyelids.	Wash eyelids with warm water containing a few drops of baby shampoo, or with over-the-counter eyelid wash. Call doctor for advice and appointment if condition doesn't clear up with home treatment.
Hazy vision, blurriness around lights, frequent changes in eyeglass prescriptions, white area visible in pupil.	Cataracts.	See cataracts, page 60.
White of eye is bloodshot; sticky or watery discharge; itching.	Conjunctivitis.	See conjunctivitis, opposite page.
Blurred vision when looking at nearby objects, eyestrain, headaches.	Presbyopia, or farsightedness. Occurs with age as lens loses flexibility.	Call doctor for advice and appointment. Eyeglasses or contact lenses can correct it.
Blurred vision when looking at distant objects.	Myopia, or nearsightedness. May run in families.	Call doctor for advice and appointment. Eyeglasses or contact lenses can correct it.
Red spot on white of eye.	Subconjunctival hemorrhage—bleeding from small blood vessels in membrane over eyeball.	Harmless, though can be alarming in appearance. Usually no apparent cause; may follow injury, coughing, or sneezing. Should clear up in 2–3 days. Call doctor for advice if painful or if bleeding recurs.

as "fulfilling the American National Standards Institute requirement." The label should also say that they "eliminate 99 percent of UVA and UVB."

➤ If you are a woman and intend to become pregnant, protect your baby by getting vaccinated for German measles if you haven't had the disease already.

➤ Wear safety glasses to prevent eye injury when playing sports, or when using power tools or caustic chemicals such as paint remover.

➤ Eat more green and yellow vegetables, which contain substances (antioxidants) that researchers believe help prevent cataracts.

FOR MORE HELP

Information line: National Eye Care Project Help Line, 800-222-3937, M–F 8–4 PST. Refers disadvantaged senior citizens to ophthalmologists who provide medical care at no cost to seniors.

Organization: Prevent Blindness America, 500 E. Remington Rd., Schaumburg, IL 60173. 800-331-2020, M–F 8–4 CST. Provides material on eye diseases and maintains a network of support groups across the country.

Organization: National Eye Health Education Program, National Institutes of Health, 301-496-5248, M–F 8:30–4:30 EST. Provides brochures, fact sheets, and general information about eye disease.

Video: *Cataracts at Time of Diagnosis.* Clear, useful overview of causes and treatments, consisting of four reports—Understanding the Diagnosis, What Happens Next?, Treatment and Management, and Issues and Answers. Time Life Medical, 1996, $19.95.

Conjunctivitis

SIGNS AND SYMPTOMS

Reddening of the whites of the eyes is common to all types of conjunctivitis. Other signs include:

In bacterial conjunctivitis:
- Discharge of pus from the eye or crusting on the eyelashes in the morning.

In viral conjunctivitis:
- Watery discharge, often from one eye only, occasionally with crusting.
- Sore throat and runny nose, with some viruses.

In allergic conjunctivitis:
- Itching eyes.
- Burning and watery eyes.
- Swelling of the tissues around eye.
- Runny nose, sneezing.

In conjunctivitis caused by environmental irritants:
- Burning and watery eyes.
- A sensation of having something in the eye.

Conjunctivitis is an inflammation of the membrane (conjunctiva) that covers the inside of the eyelid and the white of the eye. It is annoying but rarely serious. Causes include:

➤ Bacterial or viral infections (commonly called pinkeye).

➤ Allergies to substances such as grass pollen, house dust, mold, or cosmetics.

➤ Environmental irritants such as smoke and fumes.

➤ In newborns (rarely): infection from the lining of the mother's birth canal. This is a serious condition that must be treated at once, as it can cause blindness.

When caused by bacteria or a virus, conjunctivitis is highly contagious and easily spread through direct contact or by touching contaminated towels, handkerchiefs, or washcloths. A doctor can prescribe antibiotic eyedrops or ointment to quicken recovery.

Allergic conjunctivitis can be chronic or may be bothersome in allergy season. It is not contagious.

WHAT YOU CAN DO NOW

Bacterial or viral conjunctivitis:
➤ To soothe infected eyes, apply a clean, warm, damp cloth. Wash used cloths in hot water with detergent, so you don't spread the infection.
➤ If you suspect your child has infectious conjunctivitis, keep him or her at home so it won't spread. The teacher and other parents will thank you.

Conjunctivitis caused by environmental irritants:
➤ To soothe irritated eyes, use artificial teardrops, available over the counter.

Allergic conjunctivitis:
➤ Apply a cold, damp washcloth to the eyes to relieve itching.
➤ Try over-the-counter allergy eyedrops or pills to reduce redness and itching. Be aware that the pills can cause drowsiness.

WHEN TO CALL THE DOCTOR

Call for an immediate appointment:
➤ If your newborn's eyes redden and produce a discharge; this condition must be treated quickly to prevent permanent eye damage.

Call for advice:
➤ If you injure your eye; injuries can become infected and lead to corneal ulcers.
➤ If conjunctivitis affects your vision or produces severe pain or excessive discharge; this may mean a staph or strep infection.
➤ If your conjunctivitis appears to be getting worse after a week of home care; you may have a bacterial or viral infection.
➤ If you get conjunctivitis frequently.
➤ If you have symptoms of conjunctivitis that don't seem to be due to an infection, a cold, or allergies. Several eye diseases can also cause redness and tearing, including **glaucoma** (see opposite page).
➤ If you notice blurred vision, light sensitivity, and redness in the eye; these may be signs of advanced glaucoma.

HOW TO PREVENT IT

➤ Don't share eye makeup or eyedrops.
➤ Don't share handkerchiefs, towels, or washcloths.
➤ If you have conjunctivitis, don't touch your eye and then touch someone; the ailment can be spread to others.
➤ Wash your hands frequently if you have conjunctivitis, or if you live with someone who has it.
➤ If you have allergies, try to avoid common allergens like pollen, dust, mold, or pets with hair or fur.
➤ During allergy season, filter the air in your car by running the air conditioner, and keep the windows and doors in your home closed.
➤ Wear goggles if your eyes are sensitive to environmental irritants or to chemicals or fumes on the job.

FOR MORE HELP

Information line: National Eye Care Project Help Line, 800-222-3937, M–F 8–4 PST. Refers disadvantaged senior citizens to ophthalmologists who provide medical care at no cost to seniors.

Organization: National Eye Health Education Program, National Institutes of Health, 301-496-5248, M–F 8:30–4:30 EST. Provides brochures, fact sheets, and general information about eye disease.

Organization: American Academy of Ophthalmology, P.O. Box 7424, San Francisco, CA 94120-7424. 415-561-8500, M–F 9–5 PST. Provides fact sheets on eye diseases. Send a business-size, self-addressed, stamped envelope, and request a brochure on conjunctivitis.

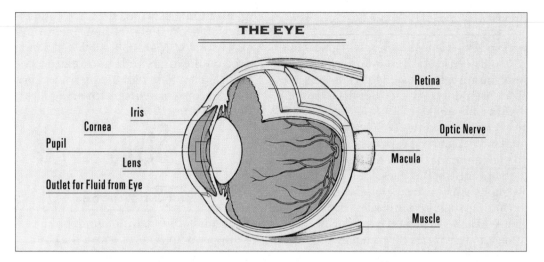

THE EYE

- Retina
- Iris
- Cornea
- Pupil
- Lens
- Outlet for Fluid from Eye
- Optic Nerve
- Macula
- Muscle

Glaucoma

Typically, there are no symptoms at first. By the time symptoms do appear, some vision may have been lost permanently, so it's very important to diagnose and treat glaucoma early.

In chronic glaucoma:
- Blurred vision.
- Progressive loss of side (peripheral) vision.
- Teary, aching eyes.
- Occasional headaches.

In acute glaucoma:
- Severe, sudden eye pain.
- Blurred vision.
- Rainbow halos around lights.
- Headaches.
- Nausea and vomiting.

In secondary glaucoma (after an injury or certain diseases):
- Blurred vision.
- Halos around lights.
- Headaches.

Think of the eye as a sink with a faucet and a drain. The "faucet" consists of cells that continually produce fluid that fills the eye. The "drain" lets out excess fluid, so the pressure inside remains constant. Glaucoma occurs when the drain becomes clogged; pressure builds inside the eye and presses on the optic nerve or on the small vessels that nourish the retina. Left untreated, glaucoma can cause permanent vision loss and even blindness.

Glaucoma is one of the most common eye problems in men and women over 60. It runs in families. People of African ancestry and those with diabetes are at greater risk than others. It may be brought on by certain drugs, such as antidepressants or some medications prescribed for asthma or irritable bowel syndrome. Those with past eye injuries may be prone to secondary glaucoma.

Chronic glaucoma, which accounts for 90 percent of cases, is often called the "sneak thief in the night" because it comes on gradually to steal away vision. Acute glaucoma accounts for fewer than 10 percent of cases; it comes on quickly and requires immediate medical attention.

Glaucoma can usually be controlled with eyedrops, pills, or injections that decrease pressure in the eye. Laser surgery, sometimes used to widen clogged drainage channels or to create new ones, is commonly done in a doctor's office. Serious cases may require further treatment.

There is no home treatment for glaucoma, so it's important for a doctor to diagnose and treat glaucoma early to prevent permanent eye damage.

➤ If you experience symptoms of glaucoma. You'll need medical attention right away.

➤ If you are being treated for glaucoma and another doctor prescribes drugs for another ailment.

➤ If you are taking eyedrops or pills for glaucoma and you experience side effects such as headaches; red eyes; a stinging sensation in the eyes; blurred vision; changes in heartbeat, pulse, or breathing; tingling of fingers and toes; drowsiness; loss of appetite; bowel irregularities; kidney stones; or easy bleeding; or you learn you have anemia.

➤ If you become drowsy, fatigued, or short of breath after taking eyedrops for glaucoma. The medication may be aggravating a heart or lung problem.

HOW TO PREVENT IT

➤ Get an eye exam every three to five years if you are 39 or older.

➤ Schedule an eye exam every one to two years if you have family members with glaucoma or severe myopia, if you have African ancestors, if you have ever had a serious eye injury, or if you are taking antidepressants or medications for asthma or irritable bowel syndrome.

➤ If you have **diabetes** (see page 269), take steps to control it.

FOR MORE HELP

Information line: National Eye Care Project Help Line, 800-222-3937, M–F 8–4 PST. Refers disadvantaged senior citizens to ophthalmologists who provide medical care at no cost to seniors.

Information line: American Foundation for the Blind, 800-232-5463, M–F 9–2 EST. Supplies free information on visual impairment, including career counseling for people who have trouble seeing.

Organization: National Eye Health Education Program, National Institutes of Health, 301-496-5248, M–F 8:30–4:30 EST. Provides brochures, fact sheets, and general information about eye disease.

Organization: Glaucoma Research Foundation, 800-826-6693, 24-hour recording. 415-986-3162, M–F 8:30– 4:30 PST. Sends free publications and coordinates a national, telephone-based support network for glaucoma patients and their families.

Styes

SIGNS AND SYMPTOMS

■ A small, red, painful bump on the upper or lower eyelid near the base of an eyelash.

■ Burning, itching, or a feeling of having something in the eye.

■ Tearing in the affected eye.

A stye is a bacterial infection of a gland at the base of an eyelash. Styes are often painful, although they are not a serious problem.

Styes usually enlarge, fill with pus, and break open within three to seven days, relieving the pain. They may also go away without bursting. They're easily spread by touching your eyelid, by squeezing the stye, or by using contaminated makeup or towels.

WHAT YOU CAN DO NOW

➤ Apply a soft, clean washcloth that has been soaked in warm water and wrung out; hold for 10 to 15 minutes. Repeat this two to four times a day, until the stye goes away.

➤ Use a new washcloth each time, so you don't spread the infection. Wash used cloths in hot water with detergent.

➤ If the stye comes to a head and bursts, carefully wash the pus from the eyelid and apply an antibiotic ointment. Don't pick at the stye.

WHEN TO CALL THE DOCTOR

➤ If the stye does not respond to home care within a week. A doctor may prescribe an-

tibiotic drops or ointment, or may lance
and drain the stye.

➤ If there is an infection elsewhere in your
body. Your doctor may prescribe a sys-
temic antibiotic.

➤ If the stye enlarges but doesn't break open
and drain.

➤ If styes keep coming back. Rarely, recurrent styes can be a sign of cancer of the
eyelid.

➤ If there are any signs of skin infection
(redness and roughness) spreading on the
eyelid.

HOW TO PREVENT IT

➤ Try to avoid touching or rubbing your
eyes. Styes can come back again if the bacteria spread.

➤ Wash your hands frequently with soap and
water.

➤ Don't share towels or washcloths.

➤ Change towels and pillowcases often.

➤ Be careful not to share eye makeup or eyedrops, and discard used cosmetics after
six months.

➤ If styes tend to recur, clean the outside of
your eyelids daily: Dip a cotton swab into
a teacup of warm water containing a few
drops of baby shampoo. Gently wash the
lashes of each closed eyelid with this solution once or twice a day.

FOR MORE HELP

Organization: American Optometric Association, 314-991-4100, M–F 7:30–5 CST.
Distributes free pamphlets on eye and vision problems.

Organization: National Eye Health Education Program, National Institutes of
Health, 301-496-5248, M–F 8:30–4:30
EST. Provides brochures, fact sheets, and
general information about eye disease.

Eyes

Ears

◆

Airplane Ears

SIGNS AND SYMPTOMS

- Feeling of fullness in the ears.
- Moderate to severe pain or discomfort inside the ears.
- Possibly some temporary hearing loss.
- Dizziness.
- Ringing in the ears.

The condition called "airplane ears" (barotrauma) often occurs when you take a plane trip, especially if you have a **cold** (see page 90), **sinusitis** (see page 95), or **allergies** (see page 85). But you don't have to fly to get airplane ears. It can happen any time rapid air-pressure changes occur—while riding in an elevator in a high-rise, for instance, or while scuba or skin diving.

The problem is in the middle ear, which is most affected by changes in air pressure. The middle ear is connected to the back of the nose by a tube called the eustachian tube (see illustration, page 72) that can become blocked or swollen. If it does, it can cause uncomfortable pressure to build in the ears, especially during descents.

WHAT YOU CAN DO NOW

➤ Simply swallowing can help. This activates the muscle that opens the tube leading to the middle ear. Try this just before and during the plane's descent; chew gum or suck on candy so you'll swallow more often. Yawning works the same way.
➤ Avoid sleeping during descent.

If swallowing and yawning don't work, try this more active way to unplug your ears:

➤ Take a deep breath through your mouth; then hold your nose and try to breathe out gently while keeping your mouth closed. This can help force air through the tubes between your nose and ears. You may have to do this several times during descent.

If you're flying with an infant:

➤ Give your baby something to drink or a pacifier during landing. Babies can't "pop" their ears on purpose, but sucking on a bottle or pacifier may do the trick.
➤ Wake your infant prior to descent.

WHEN TO CALL THE DOCTOR

➤ If your ears don't clear, or if pain persists for several hours after flying.
➤ If you're planning a plane trip and have recently had ear surgery. Consult with your doctor on how soon you may fly safely.

HOW TO PREVENT IT

If you have a cold, sinus infection, or allergy attack, it's best to postpone a plane trip. If you can't:

➤ Some air travelers find relief by using an over-the-counter decongestant pill or nasal spray about an hour before landing.
➤ People with allergies should take their

Ear and Hearing Problems

SYMPTOMS	WHAT IT MIGHT BE	WHAT YOU CAN DO
Severe pain and swelling within and behind ear, fluid coming from ear, fever, temporary hearing loss.	Mastoiditis—inflammation of mastoid bone behind ear.	Call doctor for immediate appointment. Antibiotics or prompt surgical drainage may be required.
Pain, partial hearing loss, discharge or bleeding from ear.	Ruptured (perforated) eardrum—typically caused by object inserted into ear. ● Serious middle ear infection (see page 71). ● Blow to ear; or injury while diving or water-skiing.	Call doctor for immediate appointment. Treatment includes medications, temporary patch over eardrum, or surgery. To relieve pain, cover ear with heating pad set on low and take painkillers.
Hearing loss, headache, earache, dizziness, and pus from ear.	Cholesteatoma—cyst in middle ear. Could be caused by repeated middle ear infections (see page 71). May wear away bone that lines ear cavity and damage bones in middle ear.	Call doctor for advice and appointment. Treatment may include operation to remove cyst.
Loss of balance, dizziness, ringing in ears, hearing loss, nausea or vomiting.	Labyrynthitis—infection usually caused by a virus, in area of inner ear that controls balance.	Call doctor for advice and appointment. Treatment includes medications and bed rest.
Repeated episodes of sudden and severe dizziness, hearing loss, or ringing in ear; loss of balance; headache; nausea or vomiting.	Ménière's syndrome—from fluid buildup in inner ear.	Call doctor for advice and appointment. Treatment includes medications and possibly surgery. Rest to reduce symptoms. Cut back on fluids and salt. Avoid alcohol, caffeine, smoking. **For more help:** Ménière's Network, EAR Foundation, 800-545-HEAR, M–F 8–4:30 CST.
Progressive hearing loss, dizziness, ringing in ear.	Otosclerosis—overgrowth of bone in middle ear. Often runs in families. More common in women; may get worse during pregnancy.	Call doctor for advice and appointment. Simplest treatment is hearing aid; surgery usually helps.

(continued)

Ear and Hearing Problems *(continued)*

SYMPTOMS	WHAT IT MIGHT BE	WHAT YOU CAN DO
Trouble hearing, particularly at higher frequencies and when there is background noise; difficulty understanding speech.	Presbycusis—age-related hearing loss. Usually begins between 40 and 50. Most common and severe in men.	Call doctor for advice and appointment. Hearing aid is usual treatment.
Full feeling, discomfort, or pain in ears during or after flying; temporary hearing loss; dizziness; ringing in ears.	Airplane ears.	See airplane ears, page 68.
Throbbing pain and/or tender lump in ear canal; discharge of pus or blood from ear.	Boil (see page 142).	Usually heals by itself. Antibiotic drops or heating pad may help.
Blocked or full feeling in ear, temporary hearing loss, pain or discomfort, ringing in ear.	Earwax (see page 73). ● Ear infection (see opposite page). ● Early sign of throat cancer (rarely).	If symptoms persist, call doctor for advice.
Earache, fever and chills, stuffy nose, blocked or full feeling in ear, muffled hearing, discharge from ear. In young children: tugging at ear, irritability, restlessness, lack of appetite.	Middle ear infection.	See ear infections, opposite page.
Itchy or blocked ear, pain or tenderness, yellowish discharge, flaky skin around ear, temporary hearing loss.	Swimmer's ear—infection of outer ear canal.	See swimmer's ear, page 73.
Earache with pain in jaw and/or face; headache; clicking noise or locked feeling when opening or closing mouth.	Temporomandibular disorder (TMD).	See temporomandibular disorder, page 193.
Ringing or buzzing in ears—noise that can't be heard by others.	Tinnitus.	See tinnitus, page 74.

Ear and Hearing Problems

SYMPTOMS	WHAT IT MIGHT BE	WHAT YOU CAN DO
Earache with sore, inflamed throat and difficulty swallowing; swollen neck glands; headache; fever; foul taste and whitish film at back of throat (adults); refusal to eat (children).	Tonsillitis (see page 99). • Throat cancer (rarely).	If symptoms persist, call doctor for advice.

medication about an hour before landing—but if it's prescription medicine, follow your doctor's directions.

FOR MORE HELP

Information line: American Speech-Language-Hearing Association, 800-638-8255, M–F 8:30–5 EST. Information specialists answer questions and provide written material on airplane ears and other disorders.

Ear Infections

SIGNS AND SYMPTOMS

In adults:
- Earache (either a sharp, sudden pain or a dull, continuous pain).
- Muffled hearing.

Sometimes accompanied by:
- Fever of 100 degrees or above, possibly with chills.
- Stuffy nose.
- Sore throat.
- Full feeling in the ear.
- Discharge of pus or blood from ear.
- Nausea or diarrhea.

In young children, especially those who aren't yet talking, watch for:
- Tugging at the ear.
- Irritability.
- Restlessness.
- Lack of appetite.
- Fever of 100 degrees or above.
- Discharge from the nose or ear.

A middle ear infection or inflammation (otitis media) is the most common cause of earaches, particularly in children. It tops the list of illnesses seen by pediatricians, but it can affect adults, too.

Ear infections are most often caused by **colds** (see page 90) or **flu** (see page 91), which swell the tissues of the middle ear (see illustration, page 72), trapping fluids and creating an ideal environment for bacteria or viruses to thrive. **Allergies** (see page 85) or irritants such as smoke or fumes can have the same effect.

Infections that continue for several weeks or happen over and over again can sometimes cause permanent hearing loss. In young children, any hearing loss is worrisome, as it may delay speech and language development; prompt treatment is essential.

An ear infection can lead to other complications, including mastoiditis (an inflammation of the mastoid bone behind the ear), perforation of the eardrum, **meningitis** (see page 56), and facial nerve paralysis.

WHAT YOU CAN DO NOW

➤ Hold a warm compress to your ear. Inhaling steam may also help.

(continued)

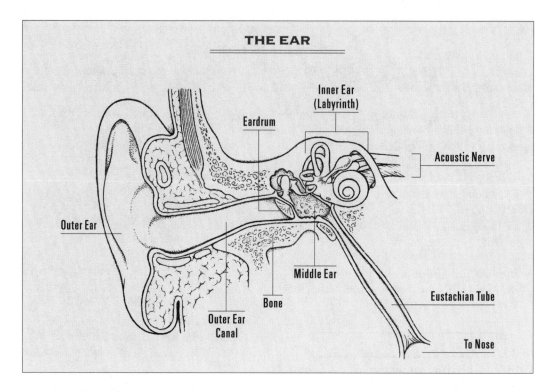

THE EAR

Inner Ear (Labyrinth)

Eardrum

Acoustic Nerve

Outer Ear

Middle Ear

Bone

Eustachian Tube

Outer Ear Canal

To Nose

➤ Gargle with salt water to soothe a sore throat and help open up blocked ears.

➤ Use pillows to raise your head when lying down. This helps drain your middle ear.

➤ Allergy sufferers may find relief with over-the-counter antihistamines. Some people use decongestant nasal sprays to help unblock the ears. But after a couple of days, sprays can lead to "rebound" congestion, worsening your condition.

➤ Over-the-counter drugs such as aspirin, ibuprofen, or acetaminophen may provide some relief. (Never give aspirin to a child under 12 who has chicken pox, flu, or any other illness you suspect of being caused by a virus, such as a bad respiratory infection; see box on **Reye's syndrome,** page 92.)

WHEN TO CALL THE DOCTOR

➤ If your child has symptoms of an ear infection or difficulty hearing.

➤ If you or your child have an earache that lasts more than two days.

➤ If your or your child's body temperature rises above 100 degrees.

➤ If you or your child frequently develop ear infections.

HOW TO PREVENT IT

➤ Remove irritants and allergy-causing agents from your home, including dust, cleaning fluids, and tobacco smoke.

➤ If you or your child are susceptible to food allergies, cut back on wheat products, corn products, or specific foods that may cause allergic reactions.

➤ Pay close attention to your baby's health—particularly if you are not breast-feeding. Bottle-fed babies are more likely to get ear infections. Hold your baby upright during bottle-feeding to prevent milk from irritating the tube that connects the back of the nose and the ear.

FOR MORE HELP

Information line: American Speech-Language-Hearing Association, 800-638-8255, M–F 8:30–5 EST. Information specialists answer questions on hearing loss; ask for the pamphlet on otitis media.

Organization: National Institute on Deafness and Other Communication Disorders Information Clearinghouse, 800-241-1044, M–F 8:30–5 EST. Ask for the ear infections information packet.

Earwax

SIGNS AND SYMPTOMS

- Blocked or plugged feeling in ear.
- Temporary, partial hearing loss.
- Ear pain or discomfort.
- Ringing in the ear.

Earwax provides a protective coating for the outer ear canal that leads to the eardrum (see illustration, opposite page). Usually earwax is soft, drains easily, and is unlikely to cause trouble.

But sometimes the wax builds up and becomes hard and dry. Then it's one of the most common causes of temporary hearing loss, especially when it mixes with dust, dirt, or water in the ear.

WHAT YOU CAN DO NOW

Infants and young children who have earwax buildup should be taken to a doctor. Adults can try the following remedies:

➤ Add one tablespoon of hydrogen peroxide to an equal amount of warm water.
  - Tilt your head, and put a dropperful of the warmed liquid into your blocked ear. Leave it there for three minutes, keeping your head tilted.
  - Let the liquid run out onto a towel or tissue. The wax should be soft enough to be wiped away from the outer ear with a cotton ball. Repeat if necessary.
  - If the wax is particularly stubborn, soften it up beforehand with three or four drops of castor oil or glycerin. You may need to do this several times.
➤ Over-the-counter liquid earwax softeners can help to loosen earwax. But don't use wax softeners if you suspect you have an **ear infection** (see page 71) or eardrum rupture (see **ear and hearing problems** chart, page 69).
➤ Use a soft rubber bulb syringe to dislodge wax by gently rinsing the ear canal with warm water or a mixture of warm water and hydrogen peroxide. Don't do this if

you have an earache, fever, discharge from your ear, or a perforated eardrum, or if you've recently had ear surgery.
➤ Never attempt to remove earwax with a cotton-tipped stick or swab. You can damage your eardrum or cause an infection.

WHEN TO CALL THE DOCTOR

Call for an immediate appointment:
➤ If you have a sudden or total hearing loss in one or both ears.
➤ If your ear secretes pus, fluid, or blood. This indicates an ear infection or a perforated eardrum.
Call for advice and an appointment:
➤ If the wax becomes so firmly lodged that home care doesn't work. You may need to have your doctor clean the ear.
➤ If your infant or young child has an earwax blockage. Don't try to remove the wax yourself.

HOW TO PREVENT IT

➤ Try wearing earplugs if you work in dusty conditions, which can trigger wax buildup.
➤ Don't let your child push objects into the ear canal. This can pack the wax in.

Swimmer's Ear

SIGNS AND SYMPTOMS

- Itchy or blocked feeling in the ear.
- Pain and tenderness in the ear, especially when moving your head or gently pulling on your earlobe.
- Watery, foul-smelling, or yellowish discharge from the ear.
- Patches of broken, flaky skin surrounding the opening of the ear.
- Temporary hearing loss or muffled hearing.

You don't have to be a swimmer to suffer from "swimmer's ear" (otitis externa), an inflammation of the outer ear canal that leads to the eardrum. It's typically caused by moisture in the ear, often from swimming, particularly in polluted water. But frequent shampooing or showering can trigger the problem as well.

The moisture causes the skin inside the ear canal to flake or crack, allowing bacteria or fungi to invade. Certain skin conditions, such as **dermatitis** (see page 144) and **psoriasis** (see page 152), can lead to swimmer's ear. Another common cause is a lack of earwax, which protects the ear canal from moisture. Swimmer's ear usually isn't serious, though it can be annoying.

Swimmer's ear often clears up on its own. If not, it responds quickly to treatment and usually disappears within a few days. Here's what you can do to speed recovery:

➤ Keep the infected ear dry. Protect your ears when showering or washing your hair. Avoid swimming.

➤ Use over-the-counter antiseptic eardrops. Or you can make your own using equal parts rubbing alcohol and white vinegar. Leave the drops in your ear for a couple of minutes, then tilt your head to let them drain out.

➤ Hold a warm compress over the ear to relieve pain. Over-the-counter drugs such as aspirin or acetaminophen may help, too. (Never give aspirin to a child under 12 who has chicken pox, flu, or any other illness you suspect of being caused by a virus, such as a bad respiratory infection; see box on **Reye's syndrome,** page 92.)

WHEN TO CALL THE DOCTOR

➤ If symptoms persist after more than four or five days of self-care. It's rare, but the infection can spread.

➤ If you have symptoms and your eardrum has ever ruptured or otherwise been injured, or if you've had ear surgery.

➤ If you have frequent bouts of swimmer's ear or already have an **ear infection** (see page 71).

➤ If you have diabetes or a weakened immune system.

HOW TO PREVENT IT

➤ Try to keep your ears moisture-free. Wear earplugs while swimming (remove them immediately after), and pull a shower cap over your ears for showering. Dry the outer parts of your ears after these activities, and use buffered alcohol eardrops, available in drug stores, to help evaporate remaining water.

➤ Squirt lanolin eardrops into your ears before you swim to protect them from the water. Tilt your head so the drops get to the bottom of the ear canal, then let the liquid drain out.

➤ Don't get any water in the ear canal for three weeks after symptoms disappear, to keep the problem from coming back.

➤ Use antiseptic eardrops if you get water in your ear and you have a tendency to get swimmer's ear.

➤ Be careful when cleaning **earwax** (see page 73) from your ears. Don't use any objects that could scratch the ear canal.

FOR MORE HELP

Organization: American Academy of Otolaryngology–Head and Neck Surgery, One Prince St., Alexandria, VA 22314. 703-836-4444, M–F 8:30–5 EST. Fax: 703-683-5100. Ask for the swimmer's ear brochure and physician referrals.

Tinnitus

SIGNS AND SYMPTOMS

■ Noise such as ringing, roaring, buzzing, humming, hissing, or whistling that only you can hear. It can be intermittent or continuous, and can vary in loudness or pitch. It's most noticeable when background noise is low.

Tinnitus affects about 50 million adults in the United States. It's not usually a sign of anything serious, and sometimes it disappears on its own or when an underlying problem is treated. But when tinnitus is especially loud and persistent, people can find it difficult to concentrate, sleep, or work. Although tinnitus sometimes accompanies hearing loss, it doesn't cause the loss.

The older you are, the more likely it is that you could have tinnitus. It has a variety of causes, including:

➤ Long exposure to loud noise.
➤ Blockage of the ear canal due to wax build-up (see **earwax,** page 73).
➤ **Ear infection** (see page 71).
➤ A perforated eardrum.
➤ Side effects of about 200 prescription and nonprescription drugs, such as aspirin, quinine, antibiotics, anti-inflammatories, diuretics, and antidepressants.
➤ Chronic **stress** (see page 212).

Tinnitus can be a symptom of other health problems, including:

➤ **High blood pressure** (see page 105).
➤ Persistent **allergies** (see page 85).

If you have tinnitus along with dizziness, you might have fluid buildup in your inner ear or damage to the small bones in your middle ear (see Ménière's syndrome and otosclerosis in the **ear and hearing problems** chart, page 69).

WHAT YOU CAN DO NOW

While there's no cure for some cases of chronic tinnitus, there are steps you can take to get relief:

➤ Cover the unwanted noise with a tape recording of soothing music or sounds, if you have trouble sleeping.
➤ Try a tinnitus masker, a small electronic instrument, worn in the ear like a hearing aid, that produces a competing but pleasant sound.
➤ Avoid alcohol, smoking, and caffeine. They can make tinnitus worse.
➤ Exercise regularly. This may bring some relief by increasing blood circulation to the head.

WHEN TO CALL THE DOCTOR

Call for an immediate appointment:
➤ If you have sudden or total hearing loss.
➤ If you have tinnitus and feel dizzy.

➤ If you have tinnitus and pain or pus in your ear.

Call for advice and an appointment:
➤ If you suspect your tinnitus is the symptom of another health problem.
➤ If tinnitus interferes with your concentration, daily activities, or sleep.
➤ If the sound distresses you.

HOW TO PREVENT IT

➤ Wear earplugs or earmuffs if you are exposed to loud noise. (Cotton balls are not sufficient because they don't block enough sound. They can also become lodged deep in the ear canal.)
➤ Don't turn up the volume when wearing earphones.
➤ Teach your children about the potential damage from loud music.
➤ Cut down on salt in your diet. Salt can cause fluid to build up in your middle ear, increasing the risk of tinnitus.
➤ Get adequate rest, avoid stress, and practice relaxation techniques.

FOR MORE HELP

Information line: American Speech-Language-Hearing Association, 800-638-8255, M–F 8:30–5 EST. Information specialists answer questions and provide written material on tinnitus and other ear disorders.

Organization: National Institute on Deafness and Other Communication Disorders Information Clearinghouse, 800-241-1044, M–F 8:30–5 EST. Ask for the tinnitus information packet.

Organization: American Tinnitus Association, P.O. Box 5, Portland, OR 97207-0005. 503-248-9985, M–F 8:30–5 PST. Fax: 503-248-0024. Ask about publications, membership information, and support group referrals.

Mouth

◆

Bad Breath

■ Offensive odor from the mouth.
■ Unpleasant taste in the mouth.
■ Inflamed and bleeding gums.

Most adults and many children have un-explained bouts of bad breath (halitosis), apart from the well-known effects of coffee, alcohol, and highly spiced or strong-smelling foods such as garlic and onions. Usually it's no cause for alarm, but it can be a sign of another health problem, such as gum disease, tooth decay (see **toothache,** page 80), **sinusitis** (see page 95), or **tonsillitis** (see page 99).

Bad breath is usually caused by bacteria, often mixed with food bits and saliva to form a foul-smelling film on the teeth called plaque. Smoking is a major culprit, too. A dry mouth also contributes to the problem, causing the familiar "morning breath." Simply not drinking enough water during the day can aggravate the condition, as can some medications, including diuretics, tranquilizers, and antihistamines.

WHAT YOU CAN DO NOW

➤ Brush and floss your teeth at least twice a day—especially after meals.
➤ Gently brush the top of your tongue with the toothbrush. Be sure to reach in back.
➤ For a quick cover-up, eat fresh parsley or mint, an orange, an apple, or celery. Or rinse your mouth with mouthwash.

WHEN TO CALL THE DOCTOR OR DENTIST

➤ If your bad breath persists for no obvious reason after you've repeatedly and thoroughly flossed and cleaned your teeth, gums, and tongue for a week.
➤ If your bad breath is accompanied by a toothache; you may have a cavity or an abscess. See your dentist.
➤ If your gums are inflamed and bleeding; this could be a sign of gum disease.
➤ If your bad breath is accompanied by a fever or cough and mucus; this can be a symptom of a lung abscess.

HOW TO PREVENT IT

➤ Brush and floss at least twice a day.
➤ Brush your tongue at least once a day.
➤ Have your teeth professionally cleaned every six months and examined by a dentist once a year.
➤ If you smoke, quit.
➤ Go light on sugar, coffee, and alcohol; spicy foods such as garlic, hot peppers, and salami; and strong-smelling foods such as anchovies and tuna.
➤ Drink lots of water throughout the day.

(continued)

Tooth and Mouth Problems

SYMPTOMS	WHAT IT MIGHT BE	WHAT YOU CAN DO
White or red patch on gums; lump, thickening, or discoloration anywhere in mouth; sore in mouth that bleeds and/or doesn't heal in 3–4 weeks; trouble swallowing; swelling in jaw or neck.	Oral cancer—tumors can occur anywhere in or around mouth or in upper throat.	Call doctor for immediate appointment. Most oral cancers are treatable if detected early. **For more help:** Cancer Information and Counseling Hotline, 800-525-3777, M–F 8:30–5 MST.
Toothache and red, swollen, or bleeding gums; sometimes earache; often fever; swelling in face; bad taste in mouth.	Tooth abscess. See toothache, page 80.	Call dentist for immediate appointment.
Red, swollen gums that sometimes bleed; bad breath; loose teeth; pus discharge in mouth.	Periodontitis—advanced inflammation of gums: end result of gingivitis (see below).	Call dentist for advice and appointment. Prompt treatment is important to avoid losing teeth. **For more help:** American Academy of Periodontology, 737 N. Michigan Ave., Suite 800, Chicago, IL 60611-2690. Write for fact sheets and brochures on periodontitis.
Reddish, shiny, swollen gums that bleed easily; bad breath.	Gingivitis—also called gum disease. Usually caused by plaque buildup on teeth.	Call dentist for advice and appointment. Treatment includes removing plaque. Brush teeth after meals or at least twice a day. Floss daily.
Swollen, painful, red gums; sore jaw; headache; bad taste in mouth; bad breath.	Impacted teeth—caused by lack of space in mouth.	Call dentist for advice and appointment. Treatment may include pulling a tooth.
Lump or sore in mouth or on tongue.	Noncancerous mouth or tongue tumors. Cause is unknown.	Call doctor for advice and appointment if lump or sore doesn't clear up after 3 weeks.
Creamy yellow patches in mouth that leave raw, red spots when rubbed.	Thrush—a fungal infection (see page 147); common in people with HIV. Can be caused by some antibiotics.	Call doctor for advice and appointment.

(continued)

Tooth and Mouth Problems *(continued)*

SYMPTOMS	WHAT IT MIGHT BE	WHAT YOU CAN DO
Painful, swollen glands under tongue, behind ear, or in neck; bad taste in mouth; dry mouth; fever.	Salivary gland disorders. Causes include mumps (see page 255) and bacterial infection.	Call doctor for advice and appointment. Treatment may include antibiotics to get rid of infection. Avoid spicy foods and citrus fruits.
Jaw, mouth, and facial pain; headache; clicking noise when opening or closing mouth.	Temporomandibular disorder (see page 193).	Call doctor or dentist for advice and appointment.
Pain and/or tightness in face and jaw muscles; toothache; worn teeth.	Tooth grinding (see page 81).	Call dentist for advice and appointment.
Gray film on gums; red, painful, bleeding gums; bad breath; bad taste in mouth.	Trench mouth—bacterial infection of gums; appears suddenly, often returns.	Call dentist for advice and appointment. Left untreated, can cause permanent gum damage, loss of teeth.

FOR MORE HELP

Information line: Richter Center for the Treatment of Breath Disorders, 800-210-2110, M–F 8AM–8PM EST. Treats people with chronic bad breath and provides information on the condition.

Canker Sores

SIGNS AND SYMPTOMS

- Small, painful, craterlike sores on the gums, tongue, and inside the lips. They are typically white, gray, or yellowish, with a red rim.
- Tingling or burning sensation just before a sore appears.
- Pain that may increase when eating or talking.
- Fever and swollen glands (sometimes).

Canker sores can occur when there is a tear or break in the flesh inside the mouth. They're a common ailment; teenagers and women are the most likely to get them. Usually you can safely ignore these sores, and they generally heal themselves within seven to ten days.

While it's unclear exactly what causes canker sores, which are similar to **cold sores** (see opposite page), some triggers include:
- ➤ Injury to the mouth's lining from chipped or jagged teeth, dental work, or dentures.
- ➤ Injury from rough toothbrushing.
- ➤ Burns from hot foods or liquids.
- ➤ Irritation from sour foods (such as lemons) or acidic foods (tomatoes or oranges).
- ➤ Food allergies.
- ➤ Vitamin and mineral deficiencies.

WHAT YOU CAN DO NOW

Many home treatments can ease the discomfort of canker sores. Try the following:
- ➤ Rinse your mouth about four times a day with a cup of warm water mixed with a half teaspoon of salt. Don't swallow.

- Use an ice cube on the sore.
- Apply a paste of baking soda and water.
- Avoid spicy, sour, or acidic foods, which may irritate the sores.
- Use an over-the-counter salve or an antiseptic mouthwash. (Look for a medicine that contains glycerin, which protects the sore, and peroxide, which fights bacteria.)

WHEN TO CALL THE DOCTOR OR DENTIST

- If you develop sores and a fever of 100 degrees or higher, or swollen glands.
- If the sores persist for longer than three weeks; this may indicate a more serious problem, such as oral cancer.
- If you have severe pain. Your doctor may prescribe painkillers or antibiotics.
- If you suspect that tooth or denture problems are causing your canker sores. Talk to your dentist; the sores are unlikely to heal until the underlying cause is fixed.

HOW TO PREVENT IT

- Clean your teeth gently with a soft brush, and floss regularly. Buy toothpaste that's free of the detergent sodium lauryl sulfate, which may dry out the mouth's lining and leave the insides of the cheeks and the gums vulnerable to irritants.
- Avoid foods that seem to trigger the sores.
- Take a multivitamin/mineral supplement.

Cold Sores

SIGNS AND SYMPTOMS

- Red or fluid-filled, painful blisters, typically on or around the lips or mouth.
- Tingling, prickling, or itching on the lips or mouth (often just before cold sores appear).
- Fever and swollen neck glands may accompany the first outbreak; after that, cold sores usually don't produce these symptoms.

Cold sores, also called fever blisters, are caused by a herpes virus. After a first outbreak, often during childhood, the virus may lie dormant for years, but it can be reactivated at any time. Possible triggers include fever, infection, physical or emotional stress, exposure to sun or extreme weather, or certain foods such as nuts, chocolate, or seeds.

Cold sores are similar to **canker sores** (see opposite page). They are a common ailment, and they usually aren't a serious health concern unless your immune system is weakened by some other disorder, such as **AIDS** (see page 214).

WHAT YOU CAN DO NOW

Cold sores usually clear up on their own within seven to ten days. You can't cure them, but to relieve pain and discomfort:
- Apply an ice cube to the affected area.
- Keep a prescription medication such as Zovirax cream on hand; used when you feel the first signals, before cold sores appear, it can make an attack less severe.
- Avoid sour, spicy, or acidic foods, which may irritate the sores.

WHEN TO CALL THE DOCTOR

Call for an immediate appointment:
- If you have a cold sore and feel any eye pain or discomfort, or if your vision is impaired. You may have a cold sore–related infection in your eye.

Call for advice and an appointment:
- If you develop sores and a fever of 100 degrees or higher and/or chills.
- If your cold sores last longer than two weeks or come back frequently.

HOW TO PREVENT IT

- Get a new toothbrush after you've had cold sores.
- Avoid kissing someone who has cold sores.
- Wear a hat and use sunblock on your lips if sun exposure appears to trigger cold sores.
- If stress seems to bring on cold sores, find ways to relax: Exercise regularly, or practice yoga or meditation.

These sores are contagious. To prevent the infection from spreading if you or people close to you have cold sores:

➤ Wash your hands often, and don't share tableware, towels, or razors.
➤ Avoid touching the infected area.
➤ Don't touch a cold sore and then your eye. This can cause a serious eye infection.

Toothache

SIGNS AND SYMPTOMS

Tooth decay:
■ An ache or sharp pain in a tooth, often when you bite or chew.
■ General soreness in teeth, gums, or jaw.
■ Bad breath or an unpleasant taste in your mouth—a sign of severe decay or an abscess (infection).

Tooth abscess:
■ Severe or sharp pain in the tooth or jaw.
■ A loose tooth.
■ Red, swollen, or bleeding gums.
■ Fever.
■ Earache.
■ Swollen glands in the neck.

The most common reason for toothache is a cavity caused by dental plaque, a sticky substance made up of food bits, saliva, and bacteria. Plaque produces acids that corrode the protective enamel on the teeth. Toothache can also be the result of something as simple as food wedged between the gum and a tooth, or something as serious as:

➤ Impacted teeth (teeth that do not fully grow out or that grow at odd angles) pressing against neighboring teeth or trapping food particles.
➤ **Tooth grinding** (see page 81), which can cause cracks in a tooth.
➤ Inflammation caused by gum disease.
➤ Pressure from sinus congestion or infection (see **sinusitis,** page 95).
➤ Jaws that don't line up correctly (see **temporomandibular disorder,** page 193).

WHAT YOU CAN DO NOW

You'll need to see the dentist, especially if you have signs of an abscess. The following home treatments can relieve some pain:

➤ Press an ice cube inside your mouth near the affected tooth, and suck on it to numb your gum.
➤ To remove trapped food particles, use dental floss. Also swish warm salt water around in your mouth.

WHEN TO CALL THE DENTIST

Call for an immediate appointment:
➤ If you have any symptoms of an abscess; you may have a serious infection that requires emergency treatment.

Call for advice and an appointment:
➤ If your toothache lasts longer than a day or two; if you have continual bouts of throbbing pain in a tooth; or if the tooth is highly sensitive to heat, cold, or pressure. You may have a cavity that requires a filling.
➤ If your gums are painful, swollen, and red; you may have an impacted tooth or gum disease.

HOW TO PREVENT IT

➤ Brush at least twice a day using a nonabrasive, fluoride-containing toothpaste and a soft-bristled toothbrush. Floss at least twice a day. Replace your toothbrush every few months.
➤ Cut down on or eliminate sweet and sticky foods, which are especially damaging to tooth enamel.
➤ Have your teeth cleaned every six months and examined by a dentist once a year.

FOR MORE HELP

Organization: American Dental Association, Department of Public Education and Information, 211 E. Chicago Ave., Chicago, IL 60611. Write for pamphlets on caring for teeth and gums.
Organization: American Academy of Periodontology, 737 N. Michigan Ave., Suite 800, Chicago, IL 60611-2690. Write to

request brochures on dental care. Include a business-size, self-addressed, stamped envelope.

Tooth Grinding

SIGNS AND SYMPTOMS

- Tension or tightness in the face and jaw muscles.
- Toothache.
- Mild to severe headache or migraine.
- Looseness or aching in the teeth, especially upon waking.
- Generalized facial pain.
- Obviously worn teeth.

Tooth grinding (bruxism) is a common problem, especially among women. It's thought to be caused by a variety of physical and emotional factors, including an abnormal bite, crooked or missing teeth, high levels of **stress** (see page 212), or a **sleep disorder** (see page 277).

Until you have symptoms, you may not realize that you're grinding or clenching your teeth, especially if you usually do it in your sleep. But you may be literally wearing down your teeth and creating cracks in them.

SENSITIVE TEETH

If a tooth feels painful after exposure to heat or cold, you could have a condition known as dentinal hypersensitivity. This occurs when enamel, the outer covering of the tooth, thins or wears away. The condition is brought on by age, receding gums, dental surgery, or repeated brushing with hard-bristled toothbrushes or "whitening" toothpastes containing abrasives.

You can help relieve hypersensitivity and prevent further damage by using a toothpaste made for sensitive teeth and a brush with soft bristles. If pain persists, see your dentist.

Mouth

WHAT YOU CAN DO NOW

- During the day, concentrate on releasing your jaw and keeping your teeth slightly apart.
- Don't chew gum, tobacco, pencils, or any other nonfood objects.
- Hold a warm washcloth to the side of your face. This may help to relax your jaw.
- If you suspect that stress is the problem, try to reduce your stress and practice relaxation techniques, such as meditation or yoga.

WHEN TO CALL THE DOCTOR

- If you still have symptoms after a month of home treatment, or if you think that an abnormal bite or a missing tooth is causing the problem. You may need to have your dentist fit you with a protective mouth guard or bite plate.
- If you have tooth pain or a jaw ache for more than a day or two. These symptoms could be the result of tooth decay (see **toothache,** page 80) or a sign of **temporomandibular disorder** (see page 193).
- If you think that stress is causing continuing problems. You may want to seek counseling or ask your dentist to prescribe a jaw muscle relaxant.

HOW TO PREVENT IT

- Develop habits to ease your stress and help you stay as relaxed as possible, especially around bedtime. Take a warm bath or shower before bed, listen to soothing music, and practice deep breathing or meditation.
- Cut down on caffeine-containing foods, such as coffee, tea, colas, and chocolate.
- Try to practice good posture. Slouching or hunching can trigger teeth clenching.

FOR MORE HELP

Organization: American Dental Association, Department of Public Education and Information, 211 E. Chicago Ave., Chicago, IL 60611. Write to request the pamphlet "Do You Grind Your Teeth?"

Nose, Throat, Lungs, & Chest

Acute Bronchitis

SIGNS AND SYMPTOMS

- Persistent, hacking, dry or wet cough that brings up green, gray, or yellowish mucus.
- Wheezing and shortness of breath.
- Pain in the upper chest, made worse by fits of coughing.
- Fever of 100 degrees or higher.

Acute bronchitis develops when the branches of the windpipe (the bronchi and bronchial tubes) that carry air to and from the lungs become swollen. This inflammation leads to increased mucus, which clogs the airways and causes the heavy cough characteristic of bronchitis.

Most people have an episode of acute bronchitis at some point in their lives, usually when a virus that causes a cold or throat infection spreads to the airways. The illness can also be brought on by irritants such as cigarette smoke, chemical fumes, or dust. If your heart and lungs are healthy, bronchitis usually clears up in several days and vanishes when the infection does.

If bouts of bronchitis continue, you may have **chronic bronchitis** (see page 88).

WHAT YOU CAN DO NOW

- ➤ Take acetaminophen or ibuprofen to fight fever and pain. (Never give aspirin to a child under 12 who has chicken pox, flu, or any other illness you suspect of being caused by a virus, such as a bad respiratory infection; see box on **Reye's syndrome,** page 92.)
- ➤ If you have a persistent, dry cough, try an over-the-counter cough medicine. (If you have a cough that is bringing up mucus, be careful not to take medicine labeled as a cough suppressant; doing so could cause mucus to build up in your lungs.)
- ➤ Stay home in a warm room.
- ➤ Inhale steam from a vaporizer or a pot of hot water, or take hot showers. This will loosen mucus in your lungs.
- ➤ Drink a lot of liquids—at least eight to ten glasses a day.

WHEN TO CALL THE DOCTOR

- ➤ If symptoms don't ease in three or four days, or if your bronchitis keeps coming back.
- ➤ If the person with bronchitis is an infant or elderly.
- ➤ If your mucus increases or becomes darker or thicker. You may have a bacterial infection that requires antibiotics.
- ➤ If you have a lung disease or heart disease and you suffer a bronchitis attack.
- ➤ If you cough up blood or if your shortness of breath gets worse.

(continued)

Breathing Problems and Coughs

SYMPTOMS	WHAT IT MIGHT BE	WHAT YOU CAN DO
Wheezing; tightening of chest or throat; itching and hives; swollen eyes, lips, and tongue; panic; stomach cramps or vomiting; bluish skin (sometimes).	Anaphylactic shock— severe allergic reaction (see page 18).	Call 911 or go to emergency facility **immediately.**
Shortness of breath, sharp chest pain, dry cough; symptoms of shock—cold hands and feet, rapid pulse, confusion, moist skin.	Collapsed lung.	Call 911 or go to emergency facility **immediately.**
Wheezing and shortness of breath; persistent, mucus-producing or dry cough.	Chronic bronchitis or emphysema (see page 88).	If skin turns blue or purple, call 911 or go to emergency facility **immediately.** Otherwise, call doctor for immediate appointment.
Shortness of breath; crushing chest pain, pressure, or squeezed feeling (possibly spreading to jaw, neck, back, or arms); sweating; nausea.	Heart attack (see page 38).	Call 911 or go to emergency facility **immediately.**
Sudden shortness of breath and sharp chest pain, cough (sometimes with bloody phlegm), anxiety, loss of consciousness (sometimes).	Blood clot that travels through body to block artery in lungs.	Call 911 or go to emergency facility **immediately.**
Wheezing; quick, shallow breathing; coughing (sometimes with thick mucus); tightness in chest; gasping for breath.	Asthma (see page 86).	If skin turns blue or person becomes confused, call 911 or go to emergency facility **immediately.** Otherwise, call doctor for immediate appointment.
"Smoker's cough" (sometimes with bloody mucus), wheezing and shortness of breath, chest pain, fatigue, weight loss, lack of appetite.	Lung cancer (see page 93). • Pneumonia (see page 94). • Tuberculosis (see page 100).	Call doctor for immediate appointment.

(continued)

Breathing Problems and Coughs *(continued)*

SYMPTOMS	WHAT IT MIGHT BE	WHAT YOU CAN DO
Cough; fever; runny nose; sore throat; muscle aches; red, itchy bumps all over body.	Measles (see page 254).	If bumps start to bleed or convulsions occur (very rare), call 911 or go to emergency facility **immediately.** Otherwise, treat at home with rest and fluids. Call doctor for advice and appointment if symptoms last longer than a week.
In children ages 6–12: first symptoms resemble cold; after 2 weeks, cough becomes almost constant and is followed by whooping sound, vomiting, choking.	Whooping cough (see page 261).	If child turns blue or stops breathing, call 911 and start **CPR** (see page 14). Call doctor for advice and appointment if symptoms linger or get worse.
Sharp, sudden chest pain that gets worse with deep breathing; fever and chills; headache; weakness; dry cough.	Pleurisy—inflammation of lining of lungs.	Call doctor for immediate appointment.
Cough, hoarseness, and lost voice (sometimes); sore throat; fever (sometimes).	Laryngitis—inflammation of voice box. May be caused by bacterial or viral infection or by strained vocal cords.	Call doctor for advice. Avoid talking, drink lots of fluids, and take nonprescription throat lozenges.
Coughing and sneezing; congestion; runny nose; sore throat; headache; aching muscles; fever and fatigue (sometimes).	Flu (see page 91). ● Cold (see page 90).	Rest, drink lots of fluids, and take over-the-counter pain medications. Do not give aspirin to child under 12 (see box on **Reye's syndrome,** page 92).

➤ If you have a temperature of 102 degrees or higher.

➤ On days with poor air quality, avoid exercise, outdoor work, or long outings.

HOW TO PREVENT IT

➤ If you smoke, quit (see **smoking and illness,** page 210). Avoid secondhand smoke and other irritating fumes.
➤ Treat colds and flu promptly.

FOR MORE HELP

Information line: National Jewish Center for Immunology and Respiratory Medicine, 1400 Jackson St., Denver, CO 80206. 800-222-5864, M–F 8–5 MST. Nurses answer questions, make referrals, and send information. 800-552-5864, recorded information on breathing problems.

Information line: American Lung Association, 800-LUNG-USA (586-4872), M–F 9–5 your time. Automatically connects you to a local ALA chapter, which provides information on bronchitis and other respiratory diseases and can refer you to support groups and programs for quitting smoking.

Allergies

SIGNS AND SYMPTOMS

Hay fever (allergic rhinitis, a respiratory allergy):
- Frequent sneezing.
- Itchy or watery eyes.
- Runny or stuffy nose.
- Itching in back of throat or on roof of mouth.

Allergic asthma:
- Sneezing, wheezing, and coughing.
- In some cases, difficulty breathing.

Food allergies:
- Outbreaks of irritated, itchy, red, or bumpy skin.
- Stomachache and/or frequent indigestion.

Drug allergies:
- Outbreaks of irritated, itchy, red, or bumpy skin, sometimes accompanied by flulike symptoms such as headache, low fever, and joint pain.

When your immune system overreacts to substances that are usually harmless, you have allergies. In fighting what it identifies as an invader, the immune system produces a chemical called histamine, which can provoke the sneezing, itching, and other symptoms associated with allergies.

Hay fever is one of the most common allergies, affecting nearly one in five Americans. Pollen, bits of animal skin called dander, household dust, and molds are the most common offenders.

Food allergies—which are relatively uncommon—occur more often in children than adults and are often outgrown by the age of three. The foods that most frequently cause allergies include nuts, eggs, and milk. Seafood and peanuts tend to produce the most severe reactions, including shock or even death in rare cases, but prompt treatment—normally with an injection of adrenaline—is usually effective. Such severe allergies are rarely outgrown. Allergies to drugs such as penicillin or to insect stings can be just as dangerous (see **bee and wasp stings,** page 20, and **anaphylactic shock,** page 18).

Many allergies can be handled at home. If yours are unusually persistent, though, your doctor might recommend prescription antihistamines, steroid nasal sprays, or shots to relieve your symptoms. Some people with allergies find relief in alternative therapies such as homeopathy, acupuncture, or herbal remedies.

WHAT YOU CAN DO NOW

➤ If you're allergic to pollen, stay indoors on days with high pollen counts.
➤ Avoid tobacco smoke and insect sprays, and stay inside on days with high pollution levels.
➤ If you have hay fever, try various over-the-counter antihistamines and keep track of which ones work best. Don't combine antihistamines with prescription medications or other over-the-counter drugs without checking with your doctor or pharmacist. (**Note:** Phenylpropanolamine—found in some decongestants—has in rare cases been linked to stroke. Use decongestants containing pseudoephedrine instead.)
➤ If you're allergic to insect stings or have severe reactions to specific foods, ask your doctor for an emergency kit with antihistamines and an adrenaline shot. Always carry the kit with you.
➤ If you frequently have itchy or watery eyes, ask your doctor about a prescription for antihistamine eyedrops.

Nose, Throat, Lungs, & Chest

Call 911 or go to an emergency facility **immediately:**

➤ If you develop a rapid heartbeat and skin welts along with flushing, itching, dizziness, and trouble breathing. You could be having a dangerous and potentially fatal reaction called **anaphylactic shock** (see page 18).

➤ If your breathing becomes extremely difficult or painful. You may be having an attack of **asthma** (see this page).

➤ If you have violent stomach cramps, vomiting, bloating, or diarrhea. This could signal a serious reaction to a food.

Call for advice and an appointment:

➤ If you have recurring allergies. Your doctor may refer you to an allergy specialist, who can test you to find out what you're allergic to.

HOW TO PREVENT IT

➤ Learn what you're allergic to, and avoid it.

➤ If you're allergic to a commonly used drug such as penicillin, wear a medical alert tag or bracelet.

➤ If you're allergic to cats or dogs, stay away from them—or at least see that your pets are bathed frequently and keep them out of your bedroom.

➤ If you're allergic to molds, keep your house clean and dry, particularly these key spots: bathrooms (especially shower stalls), refrigerator drip trays, basements, and closets.

➤ If you sneeze and cough year-round, you may be among the millions of people who are allergic to dust mites (microscopic, spiderlike bugs that live in house dust). Try to keep your house—particularly your bedroom—as dust-free as possible. Encase mattresses in plastic covers; wash your bedding weekly in hot water; and avoid carpet, upholstered furniture, and other dust-catchers. Also, vacuum regularly (use a nonporous bag) or, better yet, have someone else do it.

➤ If you have a severe food allergy, read package labels carefully. When dining out, be particularly careful to ask about ingredients.

FOR MORE HELP

Information line: National Jewish Center for Immunology and Respiratory Medicine, 1400 Jackson St., Denver, CO 80206. 800-222-5864, M–F 8–5 MST. Nurses answer questions, make referrals, and send out information. 800-552-5864, recorded information on breathing problems.

Book: *The Best Guide to Allergy,* by Nathan Schultz, M.D., Allan V. Giannini, M.D., Terrance T. Change, M.D., and Diane Wong. Humana Press, 1995, $14.50.

Book: *Empty Your Bucket: Practical Steps to Overcome Allergy and Allergic Asthma,* by Stephen Astor, M.D. Two A's Industries, 1994, $14.95.

Asthma

SIGNS AND SYMPTOMS

Mild or moderate asthma attack:
■ Shortness of breath.
■ Wheezing or whistling sounds with breathing.
■ Tightness in the chest.
■ Coughing, especially at night.

Severe attack:
■ So much difficulty breathing that you sweat.
■ A racing pulse.
■ Panic.

In asthma, muscle spasms and swelling in the branches of the windpipe (the bronchi) that carry air to and from the lungs constrict your airways and block the flow of air you need to breathe comfortably. Excess mucus may further clog the airways. As a result, you have to gasp for breath. (See color illustrations, page 168.)

Asthma attacks may come on suddenly, and they can last from 15 minutes to more than a day. They are frequently triggered by allergies to particles in the air, including pollen, dust, mold, or bits of animal skin called dander. (See **allergies,** page 85.) Smoke, exercise, cold air, some foods, emotional upset, a common cold and—according to new research—impaired lung muscles can also spark asthma. In a small percentage of people with asthma, aspirin can prompt an attack.

Asthma frequently begins during childhood, and it's more common and more serious among African-American children than others. Many youngsters seem to outgrow the illness, but it can reappear in adulthood.

Severe, untreated asthma can be fatal, but most children and adults can control their asthma by taking medications and by avoiding things that trigger an attack.

WHAT YOU CAN DO NOW

➤ Remain calm and quiet. Anxiety makes the symptoms worse.
➤ Don't lie down. You can breathe better if you sit upright and lean forward slightly.
➤ Collect in one place any medicines your doctor has prescribed. They may include a bronchodilator—a spray drug to open your airways—in an inhaler that controls the dose. Rinse your mouth with water each time you use it to prevent yeast infections in the mouth.
➤ If you're using oral medications, follow the instructions exactly. Also, write down the time you take each dose: Overdoses can be dangerous.

WHEN TO CALL THE DOCTOR

Call 911 or go to an emergency facility **immediately:**
➤ If you note the following signs of a lack of oxygen:
  ● a suffocating feeling that makes talking difficult.
  ● flaring nostrils.
  ● a sucked-in look to the skin between the ribs when inhaling.
  ● bluish lips and nails.
Call for an immediate appointment:
➤ The first time anyone in your family has severe or prolonged wheezing, coughing, or difficulty breathing.

➤ If your asthma medicine doesn't work in the time it's supposed to.
➤ If you cough up green, yellow, or bloody mucus.
➤ If you feel new, unexplained symptoms. These may be side effects of your drugs or may mean your asthma is getting worse.

HOW TO PREVENT IT

Anyone with asthma should be under a doctor's care. Ask the doctor if you should learn to use a peak flowmeter: It measures airflow and can give early warning of a coming attack. Ask, too, if you should use an inhaler for corticosteroids to reduce your bronchial swelling. Also:

➤ Keep a diary of attacks: How frequent? How severe? What happened just before? With some detective work, you can learn to recognize and avoid your triggers. Notice whether certain foods or drugs seem to bring on an attack, and avoid them.
➤ Stay away from smoke and smokers. If you smoke, quit. (See **smoking and illness,** page 210.)
➤ Stay indoors, if possible, when air pollution and pollen counts are high.
➤ In cold weather, breathe through your nose and cover your nose and mouth with a scarf.
➤ Keep your house as dust-free as possible.
➤ Get bedding that is made of nonallergenic materials.
➤ Stick with pets that don't have hair or fur.
➤ Exercise regularly but moderately. Many doctors recommend swimming—unless you react badly to chlorine—because humidity helps ease breathing. If vigorous exercise sets off an attack, talk to your doctor. Adjusting your medication may help.
➤ Take a yoga class. It can help relax you.
➤ Lower your risk of colds and flu by washing your hands often and by getting a flu shot every year.
➤ Consider getting an air-filtering machine for your bedroom.

FOR MORE HELP

Information line: National Jewish Center for Immunology and Respiratory Medicine, 1400 Jackson St., Denver, CO 80206. 800-222-5864, M–F 8–5 MST. Nurses answer questions, make referrals, and send out information. 800-552-5864, recorded information on breathing problems.

Information line: Asthma and Allergy Foundation of America, 800-727-8462, 24-hour recording. 202-466-7643, M–F 9–5 EST. Fax: 202-466-7643. Offers referrals to local support groups and lists of books, pamphlets, and videos for sale.

Video: *Asthma in Children at Time of Diagnosis.* Clear, useful overview of causes and treatments, consisting of four reports— Understanding the Diagnosis, What Happens Next?, Treatment and Management, and Issues and Answers. Time Life Medical, 1996, $19.95.

Chronic Bronchitis and Emphysema

SIGNS AND SYMPTOMS

Chronic bronchitis:
- Usually begins with a "smoker's cough"—a regular morning cough that brings up mucus.
- As the disease progresses, coughing becomes more persistent and you find yourself short of breath.
- In the final stages, coughing and wheezing are almost nonstop.

Emphysema:
In the early stages, there may be no symptoms. Later symptoms include:
- A persistent, dry cough.
- Shortness of breath: at first, only with exertion; later, with any physical activity.
- In the late stages, the chest may become distended and barrel-shaped from air trapped inside lungs.
- Weight loss.
- Recurring infections of the lungs.

Chronic bronchitis and emphysema often develop at the same time. Together, they're known as chronic obstructive pulmonary disease (COPD). They damage the lungs and the branches of the windpipe that carry air to and from the lungs (bronchi), making it difficult to breathe.

Chronic bronchitis: When you cough up mucus continually for periods of three months or more, two years in a row, you are considered to have chronic bronchitis. It is usually linked to smoking, although air pollution, secondhand smoke, and allergies can also play a role. If you don't treat it and you continue to smoke or be exposed to an irritant, you leave yourself open to other diseases, such as pneumonia or emphysema.

Chronic bronchitis affects 7.5 million Americans. Early treatment—and quitting smoking—can ease symptoms and slow the disease. In a small percentage of cases, it can be fatal.

Emphysema: When the lungs are damaged by cigarette smoke (and often, by the persistent coughing of chronic bronchitis), the millions of tiny air sacs inside them can't deliver enough oxygen to the bloodstream. You use more and more energy gasping for breath; you tire easily and lose weight. Eventually, even a short walk may leave you breathless. Because emphysema makes the heart work harder, it can lead to heart disease. It also makes you prone to lung infections such as pneumonia.

The disease, which is irreversible, usually strikes people over 50, although a small group of those with a genetic deficiency may develop symptoms in their twenties and thirties. A blood test can identify people with this problem, who absolutely should not smoke.

Emphysema kills more Americans— 13,000 a year—than any other chronic lung disease. There are two important things to remember about emphysema: 1) If you don't smoke, you have very little chance of getting it. 2) It's good to quit smoking even if you think you're in good health. In the early stages, emphysema often has no symptoms. By the time it's diagnosed, most people have lost 50 to 70 percent of their lung capacity.

HINTS ON HUMIDIFIERS

Many people with chronic dry noses and throats, sinusitis, or respiratory diseases such as bronchitis use humidifiers to boost the moisture content of indoor air so they can breathe more easily. These devices are particularly helpful for people who live in dry environments, such as parts of the American Southwest.

But humidifiers should not be used without consulting a doctor. Humid environments promote the growth of both molds and household dust mites, so humidifiers can cause serious problems for people with allergies or allergic asthma. Even people not prone to allergies may develop a hypersensitivity sometimes called "humidifier lung." Dirty humidifiers can also breed and disperse mold spores. For this reason, they should be cleaned regularly.

For more help: You can order a paper on cleaning humidifiers from the Lung Line, sponsored by the National Jewish Center for Immunology and Respiratory Medicine, by calling 800-222-5864, M–F 8–5 MST.

Treatment for these diseases is limited. A physical therapist may design a program that enables you to exercise more. Your doctor may prescribe a bronchodilator and, in later stages, pure oxygen, which you can breathe to ease shortness of breath.

WHAT YOU CAN DO NOW

➤ If you smoke, quit (see **smoking and illness,** page 210). Smoking is by far the main cause of emphysema and chronic bronchitis. But studies show that giving up tobacco—even after symptoms appear—can greatly slow lung damage.
➤ Get an annual flu shot and a vaccination against pneumonia.

➤ Stay inside if the air is unusually polluted, and avoid smoky places.
➤ Exercise moderately but regularly in good-quality air.
➤ Take good care of yourself, and if you get a lung infection, have it promptly treated.

WHEN TO CALL THE DOCTOR

➤ If you have a lingering, mild cough that doesn't go away for months.
➤ If you regularly become breathless after mild exertion, such as climbing a flight of stairs.

HOW TO PREVENT IT

➤ Don't smoke.
➤ Treat bronchitis promptly to guard against emphysema.

FOR MORE HELP

Information line: National Jewish Center for Immunology and Respiratory Medicine, 1400 Jackson St., Denver, CO 80206. 800-222-5864, M–F 8–5 MST. Nurses answer questions, make referrals, and send information. 800-552-5864, recorded information on breathing problems.

Information line: American Lung Association, 800-LUNG-USA (586-4872), M–F 9–5 your time. Automatically connects you to a local ALA chapter, which has information on COPD and other lung diseases and can refer you to support groups and programs for quitting smoking.

Book: *Shortness of Breath: A Guide to Better Living and Breathing,* by Kenneth M. Moser, M.D., et al. Tells people with bronchitis, emphysema, and serious respiratory diseases how to manage their condition. Mosby Co., 1991, $17.95.

Colds

- Runny nose.
- Sore throat and hoarseness.
- Watery eyes.
- Coughing.
- Low fever.

If you're plagued by a scratchy throat, runny nose, and cough, you probably have a viral infection of the head and throat, known as the common cold. It's likely caused by one of more than 200 cold viruses. Our bodies can work up an immunity against each one only after exposure, so it's practically impossible to become immune to colds.

You cannot catch a cold from getting your feet wet or sitting in a drafty room—you get it from the virus. But taking a few simple precautions can help protect you from this highly contagious infection.

WHAT YOU CAN DO NOW

There is no cure for the common cold, but there are things you can do to lessen your discomfort. First, stay home from work or school for the first three or four days—not only to rest and recover, but also to prevent spreading your cold to other people. Other ways to feel better:

- ➤ Drink lots of fluids to avoid dehydration.
- ➤ Take an aspirin substitute for aches and fever. (Never give aspirin to a child under 12 who has a cold, chicken pox, flu, or any other illness you suspect of being caused by a virus, such as a bad respiratory infection; see box on **Reye's syndrome,** page 92.)
- ➤ If you have a sore throat, try gargling with salt water a few times a day.
- ➤ Use over-the-counter saline nose drops to clear up a stuffy nose.
- ➤ Avoid smoking and smoky places.
- ➤ Taking one 500-milligram tablet of vitamin C four times a day may lessen the discomfort and duration of your cold, according to some researchers. But be aware that taking too much vitamin C over long periods of time can cause severe diarrhea.
- ➤ Use a cool-mist humidifier to keep your nasal passages from drying out (see box on **humidifiers,** previous page).

GIVE COLD FORMULAS THE COLD SHOULDER

Cold medicines are a $1.9 billion a year industry. Many contain far more ingredients than you need, and some may even make you feel worse.

Physicians recommend that you buy generic drugs with only one ingredient—such as aspirin, a cough suppressant, or an oral decongestant—rather than brand-name "mega" formulas, which try to tackle several symptoms at once. Some medications generally not recommended for the relief of cold symptoms are:

- ➤ **Antihistamines.** Although they help to clear up runny noses and sneezing, they can also dry out the nasal passages too much. Also, in older men, they may make urination difficult.
- ➤ **Expectorants.** There is no conclusive evidence that these medications loosen mucus.
- ➤ **Nasal decongestants.** Although they help shrink swollen nasal passages, they often have a "rebound effect," meaning that the nasal tissues may swell back up, sometimes even worse, after a few days of use.

Cough suppressants (antitussives) present another dilemma. Some coughs are "productive"—that is, they bring up mucus from the lungs—so it's better not to suppress them. Dry, hacking coughs, though, are best treated with an antitussive syrup or lozenge. The medicine may cause drowsiness, so avoid driving if you take it. Also, avoid taking decongestants with certain antidepressants (see chart on **drug combinations to avoid,** page 307).

WHEN TO CALL THE DOCTOR

Call for an immediate appointment:

➤ If you have a fever of 100 degrees or higher and facial swelling and/or severe pain in the ears; you may have a dangerous **ear infection** (see page 71).

➤ If your throat begins to hurt severely and your tonsils or throat have a white or yellow coating; you may have **tonsillitis** (see page 99) or **strep throat** (see pages 97 and 258).

➤ If you have a severe cough with thick, discolored mucus; a cough that lasts more than ten days; or bluish lips or nails. You may have **pneumonia** (see page 94).

Call for advice and an appointment:

➤ If you have a headache accompanied by pain around the face, a supersensitive upper jaw, or yellow or green mucus coming from your nose or throat; these are signs of bacterial infection in the sinuses. (See **sinusitis,** page 95.)

➤ If a fever lasts longer than four days or you have a fever of more than 102 degrees.

➤ If your cold hasn't improved after ten days or has gotten steadily worse.

HOW TO PREVENT IT

Since cold viruses can be transmitted through handshakes and can lurk on doorknobs and counters, wash your hands often, especially during cold season in the fall and winter. Also:

➤ Keep your hands away from your eyes, nose, and mouth.

➤ Move away from people who are coughing and sneezing.

➤ Drink lots of fluids.

➤ Since stress, allergies, and menstrual cycles may make you more vulnerable to infection, try to rest more and take good care of yourself when you're feeling under the weather.

Flu

SIGNS AND SYMPTOMS

■ Chills and a fever over 103 degrees.
■ Muscle aches.
■ Weakness and fatigue.
■ Headache and eye pain.
■ Dry cough.
■ Sore throat.

Flu (influenza) is a highly contagious respiratory infection caused by a virus. Flu viruses show up most frequently in winter and early spring. They change from year to year, making the rounds of schools, offices, and other places where people gather. Occasionally flu viruses mutate dramatically, leading to more severe outbreaks.

Children are most vulnerable to flu infection, but the elderly and people with lung disease or other chronic conditions have a higher risk of complications than others.

Flus and colds are similar, but flus are usually more severe, with higher fevers and aches and pains. A bad case of the flu may send a healthy person to bed for three to five days, but he or she will probably recover fully within a week or two.

WHAT YOU CAN DO NOW

The more rest you get, the sooner you'll get well. And staying home lessens the risk of infecting people at school or work: Flu continues to be contagious for three or four days after symptoms appear. To recover quickly:

➤ Drink as many fluids—water, juice, hot tea—as you can. Have some frozen juice bars for variety.

➤ Have chicken soup and bouillon; the heat may relieve the feeling of congestion.

➤ Take an aspirin substitute for aches and fever. (Never give aspirin to a child under 12 who has flu, chicken pox, or any other illness you suspect of being caused by a virus, such as a bad respiratory infection; see box on **Reye's syndrome,** page 92.)

➤ Avoid cold medicines designed to treat

more than one symptom (see box on **cold medicines,** page 90).

WHEN TO CALL THE DOCTOR

Flus are particularly dangerous for people with chronic illnesses, including cancer; diabetes; respiratory, heart, or kidney disease; cystic fibrosis; or recurring anemia. If you have one of these conditions—or if you are HIV positive—call your doctor at the first appearance of flu symptoms. Drugs can treat certain flu viruses and may help the elderly or chronically ill.

Call for an immediate appointment:

➤ If you have a recurring fever or chest pain, or if you cough up thick, discolored, or bloody mucus; you may be developing **pneumonia** (see page 94) or **bronchitis** (see page 88).

➤ If you have an earache, facial swelling, drainage from your ear, or severe pain in your face or forehead. These may indicate another illness, such as **sinusitis** (see page 95) or an **ear infection** (see page 71).

Call for advice:

➤ If your fever lasts more than three to four days or is higher than 102 degrees.

HOW TO PREVENT IT

Because flu viruses mutate from year to year, it's impossible to develop immunity. To avoid infection or lessen the severity, get a flu shot each fall—particularly if you're over 65 or you have a chronic health problem. The vaccine is not always effective, however, because the viruses it's supposed to protect against may be different from the ones that are going around in your area.

➤ If you are pregnant, you should consult your doctor before getting a flu shot.

➤ If you are allergic to eggs, or think you are, consult your doctor about whether or not to be vaccinated.

The flu virus is spread in the spray from coughs and sneezes, so keeping a distance from people who have the flu may lessen your chances of infection. In addition:

➤ Wash your hands frequently to reduce your risk of catching a cold or the flu.

➤ Avoid secondhand cigarette smoke, and if you smoke, quit.

➤ Keep your immune system healthy by following a good diet, getting adequate sleep, keeping stress levels low, and drinking lots of water.

FOR MORE HELP

Information line: Centers for Disease Control and Prevention's Voice Information System, 404-332-4555, 24-hour automated line. Choose from several topics relevant to the flu and flu shots; you can ask to receive information by voice, fax, or mail.

REYE'S SYNDROME

This rare disorder causes vomiting and sometimes leads to delirium, coma, or even death. Reye's syndrome reached its peak in the late 1970s and early 1980s, with hundreds of cases reported annually, but there are now fewer than 20 cases a year. No age group is immune, although the disease almost always strikes young people between infancy and adolescence. While its exact causes are unknown, it is associated with aspirin taken during viral infections such as chicken pox and flu.

For this reason, doctors warn that you should never give aspirin to a child under 12 who has chicken pox, flu, or any other illness you suspect of being caused by a virus, such as a bad respiratory infection. Use acetaminophen.

If your child or teenager has a viral infection, begins to vomit, and becomes drowsy or delirious, or unusually confused, disoriented, or combative, he or she may have Reye's syndrome. Call your doctor immediately.

Lung Cancer

SIGNS AND SYMPTOMS

In its early stages, lung cancer typically has no symptoms. By the time a tumor has grown large enough to cause symptoms, it's often in an advanced stage. Then, symptoms include:

- An increase in a chronic, hacking "smoker's cough," sometimes accompanied by blood-streaked mucus. These are often the first signs.
- Recurring bronchitis—an inflammation of the main air passages in the lungs.
- Shortness of breath; wheezing; dull, persistent chest pain or intermittent, sharp chest pain.
- Hoarseness.
- Pain and weakness in the shoulder, arm, or hand.
- Weight loss or loss of appetite.
- Persistent low fever.

Before cigarettes became popular, lung cancer was a relatively rare disease. Today lung cancer causes 25 percent of all cancer deaths in the United States. Although the disease remains more prevalent among men than women, lung cancer now kills more women than does breast cancer.

Smoking is by far the most common cause of lung cancer. But genes, previous lung disease, and exposure to cancer-causing substances are also factors.

When a normal cell in the lungs becomes cancerous, it begins to reproduce uncontrollably, forming a tumor, or mass of tissue, that gradually invades and destroys healthy lung tissue. If untreated, the cancer cells may spread through the blood and the lymph system to other parts of the body, where they form new tumors. Only 13 percent of all lung cancer patients live for five years or longer, but chances of survival increase significantly with early detection.

WHAT YOU CAN DO NOW

Lung cancer is not something you can treat yourself. But once it is diagnosed, your doctor will work with you to decide which treatment—surgery, chemotherapy, radiation, or a combination—is best for you.

There is much you can do to improve your chances of recovery and to stay active during treatment:

- Ask your nurse or doctor to show you exercises that strengthen your chest muscles.
- Join a support group for people with cancer and their families. Emotional support seems to aid in recovery.
- Practice good general health habits.

WHEN TO CALL THE DOCTOR

- Call for an immediate appointment if you have any symptoms. Early detection is the key to successful treatment of lung cancer.

HOW TO PREVENT IT

- Don't smoke. Even long-term smokers improve their chances of avoiding lung cancer by quitting. (See **smoking and illness,** page 210.)
- Quitting smoking will not only reduce your risk of getting lung cancer, it will reduce the risk for those close to you; the spouses of smokers have at least a 30 percent higher risk of getting lung cancer from secondhand smoke than do the spouses of nonsmokers.
- Eat plenty of fresh fruits and vegetables.
- Reduce stress through relaxation, visualization, meditation, or yoga.

FOR MORE HELP

Information line: Cancer Information Service, 800-422-6237, M–F 9–4:30 your time. Provides information, literature, access to a database of physicians, and information on clinical trials, free of charge.

Information line: American Cancer Society's Cancer Response System, 800-227-2345, M–F 9–5 local time. Provides pamphlets and makes referrals to cancer support groups in your area.

Pneumonia

Common:
- Shaking, chills, and fever as high as 105 degrees.
- Chest pain.
- Mucus that is greenish, greenish-yellow, rust-colored, or streaked with blood.
- Shortness of breath.

Sometimes:
- Sweating, rapid pulse, and rapid breathing.
- Bluish lips and nails.
- Delirium.
- Diarrhea, headache, or pain in the muscles.
- Vomiting.

Pneumonia is a serious infection in which parts of the lungs fill with pus or other liquid that clogs air sacs and prevents oxygen from reaching the bloodstream. The most common causes include:

➤ **Bacteria.** If untreated, bacterial pneumonia can sometimes result in death, particularly in people with emphysema and other chronic conditions. It can spread from the lungs to the rest of the body.

➤ **Viruses.** There is no drug therapy available for viral pneumonia, but most people recover with bed rest and adequate care.

➤ **Fungi.** Certain fungi that usually cause a mild form of pneumonia in otherwise healthy people can cause severe reactions in people with AIDS or other immune system disorders. One of the most common causes of pneumonia in people with AIDS is *Pneumocystis carinii*, which some researchers believe to be a fungus. It is usually treatable with antibiotics, though occasionally steroids such as cortisone are needed as well.

The people most likely to have severe pneumonia are those under age 2 and over 75, and people with chronic health conditions, including heart trouble, cancer, emphysema, HIV, or asthma. Alcoholics, people who have had strokes, and those who are taking anticancer drugs or other drugs that suppress the immune system also run a high risk of developing the illness. People who are bedridden are at high risk, because lying flat on the back makes it harder to cough up mucus.

Pneumonia symptoms can range from those of "walking pneumonia"—tiredness and congestion that can linger without sending you to bed—to more serious cases that require immediate hospitalization. Call your doctor for an immediate appointment if you think you have any form of the illness. In addition:

➤ Drink lots of fluids.

➤ Avoid cough suppressants if you have a wet cough: Coughing up mucus will help you recover.

➤ Try using a cool-mist humidifier in your bedroom. Clean it daily, and fill it only with distilled water (see box on **humidifiers,** page 89).

➤ Put hot compresses on your chest to make yourself more comfortable.

➤ Avoid smoking and smoky places.

➤ To prevent a relapse, which can be more serious than the first bout, be sure to take all the medicine your doctor prescribes—especially antibiotics.

Pneumonia often comes on the heels of another respiratory illness, such as a cold. Call for an immediate appointment if you have been sick and these symptoms appear:

➤ Change in color of mucus, or appearance of mucus streaked with blood.

➤ Persistent fever over 100 degrees, accompanied by chills or sweats.

➤ Shortness of breath or pain when breathing. If the recently ill person is in a high-risk category (very young, over 65, or someone with a chronic condition), be on guard for the first signs of pneumonia and arrange for prompt medical attention.

HOW TO PREVENT IT

If you are in a high-risk group, talk to your doctor about getting a vaccination for bacterial pneumonia as well as a yearly flu shot. Also:

➤ Avoid smoking, smoke-filled rooms, and heavy drinking: These all weaken your ability to fight off infection.

➤ Avoid close contact with people who have respiratory infections.

➤ Eat healthfully. Emphasize fruits, vegetables, and grains in your diet. Plant-based foods are high in vitamins and fiber; they provide a lot of nutrients without much fat, and the fiber helps speed toxins out of the body. Plants also contain many chemicals that help boost the body's immune system. (See **Eight Ways to Feel Your Best,** page 286.)

➤ Exercise several times a week. Regular physical effort and movement not only increase your energy and strength, they build your body's resistance to colds and flu. (See **Eight Ways to Feel Your Best,** page 282.)

➤ If you're bedridden, try to sit up for one or two hours after eating to avoid inhaling food particles, which can lead to developing pneumonia.

FOR MORE HELP

Information line: National Jewish Center for Immunology and Respiratory Medicine, 1400 Jackson St., Denver, CO 80206. 800-222-5864, M–F 8–5 MST. Nurses answer questions, make referrals, and send information. 800-552-5864, recorded information on breathing problems.

Organization: American Lung Association, 800-LUNG-USA (586-4872), M–F 9–5 your time. Automatically connects you to a local ALA chapter, which can send you a pamphlet on pneumonia.

Sinusitis

SIGNS AND SYMPTOMS

Acute sinusitis:
■ Stuffy nose and trouble breathing, especially when a cold lasts longer than a week.
■ Green or yellow nasal discharge, sometimes tinged with blood. It may drip into the back of your throat, making you cough.
■ Pain or pressure in or around the eyes and forehead. The pain may travel to the back of your head and be worse in the morning or when you're leaning forward.
■ A foul smell in your nose and/or bad breath.
Sometimes:
■ Fever.
■ Pain in the upper jaw.
Chronic sinusitis:
■ Nasal discharge and sinus congestion that persist or recur over a period of months.

Acute and chronic sinusitis are inflammations of the sinuses, the air-filled pockets in the bones around the nose.

When allergies, smoke, air pollution, or infections irritate your nasal passages, the membranes there swell and clog the tiny openings to your sinuses. Bacteria can grow in the mucus trapped in the sinuses, causing pressure and pain—sometimes severe—in the forehead, cheeks, or behind and around the eyes.

People who smoke, have allergies, or are frequently exposed to infection—such as schoolteachers and health care workers—are among the most likely to get sinus infections.

Symptoms of **acute sinusitis** caused by a bacterial infection usually last only a few days if treated with antibiotics. Sinusitis caused by a virus generally goes away by itself. The symptoms of **chronic sinusitis** are often milder than those of the acute form: Chronic sinusitis usually doesn't cause severe

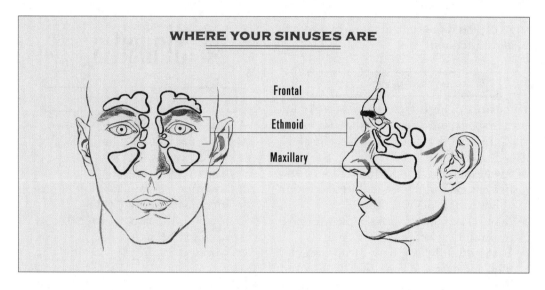

WHERE YOUR SINUSES ARE

Frontal

Ethmoid

Maxillary

headaches. It can, however, cause congestion and annoying nasal secretions for months or years. Chronic sinusitis occurs when the sinus opening is blocked for a long time, sometimes as a result of small growths in the nose called nasal polyps, or of a condition (deviated septum) in which the wall between the nostrils is crooked and reduces the flow of air.

WHAT YOU CAN DO NOW

➤ Inhale steam for temporary relief from clogged sinuses. Take a hot shower or place a warm, damp cloth over your nose.
➤ Drink plenty of liquids—at least eight to ten glasses a day.
➤ Try oral decongestants or nasal decongestant sprays. They may help you breathe more easily, but they should not be used for more than two days without consulting a doctor, because their "rebound effect" can make symptoms worse.
➤ Flushing your nose with salt water can help wash away mucus and bacteria.

WHEN TO CALL THE DOCTOR

Call for an immediate appointment:
➤ If facial swelling occurs or vision is blurry; you may have a dangerous infection.
Call for advice and an appointment:
➤ If symptoms last more than seven days without improvement; it's important to get medical attention. If a bacterial sinus

infection goes untreated, it can persist for years, causing chronic pain. Continued postnasal drip of infected mucus can lead to bronchitis, chronic cough, or asthma.

HOW TO PREVENT IT

Since sinusitis generally follows problems like allergies, colds, or the flu, it's important to treat those conditions before sinusitis can develop.
➤ If you have **allergies** (see page 85), learn what triggers them so you can manage your condition.
➤ Sleep with your head elevated to help your sinuses drain.
➤ Avoid smoky or polluted environments. If you smoke, quit.
➤ Don't blow your nose too hard.

FOR MORE HELP

Organization: National Jewish Center for Immunology and Respiratory Medicine, 1400 Jackson St., Denver, CO 80206. 800-222-5864, M–F 8–5 MST. Nurses answer questions, make referrals, and send information. 800-552-5864, recorded information on breathing problems.
Pamphlet: "Sinus Pain, Pressure, and Drainage," by the American Academy of Otolaryngology. Send a business-size, self-addressed, stamped envelope to AAO, One Prince St., Alexandria, VA 22314. Or fax your request to 703-683-5100.

Sore Throat

(see page 254) and **chicken pox** (see page 243). They can also be signals of problems like epiglottitis (a serious infection of the larynx) or mononucleosis.

SIGNS AND SYMPTOMS

- Pain when talking or swallowing.
- Throat that looks red all over or in streaks when you open wide and say "Aahhh."
- Swollen, tender glands in the upper neck.

Sometimes:
- Fever.
- Headache.
- Earache.

Strep throat:
- Sore throat that comes on suddenly, accompanied by fever, swollen neck glands, headache, or bright red tonsils.

Mononucleosis:
- Same symptoms as strep throat, plus debilitating fatigue and loss of appetite.

Sooner or later, everybody gets a sore throat. Most result from a virus—from flu or a cold or sinus infection—that invades the throat. Air pollution, allergies, tobacco smoke, and the dry air of wintertime heating can also bring on sore throats. Even sustained shouting can irritate the throat and cause soreness.

A minority of sore throats are caused by bacteria—usually streptococcus (or strep)—transmitted from an infected person. **Strep throat** is most common in children (see page 258), but it also occurs in adults. Because strep can invade other parts of the body and cause serious complications such as rheumatic fever or a severe kidney infection—and because it's impossible to diagnose without a test—you should see your doctor promptly if you suspect you have it. A doctor can take a throat culture or give you a newly developed rapid strep test. If you have the strep bacteria, a course of antibiotics should knock it out.

Painful sore throats commonly accompany childhood ailments such as **measles**

WHAT YOU CAN DO NOW

- Drink lots of liquids, preferably warm ones such as soup or herbal tea.
- Gargle with warm salt water.
- Don't smoke, and keep away from people when they're smoking.
- Take a nonaspirin pain reliever to ease pain and inflammation. (Never give aspirin to a child under 12 who has chicken pox, flu, or any other illness you suspect of being caused by a virus, such as a bad respiratory infection; see box on **Reye's syndrome,** page 92.)
- Suck on throat lozenges or cough drops to keep your throat moist.
- Use a vaporizer or humidifier to moisten bedroom air (see box on **humidifiers,** page 89).
- Don't ask your doctor for an antibiotic unless you have strep or another bacterial infection—it won't work against a virus.

WHEN TO CALL THE DOCTOR

Call 911 or go to an emergency facility **immediately:**
- If you cannot swallow liquids or you have trouble breathing.

Call for an immediate appointment:
- If you have fever over 101 degrees.
- If the glands in your neck are swollen.
- If your tonsils are bright red or have spots of white pus on them.
- If your sore throat lasts longer than the five-to-seven-day span of a typical cold.

HOW TO PREVENT IT

- Avoid cigarette smoke and other irritants.
- Stay away from people who have strep throat or a sore throat.

FOR MORE HELP

Pamphlet: "Sore Throats: Causes and Cures," provided by the American Academy of

Otolaryngology. For the pamphlet and a list of qualified physicians in your state, send a business-size, self-addressed, stamped envelope to AAO, One Prince St., Alexandria, VA 22314. Or fax your request to 703-683-5100.

Swallowing Difficulty

SIGNS AND SYMPTOMS

■ Pain or serious discomfort while swallowing.
■ Trouble getting food to go down.

Painful and difficult swallowing are not diseases in themselves, but they are often symptoms of other conditions, usually involving the throat or the tube that connects the throat to the stomach (the esophagus). (See color illustration, page 172.)

Swallowing difficulties often accompany other symptoms—such as hoarseness, fever, throat or chest pain, nausea and vomiting, headache, and weight loss—that are key to diagnosing the illness.

Obviously, an object or a piece of food (such as a fish bone) stuck in the throat may be the problem. In this case, difficult swallowing could become an emergency if a person can't breathe (see **choking,** page 25).

If you have difficulty swallowing in addition to a sore throat and possibly fever and hoarseness, you may have inflamed tonsils (see **tonsillitis,** opposite page); an infected larynx, or "voice box" (laryngitis); or an inflamed pharynx (pharyngitis), which is the area of the throat between the mouth and the esophagus.

Frequently, stomach acid flowing up from the stomach can irritate the esophagus and produce a feeling like **heartburn** (see page 121). This condition, called esophagitis, can also cause chest pain and, rarely, vomiting.

Similar symptoms occur when part of the stomach squeezes up into the chest cavity (a hiatal **hernia,** see page 123) or when the esophagus becomes narrowed by a buildup of scar tissue caused by stomach acid.

Other causes of swallowing difficulties are cancers of the mouth, esophagus, and stomach; botulism (see **food poisoning,** page 35); tetanus; **Parkinson's disease** (see page 57); multiple sclerosis; and defective nerves in the esophagus.

People with a condition called globus—usually caused by anxiety—can swallow normally, yet have the sensation of a lump in the throat or the feeling that they are choking when they swallow.

WHAT YOU CAN DO NOW

➤ For burning pain in the throat or a feeling of heartburn, take antacids.
➤ For the sensation of a lump in the throat, drink lots of water with meals and practice relaxation techniques to reduce stress.

WHEN TO CALL THE DOCTOR

Call 911 or go to an emergency facility **immediately:**
➤ If something is caught in your throat.
Call for an immediate appointment:
➤ If you have swallowing difficulties that last for more than a few days, or if they are combined with weight loss and vomiting.
Call for advice and an appointment:
➤ If you suspect you have tonsillitis, laryngitis, or pharyngitis.
➤ If you can swallow food or drink yet still feel as if you have a lump in your throat, even after trying relaxation techniques.

HOW TO PREVENT IT

➤ Do not smoke; if you do, quit. Smoking can cause oral cancer and problems of the esophagus.
➤ Take antacids to neutralize stomach acid or acid blockers to prevent stomach acid production.
➤ Avoid spicy foods and alcohol, which can worsen heartburn.
➤ If you are overweight, losing weight may reduce the swallowing difficulties and heartburn resulting from hiatal hernia.

Organization: National Digestive Diseases Information Clearinghouse, 2 Information Way, Bethesda, MD 20892-3570. Ask for the fact sheet on gastroesophageal reflux disease, which includes information on heartburn and hiatal hernia.

Book: *Gastrointestinal Health,* by Steven Peikin, M.D. HarperCollins, 1992, $12.

Tonsillitis

SIGNS AND SYMPTOMS

Mild cases:
- Sore or raw throat.
- An increasingly hoarse or "throaty" voice.

More severe cases:
- Tonsils that are red or have white or yellow spots.
- Tonsils so swollen that they fill the back of the throat.
- Tender or swollen lymph glands in the neck.
- Fever of 100 degrees or higher, headache, or vomiting.
- Ear or stomach pain.

In children:
- Refusal to eat because swallowing is painful.

In adults:
- Foul-smelling white debris and a burning sensation in the back of the throat.

A generation ago, "having your tonsils out" was almost a rite of passage for youngsters. Doctors routinely removed children's tonsils—pink masses of lymph tissue on both sides of the back of the throat—to prevent tonsillitis, a viral or bacterial infection. More recently, doctors have realized that children often outgrow the tendency to get these infections. (Adults can get tonsillitis, too, although it's more common in children.)

Furthermore, as it turns out, tonsils aren't simply a nuisance. Researchers have found that they play an active role in fighting off respiratory infections, especially in young children. Removing the tonsils is unwarranted unless children have repeated tonsil infections that cause them to miss weeks of school.

WHAT YOU CAN DO NOW

If your child's tonsils are simply red (there's no swelling or white or yellow coating) and he or she does not have a fever or any problems swallowing, you can usually get good results with home treatment.

➤ Keep your child warm and rested, with a cool-mist humidifier operating in the room if possible.
➤ Give lots of liquids, along with ice cream or frozen yogurt, to soothe the throat.
➤ Use a saltwater gargle to help dull the pain and cleanse infected tonsils.
➤ Give acetaminophen for fever and pain. (Never give aspirin to a child under 12 who has chicken pox, flu, or any other illness you suspect of being caused by a virus, such as a bad respiratory infection; see box on **Reye's syndrome,** page 92.)
➤ Sponge the face with cool water to reduce fever.

WHEN TO CALL THE DOCTOR

In children:
➤ If the tonsils have a white or yellow coating or spots on them. (Use a flashlight to look at them.)
➤ If the tonsils are so swollen that they are touching; this may mean a serious infection such as strep.
➤ If a sore throat is severe and lasts more than two days.
➤ If your child has a fever above 100 degrees or goes 24 hours without eating.
➤ If your child has greenish, yellowish, or rusty-colored mucus or experiences nausea, skin rashes, chest pain, convulsions, inflamed or painful joints, or a fever that returns after being absent for a day or two. These may signal a system-wide staph infection; sometimes tonsillitis leads to another infection in the tonsils or elsewhere.

In adults:
➤ If you have difficulty swallowing or opening your mouth, and excruciating pain in your throat or jaw.

HOW TO PREVENT IT

Encourage children to avoid bacteria and viruses by:
➤ Moving away from people who are coughing and sneezing.
➤ Not sharing cups or silverware.
➤ Washing their hands frequently.
➤ Keeping their hands away from their mouths.

FOR MORE HELP

Pamphlet: American Academy of Pediatrics, P.O. Box 927, Elk Grove Village, IL 60009-0927. Send a business-size, self-addressed, stamped envelope, and request a copy of "Tonsils and Adenoids."

ABOUT ADENOIDS

Tonsillitis should not be confused with enlarged adenoids, which often accompany a tonsil infection. The adenoids are grapelike clusters of tissue found in the upper part of the throat, behind the nose. They begin to grow when a child is about three; at about five, they usually begin to shrink, and by the teens they disappear.

A child who snores or breathes through the mouth rather than the nose, and who develops a twangy, nasal voice, may have enlarged adenoids. Swollen adenoids can cause a more serious condition known as sleep apnea, in which the child may stop breathing for several seconds at a time. (See **sleep disorders,** page 277.) Call a doctor if any of the above symptoms lasts for more than a week.

Tuberculosis

SIGNS AND SYMPTOMS

Tuberculosis (TB) infection:
■ Mild cough (sometimes).
Note: You may have an infection even if you have no symptoms at all.
TB disease:
■ Coughing, sometimes with bloody mucus.
■ Slight fever.
■ Weight loss and fatigue.
■ Night sweats.
■ Chest pain.

Tuberculosis, or TB, is a chronic infection that usually affects the lungs. But it can also spread throughout the body, particularly to the brain, kidneys, and bones.

Tuberculosis was once so commonplace that it killed one out of five adults in Europe and the United States. With the discovery of antibiotics, the disease all but disappeared until the mid-1980s, when it began to spread among people who lacked access to adequate medical care or whose immune systems had been weakened by AIDS. In addition, new types of TB appeared that outsmarted common antibiotics.

Tuberculosis develops in two stages. The first is infection, when the TB bacteria enter the lungs and multiply. Generally, the body's immune system stops the infection within two to ten weeks.

Only about 10 percent of the people who are infected with TB go on to develop the active disease, half of those within one to two years. People who develop active TB can spread it to others through close contact, usually over a long period of time. It is rarely spread by casual contact or in public transportation such as buses and airplanes.

Most TB can be treated effectively with antibiotics, with excellent recovery rates. However, the death rate for a rarer, drug-resistant TB is about 50 percent.

WHAT YOU CAN DO NOW

➤ If you have the disease, it's important to get regular medical attention and to follow your doctor's advice closely.

WHEN TO CALL THE DOCTOR

➤ If you have symptoms of the disease.
➤ If you suspect you have been exposed to tuberculosis for a long period.
➤ If you are receiving treatment for TB and new, unexpected symptoms develop.

HOW TO PREVENT IT

Most people are not at risk of getting TB, so they needn't take any special measures.

If you are in any of the following high-risk groups, however, talk with your doctor about screenings, prevention, or a preventive vaccine (the vaccine is not 100 percent effective):

➤ If you are HIV positive.
➤ If you have spent a long time with someone who has the disease, or you work in a place such as a homeless shelter, a hospital, or a residential care facility.
➤ If you are an intravenous drug user.
➤ If you have spent a long time in crowded conditions in a country where tuberculosis is known to be prevalent.
➤ If there has been TB in their school, your children should be tested.

FOR MORE HELP

Information line: National Jewish Center for Immunology and Respiratory Medicine, 1400 Jackson St., Denver, CO 80206. 800-222-5864, M–F 8–5 MST. Nurses answer questions, make referrals, and send information. 800-552-5864, recorded information on breathing problems.

Information line: Centers for Disease Control and Prevention, 404-639-1819, M–F 8–4 EST. Voice mail system allows you to hear information on TB, request brochures by mail or fax, and talk with information specialists.

Heart & Circulation

Congestive Heart Failure

SIGNS AND SYMPTOMS

- Weakness and fatigue.
- Shortness of breath during even light physical activity or while lying down. This breathlessness might cause wheezing that is mistaken for asthma.
- Need to sleep on more pillows than usual or to sleep sitting up.
- Swelling in the feet, ankles, and legs.
- Dull ache or pain in the chest.
- Persistent cough with foamy, blood-specked mucus.
- Feeling of abdominal fullness.
- Weight gain from fluid retention.
- Frequent need to urinate, especially at night.
- Swelling of neck veins.
- Nausea, vomiting, and/or loss of appetite.
- Irregular or rapid heartbeat.

Despite its frightening name, congestive heart failure is not a life-threatening disease when the causes are diagnosed and treated. It occurs when the heart muscle is damaged, usually by **high blood pressure** (see page 105), a **heart attack** (see page 38),

palpitations (see page 108), valve problems, or a condition called cardiomyopathy, which may be caused by some viruses, alcohol abuse, or inherited defects. As a result, the heart can't keep the blood circulating effectively, causing congestion and swelling, especially in the legs and ankles. Sometimes fluid collects in the lungs and makes breathing difficult. Congestive heart failure also makes it harder for the kidneys to get rid of excess sodium and water, which can make the swelling worse.

Congestive heart failure is the single most frequent reason for hospitalization in people 65 years or older. When treatment is timely and appropriate, people with congestive heart failure are often able to resume all of their regular activities.

WHAT YOU CAN DO NOW

After diagnosis:

- ➤ Get plenty of rest at first. Later, as your symptoms ease, increased physical activity (with your doctor's consent) will be very important.
- ➤ To make breathing easier when lying down, raise your head by putting a wedge under your mattress or using extra pillows.
- ➤ Put your legs up when sitting.
- ➤ Eat less salt; it increases fluid retention and swelling.
- ➤ Don't drink caffeinated beverages; if you're having heart palpitations, caffeine can make them worse.

(continued)

Chest Pain

Never ignore chest pain, especially in an adult. It's difficult to tell one kind of chest pain from another, so if it is severe or lasts more than a few minutes, call 911.

SYMPTOMS	WHAT IT MIGHT BE	WHAT YOU CAN DO
Crushing pain, pressure, or squeezing in center of chest that may spread to jaw, neck, back, or arms (often left arm); sweating, nausea, or shortness of breath.	Heart attack (see page 38).	Call 911 or go to emergency facility **immediately.**
Pain or chest tightness with breathing. In adults: sudden, sharp chest pain with increasing shortness of breath. In young people: possibly vague or minor pain that spreads to neck or back with some breath-lessness.	Collapsed lung. Sometimes occurs in young people for no apparent reason, or in adults who have asthma or chronic bronchitis. May follow a recent chest injury.	Call 911 or go to emergency facility **immediately.**
Severe, persistent, possibly ripping chest pain that may spread to abdomen and upper back; dizziness and fainting.	Aortic aneurysm—weak spot with rip or tear in main artery from heart. Usually caused by narrowed arteries (see page 107) or high blood pressure (see page 105).	Call 911 or go to emergency facility **immediately.** Surgery may be required to repair aorta.
Sharp chest pain, worse when breathing in; short-ness of breath; possibly fever.	Pleurisy—inflammation of sac around lungs; often a complication of pneumonia (see page 94) or tuberculosis (see page 100).	Call 911 or go to emergency facility **immediately.**
Dull pain, pressure, or squeezing in center of chest that may feel like indiges-tion or heartburn; may spread to jaw, neck, back, or arms (usually left arm); brought on or made worse by stress or activity, easing with rest in 30 seconds to 5 minutes.	Angina. ● Coronary artery disease. (See narrowed ar-teries, page 107, and heart attack, page 38.)	Call doctor for immediate appointment, but if symptoms persist 10 minutes or longer, call 911 or go to emergency facility **immediately.**

(continued)

Heart & Circulation

Chest Pain *(continued)*

SYMPTOMS	WHAT IT MIGHT BE	WHAT YOU CAN DO
Chest pain, breathlessness, easy fatigue, irregular heartbeat (palpitations), fainting (sometimes).	Disturbance of heart rhythm. ● Mitral valve prolapse—heart valve allows blood to leak backward; affects many more women than men, may run in families.	Call doctor for immediate appointment. For mitral valve prolapse, beta-blocker medications may ease palpitations and chest pain. Antibiotics should be taken before dental work or surgery to prevent infection of heart's lining. **For more help:** American Heart Association, 800-242-8721, M–F 8:30–5 PST.
Tightening or pain in chest, rapid heartbeat, shortness of breath, numbness or tingling in hands, fear, possibly feeling of not getting enough air.	Anxiety. ● Panic attack. ● Hyperventilation—rapid breathing that lowers level of carbon dioxide in blood. (See anxiety and phobias, page 202.)	If you can't function normally, call doctor for advice.
Burning or pressure in chest or upper abdomen, worse on bending over or lying down, especially when stomach is full; belching. Symptoms can resemble heart attack.	Heartburn. ● Esophageal reflux—stomach acid backs up into esophagus when muscle intended to prevent this becomes weak. ● Ulcer. ● Gastritis.	See heartburn, page 121, or ulcers and gastritis, page 130.
Severe burning or aching pain on one side of chest that may spread to back, unaffected by breathing; followed several days later by blistering, itchy rash.	Shingles.	See shingles, page 154.
Sharp pain that gets worse with movement or deep breathing, or when area is pressed; may follow severe coughing or sneezing, or chest injury.	Pulled muscle. ● Inflamed cartilage. ● Injured rib.	Rest, apply an ice pack (a bag of frozen peas wrapped in a dishcloth works well) several times a day, 10–15 minutes at a time.

> Use elastic support stockings to control swelling in your legs. Ask your pharmacist which kind is most appropriate for you.

| WHEN TO CALL THE DOCTOR |

Call 911 or go to an emergency facility **immediately:**
> If you experience severe chest pain or breathlessness.

Call for an immediate appointment:
> If you frequently become breathless and exhausted after mild physical activity.

Call for advice:
> If you're being treated for congestive heart failure and your symptoms get worse.
> If you gain more than a couple of pounds over a few days.

| HOW TO PREVENT IT |

> Do what you can to prevent the underlying problems, such as high blood pressure or narrowed arteries.
> If you know you have high blood pressure or heart disease, follow your doctor's advice about treating the condition.
> Avoid excessive alcohol intake.

| FOR MORE HELP |

Information line: American Heart Association, 800-242-8721, M–F 8:30–5 your time. Information specialists answer questions and send out literature.

Organization: National Heart, Lung, and Blood Institute Information Center, P.O. Box 30105, Bethesda, MD 20824-0105. 800-575-WELL, 24-hour recorded information. 301-251-1222, M–F 8:30–5 EST. Fax: 301-251-1223. Staffers respond to callers' questions and send out appropriate literature.

Book: *Your Heart: Questions You Have—Answers You Need,* by Ed Weiner and the staff of the People's Medical Society. People's Medical Society, 1992, $9.95.

High Blood Pressure

| SIGNS AND SYMPTOMS |

High blood pressure, or hypertension, is called the "silent killer" with good reason. In most cases, there are no clear warning signs, even as the condition damages your health.

Blood pressure refers to the force of blood pushing against artery walls as it courses through the body. Your blood pressure rises and falls naturally through the day with changes in your activities and emotions. But when it remains consistently high, it can force your heart to work too hard, which can threaten your health. High blood pressure is the most common of all cardiovascular diseases. It is the leading cause of **heart attack** (see page 38) and **stroke** (see page 109).

Blood pressure is measured with a device that records two numbers. The lower the numbers, the better. Your blood pressure is too high if the first number (systolic blood pressure—peak pressure when your heart beats) is consistently 140 or higher, or if the second number (diastolic blood pressure—when your heart relaxes between beats) is consistently above 90.

While the causes of most high blood pressure are unknown, the risk factors are well known—they're a combination of things you can't control and things you can. If high blood pressure runs in your family, your risk is doubled. The risk increases with age. African-Americans have a high risk. If you are overweight, under stress, or sedentary, you're also at risk. Sometimes high blood pressure is a sign of other problems, such as **diabetes** (see page 269) or kidney disease.

Fortunately, high blood pressure can be treated effectively with lifestyle changes and, frequently, medications.

Heart & Circulation

➤ If you're in a high-risk group, have your blood pressure checked as often as your doctor recommends. Your doctor can check your blood pressure; your community may offer free or inexpensive screenings; or you can buy a blood pressure cuff and check it yourself, although this takes some practice.

WHEN TO CALL THE DOCTOR

Call for emergency advice (if not available, call 911 or go to an emergency facility):

➤ If you have or suspect you have high blood pressure and you experience any of the following: recurring headaches, chest pain or tightness, frequent nosebleeds, numbness and tingling, confusion, or blurred vision.

Call for advice and an appointment:

➤ If you or someone else checks your blood pressure repeatedly over several days and it is consistently much higher than before.

➤ If you're pregnant and you develop high blood pressure. This can harm both you and your unborn child. (See **pregnancy,** page 232.)

➤ If you have high blood pressure and preventive measures and lifestyle changes don't lower it.

➤ If you're taking drugs to control your high blood pressure and you develop side effects such as drowsiness, dizziness, constipation, or impotence. You may need a different drug. But never discontinue your blood pressure medication without telling your doctor; stopping abruptly can be dangerous.

HOW TO PREVENT IT

➤ Exercise regularly—try brisk walking, swimming, or biking. If you have been totally sedentary, check with your doctor before beginning an exercise program.

➤ Make an effort to lose extra pounds.

➤ If you drink alcohol, drink moderately (no more than two 1.5-ounce drinks of hard liquor, two 12-ounce cans of beer, or two 5-ounce glasses of wine a day for men, one for women).

➤ Eat no more than 2,000 milligrams of salt a day. (One teaspoon of salt equals about 2,100 mg.) Fresh vegetables and fruits are low in salt; fast food and processed foods contain a lot of it.

➤ If you smoke, quit. (See **smoking and illness,** page 210.)

➤ Find a healthy outlet for **stress** (see page 212). Try meditation or yoga to relax.

➤ If you use birth control pills, consider a different contraceptive method. The Pill can cause high blood pressure in some women.

FOR MORE HELP

Information line: American Heart Association, 800-242-8721, M–F 8:30–5 your time. Information specialists answer questions and send literature, including publications on specific groups at risk, such as African-Americans and women.

Organization: National Heart, Lung, and Blood Institute Information Center, P.O. Box 30105, Bethesda, MD 20824-0105. 800-575-WELL, 24-hour recorded information. 301-251-1222, M–F 8:30–5 EST. Fax: 301-251-1223. Staffers respond to questions on high blood pressure and send out literature.

Pamphlets: Citizens for Public Action on Blood Pressure and Cholesterol, P.O. Box 30374, Bethesda, MD 20824. Pamphlets and brochures on high blood pressure are available.

Video: *High Blood Pressure at Time of Diagnosis.* Clear, useful overview of causes and treatments, consisting of four reports— Understanding the Diagnosis, What Happens Next?, Treatment and Management, and Issues and Answers. Time Life Medical, 1996, $19.95.

Narrowed Arteries

SIGNS AND SYMPTOMS

There may be no symptoms before narrowed arteries (atherosclerosis) have caused significant damage to your health. That's why prevention and early detection are important. Watch for symptoms of the following:

Heart disease:
- Dull chest pain (angina) or simply a feeling of tightness or heavy pressure. It's usually in the center of the chest but can spread into the arms and jaw. With rest, angina goes away in 30 seconds to five minutes.

Heart attack:
Call 911 or go to an emergency facility **immediately:**
- If the pain lasts, gets worse, occurs more often, or occurs during rest; this could mean you're about to have a heart attack.

Stroke:
Call 911 or go to an emergency facility **immediately:**
- If you experience unexplained loss of balance, coordination, speech, or vision; or the sudden onset of tingling, numbness, or paralysis in a limb.

Peripheral vascular disease:
- Muscle fatigue, weakness, or pain in the buttocks or legs during exertion, usually in the calves while walking.
- Cold feet.
- Discolored skin, sores that won't heal, and sudden, sharp pains in the legs or feet during rest.

The walls of a healthy artery are smooth and elastic, allowing blood to flow freely. But sometimes a substance known as plaque builds up inside the artery, a process called atherosclerosis. The walls of the vessel thicken, grow rough, and become stiff, narrowing the artery. (See color illustrations, page 169.)

Plaque deposits develop when there are high levels of cholesterol in the blood, a problem that runs in some families. Lack of exercise; a high-fat, high-cholesterol diet; smoking; and untreated **high blood pressure** (see page 105) or **diabetes** (see page 269) also increase your chance of developing narrowed arteries.

The risk rises with age; overweight people are more at risk than those who are lean; and men are in more danger than women, but the risk for women increases sharply once they reach menopause. Women over 35 who smoke and take birth control pills may also have a higher chance of narrowed arteries.

Most of us probably have some arteries that have narrowed significantly by the time we're in our fifties or sixties. Even before serious symptoms appear, atherosclerosis can cause tiredness or a general unwell feeling.

When the disease is more advanced, it can cause serious health problems, including:

Heart disease: This is the leading cause of death in the United States. It occurs when the arteries that supply blood to the heart muscle become narrowed. If the coronary arteries can't supply enough blood to the heart during exertion or strong emotions, you feel chest pain (angina). A heart attack occurs when a blood clot forms in a coronary artery and cuts off the flow of blood to a part of the heart. This typically happens where plaque deposits have built up and damaged the artery's walls.

Stroke: Some types of **strokes** (see page 109) occur when clots form in vessels in or leading to the brain. As in coronary artery disease, this usually happens where the vessel is narrowed by plaque.

Peripheral vascular disease: This occurs when arteries that go to the arms and legs become narrowed. While not necessarily life-threatening, it can lead to gangrene and the loss of a limb, most often a leg, if untreated.

If your doctor suspects you have narrowed arteries, he or she may recommend diet and lifestyle changes, and possibly drugs to reduce high cholesterol or control high blood pressure. Balloon angioplasty can sometimes open blocked arteries, or surgery can bypass them.

There is no quick fix. But long-term changes in lifestyle, including those described below, may slow the disease's progress or even reverse it.

Call 911 or go to an emergency facility **immediately:**

➤ If you feel crushing pain in your chest. This may be accompanied by nausea, vomiting, sweating, shortness of breath, weakness, or intense feelings of anxiety. You may be having a heart attack.

➤ If you've had chest pain before, but this time it doesn't go away in 10 to 15 minutes.

➤ If you've had chest pain before, but it's getting worse or you have it while resting.

➤ If you have any symptoms of a stroke, such as loss of speech or balance, or numbness.

Call for an immediate appointment:

➤ If you have symptoms of peripheral vascular disease such as pain in the legs or feet.

Whether or not your doctor has said that you have atherosclerosis, you can help prevent the problem from developing, slow its progress if it has begun, or perhaps even reverse it by taking the following steps:

➤ Exercise regularly. But check with your doctor before beginning an exercise program, especially if you are at risk for narrowed arteries.

➤ Include lots of whole grains, fruits, and vegetables in your diet. Go easy on meats, dairy products, and processed foods.

➤ Don't smoke. If you do, quit. Smokers have a much higher risk of narrowed arteries than do nonsmokers (see **smoking and illness,** page 210).

➤ If you have **high blood pressure** (see page 105), take steps to get it under control.

➤ Have your cholesterol level checked, and if it's too high (more than 200 milligrams per deciliter of blood), work with your doctor to lower it.

➤ If you are overweight, take steps to lose the extra pounds.

Information line: American Heart Association, 800-242-8721, M–F 8:30–5 your time. Information specialists answer questions and send literature.

Organization: National Heart, Lung, and Blood Institute Information Center, P.O. Box 30105, Bethesda, MD 20824-0105. 800-575-WELL, 24-hour recorded information. 301-251-1222, M–F 8:30–5 EST. Fax: 301-251-1223. Information specialists field questions on narrowed arteries and send out literature.

Video: *Coronary Artery Disease at Time of Diagnosis.* Clear, useful overview of causes and treatments, consisting of four reports— Understanding the Diagnosis, What Happens Next?, Treatment and Management, and Issues and Answers. Time Life Medical, 1996, $19.95.

Palpitations

Rapid heart rate:

■ An uncomfortable, persistent awareness of your heartbeat.

■ A fluttering, thumping, pounding, or racing beat in your chest.

■ Shortness of breath, chest pain, light-headedness, or fainting.

Slow heart rate:

■ Fatigue, shortness of breath, light-headedness, or fainting.

■ Nausea.

Palpitations are disturbances in the heartbeat caused by changes in the electrical impulses that control the heart muscle. Nearly everyone experiences an irregular heartbeat on occasion, and it's usually harmless. But frequent or lasting changes in the heart's rhythm can mean a serious health problem.

The risk of palpitations increases with age. Anxiety, stress, thyroid disorders, and drugs, including nicotine, caffeine, and alcohol, can also set them off. But the most important causes are underlying **high blood pressure** (see page 105) and **narrowed arteries** (see page 107). These diseases can damage the heart muscle, causing a "short circuit" in its electrical system.

Mild, recurring palpitations can often be controlled with drugs. Sometimes implantable devices such as pacemakers are used to control more severely irregular heartbeats.

high blood pressure (see page 105) and narrowed arteries (see page 107).

WHAT YOU CAN DO NOW

➤ If you experience frequent or severe palpitations, call your doctor for an immediate appointment.

WHEN TO CALL THE DOCTOR

Call for an immediate appointment:
➤ If you have fainting spells.
➤ If you notice an unusual heartbeat and feel light-headed or dizzy.
➤ If you have irregular heartbeats that are intense, painful, or more than fleeting.
➤ If you are taking drugs your doctor has prescribed for palpitations and you notice a new, irregular heartbeat pattern; or you have vomiting, nausea, diarrhea, rashes, or fainting.

HOW TO PREVENT IT

➤ Eliminate caffeine from your diet (sources include coffee, tea, chocolate, and caffeinated soft drinks).
➤ Don't smoke, don't drink alcoholic beverages, and don't take decongestants, diet pills, or stimulant drugs such as cocaine or amphetamines.
➤ Get regular exercise, such as brisk walking, jogging, swimming, or bicycling, to help regulate your resting heart rate.
➤ Find a healthy outlet for stress. Try meditation, yoga, or deep breathing.
➤ Eat balanced, low-fat meals. Your doctor may also suggest mineral supplements; calcium, magnesium, and potassium help moderate the heartbeat.

FOR MORE HELP

Information line: American Heart Association, 800-242-8721, M–F 8:30–5 your time. Information specialists answer questions and send literature.

Organization: National Heart, Lung, and Blood Institute Information Center, P.O. Box 30105, Bethesda, MD 20824-0105. 800-575-WELL, 24-hour recorded information. 301-251-1222, M–F 8:30–5 EST. Fax: 301-251-1223. Staffers field general questions and send literature.

Organization: Coronary Club, Cleveland Clinic Foundation, 9500 Euclid Ave., Cleveland, OH 44195. 800-478-4255 and 216-444-3690, M–F 9–3 EST. Fax: 216-444-9385.

Stroke

SIGNS AND SYMPTOMS

If you or a family member experience any of the following, call 911 or go to an emergency facility **immediately:**
■ Abrupt weakness or numbness of the face, arm, or leg, usually on one side of the body.
■ Sudden difficulty seeing or loss of vision, particularly in only one eye.
■ Loss of speech, or trouble talking or understanding speech.
■ Sudden and severe headache.
■ Dizziness, unsteadiness, or sudden loss of consciousness.

A stroke occurs when blood flow to the brain is interrupted. It's an emergency, since affected areas of the brain can begin to die within minutes, causing permanent damage to speech, vision, and movement. In fact, strokes are the number one cause of adult disability in the United States.

There are three main kinds of strokes:

Cerebral thrombosis, the most common, occurs when a blood clot forms and blocks circulation in an artery in the brain or leading to it. These clots usually form in arteries narrowed by fatty deposits called plaque.

Cerebral embolism occurs when a clot forms in some other part of the body, then is carried to the brain.

These two types of stroke are often preceded by a transient ischemic attack (TIA), in which a clot temporarily blocks an artery in the brain or leading to it, briefly cutting off oxygen to part of it. The symptoms are similar to those of cerebral thrombosis or embolism, but they come on rapidly and usually last only a few minutes. TIAs cause no permanent damage, but they are important warning signs of a possible stroke.

Cerebral hemorrhage occurs when a defective artery in the brain bursts and bleeds into the surrounding tissue. Sometimes a vessel on the surface of the brain breaks and bleeds into the area between the brain and the skull.

Smokers, people over 65, men, African-Americans, and those with a family history of stroke all have a higher than usual chance of having a stroke. Women using birth control pills (see **contraception health risks,** page 217) have a greater risk of stroke if they also smoke. They have an even higher risk if they are over 35 or have high blood pressure.

Depending on the location and the damage caused by a stroke, many people recover fully following physical or occupational therapy, combined with other treatment and lifestyle changes to prevent recurrences.

WHEN TO CALL THE DOCTOR

➤ Call 911 or go to an emergency facility **immediately** if you or someone else experience any of the symptoms of a stroke or a transient ischemic attack. You can reduce the risk of permanent damage by getting prompt treatment. (See page 45 for emergency procedures.)

HOW TO PREVENT IT

➤ Control your blood pressure. **High blood pressure** (see page 105) is the single most important risk factor for stroke.

➤ Find a healthy outlet for stress, such as meditation, yoga, or deep breathing.

➤ Exercise regularly, and eat plenty of low-fat, high-fiber foods—fresh fruits and vegetables and whole grains.

➤ Don't smoke. If you do, quit (see **smoking and illness,** page 210).

➤ If you have cardiovascular disease (see **narrowed arteries,** page 107), your doctor may suggest anticlotting medications such as aspirin or a prescription drug to reduce the chance of clots. Your doctor may also discuss surgical procedures to widen narrowed vessels in your neck.

➤ If you have **diabetes** (see page 269), take steps to control it. This disease can damage blood vessels and increase the risk of stroke.

FOR MORE HELP

Information line: Stroke Connection of the American Heart Association, 800-553-6321, M–F 8:30–5 CST. Information specialists field questions about stroke, send literature, and make referrals to local support groups.

Information line: National Stroke Association, 800-787-6537, M–Th 8–4:30, F 8–4 MST. Provides information about strokes and a directory of support groups.

Information line: National Institute of Neurological Disorders and Stroke, 800-352-9424, M–F 8:30–5 EST. Provides free brochures on strokes and other neurological disorders.

Video: *Stroke at Time of Diagnosis.* Clear, useful overview of causes and treatments, consisting of four reports—Understanding the Diagnosis, What Happens Next?, Treatment and Management, and Issues and Answers. Time Life Medical, 1996, $19.95.

Varicose Veins

SIGNS AND SYMPTOMS

- Swollen, twisted clusters of purple or blue veins.
- Swollen legs.
- An ache or heavy feeling in the legs.
- Itching around affected veins.
- Brown discoloring of skin.
- Sores.

In healthy veins, valves allow blood to flow only one way. Varicose veins form when these valves fail, allowing blood to back up and pool inside the vein, which makes it swell. These veins can be unsightly and painful, but they're usually not dangerous.

Varicose veins can appear anywhere, but they show up mostly on the legs, sometimes surrounded by patches of thin, red capillaries or green veins known as spiders. Hemorrhoids are varicose veins around the anus.

Varicose veins tend to run in families. Women, especially those of German or Irish descent, are twice as likely as men to develop them. Anything that puts added pressure on the legs, such as standing for long periods, pregnancy, and obesity, can cause them.

Most varicose veins develop near the surface of the skin. Deeper ones can't be seen, but the skin above them can become swollen, darkened, and hard. In severe cases, sores may develop from poor circulation, usually around the ankles. Varicose veins can be removed surgically or treated with medications.

WHAT YOU CAN DO NOW

➤ Wear elastic support stockings, available at most drugstores.
➤ Stay off your feet as much as possible.
➤ When you need to stand for long periods, take frequent breaks to sit down and put your feet up.

WHEN TO CALL THE DOCTOR

Call for an immediate appointment:
➤ If you have cut a varicose vein—it may bleed heavily. First, lie down, elevate the injured leg, and apply gentle, firm pressure with a clean cloth. Get help as soon as possible after the bleeding has slowed.

Call for advice and an appointment:
➤ If varicose veins make walking or standing painful.
➤ If you develop sores.

HOW TO PREVENT IT

➤ If you are overweight, take steps to lose the extra pounds.
➤ Exercise regularly. Activities that work the leg muscles, such as walking or jogging, help pump blood toward the heart.
➤ Don't wear garters, girdles, or other tight clothing.
➤ Don't cross your legs.
➤ Avoid long periods of sitting or standing.
➤ Sit or lie down and elevate your legs to about hip level at least twice a day for 30 minutes at a time.

FOR MORE HELP

Organization: National Heart, Lung, and Blood Institute Information Center, P. O. Box 30105, Bethesda, MD 20824-0105. 800-575-WELL, 24-hour recorded information. 301-251-1222, M–F 8:30–5 EST. Fax: 301-251-1223. Ask for information on varicose veins.

Stomach, Abdomen, & Digestive System

Colon Cancer

Cancers of the colon and rectum often show no symptoms in the early stages. Likely first warning signals include:

- Changes in bowel movements (including bleeding from the rectum, persistent constipation or diarrhea, or a feeling of being unable to empty the bowel completely) that last for more than ten days.
- Dark patches of blood in or on the stool, or long, thin "pencil stools."
- Black, sticky stools, which may indicate internal bleeding.
- Frequent gas pains, bloating, stomach discomfort, and/or abdominal cramping.
- Unexplained fatigue and weakness, weight loss, or loss of appetite.

Colon cancer is one of the most common cancers in the United States. The disease—a malignant tumor in the large intestine (see color illustration, page 174)—is most common among people over the age of 40. Anyone with a family history of this cancer or who has had colon polyps (benign tumors) or inflammatory bowel disease is considered to be at high risk, as can be people who have been heavily exposed to asbestos.

Diet also appears to contribute to the risk.

Research suggests that people who eat a lot of animal fat and don't eat enough fiber (found in fruits, vegetables, and unrefined grains) are more likely to develop the cancer than those with a low-fat, high-fiber diet.

For people whose cancer is caught early, chances are good for a full recovery. Beginning at about age 40, everyone should get an annual rectal exam. People over 50 should have an annual stool test, to screen for microscopic traces of blood, and an internal rectal exam (sigmoidoscopy) every three to five years. Anyone with a history of benign colon polyps, inflammatory bowel disease, or a family history of colon cancer may also need periodic exams in which a flexible tube is used to view the entire colon (colonoscopy).

WHAT YOU CAN DO NOW

➤ If you are diagnosed with this cancer, surgery, radiation, or chemotherapy may cure or help control it.

WHEN TO CALL THE DOCTOR

Call for an immediate appointment:
➤ If you develop symptoms of anemia (pale complexion, fatigue, rapid heartbeat).
Call for advice and an appointment:
➤ If there's a noticeable change in your bowel movement habits.
➤ If you experience bleeding from the rectum, or notice blood in or on stool or tarry stools. (Don't just assume that you have hemorrhoids.)

(continued)

Abdominal Pain

Abdominal discomfort is usually a sign of a mild disorder such as indigestion or stomach flu. But severe pain can be a medical emergency, and persistent pain may signal a serious illness.

SYMPTOMS	WHAT IT MIGHT BE	WHAT YOU CAN DO
Acute, constant pain in abdomen that radiates to back and chest; fever; nausea; vomiting; distended abdomen; clammy skin.	Pancreatitis—inflammation of pancreas.	Call 911 or go to emergency facility **immediately.** Acute pancreatitis can cause shock, which can be fatal if not treated quickly.
Extremely severe abdominal pain with or without other acute symptoms.	Intestinal obstruction. ● Appendicitis (see page 20). ● Pelvic inflammatory disease (see page 230). ● Heart attack (see page 38). ● Perforated stomach ulcer (see page 130). ● Anaphylactic shock (see page 18). ● Diabetic emergency (see diabetes, page 269). ● Poisoning (see page 41).	Call 911 or go to emergency facility **immediately.**
Pain in upper-right side of abdomen, possibly spreading to upper back, chest, or right shoulder; nausea; gas; vomiting.	Gallstones (see page 119).	In a first attack, call doctor for emergency advice. If not available, call 911 or go to emergency facility. Do not eat or drink.
Sharp pain that starts in side and moves toward groin or abdomen; frequent, painful, or blocked urination;cloudy, foul-smelling, or bloody urine; fever and chills; nausea and vomiting; sweating.	Kidney stones (see page 132).	Call doctor for immediate appointment. Meanwhile, drink lots of water to help stone pass, and take a non-aspirin pain reliever, if necessary.
Cramping or pain in abdomen, nausea, diarrhea, vomiting, fever, fatigue, weakness, intestinal gas.	Stomach flu (see nausea and vomiting, page 127).● Food poisoning (see page 35).	If, with vomiting and pain, you have blurred or double vision, muscle weakness, or difficulty speaking or swallowing, call 911 or go to emergency facility **immediately;** these may be signs of botulism, a sometimes fatal bacterial food poisoning.

(continued)

Abdominal Pain (continued)

SYMPTOMS	WHAT IT MIGHT BE	WHAT YOU CAN DO
Cramping or pain in abdomen, diarrhea, bloody stool, fever, fatigue, weight loss.	Crohn's disease. • Ulcerative colitis. • Bacterial dysentery, especially if you have been traveling overseas.	See inflammatory bowel disease, page 125. If you think you have bacterial dysentery, call doctor for immediate appointment.
Pain that increases when sore spot on abdomen is touched; severe abdominal cramping, usually worse on left side; nausea; fever; chills; diarrhea, constipation, or unusually thin stools.	Diverticulitis.	See diverticulitis, page 118.
Discomfort in abdomen or groin when lifting or bending over, swelling or bulge beneath skin in abdomen or groin.	Hernia.	See hernia, page 123.
Pain in abdomen accompanied by diarrhea or constipation, or bouts of both; excessive gas or bloating; nausea, particularly after eating; fatigue.	Irritable bowel syndrome.	See irritable bowel syndrome, page 126. (For self-care, also see diarrhea, page 116, and constipation, opposite page.)
Pain or discomfort in upper abdomen, nausea, vomiting, diarrhea, loss of appetite, belching or gas, heartburn.	Stomach ulcer. • Gastritis.	See ulcers and gastritis, page 130.
Pain and cramps after drinking milk or eating other dairy products, gas and bloating, diarrhea, nausea, rumbling sounds from abdomen.	Lactose intolerance—difficulty digesting cow's milk, cheese, butter, ice cream, and other dairy products.	Restrict or eliminate dairy products from diet. Substitute soy milk. Try acidophilus yogurt, which is tolerated better than milk.

> If you experience persistent abdominal pain, weight loss, or fatigue. These symptoms can have other causes but should be investigated promptly to rule out cancer.

HOW TO PREVENT IT

> Eat plenty of whole grains, fresh fruits, and vegetables—at least five servings of fruits and vegetables each day (especially cruciferous vegetables such as broccoli, cauliflower, and cabbage).
> Cut back on red meat and animal fats in your diet. Cooked dried beans, nuts, and soybean products such as tofu are good alternative sources of protein.
> Avoid overcooking meats and fish, and don't barbecue them.
> Increase your fiber intake. You might add bran or wheat germ to your breakfast cereal. Start with one tablespoon a day and gradually increase to three or four.

FOR MORE HELP

Hotline: Cancer Information and Counseling Hotline, AMC Cancer Research Center, 800-525-3777, M–F 8:30–5 MST. Trained staffers provide counseling, answer questions, and send pamphlets, brochures, and fact sheets.

Information line: The Wellness Community, 310-314-2555, M–F 9–5 PST. The nation's largest organization devoted solely to providing free psychological and emotional support for cancer patients and their families.

Book: *What to Do If Cancer Strikes.* To order, send $2 for postage and handling to: Cancer Research Institute, P.O. Box 5199, FDR Station, New York, NY 10150-5199, or call 800-992-2623.

Video: *Colon & Rectal Cancer at Time of Diagnosis.* Clear, useful overview of causes and treatments, consisting of four reports—Understanding the Diagnosis, What Happens Next?, Treatment and Management, and Issues and Answers. Time Life Medical, 1996, $19.95.

Constipation

SIGNS AND SYMPTOMS

- Hard, compacted stools that are difficult or painful to pass.
- A lingering feeling of fullness or incompleteness after having a bowel movement.
- No bowel movement for three days for adults, four days for children. (Depending on your diet, age, and daily activity, regularity can mean anything from three bowel movements a day to three per week.)
- Swelling, bloating, or discomfort in the abdomen.

Constipation is one of the most common medical complaints—and one of the most frustrating. It often results from our hurried, modern lifestyle: eating fast foods that are low in fiber, drinking too little water, getting too little exercise, and failing to respond promptly to the urge to move the bowels. Emotional and psychological problems can contribute to the problem, as can some drugs and vitamin and mineral supplements.

Persistent, chronic constipation may be a symptom of a more serious disorder, including **irritable bowel syndrome** (see page 126), **colon cancer** (see page 112), **diabetes** (see page 269), **Parkinson's disease** (see page 57), multiple sclerosis, or **depression** (see page 204).

WHAT YOU CAN DO NOW

Most cases respond to home treatment, such as changes in diet. If constipation isn't caused by disease, simply eating more fiber (found in fruits, vegetables, and whole grains) and drinking lots of water (at least eight glasses a day) should soften your stools and restore regularity. In addition:

> Avoid over-the-counter laxatives unless your doctor recommends them, because your body may become dependent on

Stomach, Abdomen, & Digestive System

them. If you must take a laxative, try a bulk-forming psyllium laxative, which is relatively gentle. Never take a laxative if you have abdominal pain, nausea, or vomiting, or if you are pregnant.

➤ Do not take mineral oil as a laxative unless your doctor recommends it.

➤ If infants under six months are mildly constipated, give them prune juice or other fruit juices. Toddlers, older children, and adults can have whole prunes. (Remove pits for toddlers.)

WHEN TO CALL THE DOCTOR

Occasional constipation shouldn't send you to the doctor's office, but two weeks or more of the problem should. Call for an immediate appointment:

➤ If your constipation is accompanied by fever and lower abdominal pain, and the stools you do produce are thin or loose. These symptoms may indicate **diverticulitis** (see page 118).

Call for advice and an appointment:

➤ If you have blood in your stools. This may be from an anal fissure or a **hemorrhoid** (see page 122), but it could also be a sign of bowel cancer.

➤ If constipation develops after taking a new prescription drug or vitamin and mineral supplements. You may need to discontinue or change the dosage.

➤ If you are elderly or disabled and have been constipated for a week or more; you may have an impacted stool.

➤ If your constipation is accompanied by weight loss.

➤ If an increase in dietary fiber and exercise have failed to help after two weeks.

HOW TO PREVENT IT

➤ Include moderate exercise in your daily routine. A brisk 30-minute walk should be enough to promote regularity.

➤ Be sure to drink plenty of water—at least eight glasses a day.

➤ Get lots of fiber by eating at least five servings a day of fresh fruits, vegetables, and other good sources of dietary fiber, including bran and other whole-grain cereals, raw or cooked dried fruits such as raisins and prunes, cooked dried beans, and nuts.

➤ Allow sufficient time for bowel movements, particularly after breakfast and dinner, and preferably at the same time every day.

FOR MORE HELP

Hotline: Consumer Nutrition Hotline of the National Center for Nutrition and Dietetics, 800-366-1655, M–F 9–4 CST. A registered dietitian will answer questions about constipation and give referrals to registered dietitians in your area.

Organization: International Foundation for Bowel Dysfunction, P.O. Box 17864, Milwaukee, WI 53217. 414-241-9479, M–F 9–5 CST. Provides support and educational materials on functional bowel disorders.

Book: *Gastrointestinal Health*, by Steven Peikin, M.D. HarperCollins, 1991, $19.95.

Diarrhea

SIGNS AND SYMPTOMS

■ Loose, watery stools.
■ Frequent bowel movements.
■ Abdominal pain or cramping.

Diarrhea occurs when stools are pushed through the intestines (see color illustration, page 174) before the body can absorb the water they contain. Diarrhea can be brought on by food sensitivities or **food poisoning** (see page 35), anxiety or **stress** (see page 212), too much alcohol, and some medications, especially antibiotics. Diarrhea can also result from drinking untreated water that contains giardia, a common parasite that affects the intestines, or from contact with other parasites and amoebas.

In some cases, diarrhea may indicate more serious diseases (see **diverticulitis,** next page, and **inflammatory bowel disease,** page 125).

page 212), ... page 125).

WHAT YOU CAN DO NOW

➤ Avoid eating solid food at first, to let the digestive tract rest.

➤ Sip clear, warm liquids (water, tea, or broth), sports drinks, or flat sodas (ginger ale, cola, or other sodas that have been left open to lose their fizz). Drink only small amounts for the first few hours, then as much as your stomach can handle.

➤ If your stomach tolerates the fluids, try eating bulk-adding foods such as bananas, white rice, or toast.

➤ Don't take over-the-counter antidiarrhea products for the first few hours; allow your system to expel whatever irritant or infectious agent may be causing the problem. If you do use such products, don't continue taking them for more than a day or two without consulting your doctor.

➤ While you are recovering, avoid alcohol, milk products, and fiber-rich foods such as salads and fruit.

➤ If your diarrhea is severe, be sure to avoid dehydration. The signs include dry mouth, sticky saliva, and dark yellow urine in smaller amounts than usual. Commercial rehydration drinks such as Pedialyte (for infants) and sports drinks can help replace lost fluids and minerals.

REHYDRATION RECIPE

To make an inexpensive rehydration drink at home for anyone older than 12, mix 1 quart of water with ½ teaspoon of table salt and 3 to 4 tablespoons of sugar. **Note:** For infants and children 12 and under, use only a commercial rehydration drink such as Pedialyte.

DIARRHEA IN CHILDREN

Infants and young children need special attention when they are suffering from diarrhea. If it's severe, an infant can become very dehydrated in less than a day.

➤ Infants who breast-feed should continue regular feedings. If you use formula, ask your doctor about diluting it with water to half strength for 24 to 48 hours. If the diarrhea doesn't improve, try soy-based formula until your child is better.

➤ Do not give soda, fruit juice, or sports drinks to infants or young children. To help prevent dehydration, give a few sips of a commercial rehydration drink, such as Pedialyte, every few minutes.

➤ Do not give antidiarrhea medication to infants or young children.

➤ For older babies, try feeding rice cereal, bananas, toast, and other foods that add bulk to the stool. But avoid giving babies solid food if they are vomiting.

➤ Call your doctor if you see signs of dehydration—sticky saliva, dark yellow urine, weakness.

WHEN TO CALL THE DOCTOR

Call for emergency advice (if not available, call 911 or go to an emergency facility):

➤ If the diarrhea is accompanied by severe cramping, light-headedness, chills, vomiting, or fever over 101 degrees.

➤ If you notice signs of severe dehydration—dry mouth, sticky saliva, dizziness or weakness, and dark yellow urine.

Call for an immediate appointment:

➤ If stools are bloody or tarry, or contain mucus or worms.

Call for advice and an appointment:

➤ If you have diarrhea frequently, or if it occurs while you are taking a medication.

➤ If diarrhea lasts for more than 48 hours (one day for a child under three, eight hours for an infant under six months).

Stomach, Abdomen, & Digestive System

- ➤ If you have been traveling and may have been drinking untreated water.
- ➤ If diarrhea alternates with constipation and persists for more than a few weeks. You may have **irritable bowel syndrome** (see page 126) or—though less likely—**colon cancer** (see page 112).
- ➤ If you notice signs of dehydration, which can be dangerous for the elderly as well as for young children.

HOW TO PREVENT IT

- ➤ Avoid foods that you know your body cannot tolerate well.
- ➤ When traveling in foreign countries, drink only bottled or boiled water or canned beverages. Peel fruits and vegetables.
- ➤ See **nausea and vomiting** (page 127) for suggestions about food-related diarrhea.

FOR MORE HELP

Organization: International Foundation for Bowel Dysfunction, P.O. Box 17864, Milwaukee, WI 53217. 414-241-9479, M–F 9–5 CST. Provides support and educational materials on bowel disorders.

Diverticulitis

SIGNS AND SYMPTOMS

- ■ Abdominal cramping that is usually most severe on the lower-left side.
- ■ Nausea.
- ■ Fever.
- ■ Diarrhea, constipation, or unusually thin stools.
- ■ Pain that increases when the sore spot on the abdomen is touched.
- ■ Intestinal gas.

Many people develop small pouches in the colon (the major part of the large intestine)—a fairly harmless condition known as diverticulosis.

But sometimes one or more of the pouches (see color illustration, page 174) gets in-

flamed. Then the condition is known as diverticulitis, and the results can range from mild infection to bowel blockage or breaks in the bowel wall.

People who eat mostly low-fiber foods, have constipation, or use laxatives seem to have an increased risk of diverticulitis.

Treatment may include bed rest, changes in diet, and antibiotics or other drugs. The chances of a full recovery are very good if you receive prompt medical attention. Left untreated, diverticulitis can result in serious complications requiring extensive surgery.

WHAT YOU CAN DO NOW

- ➤ If you have symptoms of diverticulitis, see your doctor.
- ➤ Never use an enema for this condition.

WHEN TO CALL THE DOCTOR

Call 911 or go to an emergency facility **immediately:**
- ➤ If you have severe abdominal pain and swelling, fever, chills, and nausea or vomiting—even if you think your symptoms are getting better. You could have peritonitis, a life-threatening infection of the membrane that lines the abdominal cavity.

Call for an immediate appointment:
- ➤ If blood appears in your stools; this may mean that you have internal bleeding.
- ➤ If severe pain continues despite treatment; you may have another abdominal disorder (see **abdominal pain** chart, page 113).

HOW TO PREVENT IT

- ➤ Eat whole-grain breads, oatmeal, bran cereals, fresh fruits, and vegetables. Add fiber gradually, though. A sudden switch to a high-fiber diet can create an uncomfortable amount of intestinal gas.
- ➤ Drink plenty of fluids (at least eight glasses of water a day), especially if you increase your fiber intake.
- ➤ Avoid foods that are difficult to digest, such as nuts, seeds, corn, and popcorn.
- ➤ Don't delay or ignore the urge to move your bowels.
- ➤ Exercise regularly to help the muscles in

your intestines retain their tone. This encourages regular bowel movements.

➤ Don't use laxatives unless your doctor recommends them. Prunes, prune juice, and psyllium seed (available in drugstores, as powder or capsules) are good natural alternatives.

➤ If you smoke, quit; smoking may aggravate the problem.

➤ Avoid caffeine, and if you drink alcohol, do so in moderation.

FOR MORE HELP

Information line: Intestinal Disease Foundation, 412-261-5888, M–F 9:30–3:30 EST. Provides telephone support, educational programs and materials, information on support groups, and physician referrals.

Organization: National Digestive Diseases Information Clearinghouse, 2 Information Way, Bethesda, MD 20892-3570. Write for a free fact sheet or information packet on diverticulitis.

Gallstones

SIGNS AND SYMPTOMS

■ Intense pain in the upper-right side or center of the abdomen, possibly spreading to the back, chest, or right shoulder.

■ Nausea and vomiting.

■ Gas and indigestion.

■ Fever and chills.

■ Jaundice—yellowish skin and eyes.

Gallstones are hard deposits of cholesterol or bile salts that develop in the gallbladder—a small, pear-shaped organ that stores a digestive juice called bile. The stones can be as small as a grain of sand or as large as a golf ball. Most gallstones are "silent stones," which produce no symptoms and cause no harm.

A gallstone attack occurs when a stone gets trapped in one of the bile ducts (the tubes that carry bile from the gallbladder to

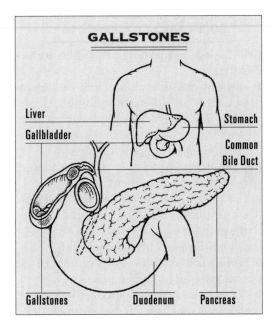

GALLSTONES

Liver · Stomach · Gallbladder · Common Bile Duct · Gallstones · Duodenum · Pancreas

the small intestine; see illustration above, and color illustration, page 174). These attacks, which can last up to several hours, generally occur within an hour or two of eating a large meal or in the middle of the night. Gallstones may cause jaundice if bile backs up into the liver.

The tendency to develop gallstones may be hereditary (they are found most often among Native Americans and Mexican-Americans). You're more likely to have them if you're obese, eat a high-fat diet, or have lost a lot of weight in a short time. If you're over the age of 40 or a woman between 20 and 60, you're at higher risk, as are pregnant women and women who have used birth control pills or estrogen replacement therapy.

For those who have frequent, painful attacks, the standard treatment is surgery to remove the gallbladder. This procedure is much less invasive than it used to be, with less pain and a quicker recovery.

WHAT YOU CAN DO NOW

➤ If you have symptoms of a gallstone attack, it's critical to get immediate medical attention.

➤ In the meantime, do not eat or drink.

Call 911 or go to an emergency facility **immediately:**
➤ If you have sudden, severe pain in the upper-right area of your abdomen. (If abdominal pain is accompanied by nausea, sweating, and shortness of breath, these symptoms may signal a heart attack.)
Call for emergency advice (if not available, call 911 or go to an emergency facility):
➤ If you think you are having your first gallstone attack or if you develop fever with the pain.
Call for an immediate appointment:
➤ If you notice a yellow discoloration of the skin and eyes (called jaundice).
➤ If you have already been diagnosed with gallstones and you have severe abdominal pain that lasts more than two hours.

HOW TO PREVENT IT

➤ Maintain your ideal body weight.
➤ Consult your doctor before trying to lose weight, and diet sensibly.
➤ According to some experts, you can cut the risk of gallstones with a diet that is high in fiber and low in fat and cholesterol.

FOR MORE HELP

Video: *Gallstones at Time of Diagnosis.* Clear, useful overview of causes and treatments, consisting of four reports—Understanding the Diagnosis, What Happens Next?, Treatment and Management, and Issues and Answers. Time Life Medical, 1996, $19.95.

Gas and Gas Pain

SIGNS AND SYMPTOMS

■ Belching.
■ Flatulence.
■ Abdominal pain or bloating.

Gas and gas pains are a normal part of the digestive process, often caused by the air you swallow as you eat and drink—especially if you eat quickly. Gas is also produced by food you're digesting. High-fiber foods such as beans, vegetables, fruits, and grains can create large amounts of gas, as can dairy foods for some people.

When air enters your stomach, you may expel it by belching, which is natural and healthy—though usually considered impolite. Even less socially acceptable is passing gas through the anus (flatulence). But what many people consider excessive gas may actually be normal. In fact, the average adult releases gas from 8 to 20 times a day.

WHAT YOU CAN DO NOW

➤ Try teas made with peppermint, chamomile, or fennel to relieve gas pains.
➤ If you need to release gas, release it—even if it means you have to leave the room.
➤ If you are suffering from severe gas pains, try lying on your back and pulling your legs up to your chest. It's easier to expel the gas in this position.

WHEN TO CALL THE DOCTOR

Call for emergency advice. If not available, call 911 or go to an emergency facility:
➤ If you have severe pain that starts close to the navel and moves to the lower-right area of the abdomen; this could be a sign of **appendicitis** (see page 20).
Call for an immediate appointment:
➤ If you have pain in the upper-right area of the abdomen; this may be a sign of a gallbladder disorder (see **gallstones,** page 119) or an **ulcer** (see page 130).
Call for advice and an appointment:
➤ If you have persistent, unexplained bloating for more than three days.
➤ If you have lower abdominal pain that decreases when you pass gas or have a bowel movement; you may have **irritable bowel syndrome** (see page 126).
➤ If you have frequent gas, are losing weight, and have pale, foul-smelling bowel movements; you could have a malabsorption disorder (inability to digest fat).

You can usually avoid excessive gas and gas pains simply by changing your diet. Keep in mind, though, that the high-fiber foods that often cause gas are also those most essential to a healthy diet. Rather than cutting down on fruits, vegetables, beans, and whole grains, try these changes to reduce gas:

➤ Buy dry beans rather than canned. Soak them overnight in water, then pour out the water and replace it with fresh water for cooking. Make sure to cook the beans thoroughly.

➤ For a good source of high-quality protein, try tofu, a fermented soy product that is easier to digest than many beans.

➤ Drink plenty of fluids.

➤ Avoid foods and snacks that are sweetened with fructose (fruit sugar) or sorbitol (an artificial sweetener), both of which can increase flatulence.

➤ Eat slowly, chew your food thoroughly, and avoid overeating. (Remember that it may take 20 to 30 minutes for a sensation of fullness to set in.)

➤ Take a walk after meals. Moderate exercise improves digestion and helps move gas through your system more quickly.

➤ Avoid carbonated drinks, chewing gum, and drinking through a straw; these can increase the amount of air that gets into your stomach.

FOR MORE HELP

Hotline: Consumer Nutrition Hotline of the National Center for Nutrition and Dietetics, 800-366-1655, M–F 9–4 CST. Registered dietitians answer questions about gas and give referrals to registered dietitians in your area.

Heartburn

SIGNS AND SYMPTOMS

- A burning feeling in the chest, just behind the breastbone, that occurs after eating and lasts from a few minutes to several hours.
- Chest pain, especially after bending over or lying down.
- Burning in the throat; or hot, sour, or salty-tasting fluid at the back of the throat.
- Mild pain in the upper abdomen.
- Belching (sometimes).

Heartburn has nothing to do with the heart. Also known as acid indigestion or reflux, heartburn is an irritation of the esophagus (the muscular tube between the throat and the stomach) caused by stomach acid that's escaping into it.

This unpleasant condition can be triggered by overeating or too much pressure on the abdomen (frequently because of obesity or pregnancy). Eating spicy, acidic, or fatty foods, in particular, can lead to heartburn, as can drinking alcohol. So can certain medications—especially aspirin, ibuprofen, and some antibiotics—and smoking, which stimulates the release of stomach acid.

Heartburn is common. If you feel it often, it may cause serious problems, such as bleeding or scarring in the esophagus. As an occasional source of discomfort, however, it isn't dangerous. Medication or changes in your lifestyle will generally take care of it.

WHAT YOU CAN DO NOW

Many physicians recommend taking over-the-counter remedies such as antacids for occasional heartburn. But don't take antacids without first checking with your doctor if you have **high blood pressure** (see page 105), an irregular heartbeat, kidney disease, intestinal problems, chronic heartburn, or any symptoms of **appendicitis** (see page 20). Pregnant women and nursing mothers should consult a physician before taking any medication, including antacids.

Try these natural alternatives:

➤ Drink ginger tea for quick relief.

➤ Avoid lying down for two to three hours after eating. If you must recline, lie on your left side; in this position, your stomach is lower than your esophagus, so the acids are less likely to back up.

➤ Cut down on coffee, smoking, and excessive alcohol.

➤ Practice relaxation techniques to help relieve stress.

➤ Raise the head of your bed four to six inches by putting something like bricks or phone books under the legs, or by placing a foam-rubber wedge under your bottom sheet.

WHEN TO CALL THE DOCTOR

Call 911 or go to an emergency facility **immediately:**

➤ If you have severe chest pain or pain radiating into your arms and shoulders. This could signal a heart attack.

Call for advice and an appointment:

➤ If you've tried the suggestions above, but your symptoms persist.

HOW TO PREVENT IT

Many of the remedies for heartburn will also help prevent it. In addition:

➤ Maintain a reasonable weight.

➤ Avoid foods and drinks that can aggravate the problem. These may include tomatoes, citrus fruits, garlic, onions, chocolate, coffee and tea, alcohol, peppermint, and carbonated drinks.

➤ Cut down on dishes that are high in fats and oils.

➤ Eat small, frequent meals (four or five a day) instead of three large ones.

➤ Avoid eating just before bedtime.

➤ Get plenty of rest and exercise.

➤ Don't smoke. Nicotine relaxes a muscle that allows gastric juice to escape from the stomach into the esophagus.

➤ Avoid aspirin, ibuprofen, and other non-steroidal anti-inflammatory drugs.

FOR MORE HELP

Hotline: Consumer Nutrition Hotline of the National Center for Nutrition and Dietetics, 800-366-1655, M–F 9–4 CST. A registered dietitian will answer questions about heartburn and give referrals to registered dietitians in your area.

Organization: National Digestive Diseases Information Clearinghouse, 2 Information Way, Bethesda, MD 20892-3570. Write for the packet on heartburn (gastroesophageal reflux disease) and a publications list.

Hemorrhoids

SIGNS AND SYMPTOMS

■ Bright red blood that may appear in the stool or on toilet tissue.

■ Pain during bowel movements.

■ Painful swelling or a lump near the anus.

■ Itching in or around the anus.

■ Mucous discharge from the anus.

Hemorrhoids are inflamed or swollen veins either inside or outside the anus. This painful condition, also known as piles, may result from straining to pass hard, compacted stools during bouts of **constipation** (see page 115). It may also be connected to heredity, aging, pregnancy, chronic diarrhea, and the overuse of laxatives. The irritation typically lingers for several days and often recurs. Still, it generally gets better with home treatment.

WHAT YOU CAN DO NOW

➤ Sitz baths are a time-honored remedy to ease the irritation: Sit in warm (not hot) water for 10 to 15 minutes several times a day, especially after a bowel movement.

➤ Bathe regularly to keep the anal area clean, but be gentle. Excessive scrubbing, especially with soap, can worsen burning and irritation.

- For external hemorrhoids, dab the area with witch hazel or apply a cold compress.
- Insert a dab of petroleum jelly just inside the anus to make bowel movements easier and less painful.
- Resist the temptation to scratch hemorrhoids; you'll further irritate the veins and intensify itching.
- Be gentle when wiping. Dampen your toilet paper first, or use cotton balls or alcohol-free baby wipes.

WHEN TO CALL THE DOCTOR

- If bleeding persists for more than a few days. You could have a more serious problem, such as **colon cancer** (see page 112).
- If you have persistent or severe pain. You may require treatment (which can include outpatient surgery) to remove or shrink the hemorrhoids. This may signal another problem that needs medical attention.

HOW TO PREVENT IT

- To produce soft, easily passed stools, eat plenty of fruit, vegetables, bran cereals, and whole-grain bread. (If you are pregnant, consult your doctor before making changes in your diet.) Also, drink lots of liquids such as water or fruit and vegetable juices (at least eight glasses a day).
- Cut back on meat, animal fat, and alcoholic drinks.
- Establish a regular time for your bowel movements.
- Since long periods of sitting reduce blood flow around the anus and may contribute to hemorrhoids, take frequent breaks if you have a sit-down job.
- Tone up and strengthen the anal sphincter muscles by doing an easy exercise called the buttock press: Rhythmically tighten and relax the buttock muscles and anal sphincter muscles.
- Try doing yoga, which enhances blood flow, reducing pain and inflammation in hemorrhoidal tissue.
- Don't sit on the toilet for more than five to ten minutes at a time.
- Don't sit on a "doughnut" cushion; these can trap blood in the swollen veins.

FOR MORE HELP

Hotline: Consumer Nutrition Hotline of the National Center for Nutrition and Dietetics, 800-366-1655, M–F 9–4 CST. A registered dietitian will answer questions about hemorrhoids and give referrals to registered dietitians in your area.

Organization: National Digestive Diseases Information Clearinghouse, 2 Information Way, Bethesda, MD 20892-3570. Write for a free fact sheet about hemorrhoids and a publications list.

Hernia

SIGNS AND SYMPTOMS

- An obvious swelling or bulge beneath the skin in the abdomen or groin. It may disappear when you lie down, and it may be tender.
- A heavy feeling in the abdomen, sometimes accompanied by ongoing constipation.
- Discomfort in the abdomen or groin when lifting or bending over.
- In severe cases, pain in the abdomen, nausea, and vomiting.
- Chronic heartburn, belching, or regurgitation. These could signal a hiatal hernia (see illustration, next page), which occurs when part of the stomach or lower esophagus squeezes into the chest cavity.

A hernia is a bulge—usually visible—caused by a lump of tissue that squeezes through a hole or weak spot in a surrounding muscle. Although it can occur in many places in the body, it is most common in the abdominal wall. (See illustration next page, and color illustration, page 174.) If there is a weak point, pressure from extra body weight, from lifting a heavy object, or from straining during bowel movements can force the muscle apart, allowing part of an internal organ or some tissue to push its way through.

Ninety percent of all abdominal hernias occur in men. Sometimes a weakness in the covering of the muscle, which allows a hernia to form, is present at birth. More often, it occurs later in life. Poor nutrition, excess pounds, smoking, and muscle strain or over-exertion all can make hernias more likely.

Most hernias can simply be pushed back into place, by you or by a doctor, but eventually they will protrude again. If the hernia consists of intestine poking through the abdominal wall (see illustration below), it could block the passage of the organ's contents, resulting in abdominal pain, nausea, and vomiting. Another danger is an internal strangulation, which occurs when surrounding tissue squeezes against the protruding organ and constricts or cuts off its blood supply. If it goes untreated, this condition can result in gangrene of the bowel.

In many cases, even hernias that are not serious slowly worsen and may need to be repaired surgically.

WHAT YOU CAN DO NOW

➤ Call your doctor if you suspect you have a hernia. Sometimes hernias require urgent medical care.
➤ Avoid straining or heavy lifting.

WHEN TO CALL THE DOCTOR

Call 911 or go to an emergency facility **immediately:**
➤ If you know you have a hernia, and you are nauseated and vomiting, or are unable to have a bowel movement or pass gas. These symptoms could indicate an obstructed or strangulated hernia.
Call for advice:
➤ If you suspect you have a hernia.

HOW TO PREVENT IT

➤ If you are overweight, try to lose some weight to ease the pressure on your abdominal muscles.
➤ Avoid lifting heavy objects.
➤ Don't strain when having a bowel movement (see **constipation,** page 115).
➤ Practice good nutrition, both to avoid constipation and to enhance muscle strength.
➤ Don't smoke. If you do, quit. Chronic coughing from bronchial irritation makes a hernia more likely and also can make one recur.
➤ Do regular, gentle exercises to tone and strengthen your abdominal muscles.

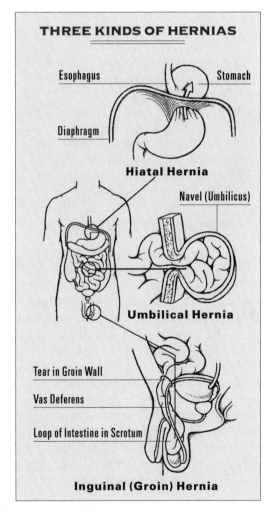

THREE KINDS OF HERNIAS

Esophagus   Stomach

Diaphragm

Hiatal Hernia

Navel (Umbilicus)

Umbilical Hernia

Tear in Groin Wall

Vas Deferens

Loop of Intestine in Scrotum

Inguinal (Groin) Hernia

AN ABDOMINAL EXERCISE

Here's a quick and easy exercise you can do every day to strengthen your stomach muscles and help prevent abdominal hernias: Lie on your back with your knees bent and your feet flat on the floor. Keeping your shoulders on the floor, lift your buttocks and back. Repeat ten times.

Organization: National Digestive Diseases Information Clearinghouse, 2 Information Way, Bethesda, MD 20892-3570. Write for a free fact sheet and/or an information packet on hernias.

Inflammatory Bowel Disease

SIGNS AND SYMPTOMS

Most common:
- Abdominal pain (in Crohn's disease, often in the lower-right side of the abdomen; in ulcerative colitis, in the left side).
- Persistent, severe diarrhea.
- Bloody stools or rectal bleeding.

Less common:
- Fever.
- Fatigue.
- Weakness.
- Skin rashes.
- Arthritis-like pains in the joints.

Inflammatory bowel disease (IBD) is the name given to a group of chronic intestinal disorders with similar symptoms and complications. The most common are Crohn's disease and ulcerative colitis.

In Crohn's disease, parts of the digestive tract (see color illustration, page 174) become inflamed, making digestion difficult and weakening the entire body. In ulcerative colitis, tiny ulcers in the colon flare up and sometimes cause bloody stools or painful attacks of diarrhea. Both are potentially serious conditions, but only in rare cases are they fatal.

The cause of IBD is unknown. Anyone can get it, including young children; most cases are diagnosed before the person is 30. Although there is no known cure, modest changes in diet and appropriate medication can often help control the symptoms. Some serious cases of IBD call for surgery to remove the diseased part of the bowel.

Both the symptoms and the severity of IBD are unpredictable. See your doctor if you suspect you have IBD; proper diagnosis and treatment can prevent it from getting worse.

WHAT YOU CAN DO NOW

➤ If you have repeated bouts of diarrhea, be very careful not to let yourself get dehydrated (see **diarrhea,** page 116).

In addition, your doctor may recommend that you:

➤ Maintain a balanced diet. Because diarrhea and poor digestion rob the body of essential fluids and nutrients, good nutrition is crucial.

➤ Avoid foods that irritate the colon. To check for sensitivities, avoid a suspected food for 10 to 30 days; then try it. If your symptoms flare up, eliminate the food from your diet. (Common irritants are spicy or high-fiber foods, dairy products, eggs, and wheat.)

➤ Avoid alcohol.

➤ Avoid aspirin.

➤ Because you may be at greater risk of **colon cancer** (see page 112), discuss routine screening with your doctor.

WHEN TO CALL THE DOCTOR

Call for an immediate appointment:

➤ If you have a sudden attack of abdominal pain, fever, and the urge to pass gas or to have a bowel movement. You may be in the initial stage of **appendicitis** (see page 20).

➤ If you have rectal bleeding with clots of blood in your stool; this could indicate a severe stage of colitis.

Call for advice and an appointment:

➤ If diarrhea lasts more than 48 hours. You may be at risk of dehydration.

➤ If you have the most common symptoms of IBD. These could point to other conditions as well, such as the less serious **irritable bowel syndrome** (see next page).

- Nausea, particularly after eating.
- Headaches, fatigue, depression, or anxiety.
- A feeling that bowel movements aren't complete.

During digestion, food is pushed through the intestinal tract by waves of synchronized muscle contractions. Irritable bowel syndrome occurs when these contractions become irregular and disrupt the process. IBS, also called spastic colon, is the most common of all digestive disorders, affecting at least 10 to 15 percent of adults at some time in their lives. It does not lead to any life-threatening bowel diseases. It can be difficult to treat, however, because no one is sure what causes it. Some experts think it is brought on—or made worse—by tension and stress or a poor diet.

HOW TO PREVENT IT

There is no known way to prevent Crohn's disease or ulcerative colitis. Avoiding certain foods, however, may help minimize irritation to the colon.

FOR MORE HELP

Information line: Intestinal Disease Foundation, 412-261-5888, M–F 9:30–3:30 EST. Provides telephone support, educational programs and materials, information on support groups, and physician referrals.

Organization: Crohn's and Colitis Foundation of America, 800-343-3637. Ask for a free information packet or information on support groups.

Irritable Bowel Syndrome

SIGNS AND SYMPTOMS

Symptoms of irritable bowel syndrome (IBS) can differ markedly from one person to another but may include:
- Diarrhea or constipation, or alternating bouts of these over several months.
- Abdominal cramps or pain.
- Excessive gas or bloating.

WHAT YOU CAN DO NOW

If you have symptoms of IBS, schedule an appointment with your doctor. You should get a diagnosis to rule out more serious disorders (see **abdominal pain** chart, page 113). In the meantime, self-care can help relieve your discomfort:
- ➤ If you're suffering from **diarrhea** or **constipation,** see pages 116 or 115.
- ➤ Experiment with changes in your diet. Try cutting down on fatty foods or avoiding possible irritants such as eggs, dairy products, spicy foods, coffee, and diet foods containing sorbitol.
- ➤ Try eating smaller meals four or five times a day to make digestion easier.
- ➤ If you smoke, quit.
- ➤ Include exercise and relaxation in your daily routine.
- ➤ Seek psychological counseling if you suspect that stress is a cause of the problem.

WHEN TO CALL THE DOCTOR

Call for an immediate appointment:
- ➤ If you have pain in the lower-left side of your abdomen, fever, and (possibly) a change in the frequency of bowel move-

ments; you may have **diverticulitis** (see page 118).

➤ If you have a fever and diarrhea, or awaken at night with diarrhea, and you have been losing weight unexpectedly. Such symptoms may be signs of **inflammatory bowel disease** (see page 125).

Call for advice and an appointment:

➤ If you discover blood or mucus in your stools, or if the frequency or consistency of your stools has changed; this could signal colon polyps or **colon cancer** (see page 112).

➤ If your symptoms interfere with your normal activities.

HOW TO PREVENT IT

➤ Because the causes of irritable bowel syndrome are unknown, the best advice is to take care of your overall health: Eat sensibly and take steps to ease the stress in your life (see **stress,** page 212).

FOR MORE HELP

Information line: Intestinal Disease Foundation, 412-261-5888, M–F 9:30–3:30 EST. Provides telephone support, educational programs and materials, information on support groups, and physician referrals.

Organization: International Foundation for Bowel Dysfunction, P.O. Box 17864, Milwaukee, WI 53217. 414-241-9479, M–F 9–5 CST. Provides support and materials on functional bowel disorders.

Newsletter: *Nutrition Action.* Provides clear, useful advice on good nutrition and diet. Published by the Center for Science in the Public Interest, 1875 Connecticut Ave. NW, Suite 300, Washington, DC 20009. 202-332-9110, M–F 9–5 EST. $24 for a one-year subscription.

Nausea and Vomiting

SIGNS AND SYMPTOMS

Nausea and vomiting are sometimes accompanied by one of the following:

■ Diarrhea.
■ Abdominal cramps or pain.
■ Fever, weakness, and fatigue.
■ Headache.
■ Loss of appetite.

Although nausea and vomiting happen a lot and are usually not serious, they can be worrisome. In children and young adults, they most often result from the viral infection commonly called stomach flu. In these cases, vomiting and diarrhea usually disappear within two to three days, but weakness and fatigue may last about a week.

In elderly people, medications and ulcers are more often the culprits (see **ulcers and gastritis,** page 130). Less common causes are bacterial and parasitic infections (see box on previous page), food **allergies** (see page 85), and drinking too much alcohol.

Another cause is **food poisoning** (see page 35), which you can get from eating food contaminated with viruses, bacteria, or chemicals. In this case, you will usually also have abdominal cramps and sometimes diarrhea, headache, dizziness, or fever and chills. The vomiting may leave you dehydrated.

Mild food poisoning lasts only a few hours or at worst a day or two, but some types— such as botulism and certain forms of chemical poisoning—are severe and possibly life-threatening unless you get prompt medical treatment.

WHAT YOU CAN DO NOW

If you think you might have severe food poisoning or chemical poisoning:

➤ Call the local poison control center listed in your phone book. Trained specialists there can help you determine the possible source and whether you need medical

Rectal Bleeding and Itching

SYMPTOMS	WHAT IT MIGHT BE	WHAT YOU CAN DO
Bloody stools, painful abdominal cramping and swelling, nausea and vomiting, constipation, weakness or dizziness.	Intestinal obstruction—blockage of small or large intestine. • Scarring from abdominal surgery. • Strangulated hernia (see page 123). • Colon cancer (see page 112). • Diverticulitis (see page 118). • Foreign object in digestive tract.	Call 911 or go to emergency facility **immediately.**
Bright red rectal bleeding that occurs after injury, anal intercourse, or insertion of foreign object into rectum.	Tear in sphincter muscle or skin around anus.	Call doctor for emergency advice. If not available, call 911 or go to emergency facility **immediately.**
Watery diarrhea containing blood, mucus, or pus; abdominal cramps or pain; nausea and vomiting; fever; muscle aches or pain; rapid dehydration and weight loss.	Dysentery—contagious bacterial infection of intestinal tract.	Call doctor for immediate appointment. Drink lots of fluids, and don't take over-the-counter stomach medications.
Painful anal itching at night, especially in children; restless sleep and irritability.	Pinworms—common intestinal parasites.	Call doctor for advice and appointment. If antiworm medication is prescribed, follow directions carefully.
Frequent, painful, or difficult bowel movements; soreness in rectal area; blood or mucus discharge; abdominal cramps; constipation.	Proctitis—inflammation of rectum and anal tissues. • Bacterial or viral infection. • Inflammatory bowel disease (see page 125). • Sexually transmitted disease (see chart, page 215). • Colon cancer (see page 112). • Injury from anal intercourse.	Call doctor for advice and appointment. Take frequent warm baths to relieve discomfort. Eat high-fiber foods and drink at least 8 glasses of water a day to soften stools.
Bloody stools, persistent diarrhea, nausea, cramps or pain in lower-right side of abdomen.	Crohn's disease.	See inflammatory bowel disease, page 125.

Rectal Bleeding and Itching

SYMPTOMS	WHAT IT MIGHT BE	WHAT YOU CAN DO
Recurrent episodes of diarrhea with mucus and blood, pain in left side of abdomen that lessens after bowel movements.	Ulcerative colitis.	See inflammatory bowel disease, page 125.
Itching in anal area or bright red blood in stool, pain during or after bowel movements.	Inflamed blood vessels in anus (see hemorrhoids, page 122). ● Split or tear in skin around anus (anal fissure). ● Psoriasis (see page 152).	Take warm baths, especially after painful bowel movements. Include lots of fiber and plenty of fluids in diet (see constipation, page 115). See doctor if it persists.
Itching around anus.	Often no clear cause. In older people, may be dry skin related to advancing age.	After bowel movements, gently clean anal area with moist, undyed tissue or premoistened towelettes. Avoid soap, which can make itching worse.

treatment. (If you can't find the local center in your phone book, call information or a local hospital.)

If you have mild vomiting and diarrhea:

➤ Don't take any antinausea or antidiarrhea medication for 24 hours after your symptoms develop, unless a doctor recommends it. Vomiting and diarrhea are the body's way of expelling whatever irritant or infectious agent may be causing the problem. (Medication may be necessary for children, who become dehydrated more quickly.)

➤ Once you can keep fluid in your stomach, drink clear liquids for about the next 12 hours. Then, for a full day, eat bland foods—such as rice, cooked cereals, baked potatoes, and clear soups—if your stomach can tolerate them.

➤ Get plenty of rest until symptoms are gone. Because you can lose lots of fluid from repeated vomiting, dehydration is a potential danger, especially in children and older adults. Symptoms include dry mouth, sticky saliva, dizziness or weakness, dark yellow urine, and sometimes excessive thirst. For advice about replacing lost fluids, see **diarrhea,** page 116. If you cannot keep liquids down and are becoming severely dehydrated, you will need to go to a hospital for intravenous fluid replacement.

WHEN TO CALL THE DOCTOR

Call 911 or go to an emergency facility **immediately:**

➤ If, along with vomiting and abdominal pain, you experience blurred vision, muscle weakness, difficulty speaking or swallowing, or muscle paralysis. These may be signs of botulism, a rare but sometimes fatal type of bacterial food poisoning.

➤ If you have symptoms of chemical food poisoning—vomiting, diarrhea, sweating, dizziness, excessively teary eyes, great amounts of saliva, mental confusion, and stomach pain—about 30 minutes after eating. This is often caused by pesticides or by eating food kept in tainted containers, and can be life-threatening.

➤ If you vomit blood or anything that looks like coffee grounds.

Call for an immediate appointment:

➤ If you have bloody or tarry stools; this can signal internal bleeding.
➤ If you develop signs of dehydration—dry mouth, sticky saliva, dizziness or weakness, dark yellow urine, and, sometimes, excessive thirst. Dehydration is extremely serious in infants; (see **diarrhea in children** box, page 117).
➤ If you have intense pain or swelling in the abdomen, rectum, or anus; you may have a serious abdominal disorder (see **abdominal pain** chart, page 113).

Call for advice:

➤ If your symptoms recur after treatment; you may have an underlying problem such as an intestinal **parasite** (see box on page 126).
➤ If your vomiting and diarrhea are severe and last longer than two or three days.
➤ If you have a fever of 101.5 or higher.

HOW TO PREVENT IT

To avoid catching viral stomach flu:

➤ Keep your immune system strong with plenty of rest, exercise, and a healthy diet.
➤ Wash your hands frequently.

To prevent food poisoning:

➤ Don't thaw frozen meat at room temperature. Let meat thaw in the refrigerator, or thaw it quickly in a microwave oven and cook it immediately. Be sure that frozen food (especially poultry) is completely thawed or defrosted before cooking, so that it will cook all the way through and any bacteria will be killed.
➤ At picnics or anywhere else, be especially careful not to eat moist foods that have been out in the sun long enough to become warm. Avoid uncooked, marinated food and raw meat, fish, or eggs. Cook all such food well.
➤ Using soap and hot water, carefully wash your hands and any countertops, cutting boards, and utensils touched by uncooked meat, fish, and poultry.
➤ Refrigerate perishable items immediately. Set your refrigerator at 37 degrees, and never eat dairy products or cooked meat if they have been out of a refrigerator more than two hours.

➤ Be sure that all members of your household wash their hands with soap and water after using the toilet and before preparing food or eating.
➤ Don't eat any food that looks or smells spoiled, or any food in bulging cans or cracked jars—a signal that the contents have gone bad.
➤ Don't eat wild berries, mushrooms, or other plants unless you are sure of what they are.

Ulcers and Gastritis

SIGNS AND SYMPTOMS

■ Pain or discomfort in the upper part of the abdomen.
■ Nausea.
■ Vomiting.
■ Loss of appetite.
■ Belching or gas.
■ Heartburn.
■ Dark or bloody stools.

Stomach ulcers are sometimes called peptic ulcers. They are holes or breaks in the protective lining of the stomach, the tube between the throat and the stomach (esophagus), or the upper part of the small intestine (duodenum). Although one out of ten Americans will develop a stomach ulcer sometime, the causes are often unclear. Researchers suspect that in many cases a common bacterium called *Helicobacter pylori* predisposes a person to develop a stomach ulcer. The repeated use of anti-inflammatory medications such as aspirin and ibuprofen can also cause ulcers. Other contributing factors may include:

➤ **Stress** (see page 212).
➤ Smoking and heavy drinking.
➤ An overactive stomach that produces too much stomach acid.
➤ Too little mucus to protect the stomach lining.

Fortunately, stomach ulcers are relatively easy to treat. In most cases involving bacteria, they can be cured with antibiotics, usually in combination with another drug.

The bacteria associated with ulcers can also cause gastritis—a medical term for inflammation of the stomach lining. In some people, but not all, gastritis may cause symptoms like those of indigestion, including upper abdominal pain, nausea, and vomiting.

Although the symptoms are similar to those some people get from heavy smoking, eating fatty or spicy foods, or overeating, gastritis is not caused by any of these habits.

For mild cases of gastritis, your doctor may recommend over-the-counter antacids. If he or she suspects bacteria, you will probably need antibiotics. Untreated gastritis can cause serious damage.

WHAT YOU CAN DO NOW

➤ Schedule an examination with your doctor if you think you have a stomach ulcer or gastritis.
➤ Avoid aspirin, ibuprofen, and other nonsteroidal anti-inflammatory drugs.
➤ Drink lots of water and other liquids to prevent dehydration, but avoid milk, which can increase acid secretion.
➤ Take antacids.

WHEN TO CALL THE DOCTOR

Call 911 or go to an emergency facility **immediately:**
➤ If you vomit blood or material that looks like coffee grounds; these symptoms indicate internal bleeding.
➤ If you feel faint, cold, and clammy, or you actually do faint. These may be symptoms of shock, usually resulting from massive blood loss.

Call for an immediate appointment:
➤ If you develop symptoms of an ulcer along with severe back pain; your ulcer may be perforating the stomach or duodenum wall.
➤ If you have an ulcer and develop symptoms of anemia, such as fatigue and a pallid complexion; your ulcer may be bleeding.
➤ If you pass stools that appear dark red, bloody, or black.

Call for advice and an appointment:
➤ If you have severe stomach pain.
➤ If you have symptoms of a stomach ulcer or gastritis that last more than two weeks.

HOW TO PREVENT IT

➤ Minimize use of aspirin and ibuprofen.
➤ If you smoke, quit.
➤ Do what you can to reduce stress.
➤ If you drink alcoholic beverages, do so in moderation.
➤ Avoid foods that upset your stomach.
➤ To prevent an ulcer from recurring, carefully follow instructions for any ulcer drugs you are taking.

FOR MORE HELP

Organization: National Digestive Diseases Information Clearinghouse, 2 Information Way, Bethesda, MD 20892-3570. Write for a free fact sheet and information packet on gastritis and helicobacter, the bacterium frequently associated with gastritis and ulcers.

Video: *Ulcers (Gastrointestinal) at Time of Diagnosis.* Clear, useful overview of causes and treatments, consisting of four reports—Understanding the Diagnosis, What Happens Next?, Treatment and Management, and Issues and Answers. Time Life Medical, 1996, $19.95.

Urinary System

◆

Kidney Stones

SIGNS AND SYMPTOMS

- Waves of sharp pain—usually on one side of the body—that start in the back below the ribs and move toward the groin.
- In men, pain in testicles and penis.
- Interruption of the stream during urination.
- Frequent urge to urinate, but inability to pass more than small amounts of urine at a time.
- Bloody or dark urine.
- Nausea and vomiting.

You may also have a kidney infection if you have:

- Fever.
- Painful urination.
- Cloudy urine.

Kidney stones are just what they sound like: hard lumps that form in the kidneys, most often from excess calcium.

The kidneys filter waste products out of the blood and mix them with water to make urine. Stones that form in a kidney must pass through one of the tubes (ureters) that connect the kidneys to the bladder (see illustration, page 174). From there, the stones can pass out of the body with the urine.

Some stones pose no problems. But most stones cause excruciating pain as they move

from the kidneys to the bladder—a journey that can take a few hours to several days. Fortunately, the pain and other symptoms go away once the stone is passed.

Sometimes a stone gets trapped in one of the tubes leading to the bladder, blocking the flow of urine. Doctors can often destroy such stones with bursts of shock waves, turning them into powder that is then easily washed out with the urine. This treatment has made surgery unnecessary in most of these cases.

Kidney stones tend to run in families, and they affect many more men than women. People with gout (see **arthritis,** page 158), **irritable bowel syndrome** (see page 126), Crohn's disease (see **inflammatory bowel disease,** page 125), and chronic urinary tract infections (see **painful urination,** page 134) are more likely to develop them. Kidney stones are also more common in hot climates: When people sweat a lot and don't drink enough liquids, their urine has a higher concentration of the materials that turn into stones.

WHAT YOU CAN DO NOW

➤ If you're having a kidney stone attack, drink lots of water—at least eight to ten eight-ounce glasses a day. This will help flush the stone out of your system and will discourage new ones from forming.
➤ Take an over-the-counter pain reliever or a pain reliever prescribed by your doctor.

(continued)

Urinary Problems

SYMPTOMS	WHAT IT MIGHT BE	WHAT YOU CAN DO
Passing no urine or very little; weight gain and swelling of ankles and face.	Advanced kidney disease. ● Kidney failure—when both kidneys stop working.	Call 911 or go to emergency facility **immediately** if you also have chest pains or difficulty breathing. Otherwise, call doctor for immediate appointment.
Frequent urination, with excessive thirst.	Diabetes (see page 269). ● Disorder of pituitary gland, which regulates body's fluid balance.	Call doctor for immediate appointment if you also have fever, chills, nausea, vomiting, low back pain, or severe dehydration or discomfort.
Frequent urge to urinate, but passing only small amounts of urine.	Infection of bladder or tube that carries urine out of body. ● Prostate problem (see page 222). ● Kidney stones (see opposite page). ● Sexually transmitted disease (see chart on page 215). ● Interstitial cystitis—inflamed bladder wall.	Call doctor for immediate appointment if you also have fever, chills, nausea, vomiting, low back pain, or severe dehydration or discomfort. See also painful urination, page 134.
Painful urination.	Infection of bladder or tube that carries urine out of body. ● Kidney stones (see opposite page) or other kidney disease. ● Sexually transmitted disease (see chart on page 215). ● Pelvic inflammatory disease (see page 230). ● Prostate problem (see page 222). ● Vaginal problem (see page 237).	Call doctor for immediate appointment at onset of acute pain or discomfort during urination. See also painful urination, page 134.
Blood in urine.	Kidney stones (see opposite page) or other kidney disease. ● Prostate problem (see page 222). ● Bladder infection. ● Bladder or kidney cancer. ● Injury to kidneys or bladder.	Call doctor for immediate appointment, particularly if you are having difficulty urinating. See also painful urination, page 134.

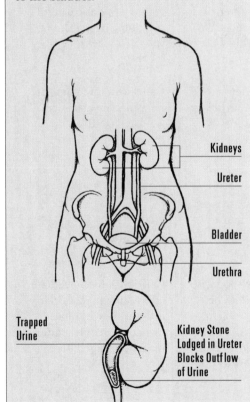

WHEN TO CALL THE DOCTOR

➤ If you have waves of sharp pain in your side, back, or abdomen.
➤ If urination is difficult or painful.
➤ If you have blood in your urine.
➤ If you develop fever with your symptoms.

HOW TO PREVENT IT

Recurrences are common, so take the following steps to try to prevent them:
➤ Drink at least eight glasses of water a day—more in hot weather.
➤ Ask your doctor about prescribing drugs or changes in your diet.

FOR MORE HELP

Information line: National Kidney Foundation Information Center, 800-622-9010, M–F 8:30–5:30 EST. Information specialists answer questions and send appropriate literature.

Organization: National Kidney and Urologic Diseases Information Clearinghouse, Box NKUDIC, 3 Information Way, Bethesda, MD 20892-3580. Sends information on kidney disorders.

Book: *The Kidney Stones Handbook: A Patient's Guide to Hope, Cure, and Prevention,* by Gail Golomb. Four Geez Press, 1994, $12.95.

Painful Urination

SIGNS AND SYMPTOMS

■ Burning, stinging, or other discomfort when urinating.
■ Frequent urination, but with small amounts of urine passed each time.
■ Cloudy, strong-smelling, or blood-tinged urine.
■ Yellow discharge from the urinary tube (urethra).
■ Pain in the lower abdomen or lower back.
■ In women, pain experienced during sexual intercourse.

Many conditions and disorders can cause painful urination, but urinary tract infections are most often responsible.

Although normal urine contains no bacteria, bacteria are always present on your skin and in the anal area. Urinary tract infections occur when bacteria get into the urinary tract and travel up the tube (urethra) connecting the bladder to the outside of the body. There they multiply, causing pain, swelling, and redness. This infection of the bladder is called cystitis, and it is the most common urinary tract infection.

The urethra can also become infected, as can the kidneys if the bacteria reach them.

KIDNEY STONES

A kidney stone causes pain when it passes through the ureter, one of the two tubes leading from the kidneys to the bladder.

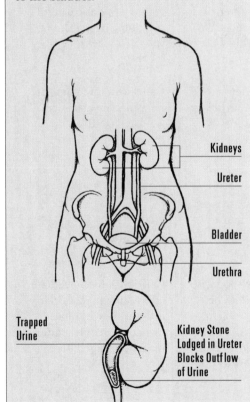

Kidneys
Ureter
Bladder
Urethra
Trapped Urine
Kidney Stone Lodged in Ureter Blocks Outflow of Urine

Adult women are especially likely to get urinary tract infections, and sexually active women are particularly at risk, because during sexual intercourse, infection-causing bacteria can move from the urethra—situated near the vagina—into the bladder. Women may get these infections if they use a diaphragm for contraception, because it can irritate the urethra.

People with diabetes and weakened immune systems are also at increased risk of infection, as are those with kidney stones and other urinary blockages, or people who must use catheters (see **diabetes,** page 269, and **kidney stones,** page 132). The likelihood of your developing a urinary tract infection increases as you grow older.

Though urinary tract infections are painful and bothersome, they usually can be treated successfully with antibiotics.

WHAT YOU CAN DO NOW

➤ Avoid caffeine, alcohol, and spicy or very acidic foods—which may further irritate the bladder.
➤ Drink eight to ten glasses of water a day to dilute the concentration of bacteria in your urine. (But don't drink lots of water if you're going to see your doctor; this can dilute your urine sample, skewing the results of your test.)
➤ Use a heating pad or hot-water bottle to ease your pain.
➤ Eat plain yogurt if you get a yeast infection after taking antibiotics prescribed for your urinary tract infection. The bacteria in the yogurt help control yeast.

WHEN TO CALL THE DOCTOR

Call for an immediate appointment:
➤ If you have a sharp pain that comes in waves, beginning in the back below the ribs and moving toward the groin; you may have kidney stones.
➤ If you have a rapidly rising fever and sudden, intense pain in your back, near or above your waistline; you may have a kidney infection.
➤ If your urine looks bloody or very cloudy.

➤ If painful urination is accompanied by an abnormal discharge from the penis or vagina; you may have a **sexually transmitted disease** (see chart on page 215).
➤ If you are a woman and painful urination is accompanied by tenderness and a dull ache or pain in your lower back and abdomen; pain during intercourse; and/or irregular, missed, or unusually heavy menstrual periods. You may have endometriosis (see page 227) or **pelvic inflammatory disease** (see page 230).

Call for advice and an appointment:
➤ If you are a man and painful urination is accompanied by a frequent need to urinate, an interrupted urinary stream, painful ejaculation, or pain in the pelvis or lower back. You may have a **prostate problem** (see page 222).
➤ If you experience painful urination or the other symptoms of a urinary tract infection.
➤ If your symptoms don't go away or if they come back despite treatment.

HOW TO PREVENT IT

➤ Drink eight glasses of fluids—including lots of water—each day. Try cranberry juice, too, which can sometimes discourage an infection from developing.
➤ Don't postpone urinating when you have the urge to go. And empty your bladder completely every time you urinate.
➤ Wash before and after sex, and ask your partner to do the same.
➤ Urinate after sex; this helps flush out bacteria that may have entered the urinary tract during intercourse.
➤ Take showers instead of baths.
➤ Avoid bubble bath and scented personal hygiene products. Use a mild, unscented detergent to launder underwear; scented or harsh products can irritate the skin around the urethra, making infection more likely.
➤ Wear cotton-crotch underwear and loose-fitting clothes.
➤ Wash genitals with plain water once a day.
For women:
➤ If you use a diaphragm, wash it after each use with warm, soapy water, then carefully

rinse it and dry it. If you have repeated infections, ask your doctor to check whether it fits properly. If a different size doesn't help, consider using another method of birth control.

➤ To keep the urinary tract free of bacteria, always wipe yourself from front to back after using the toilet.

FOR MORE HELP

Organization: Bladder Health Council, 300 W. Pratt St., Suite 401, Baltimore, MD 21201. Write to request information.

Organization: National Institute of Diabetes and Digestive and Kidney Diseases, 301-496-3583, M–F 9–5 EST. Distributes information on kidney and urinary tract disorders.

Organization: Interstitial Cystitis Association of America, P.O. Box 1553, Madison Square Station, New York, NY 10159. Send a business-size, self-addressed, stamped envelope to receive information.

Book: *Overcoming Bladder Disorders,* by Rebecca Chalker and Kristene E. Whitmore, M.D. HarperPerennial, 1990, $12.50.

IF YOU'RE PREGNANT

Urinary tract infections in pregnant women sometimes move up to the kidneys, where they can quickly become dangerous. For this reason, many doctors suggest regular urine testing during pregnancy. If you are pregnant and you experience painful urination or any of the other symptoms listed here, call your doctor for an immediate appointment.

Urinary Incontinence

SIGNS AND SYMPTOMS

■ Leaking a small amount of urine when coughing, exercising, laughing, or otherwise putting pressure on the bladder.

■ Uncontrollable urge to urinate.

■ Urinating without knowing it.

More than 10 million Americans, mostly older people, have trouble controlling the flow of urine from their bladder, a condition called urinary incontinence. There are several varieties, most of which can be limited or cured.

In stress incontinence, the muscles that close off the tube that carries urine outside the body (urethra) sometimes get too weak to withstand a sudden increase in pressure. When you sneeze, cough, or otherwise put pressure on the bladder, a little urine often escapes. Childbirth or obesity can weaken key muscles and contribute to this problem.

In urge incontinence, also called irritable bladder, you may suddenly need to urinate and be unable to control it. This condition may be traced to a urinary tract infection, but it could also be caused by **stroke** (see pages 45 and 109), **Alzheimer's disease** (see page 50), or **Parkinson's disease** (see page 57).

Overflow incontinence, or an unstable bladder, can occur when you no longer feel the sensation that tells you when it's time to urinate. Rather than being wholly emptied several times a day, your bladder is always at least partially full. For that reason, urine leaks out, usually in dribbles. This condition may be linked to **diabetes** (page 269), nerve disorders, or an enlarged prostate gland that blocks the flow of urine (see **prostate problems,** page 222). In women, it may result from a large fibroid or ovarian tumor.

Sometimes the causes of incontinence are temporary and easily remedied. It may be the first and only symptom of a urinary tract infection, so clearing up the infection will usually cure the incontinence as well. Some drugs, including sleeping pills, diuretics, and tranquilizers, can make it hard to control your bladder. The problem may be easily fixed if your doctor can take you off a drug that's causing bladder trouble or prescribe a different one.

Incontinence generally doesn't pose a risk to health. What's important is to take steps to treat it. Even if it can't be cured entirely, it can almost surely be controlled so that it won't interfere with your daily life.

WHAT YOU CAN DO NOW

➤ Cross your legs if you feel a sneeze or cough coming on. Researchers who tested this technique say it is a safe, simple way to cut down on or even eliminate stress incontinence.

➤ Keep a diary of when you urinate unexpectedly. Note how much urine is lost and what you were doing at the time. This information will help your doctor determine the kind or kinds of incontinence you're experiencing and make treatment more effective.

➤ Wear disposable, absorbent undergarments if you're going out and are worried about an accident. It's important to continue your normal activities and avoid one of the dangers of incontinence: social isolation. But think of this only as a short-term solution. Wearing them too long can cause rashes and other complications.

➤ Practice bladder training to relieve your symptoms:
  ● Schedule a trip to the bathroom every hour, whether or not you have to urinate. Work up to a three-hour or four-hour interval by lengthening the time between toilet visits by 15 to 30 minutes every two days.
  ● If you need to urinate between these scheduled visits to the toilet, relax and stay where you are until the urge is gone, then find a bathroom.

➤ Avoid drinking a lot of liquid while you are away from home.

WHEN TO CALL THE DOCTOR

➤ If you are experiencing any bladder control problems.
➤ If you have signs of an infection, such as fever or pain during urination.

HOW TO PREVENT IT

➤ Practice the following exercises, which tone the muscles that control urination: As you start and stop the flow of urine, sense which muscles you're working. Later, contract and release them—at least 15 to 20 squeezes, three times a day. After some practice, tighten the muscles for at least ten seconds each time. The exercises are completely private: You're the only one who will know you're doing them.
➤ Lose extra pounds and exercise regularly. Excess body weight puts pressure on the bladder muscles.
➤ Eat a lot of fresh fruits and vegetables and whole grains to avoid constipation. The straining that accompanies constipation can weaken bladder muscles.
➤ Avoid caffeine and alcohol, which can irritate the bladder and trigger leaks.
➤ Ask your doctor about using biofeedback to treat your incontinence.

FOR MORE HELP

Hotline: Simon Foundation for Continence, 800-237-4666, 24-hour line. Information specialists answer questions and send incontinence information packets. Call 708-864-3913, M–F 9–5 CST for information on support groups.

Organization: Help for Incontinent People, 800-252-3337 or 803-579-7900, M–F 8–5 EST. Provides literature and referrals to health care providers experienced in treating incontinence.

Book: *Staying Dry: A Practical Guide to Bladder Control,* by Kathryn L. Burgio, K. Lynette Pearce, and Angelo J. Licco. Johns Hopkins University Press, 1989, $12.95.

Skin, Scalp, & Nails

◆

Acne

Acne appears to be linked to an excess of sebum, an oily substance that lubricates the skin. When sebum plugs up a hair follicle, forming a whitehead or blackhead, bacteria grow inside the blocked follicle and cause inflammation. This can result in a pimple or, in rare cases, a boil or cyst. Acne is an outbreak of many pimples, blackheads, whiteheads, or nodules.

While adolescents are most likely to get acne, it occurs in all age groups, including newborns. You may be prone to acne:

➤ If you have a family history of acne.
➤ If your male hormones (found in both males and females) increase, especially during puberty.
➤ If you experience hormonal changes due to menstrual periods, pregnancy, or oral contraceptive use.

➤ If you take certain drugs, such as lithium or corticosteroids (anti-inflammatories).
➤ If you use creams, oils, cosmetics, or other substances that block the skin's pores.

Despite conventional wisdom, stress, poor hygiene, and a poor diet don't appear to cause acne, although they can make it worse.

WHAT YOU CAN DO NOW

➤ Wash the affected area twice a day with mild, oil- and fragrance-free soap. Avoid overwashing, which may aggravate acne.
➤ Shampoo your hair regularly. Oily hair may worsen the condition.
➤ Shave as infrequently as possible. Men with acne should also take care when shaving to avoid nicking pimples. If you have severe acne, always use a fresh blade to avoid infection.
➤ Thoroughly remove cosmetics. Use only hypoallergenic, fragrance-free makeup made for acne-prone skin.
➤ Try an over-the-counter treatment that contains benzoyl peroxide (an antibacterial agent) or salicylic acid (a mild peeling agent that helps unblock pores).
➤ Don't pop, pick, scratch, or squeeze your pimples. This may lead to scarring.

WHEN TO CALL THE DOCTOR

➤ If your acne doesn't get better after two to three months of over-the-counter treatments; you may need more aggressive treatment.
➤ If you have a large number of pimples, if

Rashes

Rashes can be caused by a variety of conditions ranging from minor to serious. This list includes some of the most common ailments associated with rashes, as well as some potentially life-threatening illnesses. If you have any concern about a rash, call your doctor for advice. If your child has a rash, or if you and your child have the same rash, see also the **children's rashes** chart (page 241).

SYMPTOMS	WHAT IT MIGHT BE	WHAT YOU CAN DO
Itchy, red bumps anywhere on body; swelling of eyes, lips, and tongue; weakness; shortness of breath; sweating; rapid heartbeat.	Anaphylactic shock— severe, sudden, life-threatening allergic reaction to foods, drugs, or insect bites. (See page 18.)	Call 911 or go to emergency facility **immediately.**
Possibly bumpy, deep red or purplish rash; fever; stiff neck; headache; sensitivity to light.	Meningitis (see page 56).	Call 911 or go to emergency facility **immediately.**
Rash resembling sunburn, often on palms of hands or soles of feet; sudden high fever (above 102); vomiting and diarrhea; headache; weakness; fainting; dizziness; confusion.	Toxic shock syndrome (see page 236).	Call 911 or go to emergency facility **immediately.** If you are using tampon, menstrual sponge, diaphragm, or cervical cap, remove it immediately after calling.
Itchy, raised, red or pink patches (sometimes with white centers) that may come and go, anywhere on body.	Hives (see page 149).	Call 911 or go to emergency facility if you also have wheezing, dizziness, and difficulty breathing. This may be anaphylactic shock (see page 18).
Pink rash that starts near wrists and ankles, then spreads to face, torso, and other areas; often accompanied by fever, chills, and severe headache.	Rocky Mountain spotted fever. Caused by microorganism that enters body through tick bite. Illness gets its name from area where first reported. Now widespread. (See tick bites, page 46.)	Call doctor for immediate appointment. Can be life-threatening if untreated. Get tested for Rocky Mountain spotted fever and Lyme disease (see next page of chart).
Butterfly-shaped, red rash on cheeks and nose; fever, fatigue, joint pain, swelling.	Lupus (see page 275).	Call doctor for immediate appointment.

(continued)

Rashes *(continued)*

SYMPTOMS	WHAT IT MIGHT BE	WHAT YOU CAN DO
Red rash that may look like bull's-eye, spreading up to several inches from tick bite; followed within a month by fever, headache, lethargy, and joint pain.	Lyme disease (see page 276). Caused by microorganism that enters body through tick bite. (See tick bites, page 46.)	Call doctor for immediate appointment. Get tested for Lyme disease and Rocky Mountain spotted fever. If you can find tick, remove with tweezers; don't squeeze or twist it.
Burning or tingling skin followed by painful, blistery, red rash; usually on only one side of torso, buttocks, or face.	Shingles (see page 154).	Call doctor for immediate appointment.
Itchy, red skin with thickened patches anywhere on body.	Eczema (see page 146). ● Dermatitis (see page 144).	Call doctor for advice and appointment.
Raised patches of pink, itchy skin with white scales, usually on knees, elbows, and scalp.	Psoriasis (see page 152).	Call doctor for advice and appointment.
Small, pus-filled, pimplelike eruptions anywhere on body.	Folliculitis—bacterial infection of hair follicles. May be caused by shaving or by clothing, especially wet athletic wear, that rubs against skin .	Use over-the-counter antibacterial soap or ointment. If infection worsens or persists after 2 weeks of home care, call doctor for advice and appointment.
Itchy, red, flaky, or scaly patches that appear on just one part of body; can affect feet, genitals, skin, and nails.	Fungal infection (see page 147). Possibly ringworm— infection that can be caught from another person or even from dog or cat; common in children.	Use over-the-counter antifungal creams, powders, and ointments. If rash worsens or persists after 2 weeks of home care, call doctor for advice and appointment.
Extreme itchiness (especially at night); rough, red, sandpaperlike rash in folds of body—between fingers, on wrists and elbows, breasts, buttocks, or waist.	Scabies.	See lice and scabies, page 150.

WHAT IS ROSACEA?

Rosacea (rose-AY-sha) is a rash often misdiagnosed as acne. It can cause a swollen, red nose; puffy cheeks; and a persistent blush on other parts of the face. Rosacea occurs when miniature blood vessels enlarge, usually on the cheeks, nose, and forehead. Sometimes red, pus-filled spots appear, but there won't be any blackheads or whiteheads. People who have rosacea may also get **conjunctivitis** (see page 63).

The cause of rosacea is unknown, though it especially affects women over 30. It comes and goes, and seems to be made worse by hot or spicy food, alcohol or caffeine, extreme temperatures or strong sunlight, and rubbing or massaging the face.

While the condition is harmless, it is often unsightly and may worsen over time. If you think you have rosacea, you should see your doctor for proper diagnosis and treatment.

your acne causes you embarrassment, or if you have signs of scarring. A skin specialist (dermatologist) may prescribe a drug to prevent the acne from getting worse and causing scars.

➤ If your skin is abnormally flushed around your cheeks and nose; you may have rosacea (see box above.)

HOW TO PREVENT IT

Since it's partly genetic and partly hormonal, doctors believe there's nothing you can do to prevent acne.

FOR MORE HELP

Information line: National Institute of Arthritis and Musculoskeletal and Skin Diseases Information Clearinghouse, 301-495-4484, M–F 8:30– 5 EST. Staffers answer questions and send information on acne.

Organization: American Academy of Der-

matology, 930 N. Meacham Rd., P.O. Box 4014, Schaumburg, IL 60168-4014. 708-330-0230, M–F 8:30–5 CST. Send a business-size, self-addressed, stamped envelope for pamphlets on acne and rosacea. Also provides doctor referrals.

Blisters

SIGNS AND SYMPTOMS

■ Sore, fluid-filled bubbles of skin, sometimes appearing in clusters. They range in size from a pinpoint to more than several inches across.
■ Itching and inflammation (sometimes).

Most blisters form as a result of friction, caused by simple movements such as the rubbing of a shovel handle or the pinch of a new pair of running shoes. Insect bites, viruses, certain skin disorders such as contact **dermatitis** (see page 144), and some drugs and chemicals can also cause them. Blisters from **burns** (see page 22) can occur from exposure to extreme heat or cold.

WHAT YOU CAN DO NOW

Usually no treatment is necessary since new skin forms underneath the affected area and the fluid is simply absorbed.
Friction blisters:
➤ Popping a blister increases the risk of infection, so it's best to leave a small one alone. To drain a large, painful blister: Cleanse the area with alcohol. Using a sterile needle, gently pierce one side of the blister and let it drain. Then apply antibiotic cream and cover it.
➤ Don't pull off or cut away the loose skin from a broken blister. The new skin underneath needs this protective cover.
➤ Cover a broken blister to protect it. Use an ordinary adhesive bandage for a small blister or a gauze pad and adhesive tape for a large one. Change the bandage daily, or more often if it gets wet.

Burn blisters:
- ➤ Flush the affected area immediately with lots of cool water or a saline solution. Don't rub or place ice on burns.
- ➤ Never pop a burn blister.

WHEN TO CALL THE DOCTOR

- ➤ If a blister has been caused by a burn, affects a large area, and is very painful; blisters indicate a second-degree burn. Some second- and all third-degree burns require a doctor's care.
- ➤ If the fluid in the blister isn't clear. White, yellow, or green discharge may signal infection.
- ➤ If your blisters are the result of a skin disorder or contact with chemicals or other toxic agents.

HOW TO PREVENT IT

- ➤ Wear gloves during activities that you do only occasionally, such as shoveling snow, sweeping, or raking.
- ➤ Have your feet measured when you buy shoes, and wear only shoes that fit.
- ➤ Have your shoes repaired regularly. Worn soles don't protect the feet, and worn linings can chafe the skin.
- ➤ Keep your feet dry. Wear absorbent, hole-free socks. Dust your feet with an antifungal powder if they tend to sweat.
- ➤ Put petroleum jelly or moleskin pads on areas, such as the heel, where socks are likely to rub. Wear socks that fit well; socks that bunch up can cause blisters.

FOR MORE HELP

Information line: American Podiatric Medical Association, 800-FOOTCARE, 24-hour recording. Takes requests for free brochures on care of the feet.

Pamphlet: American Academy of Orthopaedic Surgeons, 800-824-BONES, 24-hour recording. Ask for pamphlet titled "If the Shoe Fits, Wear It."

Boils

SIGNS AND SYMPTOMS

- ■ Inflammation, tenderness, pain, or throbbing of a lump under the skin.
- ■ A red and swollen lump with a white or yellow, pus-filled center under the skin (after several days).

A boil may appear to be a nasty pimple, but it's actually the result of staph bacteria that have invaded a blocked hair follicle or oil gland and infected it. The bacteria, along with white blood cells and dead skin cells that accumulate at the site, form pus and cause swelling.

Boils generally appear on the face, neck, scalp, buttocks, armpits, or, sometimes, a woman's nipple. A cluster of boils is known as a carbuncle—a rarer and more serious form that requires medical attention.

Boils are common ailments, and usually minor ones. People with diabetes or immune-system problems and those exposed to certain industrial chemicals are more likely to get them. So are people who are in generally poor health, who lack adequate hygiene or a good diet, or who overuse corticosteroids such as cortisone.

WHAT YOU CAN DO NOW

- ➤ Wash the infected area gently with antibacterial soap.
- ➤ Apply warm compresses (cloths soaked in hot water and wrung out), which help bring the boil to a head.
- ➤ Put an over-the-counter antibacterial ointment on the boil to keep the infection from spreading.
- ➤ Don't squeeze or lance the boil yourself; that could spread the infection. A typical boil will burst of its own accord after about 10 to 14 days. When it does, hold a warm, clean compress against it to remove all the

pus. Next, apply antibacterial ointment and cover the boil loosely with an adhesive bandage to prevent reinfection.

➤ Boils are contagious, so wash your hands thoroughly and launder towels, clothes, and bed linens in hot water and detergent to avoid spreading the infection.

WHEN TO CALL THE DOCTOR

➤ If you have a boil on your face, a cluster of boils, or boils accompanied by a fever. You could develop a more serious infection.
➤ If the pain is excruciating. A physician may lance and drain the boil.
➤ If you get boils frequently. Your doctor will want to find out what is causing them.

HOW TO PREVENT IT

➤ Shower or bathe regularly.
➤ If you're prone to getting boils, apply an antibacterial cream after shaving.
➤ Take care of minor skin injuries promptly.
➤ Avoid sharing towels, linens, clothes, or athletic equipment with anyone.
➤ Eat balanced meals that include lots of fresh fruit and vegetables.

Corns and Calluses

SIGNS AND SYMPTOMS

Corns:
■ Areas of thick, hard, dead skin on the tops or sides of toe joints or between the toes.

Calluses:
■ Patches of rough, thick, dead skin on the soles of the feet, the palms of the hands, or any other area subject to friction.

As annoying as corns and calluses can be, they form to protect the skin. They're very common and usually do not cause a problem unless they build up or crack open, which can be painful.

Corns generally show up on the feet, while calluses develop on the hands, feet, or anywhere friction occurs repeatedly—even on a violinist's chin.

Most corns and calluses that develop on the feet are caused by badly fitting shoes. Tapered, narrow-toed shoes and open-backed, high-heeled sandals are the worst offenders, putting too much pressure on the toes and making women much more likely to have these particular foot problems.

WHAT YOU CAN DO NOW

➤ Place a corn pad on the toe to help ease the pressure on a corn.
➤ Use a pumice stone or callus file to gently rub dead skin off a callus or hard corn.
➤ Soak a cracked callus in warm (not hot), soapy water. Rub it lightly with a pumice stone, and apply a moisturizing lotion or a hydrocortisone cream.

WHEN TO CALL THE DOCTOR

➤ If you have constant pain, redness, swelling, or discharge in the affected area. This could mean you have an infection.
➤ If you get corns or calluses and you are diabetic or have circulatory problems. You are at risk of getting a secondary infection, and you should see a doctor before trying home care.
➤ If self-care doesn't work, and you think the way you walk is causing the problem. A foot specialist (podiatrist) may prescribe custom-made shoe inserts (orthotics).

HOW TO PREVENT IT

➤ Have your feet measured by an experienced shoe salesperson, and wear only shoes that fit properly. Allow up to half an inch between your longest toe and the front of the shoe. Make sure toes can wiggle freely, and avoid pointed shoes and high heels.
➤ Keep your shoes in good condition by taking them for regular repairs. Worn soles give little protection from the shock of walking on hard surfaces, and old linings

can chafe the skin. Worn heels increase uneven pressure on the heel bone.

➤ Keep your feet dry, and make sure they don't rub against your shoes. Wearing socks or nylons and using talcum powder will help. (If wool or synthetic fibers make your feet sweat, wear cotton socks.)

➤ Rub away areas of skin buildup on the feet before they turn into corns or calluses. After bathing, rub the area gently with a pumice stone or callus file—available in drugstores.

FOR MORE HELP

Information line: American Podiatric Medical Association, 800-FOOTCARE, 24-hour recording. Takes requests for free brochures on care of the feet.

Pamphlet: American Academy of Orthopaedic Surgeons, 800-824-BONES, 24-hour recording. Ask for pamphlet titled "If the Shoe Fits, Wear It."

Dermatitis

SIGNS AND SYMPTOMS

One or more of the following, depending on the type of dermatitis:

■ Dry, reddish, itchy, thickened patches of skin on any part of the body.

■ A pink or red rash on an area that has been exposed to an irritant.

■ Circular patches of blistery, scaly, or crusted skin, usually on the legs, buttocks, hands, or arms.

■ Greasy, yellowish scales on the scalp, eyebrows, ears, or nose.

■ Scaly, reddened skin, sometimes with craterlike sores, on lower legs.

Dermatitis is another name for a skin irritation or rash. Dry, red, itchy skin is usually the first symptom; this may be followed by crusty scales or oozing blisters. There are several types of dermatitis, which vary according to the kind of rash and its location.

Contact dermatitis (red bumps and blisters that often weep and crust over) can appear anywhere on the body. It's usually caused by an irritation or allergy to a skin-care product or a plant such as poison ivy or poison oak. Common chemical irritants include detergents, soaps, chlorine, and some synthetic fibers. Wearing new clothes without washing them first can also cause contact dermatitis, as can leather, nickel-plated jewelry, rubber or latex gloves, or perfumes and other ingredients in cosmetics (see box on opposite page).

Another type, **nummular dermatitis,** is marked by coin-shaped, red, oozing patches that usually appear on the arms and legs. Older people who have dry skin or who live in dry places tend to get it, though its causes include other skin disorders and stress. Taking very hot showers can make it worse.

Seborrheic dermatitis (known as cradle cap in babies) is a red, scaly rash that appears mainly on the scalp and face. Its cause is unknown, but it may be aggravated by blocked oil glands or stress. It is common in people with immune disorders such as **AIDS** (see page 214).

Stasis dermatitis is a scaly, dry, reddish rash, usually on the lower legs and ankles. It is caused by poor circulation.

Extreme, persistent itchiness anywhere on the body may be **eczema** (see page 146), also known as atopic dermatitis.

WHAT YOU CAN DO NOW

➤ If you have signs of contact dermatitis, try to find the cause and, if possible, get rid of the irritation. If you discover, for example, that nickel-plated jewelry or foundation makeup is the problem, you can simply stop wearing them.

➤ If you suspect an allergy to cosmetics or chemicals, do an at-home patch test. Apply a small amount of the potential irritant to your arm, and cover the spot with an adhesive bandage (if you're allergic to adhesive, use gauze and paper tape). If you develop a red, itchy rash within 48 hours, then you'll know the substance is an irritant.

- Mix oatmeal or cornstarch into a warm (not hot) bath to soothe mild skin inflammations and relieve itching. Don't stay in the bath longer than 30 minutes, because water can strip sensitive skin of oils. Use mild, fragrance-free soaps or cleansers.
- Rub petroleum jelly or fragrance-free moisturizing lotion on dry, scaly skin; use calamine lotion on an oozing rash.
- For dermatitis on the scalp, try a tar shampoo. Stay out of the sun for a few hours after using it, since it increases the risk of sunburn on the scalp. (Never use this shampoo on children—it's too harsh. Use a baby shampoo instead, and wash your child's hair every day.)
- If you have red, oozing sores, apply washcloths that have been soaked in warm, salty water and wrung out. Then use an over-the-counter hydrocortisone cream.
- If you have stasis dermatitis on your lower legs and ankles, rest frequently with your legs elevated above hip level. Support stockings may also help.

WHEN TO CALL THE DOCTOR

- If your skin doesn't get better after two or three weeks of using over-the-counter creams or medicated shampoos.
- If you have sores that ooze pus or your skin shows other signs of infection.

HOW TO PREVENT IT

- If you know you've been exposed to a chemical irritant, wash your skin with a mild cleanser and water as soon as possible. For poison ivy and other plant irritants, wash the exposed areas with cold water and strong soap to remove the oil as soon as possible. Then wash the clothes you were wearing and any outdoor gear you were using.
- Use a humidifier at home and at work to keep the air from getting too dry (see box on **humidifiers,** page 89).
- Wear loose-fitting, natural-fiber clothing. Untreated cotton is ideal for sensitive skin.
- Avoid nickel-plated jewelry, especially earrings. Surgical stainless steel is the safest choice, and most people aren't bothered by 14- or 18-karat gold or sterling silver.
- Avoid contact with any substances that you suspect cause irritation.
- When washing dishes or handling chemicals, wear thin cotton gloves under rubber gloves to protect your hands.
- After bathing, moisturize your skin with fragrance-free, preservative-free lotion.

THE COSMETIC CONNECTION

If a rash develops on your face, neck, or scalp, the prime suspect could be one of your skin-care or cosmetic products. Deodorants, shampoos, makeup, perfumes, aftershaves, and suntan lotions can all irritate the skin.

The offending ingredient is usually a scent or preservative, but be wary of "unscented" products, too. They still may contain fragrances or other irritating chemicals. "Fragrance-free" is a better choice.

The claim that a cosmetic or skin-care product is hypoallergenic, nonallergenic, or organic can also be misleading, since no product is risk-free for everyone. If you have sensitive skin, you must choose your skin-care products with care. Start with fragrance-free products for sensitive skin, and try different brands until you find one that doesn't cause a rash.

FOR MORE HELP

Organization: American Academy of Dermatology, 930 N. Meacham Rd., P.O. Box 4014, Schaumburg, IL 60168-4014. 708-330-0230, M–F 8:30–5 CST. Send a business-size, self-addressed, stamped envelope for pamphlets on dermatitis. Also provides doctor referrals.

Eczema

SIGNS AND SYMPTOMS

- Very itchy, red, dry, scaly, blistered, or swollen patches of skin, usually on the wrists, hands, face, scalp, and creases of the knees and elbows.
- Oozing, crusting, thickening, or discoloration of the affected skin area (sometimes).

Eczema (atopic dermatitis) is one of the most common skin irritations (see **dermatitis,** page 144). It usually runs in families and is often associated with allergies, asthma, and stress. It can also be triggered by chemical irritants, weather extremes, sweating, and infections. Infants are prone to eczema, although many grow out of it before they turn two. If it persists after that age, a child is likely to have chronic eczema.

Eczema is rarely a serious health problem, but its symptoms can be persistent, uncomfortable, and annoying.

WHAT YOU CAN DO NOW

- ➤ Soothe itchiness and keep skin moist by taking warm (not hot) baths. Use a mild cleanser or fragrance-free soap sparingly, and don't scrub or towel your skin vigorously. Apply a fragrance-free moisturizer after bathing.
- ➤ In an older child or an adult, apply over-the-counter hydrocortisone cream. Avoid using lotions that contain preservatives, oils, or perfumes.
- ➤ Try an over-the-counter antihistamine to relieve itching.
- ➤ Wear loose, comfortable, cool clothing; sweating can make eczema worse. Avoid synthetic and wool fabrics, which may irritate the skin.
- ➤ Wear soft, cotton gloves or mittens to bed to limit scratching while asleep. This can be especially helpful for children.
- ➤ Relax and relieve stress by taking brisk walks or getting other exercise regularly.

- ➤ Try not to eat foods that seem to make your eczema flare up; some people report problems from cow's milk, eggs, wheat flour, nuts, and citrus juices.

WHEN TO CALL THE DOCTOR

Call for an immediate appointment:
- ➤ If you get a yellowish or light brown crust or pus-filled blisters on top of eczema patches. You may have a bacterial infection that needs treatment with antibiotics, or a rare but potentially serious complication caused by a herpes virus.

Call for advice and an appointment:
- ➤ If your condition doesn't get better after a week or two of home care, or if it keeps coming back. Your doctor may suggest more aggressive treatment.
- ➤ If you develop an unexplained itchy rash, and eczema or asthma runs in your family.

HOW TO PREVENT IT

- ➤ To keep skin from getting dry, take short, warm (not hot) showers or baths, and apply moisturizer immediately afterward.
- ➤ To keep your hands from getting dry and chapped, wear mittens or gloves in cold

---

ITCHING

Everybody gets itchy skin at one time or another, and often the cause is something as simple as an insect bite or dry skin. These kinds of minor ailments usually clear up on their own or are easily treated at home with moisturizing lotion or, in more persistent cases, over-the-counter hydrocortisone cream.

More rarely, itching can be a sign of a more serious disorder, such as anemia, kidney failure, or skin cancer. If you have itching accompanied by a rash, see the **rashes** chart (page 139). If you have an unexplained, persistent itch that lasts longer than ten days, call your doctor for advice and an appointment.

weather. Wearing cotton gloves under wool or synthetic-fiber gloves will help prevent irritation. Use cotton-lined rubber gloves when you are hand-washing clothes and dishes.

➤ Avoid as many skin irritants and allergy-causing agents as you can. These include soaps, detergents, fragrances, dust, pet hair, tobacco smoke, and foods that seem to make your eczema worse.

➤ Learn to spot potentially stressful situations, and practice relaxation techniques, such as yoga or meditation.

FOR MORE HELP

Information line: National Eczema Association, 810 River Rd., Fair Haven, NJ 07704. 800-818-SKIN, 24-hour line. Provides educational materials and services for people with eczema.

Organization: American Academy of Dermatology, 930 N. Meacham Rd., P.O. Box 4014, Schaumburg, IL 60168-4014. 708-330-0230, M–F 8:30–5 CST. Send a business-size, self-addressed, stamped envelope for a pamphlet on eczema. Also provides doctor referrals.

Fungal Infections

SIGNS AND SYMPTOMS

Athlete's foot:
■ Itching, scaling, and redness that usually start between the toes.
■ Dryness, flaking, or blisters on the toes or soles of the feet.
■ Toenails that thicken and become layered or scaly and yellowish.
■ Odor, in severe cases.

Jock itch:
■ Itchy, red bumps in the groin area and on the genitals of men. Rash may extend to the buttocks and inner thighs.

Yeast infection:
■ Thick, white, cheesy vaginal discharge.

■ Itching, pain, or tenderness in the genital area (men or women). In men, the head of the penis may be inflamed.
■ Pain or soreness during sex.
■ Frequent urination that may sting or burn.
■ Creamy yellow or white coating in the mouth or on the tongue that can be easily scraped off and may be painful (thrush).
■ A red, itching rash with flaky white patches on moist skin areas, such as around the genitals, between the buttocks, or under the breasts.

More people get athlete's foot (tinea pedis) than any other fungal infection. Although it can be annoying and unpleasant, it's easy to control if treated promptly.

The fungus that causes athlete's foot is similar to the ones that cause jock itch and yeast infections. It breeds in closed, damp environments and feeds on dead skin cells. Walking barefoot in the shower at a gym and around pools may increase your chance of getting athlete's foot. Moisture, sweating, and poorly ventilated shoes are likely to make it worse.

Jock itch (tinea cruris) is a fungal infection in the groin that most men get sometime in their lives. Women can get an infection similar to jock itch. The culprit in women is a yeast infection, which occurs when a particular fungus that's already in the body overgrows and displaces the helpful bacteria that normally keep it under control. It begins in the vagina and may spread if left untreated. Taking oral antibiotics or birth control pills can make you more likely to get the infection, as can pregnancy. Men, too, can get yeast infections, which irritate the penis.

People who are particularly prone to fungal infections include those who perspire a lot or who are overweight and likely to have folds of skin that rub together. If your immune system is weakened, you're likely to get them, too.

Athlete's foot, jock itch, and yeast infections can usually be cured quickly.

Athlete's foot:

➤ Wash daily, and dry carefully between the toes after showering or swimming.

➤ Apply an over-the-counter antifungal powder or cream to your feet, and sprinkle some powder in your shoes every day.

➤ Wash athletic shoes at least once a week.

➤ Wear clean cotton socks, and alternate the shoes you wear each day. Fungi take 24 hours to die.

➤ Take your shoes and socks off at home to give your feet plenty of air.

Jock itch:

➤ Use an antifungal powder, cream, or spray two or three times a day until the rash goes away; keep using the medication for at least a week after that, to make sure the fungus is dead.

➤ Change your underwear and athletic supporter daily. Wash them in hot water.

➤ Dry your groin well after showering. You can even use a hair dryer on the lowest setting to dry the area thoroughly.

Yeast infection:

➤ Use condoms or stop having sex until you get treatment if you have a vaginal yeast infection (it is contagious).

➤ Use an over-the-counter yeast medication as directed.

➤ Wear clean cotton underwear, and avoid panty hose.

WHEN TO CALL THE DOCTOR

Athlete's foot:

➤ If your foot has an odor that doesn't go away after treatment at home—a sign that you have a severe case.

➤ If your rash starts to spread or if there's no improvement after two weeks of self-care. Once athlete's foot spreads, it is difficult to get rid of and often returns.

➤ If the infection has reached your nails. This condition is hard to clear up. It also makes your nails more prone to bacterial infection, because moisture gets trapped in the cracks.

Jock itch:

➤ If over-the-counter treatments fail to work after a couple of weeks.

➤ If you develop an open sore that oozes pus; this is a sign of a secondary infection.

➤ If the rash spreads, gets worse, or keeps coming back.

Yeast infection:

➤ If you suspect you have one and you have failed to get better after using an over-the-counter medication. Once a diagnosis is confirmed, your doctor will prescribe antifungal suppositories, creams, or tablets for you (and possibly your partner).

HOW TO PREVENT IT

➤ Wash daily and dry thoroughly.

➤ Avoid tight shoes and underwear, especially in hot weather.

Athlete's foot:

➤ Wear sandals as much as possible, go barefoot at home to air your feet, and wear plastic sandals or thongs in public dressing rooms and showers.

Jock itch:

➤ Change your clothes as soon as you finish working out, and avoid sharing towels at the gym. Jock itch is mildly contagious.

Yeast infection:

➤ Don't use feminine hygiene sprays or douches, which may kill the helpful bacteria that can ward off a fungus.

➤ Don't wear nylon underwear. It doesn't allow the skin to breathe, creating an environment where fungi can flourish. Avoid noncotton athletic wear as well.

➤ Wash your workout clothes after each use in very hot water.

➤ If you have repeated bouts of the infection and you take oral contraceptives, consult your doctor about changing your birth control method.

➤ If you use a steroid inhaler for asthma, be sure that you rinse your mouth well after each use to prevent thrush from developing (see **asthma,** page 86).

FOR MORE HELP

Information line: American Podiatric Medical Association, 800-FOOTCARE, 24-hour recording. Ask for pamphlets on athlete's foot.

Organization: National Women's Health Network, 514 10th Street NW, #400, Washington, DC 20004. 202-347-1140, M–F 9–5:30 EST. Send an $8 check for an information packet on yeast infections.

Hives

SIGNS AND SYMPTOMS

- Itchy, raised, red or pink swellings on the skin (called weals). Each swelling may range in size from smaller than a pea to the size of a dinner plate.
- Weals that occur in groups.
- A weal with a whitish center, rimmed by a red rash.
- Weals that itch or burn and sting. New ones may develop as the old ones fade.
- Swelling on the lips, tongue, eyelids, mucous membranes, or genitals. Swelling may also occur on the backs of the hands and feet.

When an irritant invades your body, your immune system unleashes various chemicals, including histamine, to fight the irritant. This high histamine level can cause a temporary outbreak of hives. Many people—about one out of five—get hives at some point in their lives.

Substances that can provoke hives in vulnerable people include milk, eggs, nuts, shellfish, berries, food additives, and medicines such as penicillin and aspirin. So can insect bites, sunlight, extreme heat or cold, pressure on the skin, and sometimes infections. Stress can make hives worse.

One form of hives, known as angioedema, causes deep swelling in skin tissues such as the lips, tongue, eyelids, or genitals. This kind of swelling usually lasts 24 hours or more. Most other hives go away on their own within a few days or weeks. If they last longer than six weeks, you and your doctor may need to determine the exact cause.

WHAT YOU CAN DO NOW

- ➤ Take an antihistamine to reduce your allergic reaction and relieve discomfort.
- ➤ Soothe your skin with cold compresses or calamine lotion.
- ➤ Take a cool bath with a few tablespoons of oatmeal and cornstarch added.
- ➤ Relax with a book, some music, or a movie on videotape—tension tends to make hives worse.

WHEN TO CALL THE DOCTOR

Although generally harmless, hives can accompany more serious, and sometimes fatal, conditions. Call 911 or go to an emergency facility **immediately:**

- ➤ If you have hives accompanied by hoarseness, wheezing, cold sweats, nausea, dizziness, or difficulty breathing after a bee sting, insect bite, eating, or taking a medication; you may be experiencing **anaphylactic shock** (see page 18). If you have an emergency kit, administer the adrenaline injection.
- ➤ If burning sensations or itchy weals develop in your throat.

Call for advice:

- ➤ If you develop hives after taking medication; you may be experiencing an allergic reaction.
- ➤ If you have recurring hives over a period of a month or more.

HOW TO PREVENT IT

Finding the cause of your outbreak is the most important thing you can do. If you are reacting to a food, you will feel the hives begin within two hours after you start eating. To help identify the food:

- ➤ For a few days, eat foods that you think will not make you break out. (Some doctors recommend lamb and boiled rice.)
- ➤ Gradually add other foods back into your diet, watching carefully for a reaction.
- ➤ In a notebook, keep a list of what you eat as well as your activities and the products that you use, to discuss with your doctor.

Information line: American Academy of Allergy and Immunology, 800-822-2762, 24-hour line, 365 days a year. Ask for brochures on subjects relating to allergies and hives, as well as referrals to allergists.

Organization: Food Allergy Network, 800-929-4040, M–F 9–5 EST. Provides information, support, and a regular newsletter to people who have food allergies.

Ingrown Toenails

SIGNS AND SYMPTOMS

■ Pain, swelling, or redness on one or both sides of the toenail, usually on the big toe.

Ingrown toenails occur when the sharp corners or sides of the nail press into the flesh, typically because the toenails are cut too short or because tight shoes or hosiery press the nail into the toe. Repeatedly jamming toes into the ends of shoes can contribute to the problem. It also seems to run in some families.

Ingrown toenails sometimes become inflamed or infected, but they're easily treated at home. Infections can be treated with antibiotics, and severely ingrown nails can be cut away by a doctor using local anesthetic.

WHAT YOU CAN DO NOW

➤ Trim the excess nail, and put a strip of sterile cotton under the corner of the nail to lift it away from the skin. Change the cotton daily until the nail grows out.

➤ If there's redness, clean the area with hydrogen peroxide, then apply an over-the-counter antibacterial first-aid cream. Cover the nail with a bandage.

➤ Soak your foot in warm water or apply a warm compress if your toe aches from the ingrown nail.

➤ If it hurts a lot, take an over-the-counter painkiller.

WHEN TO CALL THE DOCTOR

➤ If redness or swelling around the nail is accompanied by severe pain or discharge.

➤ If you cannot trim the ingrown nail.

➤ If you have diabetes and an ingrown toenail becomes infected.

HOW TO PREVENT IT

➤ Always cut your toenails straight across using nail clippers, and leave enough so some of the white nail at the end still shows. If your nails are very hard, soften them by soaking your feet first.

➤ Wear comfortable hosiery and shoes (you should be able to wiggle your toes).

➤ When you buy new shoes, do it at the end of the day, when your feet are at their largest (they tend to swell during the day).

➤ Avoid pointed shoes.

➤ Don't expect to break in new shoes that pinch. They should be comfortable when you try them on.

FOR MORE HELP

Information line: American Podiatric Medical Association, 800-FOOTCARE, 24-hour recording. Takes requests for free brochures on care of the feet.

Pamphlet: American Academy of Orthopaedic Surgeons, 800-824-BONES, 24-hour recording. Ask for pamphlet titled "If the Shoe Fits, Wear It."

Lice and Scabies

SIGNS AND SYMPTOMS

Both lice and scabies:
■ Intense itching.
■ Marks and sores on the body from scratching (sometimes).

Head lice:
■ Itchy scalp.
■ Small, grayish-white, football-shaped eggs (nits) clinging to hairs close to the scalp.

- Crusty infection on the scalp.
- Grayish insects (lice) as long as an eighth of an inch, sometimes visible at the nape of the neck or behind the ears.

Body lice:
- Red, raised bumps (bites) on the shoulders, trunk, and buttocks.
- Nits found on clothing, especially in the seams of underwear.
- Headache, fever, and sick feeling accompanying swelling and infection of bites (in severe cases).

Crab lice ("crabs"):
- Itching in the genital region.
- Tiny crablike insects (the size of a flake of dandruff or smaller) on the skin in the crotch area.
- Small dark specks (crab feces) left on underwear.

Scabies:
- General itching that gets worse just after going to bed.
- A rough, red, sandpaperlike rash with itchy, raised bumps, mainly on the wrists, elbows, breasts, genitals, around the waist, and on the webs between the fingers.
- Dotted lines or wavy gray ridges like pencil marks on the skin.
- Large areas of crusty, thickened, itchy skin (Norwegian scabies).
- In adults, itching from the neck down only. (Babies and young children may have itching on the face.)

As bad as the itching caused by lice and scabies is, it's often overshadowed by the embarrassment that accompanies an infestation of these tiny pests. But there's no reason for shame: Lice and scabies can infest anyone, anywhere. In fact, in recent years there has been an epidemic of head lice in the United States, with 6 million to 12 million cases reported yearly.

Lice are wingless insects that feed on human blood. Three distinct types take up residence on the scalp, the body, and the pubic region, respectively. Lice are most commonly detected from August through November, and they are easily spread by physical contact or by sharing clothes, combs, and bedding. Crab lice, the kind that infests the pubic area, are usually spread by sexual contact, but they can also be contracted from toilet seats.

Scabies is an allergic reaction caused by a burrowing mite that lays eggs in tunnels under the upper layer of human skin. A rash begins to itch about two weeks after infestation. By the time you realize you have scabies, you may already have an extensive infestation. Scabies is usually transmitted through close physical contact, including sex, and through sharing clothes.

While lice and scabies are very annoying, rapid treatment usually gets rid of them.

WHAT YOU CAN DO NOW

The most effective way to rid yourself of lice and scabies, according to many experts, is to cover the affected part of the body with an over-the-counter shampoo or cream that contains permethrin, pyrethrin, or pyrethrum.

Head lice:
- ➤ Cover the scalp with a lotion or shampoo containing 1 percent permethrin (or pyrethrin), following package directions.
- ➤ To soften and remove nits, shampoo hair in warm water and then comb the nits out with a fine-tooth comb while the hair is still wet. (Give haircuts to young children to make the process easier.)
- ➤ Vacuum thoroughly, and wash sheets, towels, and clothes in hot water; dry for at least 20 minutes in a dryer set on high. Iron or dry-clean clothes that can't be washed. Seal stuffed animals and pillows that can harbor lice in plastic bags, and keep them out of the reach of children for at least 20 days.
- ➤ Boil combs, curlers, and brushes.
- ➤ If your child has repeated infestations of head lice and you want an alternative to pyrethrin shampoos, some doctors recommend this: Mix 50 drops of tea tree oil (available in health food stores) in two ounces of warm olive oil; apply it to the hair and scalp. Cover with a shower cap and a hot, moist towel for two hours. Then rinse the hair well and comb out the nits with a fine-tooth comb.

Body lice:
➤ Bathe with soap and water.
➤ Apply an antilouse cream to the entire body.
➤ Vacuum floors, and wash clothes and linens as directed for head lice.

Crab lice:
➤ Use an antilouse shampoo according to package directions.
➤ Ask your doctor to test you for other sexually transmitted diseases.
➤ Be sure that your sexual partner is treated.

Scabies:
➤ Call your doctor for an immediate appointment. The most effective, safe treatment (a preparation containing 5 percent permethrin or pyrethrin) is available only by prescription.
➤ Wash clothing and linens as directed for head lice.
➤ Be sure that all family members and people with whom you've been in close contact are treated at the same time.

Lice and scabies:
➤ Because all louse and scabies removers are poisons, it is important to wait at least ten days between treatments. Your skin may continue to itch long after the mites and lice are dead.
➤ Don't try drastic home remedies such as scrubbing with harsh soaps or dousing yourself with kerosene.

WHEN TO CALL THE DOCTOR

Lice will almost always respond to one thorough home treatment. But be sure to call your doctor:
➤ If you have any form of scabies.
➤ If you are unsure of the cause of your itching; other rashes and conditions can mimic the symptoms of scabies.
➤ If you become reinfested after treatment.
➤ If your sores become infected and ooze.
➤ If you have lice on your eyelashes; your doctor may need to remove the pests.
➤ If a baby or young child is infested.
➤ If the itching is driving you crazy.
➤ If you develop a rash or have a seizure after using a medicated cream or shampoo.

Warning:
➤ The chemical lindane, used in some treatments for lice and scabies, is no longer recommended because it is a neurotoxin that can cause convulsions and other problems. Ask your doctor for an alternative.

HOW TO PREVENT IT

Head lice:
➤ Use a flashlight to check your children for lice, especially from August through November. Look for bites, nits, or lice at the nape of the neck and behind the ears.

All infestations:
➤ Wash clothes after one or two wearings.
➤ Wash towels and linens frequently.
➤ Bathe or shower regularly.
➤ Don't share hats, combs, headphones, and other personal items.
➤ Practice safe sex, and share sexual histories with new partners.

FOR MORE HELP

Information line: National Pediculosis Association, P.O. Box 610189, Newton, MA 02161-0189. 617-449-6487, M–F 9–4 EST. Ask for information on screening programs, educational materials, and the latest methods of treatment.

Organization: American Academy of Dermatology, 930 N. Meacham Rd., P.O. Box 4014, Schaumburg, IL 60168-4014. 708-330-0230, M–F 8:30–5 CST. Send a business-size, self-addressed, stamped envelope for a pamphlet on scabies. Also provides doctor referrals.

Psoriasis

SIGNS AND SYMPTOMS

■ Pink, raised patches of skin covered with flaky, white scales, possibly itchy or painful—most often on knees, elbows, and scalp, less often in armpits, under breasts, on genitals, and around the anus.
■ Pitted fingernails that may loosen or become crumbly.

- Raised areas on the hands and feet that may crack or form blisters filled with pus.
- Stiffness and inflammation in fingers and toes, from a form of arthritis associated with 10 percent of psoriasis cases.
- Small, scaly patches triggered by a sore throat and strep infection (mostly in teens and young adults).

The scales of psoriasis are dense piles of dead skin formed when cells in the outer layer (the epidermis) multiply faster than they can be worn away. The condition, which is not contagious, sometimes runs in families. It shows up most often in people between 10 and 30 years old.

Skin injury and infection are among the suspected causes. Another suspect is emotional stress, though some experts caution against attributing psoriasis to stress. More often, the condition itself brings on feelings of low self-esteem and depression—making dealing with the emotions an important part of the overall therapy.

Some people keep psoriasis in check by using moisturizers. Others, especially those who have it on their hands and feet or on more than 30 percent of their body, may need to use stronger measures.

Although there isn't a cure, most psoriasis can be helped by a mixture of medical treatment and home care. Some commonly used medical treatments include steroid creams, ultraviolet light treatments, and oral medications, including methotrexate, an anti-cancer drug.

WHAT YOU CAN DO NOW

➤ Follow your doctor's skin-care instructions faithfully, even though they may be time-consuming.
➤ Don't pick at your scales: This can cause new scales to form.
➤ Soak the patches in warm, not hot, water. When the scales are plumped up with water, gently remove whatever will come away easily with a loofah sponge or pumice stone.
➤ Apply moisturizers to trap water in the skin. Petroleum jelly and cooking oil will do the job inexpensively.
➤ Sunbathing helps clear up the skin. The trick is to stay in the sun until just before you burn—talk with your doctor about finding the right balance.
➤ If you suspect that your flare-ups are triggered by stress, consider learning stress-management techniques such as yoga or meditation.

WHEN TO CALL THE DOCTOR

Call for an immediate appointment:
➤ If you develop pus-filled blisters or your whole body is red and scaly; you may need emergency treatment.

Call for advice:
➤ If psoriasis flares up whenever you have a sore throat, ask your doctor for medication to combat a sore throat at the first sign of illness.
➤ If symptoms don't respond to home care.

HOW TO PREVENT IT

There is no known way to prevent psoriasis.

FOR MORE HELP

Information line: National Psoriasis Foundation, 800-723-9166, M–F 9–5 PST. Staffers answer questions about causes, treatments, physician referrals, and legal matters. They also send out pamphlets and a newsletter.

Information packet: National Institute of Arthritis and Musculoskeletal and Skin Diseases Information Clearinghouse, 301-495-4484, 24-hour line. Request a packet of recent articles on psoriasis.

Shingles

The first symptoms of shingles vary widely from person to person and can resemble other sources of pain, including muscle strain or a heart attack. Watch for:

- Mysterious pain (sometimes pulsating or seemingly unbearable) and tingling, itching, or extreme sensitivity in an area of skin on only one side of the body or face.
- Fever and headache.
- A red, blistering rash in a band on one side of the body. This rash may show up one to three days after the first symptoms; if confined to one side of the body, it almost always indicates shingles. In very rare cases, the rash may appear on both sides of the body.
- Fluid-filled blisters that scab over, usually in two to three weeks.
- Pain and sensitivity to touch that may last longer than the blisters.

Thought chicken pox was behind you? Think again. Anyone who has had chicken pox has a chance of getting shingles as an adult. That's because chicken pox and the painful blistering of shingles are caused by the same herpes virus. Instead of going away when the chicken pox sores dry up, the virus hides in the nerve cells near the spine, sometimes for decades. Later, perhaps because the immune system is weakened or stressed, the virus reappears in its new form, inflaming particular nerve pathways.

Shingles is most common in adults over 50, and half of people over 85 have had it. People with immune systems compromised by AIDS, Hodgkin's disease, leukemia, or some kinds of drugs are also more likely to get shingles.

You can't catch shingles from someone. But if you've never had chicken pox, there's a small chance that you will get chicken pox when you come in contact with fluid from the broken blisters of someone with shingles. Newborns, in particular, are at high risk.

In the worst-case scenario, affecting 10 to 15 percent of people with shingles, the condition can cause shooting, burning pain that continues for a month or more after the blisters have gone away. In fact, this severe shingles pain (called postherpetic neuralgia) is the leading cause of suicide among people over 70 who suffer unmanageable pain. Antiviral drugs are now available that halt the disease, however, and the chances of developing this type of chronic pain are reduced if shingles is treated promptly.

Most people who get shingles recover fully in a few weeks, and recurrences are rare.

- Call your doctor for advice when you notice the first symptoms of shingles. The earlier you take an antiviral medication, the better your chances of avoiding the pain that shingles can cause.
- Use cool compresses or ice packs to dull the pain.
- Take over-the-counter pain relievers.
- Relieve the itching with calamine lotion.
- Ask your doctor about using over-the-counter capsaicin cream, made from the fiery substance in chili peppers, to help alleviate the severe pain of postherpetic neuralgia. Use it only after the blisters are completely healed.
- Put a few tablespoons of oatmeal or cornstarch in your bathwater.
- Do not scratch; the blisters can become infected or leave scars.
- If you have severe chronic pain, consider joining a chronic pain support group.

Call your doctor for emergency advice (if not available, call 911 or go to an emergency facility):

- If you have eye pain or a fluid-filled blister on your face; you may be at risk of getting herpes in your eye, which can lead to blindness.

Call for an immediate appointment:

➤ If you have a fever over 101 degrees or swelling, redness, and pus; this can signal a generalized infection or a bacterial infection in the blisters.

➤ If the pain becomes too great to bear. Call for advice:

➤ If you develop symptoms of shingles.

HOW TO PREVENT IT

There is no known way to prevent shingles. A vaccine for chicken pox is now available, but its effects on shingles are unknown.

FOR MORE HELP

Information line: National Institute of Neurological Disorders and Stroke, 800-352-9424, M–F 9–5 EST. Ask for publications on shingles and postherpetic neuralgia.

Information line: American Chronic Pain Association, P.O. Box 850, Rocklin, CA 95677. 916-632-0922, 24-hour line. Ask for literature and information about support groups run by and for those with chronic pain.

Skin Cancer

SIGNS AND SYMPTOMS

Basal cell carcinoma:

■ A pearly or translucent skin growth, often with a dent in the center and raised edges, that gradually expands.

■ A patch of skin that itches, bleeds, hurts, or forms a scab.

■ An open sore that fails to heal in one month or that closes and reopens.

Squamous cell carcinoma:

■ Reddish or brownish, rough, scaly patches on skin that has been exposed to sunlight (often the first sign of this cancer).

■ A persistent, scaly patch that sometimes crusts or bleeds.

■ A raised growth that looks like a wart and sometimes bleeds.

■ A firm, fleshy lump that gets bigger and bigger.

Malignant melanoma:

■ A mole that changes in appearance; it may become scaly or ooze, bleed, or enlarge.

■ A dark area of the skin that feels itchy, or the sudden appearance of a "bubbly" mole.

■ Dark spots or moles that have these "ABCD" traits: Asymmetrical; Border: blurry; Color: uneven; Diameter: larger than a pencil eraser.

About half of Americans living to age 65 will develop skin cancer at least once. (See color illustrations, page 166.) There are three main kinds:

Basal cell carcinoma: the most common kind in Caucasians; often found on the face. It develops slowly and usually doesn't send cancer cells to other parts of the body.

Squamous cell carcinoma: usually found on the face, lips, or rim of the ear. It grows more quickly than basal cell and can form large masses. If neglected, it can spread to other parts of the body.

Malignant melanoma: the most aggressive type of skin cancer. A cancer of the dark-pigmented cells that produce melanin, it frequently spreads to other parts of the body and can be fatal if left untreated.

People who had at least one bad sunburn as children have a greater chance of getting skin cancer later in life than those who did not. The risk rises for people who live in Sun Belt states; work outside; have two or more relatives who have had skin cancer; or have light-colored eyes, red or blond hair, and skin that freckles easily. If you have brown or black skin, you are less likely to get skin cancer, but you still run a risk.

The good news is that skin cancer is nearly always curable if diagnosed in time. And because exposure to the sun is the main cause, skin cancer is preventable.

➤ Don't delay going to a doctor if you suspect you have skin cancer. The earlier it's diagnosed, the better your chance of successful treatment.

WHEN TO CALL THE DOCTOR

Call for an immediate appointment:
➤ If you have an itchy mole or a dark spot or bump that changes color, bleeds, or oozes. (See color illustrations, page 167.)

Call for advice:
➤ If you see any of the signs of skin cancer.
➤ If what looks like a pimple crusts over, doesn't go away, and gets bigger.
➤ If you develop a lump on or beneath an area of your skin normally exposed to the sun and it doesn't disappear after two weeks of home treatment with warm compresses.

HOW TO PREVENT IT

Since sun exposure causes 90 percent of skin cancers, the best way to prevent them is to avoid that exposure as much as you can.
➤ Apply a sunscreen of SPF 15 or higher 30 minutes before you go outside for any length of time, and wear a hat, long-sleeved shirt, and long pants. (Remember that ultraviolet rays can penetrate haze.) Avoid being outdoors between 10AM and 2PM (or if possible, 4PM), when the sun's rays are most intense.
➤ Don't go to tanning salons—they use harmful ultraviolet light.
➤ Don't use suntan oil; it doesn't protect your skin.
➤ Do a skin self-exam periodically (see box at right). If you are light-skinned, have freckles, burn without tanning, or have a family history of skin cancer, visit your doctor for an initial checkup and help in recognizing danger signs.

FOR MORE HELP

Information line: Cancer Information Service, 800-422-6237, M–F 9–4:30 your time. In English and Spanish. Offers literature, treatment information, access to a database of clinical trials, and referrals to cancer-related community resources.

Information line: American Cancer Society, 800-227-2345, M–F 9–5 your time. Offers information about classes and activities in your area.

Video: *Skin Cancer at Time of Diagnosis.* Clear, useful overview of causes and treatments, consisting of four reports—Understanding the Diagnosis, What Happens Next?, Treatment and Management, and Issues and Answers. Time Life Medical, 1996, $19.95.

SIMPLE STEPS TO SAVE YOUR SKIN

■ Standing in front of a mirror, examine your front and, using a hand mirror, your back. Look for any abnormal lumps or new growths. (See color illustrations, page 167.)
■ Raise your arms and turn to the right and left as you examine your sides and underarms.
■ Bend your arms and look carefully at them from fingertips to shoulders, including the undersides.
■ Sit down and use the hand mirror to look at the backs of your legs, the soles of your feet, and the spaces between your toes.
■ Use the hand mirror to look at the back of your neck and your scalp, or ask someone to check these areas for you.

Warts

Common warts:

■ Small, hard, rough, raised growths that usually appear on the skin of the hands and fingers.

Plantar warts:

■ Same hard growths as common warts but on the soles of the feet, sometimes making walking painful.

Flat warts:

■ Groups of up to several hundred small, flat growths, often found on the face, neck, chest, knees, hands, wrists, or forearms.

Filiform warts:

■ Thin, threadlike growths that take root on the face or neck.

Genital warts:

■ Itchy, small bumps, round or flat, sometimes in groups, that appear on or near the genitals.

In folklore, warts come from handling frogs or toads. But the real source is any one of the more than 60 varieties of the human papilloma virus.

Most warts, except the genital variety, are not very contagious. You develop them by coming into contact with skin shed from a wart (either your own or someone else's). The virus enters through a cut or nick in the skin, causing skin cells to multiply rapidly, creating a new wart.

Children, young adults, and people with immune system deficiencies are most likely to get warts. In children, warts nearly always go away on their own within a year or so, but in adults they may take longer or need to be removed.

WHAT YOU CAN DO NOW

If you don't mind your warts, relax; they're harmless. If they bother you, you can probably get good results removing them at home. If you're over 45 and a new wart appears, check with a doctor before trying home care.

➤ The standard method for removing warts, when they are not on the face or the genitals, is to use an over-the-counter wart remover (salicylic acid). It gently peels the surface of the wart away until the body's immune forces can attack the virus lodged inside. You may need many applications to get the job done.

➤ Plantar warts often extend below the surface of the skin; removal may require the help of a skin specialist (dermatologist). Using padded insoles in your shoes may reduce discomfort.

WHEN TO CALL THE DOCTOR

➤ If you or your partner have genital warts, which can be contagious and also have been associated with cervical cancer in women (see **sexually transmitted diseases** chart, page 215).

➤ If you are over 45 and you find a new wart. Your doctor will want to check it to make sure it's not **skin cancer** (see page 155; see also color illustration, page 166).

➤ If you want a wart on your face removed, and you don't want to risk scarring.

➤ If you have a wart that does not respond to home treatment, particularly if it bleeds or changes color.

HOW TO PREVENT IT

➤ Don't scratch existing warts—it may cause them to spread.

➤ When shaving, use an electric razor to avoid the small nicks and scratches that may give viruses a point of entry.

➤ Don't touch other people's warts.

➤ When using public showers, wear sandals or other footwear.

FOR MORE HELP

Organization: American Academy of Dermatology, 930 N. Meacham Rd., P.O. Box 4014, Schaumburg, IL 60168-4014, 708-330-0230, M–F 8:30–5 CST. Send a business-size, self-addressed, stamped envelope for a pamphlet on warts. Also provides doctor referrals.

Muscles, Bones, & Joints

◆

Arthritis

Osteoarthritis:
- Joint pain that is made worse by movement.
- Stiffness in the morning.
- Knobby growths on the joints of the fingers.

Rheumatoid arthritis:
- Painful, red, swollen joints that may feel warm.
- Low fever, loss of appetite, and weight loss; feeling "sick all over."
- Stiffness in the morning.
- Skin lumps, usually on the elbows, fingers, or buttocks.
- Dry eyes and mouth.

Gout:
- Severe, sudden pain in a joint, often the wrist, big toe, or knee.
- Redness, swelling around joint.
- Fever.

Arthritis is an inflammation of the joints usually caused by wear and tear, injury, or infection. Some arthritis seems to run in families. There are more than 100 types of arthritis, ranging from mild to disabling. The three most common types are:

Osteoarthritis: This condition is marked by chips and cracks in the smooth cartilage that lines the joints (see color illustration, page 163). The bone ends may rub together and develop growths called spurs. Osteoarthritis affects about half of those over 65, usually in the hands or in large weight-bearing joints such as the knee and the hip.

Rheumatoid arthritis: In this type of arthritis, the lining of the capsule surrounding a joint becomes inflamed and thickened, causing swelling, pain, and stiffness. Organs such as the eyes and lungs may become inflamed as well. The cause is believed to be autoimmune (the body's immune system attacking itself). It usually affects those between 20 and 50 years old, and more women than men.

Gout: It usually occurs in men over 40 and is caused by elevated blood levels of uric acid, one of the body's waste products, which forms crystals in the joints. The immune system reacts to these crystals as if to a foreign invader, and the joint becomes inflamed and painful. Symptoms subside in about a week.

Treatment of arthritis depends on the type and severity. Most can be treated effectively with pain relievers, anti-inflammatories, and gentle exercise to keep the bones and muscles strong. Recurrent gout can be treated with medications to reduce uric acid in the blood. In more severe cases of osteoarthritis and rheumatoid arthritis, surgery may smooth roughened joint surfaces or replace a damaged joint.

WHAT YOU CAN DO NOW

➤ For rheumatoid arthritis, take aspirin, or the anti-inflammatory pain reliever

Neck Pain

SYMPTOMS	WHAT IT MIGHT BE	WHAT YOU CAN DO
Severe headache followed by neck pain and stiffness; sometimes accompanied by nausea, drowsiness, or sensitivity to light.	Meningitis—infection of tissue around brain (see page 56).	Call 911 or go to emergency facility **immediately.**
Severe pain and/or swelling in neck following injury; numbness, muscle weakness, or paralysis below injured area; lack of bladder or bowel control; shock.	Spinal cord injury (see head, neck, and back injuries, page 37).	Call 911 **immediately.** Never attempt to move someone who may have a spinal cord injury.
Intense neck pain, especially when moving head; or tingling, numbness, or weakness in one arm.	Protruded disk irritating or pressing on a nerve (see low back pain, page 182).	With sudden numbness or weakness, call doctor for emergency advice; if not available, call 911 or go to emergency facility. Otherwise, call doctor for advice and appointment. Take pain relievers (see box, page 301), and rest.
Pain and stiffness that begin in neck and move to shoulders, upper arms, hands, or back of head; numbness or tingling in arms, head, and fingers; weakness in arms and legs.	Cervical spondylosis—breakdown of joints in neck that may put pressure on nerves and muscles.	With numbness and tingling, call doctor for immediate appointment. Otherwise, call for advice and appointment. Apply moist heat. Sleep with thin pillow under head and thin, rolled-up towel under neck.
Pain and tenderness in front of neck, fever, swelling.	Thyroiditis (see thyroid problems, page 279).	Call doctor for immediate appointment.
Neck pain or stiffness that starts within 24 hours of a jolt (such as car stopping suddenly); may be accompanied by dizziness, headache, vomiting, or difficulty walking.	Whiplash—also known as cervical acceleration/deceleration injury.	Call doctor for immediate appointment. Wear soft, padded collar to immobilize neck. Sleep with thin pillow under head and thin, rolled-up towel under neck. Apply ice pack, and take pain relievers (see box, page 301).

(continued)

Neck Pain *(continued)*

SYMPTOMS	WHAT IT MIGHT BE	WHAT YOU CAN DO
Neck stiffness that may be accompanied by pain or swelling in other joints.	Arthritis.	See arthritis, page 158.
Neck stiffness or pain on waking, or when sitting or standing.	Strained neck muscles or joints from sleeping or sitting in awkward position.	Sleep with thin pillow under head and thin, rolled-up towel under neck. If stiffness or pain persists beyond 24 hours, call doctor for advice and appointment.
Pain with swelling or lump on side or back of neck.	Swollen lymph nodes from infection somewhere in body.	See infections, page 274.

recommended by your doctor. If these medicines upset your stomach, try an "enteric-coated" brand. Those with osteoarthritis should use acetaminophen. Those with gout should not take aspirin. (See **pain relievers** box, page 301.)
➤ Apply heat or cold packs to painful or stiff joints. Try taking warm baths, too.
➤ Apply an over-the-counter cream or lotion containing capsaicin or an over-the-counter cream containing methyl salicylate for pain relief.
➤ Use electric can openers and enlarged grips for pens or tools to ease the strain on painful joints.
➤ Don't grip objects tightly for long periods.
➤ Make sure you get plenty of rest.

WHEN TO CALL THE DOCTOR

➤ If you develop joint pain or stiffness that interferes with normal activities.
➤ If you experience fever or chills along with other arthritis symptoms. You could have infectious arthritis, which is caused by a bacterium.
➤ If you develop the acutely painful symptoms of gout.
➤ If your arthritis is not improving.

HOW TO PREVENT IT

Osteoarthritis:
➤ Exercise regularly and moderately to keep your muscles and bones strong.
➤ Maintain a healthy weight; this lessens the pressure on weight-bearing joints.
➤ Avoid repetitive activities, such as typing, that lead to joint overuse.
➤ Maintain good posture; it lessens the stress on joints.

Rheumatoid arthritis:
There's no known prevention for rheumatoid arthritis.

Gout:
➤ Control your weight, but don't fast; fasting can raise levels of uric acid.
➤ Don't drink heavily (no more than two 1.5-ounce drinks of hard liquor, two 5-ounce glasses of wine, or two 12-ounce cans of beer a day for men, one for women). Also, control high blood pressure. Both are associated with gout.
➤ Avoid protein-rich foods such as organ meats, shellfish, and dried beans, which are all associated with gout.
➤ Drink plenty of water.

(continued on page 177)

The Body Illustrated

Each part of the human body works with other parts to keep the whole system in good repair—usually. Sometimes, as you can see in the remarkable illustrations beginning on this page, something breaks down: Thinning cartilage in a joint can lead to arthritis, for example; thickening of artery walls to a heart attack; or aging of the lens of the eye to cataracts.

CATARACT LENS REPLACEMENT

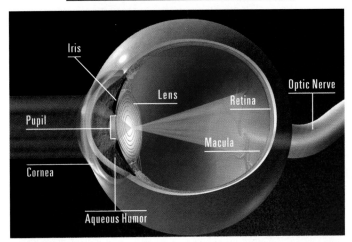

The healthy eye acts like a camera. The cornea and the lens focus light on the retina; from there, signals travel through the optic nerve to the brain and are translated into images. A cataract—clouding of the lens—distorts the focus, blurs vision, and can cause blindness.

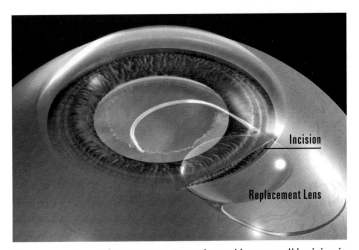

Surgeons can repair a severe cataract by making a small incision in the cornea, popping out the cloudy lens, and slipping a clear plastic replacement into the pouch where the original sat. The incision is usually stitched with special thread that does not have to be removed.

Back pain strikes half of all Americans every year. The lower back (lumbar region) supports 70 percent of the body's weight and is often affected by chronic pain. Even sitting at a desk can cause back pain.

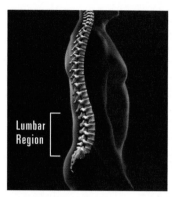

Lumbar Region

The spine consists of a column of 26 individual bones, the vertebrae. The spinal cord, a thick bundle of nerves, runs through the column.

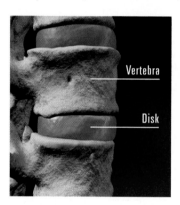

Vertebra

Disk

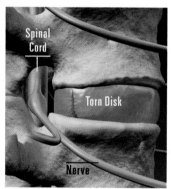

Spinal Cord

Torn Disk

Nerve

Disks between the vertebrae allow movement in the spinal column. They act as shock absorbers, cushioning the impact of walking and other motion. They have a tough outside shell and a soft gel-like center. Aging and stress on the spine can cause the shell of a disk to bulge and tear.

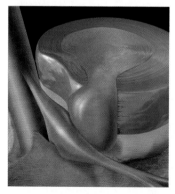

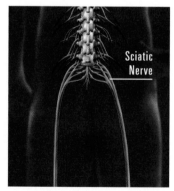

Sciatic Nerve

The bulging disk, which sometimes leaks its contents, may press on a nerve. When that happens to the sciatic nerve, pain and numbness may be felt in the legs. That's because the sciatic nerve, which starts at the base of the spine, carries nerve impulses down the legs to the feet.

Arthritis is a name for many kinds of inflammation and pain in the joints. Nearly 16 million of us have a touch of the "wear and tear" type (osteoarthritis), which is most common in people over 45.

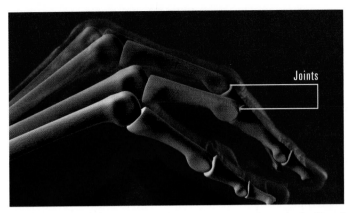

Joints

The highly mobile joints of the hands are often the first to feel stiff and painful. Other joints that commonly become arthritic are in the neck, knees, hips, spine, and big toes. Here's how osteoarthritis progresses:

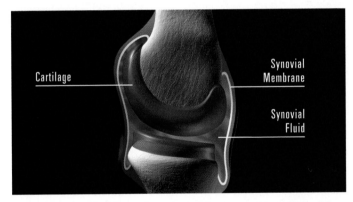

Cartilage

Synovial Membrane

Synovial Fluid

In a young joint, the place where the two bones meet is cushioned by a layer of smooth cartilage. The joint itself is sealed in a capsule filled with synovial fluid—a thick lubricant resembling egg white.

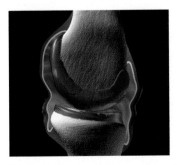

Bone Spur

Loose Body

With age, the cartilage develops pits and becomes frayed. Unprotected, rough surfaces of bone rub against each other. They may also develop small bumps—spurs—that cause pain. Bits of bone and cartilage, called loose bodies, may break free and float in the joint space, causing additional pain and restricting movement of the joint.

Though it looks hard and solid, bone is built around a porous core, which keeps it both light and strong. Osteoporosis, the gradual weakening of the bone core, affects 25 million Americans, most of them women.

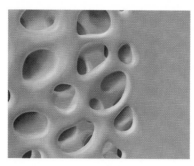

The center of the bone is honeycombed with open spaces. Surrounding and protecting this core is a hard, compact layer. In both, special cells constantly tear down and rebuild calcium deposits.

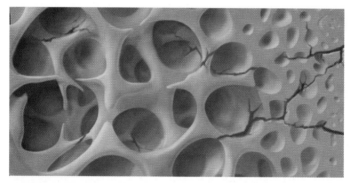

If withdrawals of calcium exceed deposits, tearing down outstrips rebuilding, and osteoporosis develops. The bridges of bone between the open spaces become thin, brittle, and easily broken.

When the bones of the spine have been weakened by osteoporosis, even the pressure of normal body weight can cause them to develop networks of tiny cracks called compression fractures.

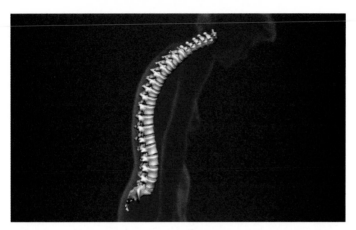

Over time, these small fractures can lead to chronic back pain, loss of height, and the curvature of the spine known as dowager's hump.

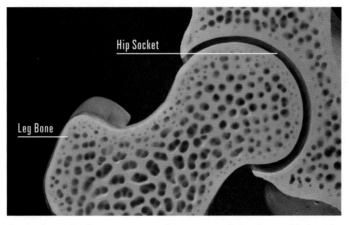

Hip Socket

Leg Bone

Sometimes the first symptom of osteoporosis is a bone that breaks for no apparent reason. Bones with large porous areas, like the bones of the hip joint, are especially vulnerable to fractures.

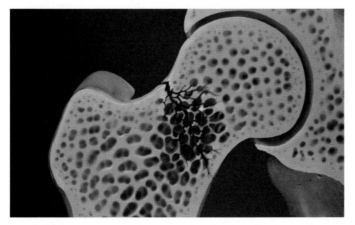

Minor falls and jolts that wouldn't hurt a younger person—even sitting down too quickly—can damage and break weakened bones.

Skin cancer affects one in six people in this country. Most skin cancers are caused by harmful ultraviolet (UV) rays from the sun and can easily be prevented by staying out of the sun and wearing sunscreen.

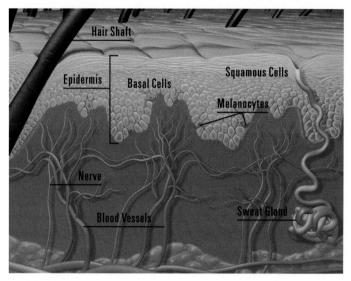

The top layer of the skin (the epidermis) is made of three kinds of cells: squamous cells, basal cells, and melanocytes. Cancer occurs when skin cells begin to reproduce uncontrollably, forming tumors.

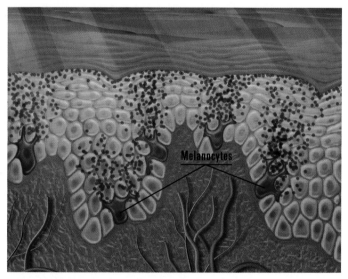

A tan is the skin's emergency response to UV rays from the sun. When UV light hits, melanocytes try to repair the damage by releasing more melanin, a dark pigment, and multiplying faster than usual. Also, over time, elastic tissues in the lower layer begin to wrinkle and sag.

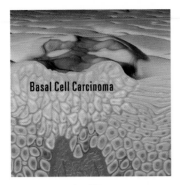

Basal Cell Carcinoma

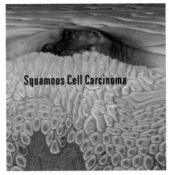

Squamous Cell Carcinoma

When a basal cell becomes cancerous, it produces a cluster of cells—called a carcinoma—which may look like a shiny, waxy pimple. When a squamous cell becomes cancerous, it forms a rough, thick carcinoma that may have a hard crust on its surface.

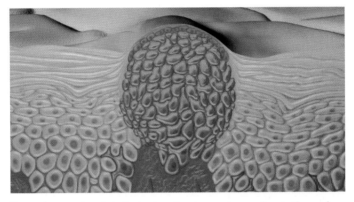

Sometimes a closely knit cluster of melanocytes pushes to the surface of the skin, forming a dark and compact, but harmless, mole.

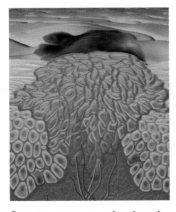

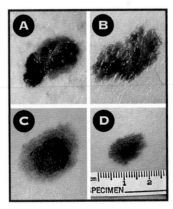

Sun exposure can stimulate the melanocytes to multiply wildly into a cancerous tumor known as a malignant melanoma. Sometimes cells from a melanoma break away and form cancerous tumors in other parts of the body.

These signs distinguish a melanoma from a normal mole:
Asymmetrical shape.
Borders are blurry.
Color varies within mole.
Diameter larger than a pencil eraser.

Most of the 12 million people with asthma feel as if they can't get enough air into their lungs during an attack. The reason is that they can't get "old" air out of their lungs when the airways become narrowed.

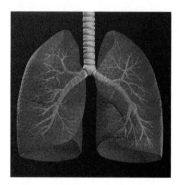

When you breathe in, air travels into each lung through bronchial tubes that branch into smaller and smaller passageways.

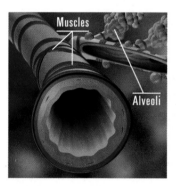

Finally, air reaches the tiny, grapelike alveoli, which pass oxygen from the air into the bloodstream. When a person with asthma inhales dust, pollen, or any other allergy-causing substance, the lining of the bronchial tubes swells. The person may wheeze when breathing.

The muscles around the bronchial tubes can also start to tighten, making breathing even more difficult. People with asthma may use as much as 25 times more effort to take a breath than people without it. In a severe attack, the lining of the bronchial tubes produces sticky mucus, further restricting lung capacity and causing a weak cough.

Atherosclerosis is a thickening and hardening of the arteries. The process can start as early as childhood and can continue unnoticed for decades until the buildup causes a heart attack or stroke.

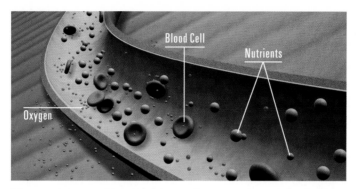

The arteries carry blood rich in nutrients, oxygen, and other substances, including cholesterol, from the heart and lungs to the body.

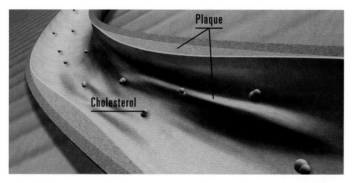

Over time, the walls of an artery may collect dense streaks of minerals and fats. (Cholesterol is depicted here without other blood components.) These streaks, which bulge from the wall, are called plaque.

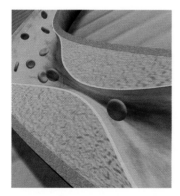
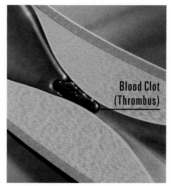

As plaque continues to narrow an artery, it restricts the amount of blood that can flow through. Its bulging, uneven surface also allows blood clots to form easily. A clot that wedges in a narrowed spot and blocks the flow of blood entirely can cause a heart attack or stroke.

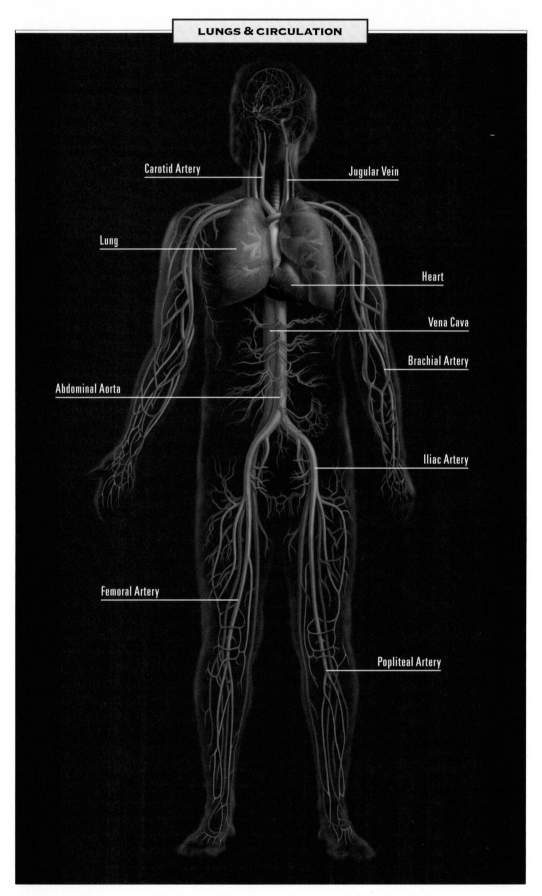

Carotid Artery

Jugular Vein

Lung

Heart

Vena Cava

Brachial Artery

Abdominal Aorta

Iliac Artery

Femoral Artery

Popliteal Artery

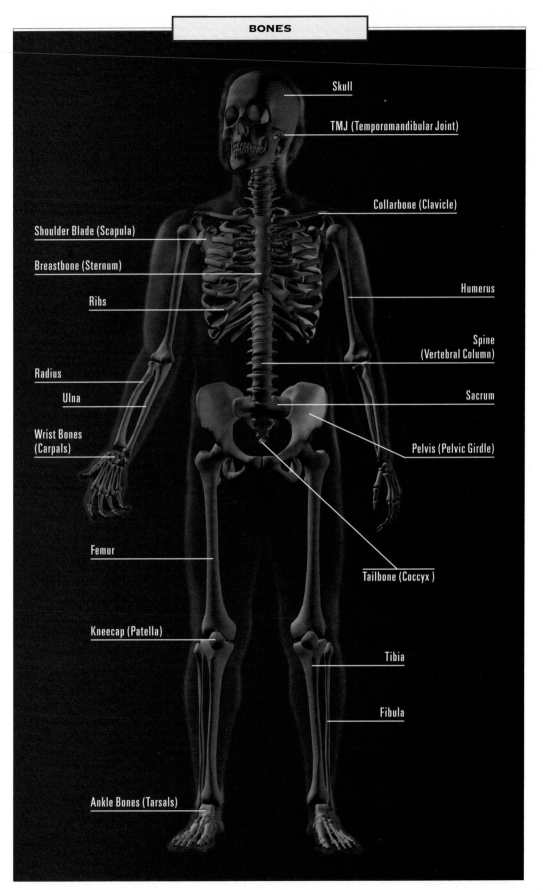

Skull

TMJ (Temporomandibular Joint)

Collarbone (Clavicle)

Shoulder Blade (Scapula)

Breastbone (Sternum)

Ribs

Humerus

Spine
(Vertebral Column)

Radius

Ulna

Sacrum

Wrist Bones
(Carpals)

Pelvis (Pelvic Girdle)

Femur

Tailbone (Coccyx)

Kneecap (Patella)

Tibia

Fibula

Ankle Bones (Tarsals)

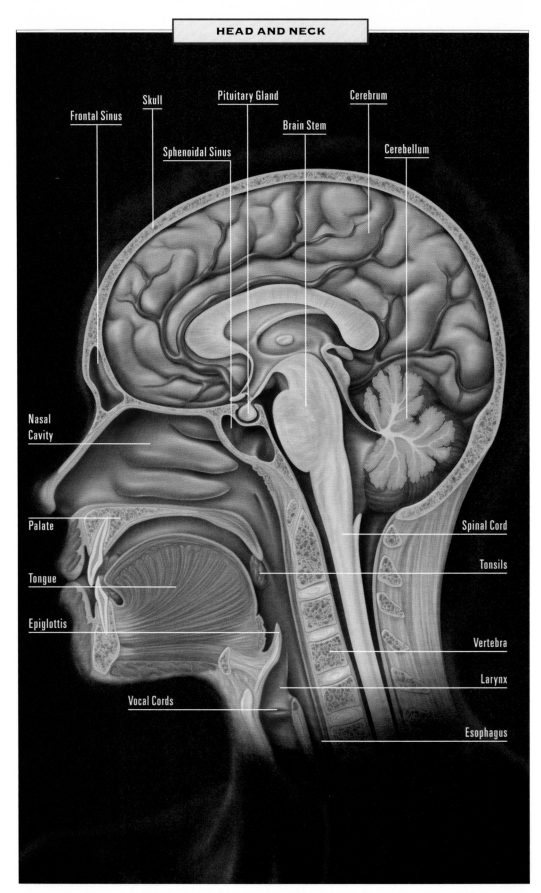

Frontal Sinus

Skull

Pituitary Gland

Cerebrum

Brain Stem

Sphenoidal Sinus

Cerebellum

Nasal Cavity

Palate

Tongue

Epiglottis

Vocal Cords

Spinal Cord

Tonsils

Vertebra

Larynx

Esophagus

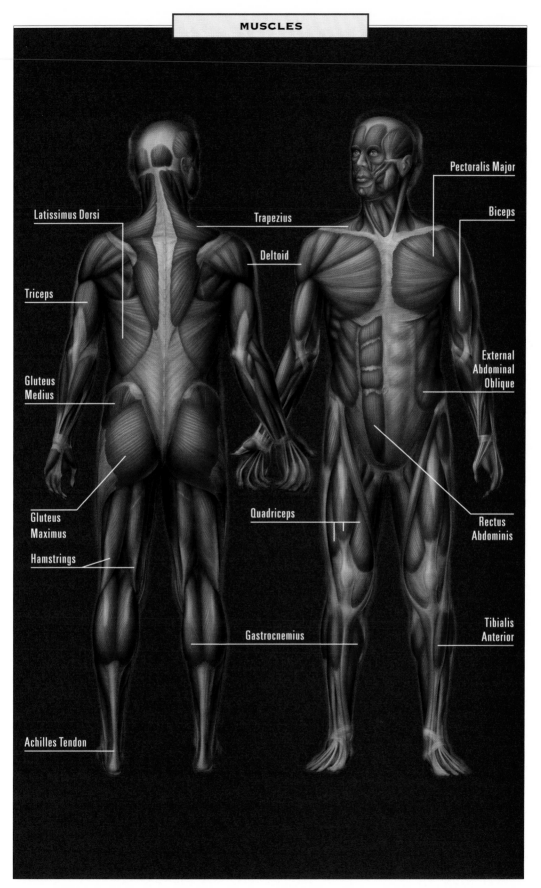

Latissimus Dorsi

Trapezius

Pectoralis Major

Biceps

Deltoid

Triceps

External
Abdominal
Oblique

Gluteus
Medius

Gluteus
Maximus

Quadriceps

Rectus
Abdominis

Hamstrings

Tibialis
Anterior

Gastrocnemius

Achilles Tendon

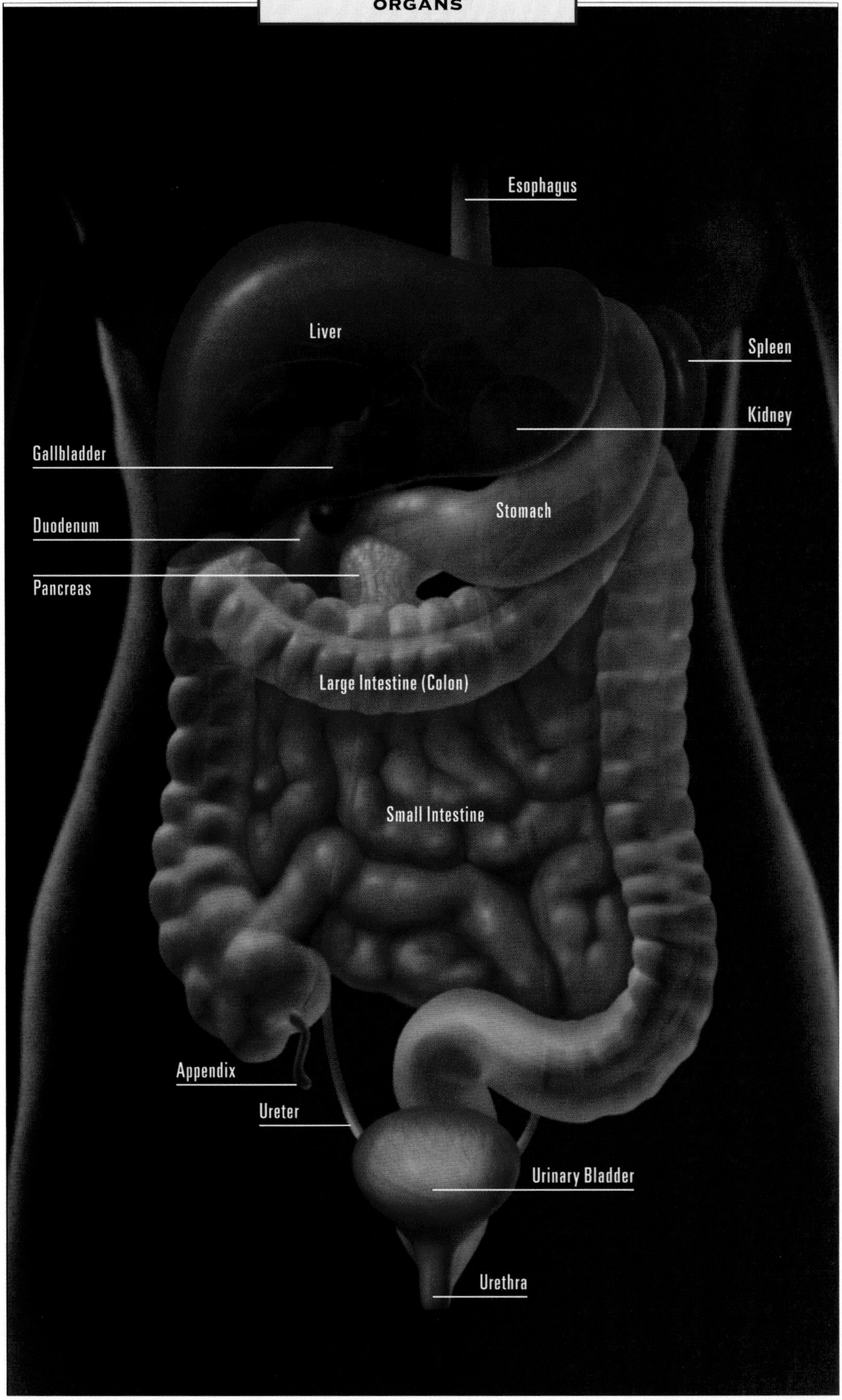

Esophagus

Liver

Spleen

Kidney

Gallbladder

Duodenum

Stomach

Pancreas

Large Intestine (Colon)

Small Intestine

Appendix

Ureter

Urinary Bladder

Urethra

The male and female reproductive systems produce and store the cells that combine to make new human beings. When a woman's egg and a man's sperm cell join, the fertilized egg is a tiny speck weighing less than one-twentieth of a millionth of an ounce.

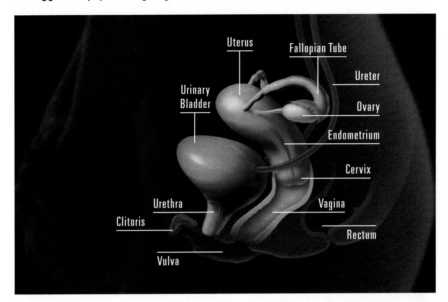

Six months before a girl is born, her ovaries contain all the eggs she'll ever have— 200,000 of them. As she reaches her teens, her ovaries begin releasing one or more of the eggs every month into the fallopian tubes, which carry them to the uterus. If an egg is not fertilized, the lining of the uterus (endometrium) will shed during menstruation. Occasionally fragments of endometrial tissue develop outside of the uterus (endometriosis), causing painful menstruation.

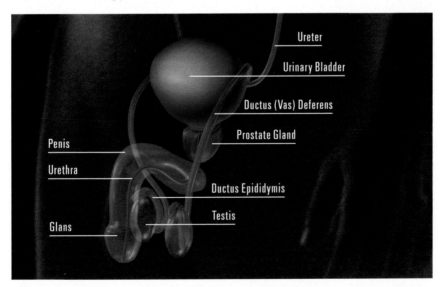

Sperm produced in a man's testes move on to the ductus epididymis, where they mature. When a man ejaculates, he releases 300 to 500 million sperm cells. The prostate gland, which produces fluid that makes sperm more active, often becomes enlarged as a man grows older. The enlarged gland may squeeze the urethra and make urination difficult.

Referred pain: Ever wonder how it can be that a person having a heart attack sometimes feels pain not in the heart but in the shoulder, chest, and left arm? The answer is "referred pain." Pain from an internal organ is sometimes referred to—that is, felt in— other locations served by nerves from the same part of the spinal cord as the organ.

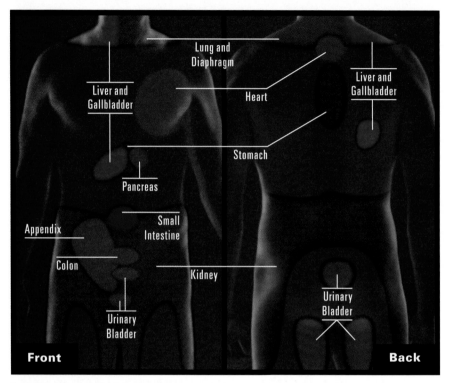

Front   Back

Pain from an internal organ often shows up in or just under the skin, in spots over the organ, or sometimes far from it. For example, pain from liver and gallbladder trouble (green) may be felt in the right side of the neck, the front of the chest, or the right shoulder blade; and from the stomach (orange), high in the abdomen and between the shoulders.

Pain in the face (indicated by the shaded areas) often signals an underlying problem.

If pain gets worse when you bend your head forward, you may have a sinus infection.

If throbbing pain gets worse at night, you may have a tooth abscess.

If your nose and one eye are runny, accompanied by a headache, you may have a migraine.

If your eye is blood-shot, vision blurry, and pain intense, you may have acute glaucoma.

(continued from page 160)

FOR MORE HELP

Organization: Arthritis Foundation, P.O. Box 7669, Atlanta, GA 30357-0669. 800-283-7800, 24-hour recording. Gives free information, from basic facts about arthritic conditions to tips on exercise and management of chronic pain. Also provides services through local chapters. Membership starting at $20 includes a subscription to *Arthritis Today* magazine.

Book: *Arthritis: What Exercises Work,* by Dava Sobel and Arthur C. Klein. Exercises that help arthritis. St. Martin's Press, 1993, $19.95 hardcover, $10.95 paperback. To order, call 800-221-7945.

Video: *Arthritis at Time of Diagnosis.* Overview of causes and treatments, consisting of four reports—Understanding the Diagnosis, What Happens Next?, Treatment and Management, and Issues and Answers. Time Life Medical, 1996, $19.95.

Bunions and Hammertoes

SIGNS AND SYMPTOMS

Bunion:
- A lump on the side of the joint connecting the big toe to the foot.
- A big toe that points inward or outward.
- Pain, swelling, or stiffness in the joint.

Hammertoe:
- A toe (frequently the second one) bent in a clawlike position.
- A corn at the top of the toe.
- Pain in the toe.

One in six people in the United States has a foot problem, and two of the most common complaints are bunions and hammertoes. Both tend to run in families, but shoes that don't fit well can cause them or make them worse.

Bunions, while usually harmless, can be very uncomfortable. And a bunion may become inflamed when a tight shoe rubs against it. Long-term pressure can cause **bursitis** (see page 179).

A hammertoe occurs when the tendons in the toe become permanently contracted, bending it downward so it can't straighten out. Where the toe rubs constantly against shoes, a painful **corn** (see page 143) can develop. For some people, the resulting discomfort may interfere with walking and standing.

These ailments can be prevented or helped with shoes that fit well (you should be able to wiggle your toes in them). Severe cases can be corrected by surgery.

WHAT YOU CAN DO NOW

Self-care won't get rid of a bunion or hammertoe, but it can ease the pain.
- Wear well-designed, comfortable shoes to relieve pressure on the foot.
- For temporary relief around the house, wear old shoes with a hole cut out for the bunion.
- Buy toe caps (padded sleeves that go around the top of a toe) to relieve the pain of a hammertoe.
- Soak your feet in warm water.
- Take over-the-counter medications to relieve pain (see box, page 301).

WHEN TO CALL THE DOCTOR

- If you have long-term redness, pain, or inflammation.
- If the condition hurts so much that you find it hard to walk, wear shoes, or do normal activities.
- If you have diabetes or poor circulation and notice irritated skin over a bunion or hammertoe; it can become infected and lead to serious problems, such as tissue death.

(continued)

Shoulder Pain

SYMPTOMS	WHAT IT MIGHT BE	WHAT YOU CAN DO
After injury, severe pain and tenderness in shoulder, especially when moving; numbness and tingling in arm; joint may look mis-shapen.	Shoulder dislocation (see fractures and dislocations, page 35).	Call doctor for emergency advice. If not available, call 911 or go to emergency facility.
Sudden joint pain along with flu or other infection.	Side effect of infection.	To ease pain and inflammation, take over-the-counter pain relievers (see box, page 301). If temperature is over 101, call doctor for immediate appointment.
Pain and swelling around shoulder, painful movement, fever (sometimes).	Bursitis (see opposite page).	If temperature is over 101, call doctor for immediate appointment; bursa may be infected.
Pain and stiffness that begin in neck and move to shoulders; numbness or tingling in arms, hands, and fingers; weakness in arms and legs.	Cervical spondylosis—a breakdown of joints in neck that may put pressure on nerves and muscles.	With numbness and tingling, call doctor for immediate appointment. Otherwise, call for advice and appointment. Apply moist heat. Sleep with thin pillow under head and thin, rolled-up towel under neck.
Severe pain during movement, difficulty moving arm in any direction, ache when not being used.	Frozen shoulder—inflammation of shoulder joint from lack of use (usually because of injury).	Call doctor for advice and appointment. Use RICE treatment (see box, page 190). Begin rehabilitation program promptly.
Pain or recurring dull ache in shoulder, difficulty raising or lowering arm, weakness in shoulder.	Rotator cuff injury—inflammation of tendons that hold shoulder in place.	Call doctor for advice and appointment.
Pain and stiffness in shoulders (and sometimes other joints).	Arthritis.	See arthritis, page 158.

Shoulder Pain

SYMPTOMS	WHAT IT MIGHT BE	WHAT YOU CAN DO
Pain in distinct spot that is worse with movement and follows injury, overexertion, or heavy lifting.	Strained or torn tendon, ligament, or muscle.	See sprains and strains, page 44.
Pain and tenderness in shoulder, often worse at night; muscle spasms.	Tendinitis.	See tendinitis, page 194.

HOW TO PREVENT IT

➤ Wear shoes that don't pinch your toes. Avoid pointed, high-heeled shoes.
➤ Fit new shoes to your larger foot. Most people's feet are not exactly the same size.
➤ Shop for new shoes at the end of the day, when your feet are at their largest (they tend to swell during the day).
➤ If you have early signs of a bunion or hammertoe, see your doctor or podiatrist and ask about orthotics, custom-made shoe inserts that can reduce the risk of foot problems.

FOR MORE HELP

Information line: American Podiatric Medical Association, 800-FOOTCARE, 24-hour recording. You can request free brochures on 40 different foot topics.

Organization: American Academy of Orthopaedic Surgeons, 800-824-BONE, 24-hour recording. Ask for free brochures on subjects such as how to select new shoes and how to exercise without injury.

Bursitis

SIGNS AND SYMPTOMS

■ Pain and swelling in or near a joint.
■ In bursitis of the shoulder, pain moving into the neck, arms, or fingers.
■ Fever, if caused by infection.

Where your bones, tendons, and ligaments move against each other, they are cushioned by small, fluid-filled sacs called bursae. These sacs help joints move smoothly through a full range of motion. Bursitis occurs when a bursa becomes inflamed through sustained pressure, overuse, infection, or injury.

Athletes and people engaged in heavy lifting or repetitive motions such as hammering tend to get bursitis. Working for long periods in unusual positions can also bring it on. Calcium deposits near bursae at the joints can aggravate it. Bursitis can also be an early sign of arthritis.

Bursitis is usually not serious and gets better in one to two weeks, provided you rest the area involved and take a break from the activity that caused the pain. Bursitis may recur, however, and can become chronic.

Bursitis responds well to applications of cold or heat, physical therapy, anti-inflammatory medicines, and gentle exercise to help restore normal movement and prevent stiffness. In severe cases, a doctor may need to withdraw fluid from the bursa, inject medications to reduce inflammation and ease discomfort, or surgically remove the bursa.

➤ Rest the painful area.
➤ Take an over-the-counter anti-inflammatory such as aspirin or ibuprofen to relieve pain and reduce swelling (see **pain relievers** box, page 301).
➤ When pain starts, hold an ice pack (a bag of frozen peas wrapped in a washcloth works well) on the spot for 20 minutes, three to four times a day for two days, to reduce swelling. After two days, or if pain keeps coming back, apply warmth for 15 to 20 minutes, three to four times a day, to relieve the pain.

WHEN TO CALL THE DOCTOR

Call for an immediate appointment:
➤ If your temperature is over 101 degrees or if the skin around the affected area turns red and swollen; you may have an infection of the bursa.
Call for advice and an appointment:
➤ If pain or swelling continues for more than two weeks despite rest and home care; you may have chronic bursitis or the onset of arthritis.

HOW TO PREVENT IT

➤ Warm up before exercise; cool down afterward (see **overuse injuries,** page 189).
➤ Wear protective gear when you're playing contact sports.
➤ Avoid extremely repetitive or strenuous activities such as hammering or kneeling on a hard surface.
➤ If you have to do repetitive work, change your position often and take five- to ten-minute breaks every hour.
➤ To prevent bursitis in the feet, don't wear high heels or badly worn running or walking shoes.
➤ To avoid bursitis in the hip, sit on cushioned chairs.
➤ Regular stretching or yoga can help prevent damage to bursae.

FOR MORE HELP

Organization: Arthritis Foundation, P.O. Box 7669, Atlanta, GA 30357-0669. 404-872-7100, M–F 9–5 EST. Offers brochures and information. Also provides support groups through local arthritis chapters.
Organization: American Chronic Pain Association, P.O. Box 850, Rocklin, CA 95677. 916-632-0922, 24-hour line. Ask for literature and information about support groups for those with chronic pain.

Carpal Tunnel Syndrome

SIGNS AND SYMPTOMS

■ Numbness and tingling in the thumb and first three fingers.
■ Shooting pains through the hand, wrist, and sometimes forearm.
■ Pain that may be worse at night, interfering with sleep.
■ Weakness in the hands and fingers (in severe cases).

The disabling pain and numbness of carpal tunnel syndrome (CTS) arise in a nerve that runs through a narrow channel of ligaments and wrist bones (called carpals). Symptoms appear suddenly or gradually as the nerve is squeezed by fluid or inflamed tissue in the carpal tunnel. The condition often results from repeated use of the wrists in strenuous sports or in the workplace, particularly when using a computer keyboard.

CTS is also common in women when pregnancy or menopause causes fluid buildup in the tissues. Diseases such as **arthritis** (see page 158), **diabetes** (see page 269), and hypothyroidism (see **thyroid problems,** page 279) may cause the disorder.

CTS can usually be treated effectively if it's caught early; left untreated, it can cause permanent nerve and muscle damage. For persistent pain, injections of anti-inflammatories into the wrist may help. Severe pressure on the nerve can sometimes be relieved by an operation done in the doctor's office.

WHAT YOU CAN DO NOW

➤ Rest the hand and wrist when possible.
➤ If you have trouble sleeping, wear a wrist splint (available at drugstores) at night to reduce pressure on the nerve.
➤ At work, wear a wrist splint if it relieves your pain.

➤ Take anti-inflammatories such as ibuprofen or aspirin to reduce pain and swelling.
➤ To ease discomfort, apply a cold pack for ten minutes at ten-minute intervals for one hour (a bag of frozen peas wrapped in a washcloth works well).

WHEN TO CALL THE DOCTOR

➤ If pain and other symptoms persist or get worse despite a month of home care.

(continued)

Muscles, Bones, & Joints

STRETCHES TO HELP YOUR WRISTS

If you regularly perform repetitive tasks, try doing these exercises three times a day. Rotate your tasks throughout the day and try to take a five-minute break every hour.

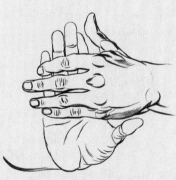

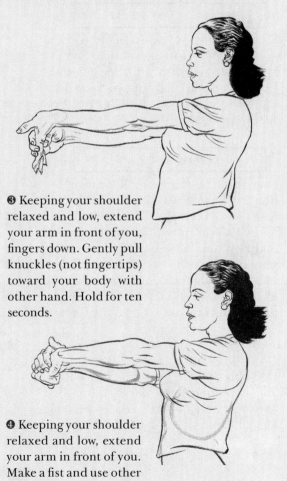

❶ Close your fist tightly, then release, spreading fingers wide. Repeat five times.

❷ Keeping your shoulder relaxed and low, extend your arm in front of you, palm out, fingers up. Use your other hand to pull back on your knuckles (not fingertips). Hold for ten seconds.

❸ Keeping your shoulder relaxed and low, extend your arm in front of you, fingers down. Gently pull knuckles (not fingertips) toward your body with other hand. Hold for ten seconds.

❹ Keeping your shoulder relaxed and low, extend your arm in front of you. Make a fist and use other hand to gently flex the wrist down and toward your body.

HOW TO PREVENT IT

➤ Change your hand position often when working, and take frequent breaks.

➤ Make sure your hands are in line with your forearms as you work, not cocked backward. Use a wrist pad, available in office supply stores, when you type.

FOR MORE HELP

Organization: Association for Repetitive Motion Syndromes (ARMS), P.O. Box 514, Santa Rosa, CA 95402. 707-571-0397, 24-hour answering machine. Sends information packet and answers general questions.

Organization: Arthritis Foundation, P.O. Box 7669, Atlanta, GA 30357-0669. 404-872-7100, M–F 9–5 EST. Offers free information and brochures on CTS, exercise, and pain management.

Book: *Repetitive Strain Injury: A Computer User's Guide,* by Emil Pascarelli, M.D., and Deborah Quilter. A guide to treating and preventing these injuries. John Wiley & Sons, 1994, $14.95. To order, call 800-225-5945.

Low Back Pain

SIGNS AND SYMPTOMS

■ Pain low in the back, possibly severe. It may come on suddenly or slowly; it may be constant or occur only at certain times of the day or when you are in a certain position; it may be confined to one place or move to other parts of your back.

■ Numbness, tingling, or a shooting pain in your legs or buttocks, usually on one side only.

■ Pain that is aggravated by coughing, sneezing, or twisting.

■ Stiffness.

Call a doctor immediately if you also have these symptoms of nerve damage:

■ Any numbness or weakness, especially numbness around your groin or rectal area.

■ Trouble controlling your bladder or bowels.

■ Weakness in one or both legs.

Back pain strikes about 80 percent of Americans at some point during their lives, and by far the most common complaint is low back pain.

(continued)

Back Pain

SYMPTOMS	WHAT IT MIGHT BE	WHAT YOU CAN DO
Persistent back pain, especially at night; numbness, tingling, and muscle weakness that gets worse; in some cases, loss of bladder or bowel control.	Spinal tumor.	With loss of bladder or bowel control, call doctor for emergency advice; if not available, call 911 or go to emergency facility. Otherwise, call doctor for immediate appointment.
Severe low back pain made worse by bending, twisting, coughing, or lifting (pain may shoot down one leg); in severe cases, loss of bladder or bowel control.	Protruded disk irritating or pressing on a nerve. (See low back pain, opposite page.)	With loss of bladder or bowel control, call doctor for emergency advice; if not available, call 911 or go to emergency facility. Otherwise, call doctor for advice and appointment, take pain relievers (see box, page 301), and rest.
Occasional or frequent low back pain that may be worse at night; back or hip stiffness in morning that improves with activity; pain and stiffness in rib area; neck or chest pain; fatigue, weight loss, and poor appetite; fever; eye pain; blurred vision.	Ankylosing spondylitis— a rare inflammatory form of arthritis that chiefly affects spinal column, usually in men under age 40.	Call doctor for advice and appointment. Physical therapy, strength training, massage, and anti-inflammatory over-the-counter pain relievers (see box, page 301) may help ease discomfort.
Numbness, weakness, and/or mild pain in back and legs; worsens when walking, eases when sitting.	Spinal stenosis—narrowing of spinal canal due to arthritis, thickened ligaments, or bulging disks.	Call doctor for advice and appointment. If overweight, weight loss and exercise to strengthen abdominal muscles may help.
Pain and stiffness in back, buttocks, and thighs; difficulty moving or bending.	Arthritis.	See arthritis, page 158.
Soreness and stiffness after exertion or injury, or soreness that develops gradually during night; may spread to buttocks and thighs.	Back sprain or strain (see low back pain, opposite page).	Rest for a few days; return to activities when comfortable. If necessary, take over-the-counter pain relievers (see box, page 301).

(continued)

Back Pain *(continued)*

SYMPTOMS	WHAT IT MIGHT BE	WHAT YOU CAN DO
Aching, pain, and stiffness in back muscles (also pain elsewhere); points on body feel sore when pressed; fatigue, headaches, and insomnia.	Fibromyalgia.	See box on fibromyalgia, page 268.
Backache; easily broken bones, especially in spine, wrists, and hips; stooped or hunched posture.	Osteoporosis.	See osteoporosis, page 188.
Pain in lower back of women more than four months pregnant.	Stress on back from extra weight. • Sign of early labor.	See pregnancy, page 232.

THE SPINE

The curves of the spine give it strength and allow humans to walk upright.

Cervical Region

Thoracic Region

Lumbar Region

Sacral Region

Coccygeal Region

The spinal column is a series of bones cushioned by small shock absorbers (disks) and surrounded by muscles and ligaments. (See color illustrations, page 162.) Most low back pain comes from muscle or ligament strain, disk problems, or some combination of these. In most cases, the pain goes away on its own, though for many it may recur.

Disks break down somewhat with age or from repeated bending and twisting. In some cases, a swollen disk may press on a nerve in the lower back and send pain down the buttocks or legs. Most disk problems resolve themselves over time, with proper care. In severe cases, surgery to remove the disk may help, although most experts now believe that disk surgery is often unnecessary.

WHAT YOU CAN DO NOW

➤ If you have pain while driving, use a pillow or rolled-up towel to support the curve in the small of your back.
➤ If back pain disturbs your sleep, put pillows beneath your knees when lying on your back.
➤ If you sleep on your side, bend your knees and place a pillow between them.
➤ Don't sleep on your stomach.
➤ Use acetaminophen, aspirin, or ibuprofen. (See **pain relievers** box, page 301.)

> For the first two days after back pain begins, apply an ice pack to the painful area for five to ten minutes at a time. After two days, apply heat from a heating pad or take hot showers.

WHEN TO CALL THE DOCTOR

Call for emergency advice (if your doctor is not available, call 911 or go to an emergency facility):
> If your back pain is combined with symptoms of nerve damage, particularly loss of bladder or bowel control.

Call for advice and an appointment:
> If back pain is severe or disrupts your normal activities.
> If the pain doesn't go away within a few days or keeps coming back.

HOW TO PREVENT IT

> Exercise regularly. Avoid exercises that twist or wrench your body, or anything that seems to make your back pain worse. Walking, swimming, and even walking in a pool are ideal.
> Do exercises to strengthen the abdominal muscles (always do sit-ups with your knees bent). Also, stretch the muscles that run parallel to your spine (lie flat on your back, pull one knee, then the other, toward your chest). Consult a book or specialist to develop a program that's right for you and your back.
> Try yoga. Both back pain sufferers and doctors give it high ratings for building strength and flexibility. It also helps you relax and reduce stress.
> Wear comfortable, low-heeled shoes.
> If you sit for long periods, make sure your work surface is at a comfortable height and that your chair provides good lower-back support. Walk around for a few minutes every half hour or so. If sitting is uncomfortable, try arranging your work area so you can stand while resting one foot on a low block.
> Don't lift and twist at the same time. Lift with your legs, not your back, and lift as little weight each time as possible.

> Lose weight if you need to. A big belly puts strain on the lower spine.

FOR MORE HELP

Hotline: Back Pain Hotline at Texas Back Institute, 800-247-2225, M–F 8–5 CST. Nurses call back (usually within one hour) to answer questions and send free literature, including illustrated back exercises.

Booklet: *Acute Low-Back Problems in Adults,* Agency for Health Care Policy and Research. Outlines recent developments in low back pain research and care. For a free copy, call 800-358-9295.

Book: *Good News for Bad Backs,* by Robert L. Swezey, M.D., and Annette M. Swezey. Advice, exercise tips, and treatment options. Cequal Publishing, 1995, $12.95. To order, call 800-350-2998.

Video: *Back Pain (Lower Back) at Time of Diagnosis.* Clear, useful overview of causes and treatments, consisting of four reports—Understanding the Diagnosis, What Happens Next?, Treatment and Management, and Issues and Answers. Time Life Medical, 1996, $19.95.

Muscle Cramps

SIGNS AND SYMPTOMS

■ A sudden, sharply painful tightening of a muscle.
■ A muscle that is hard to the touch.
■ In some cases, visible twitching of the muscle.
■ Heat cramps: sudden, severe spasms in the arms, legs, and sometimes the abdominal muscles.

A muscle cramp can happen at unexpected moments—in bed, during a walk, after working in the garden. The muscle contracts with great intensity and stays contracted, typically for about a minute, before relaxing.

(continued)

Leg Pain

SYMPTOMS	WHAT IT MIGHT BE	WHAT YOU CAN DO
Severe leg pain, swelling, and tenderness after an injury; you can't move leg.	Bone fracture (see fractures and dislocations, page 35).	Call 911 or go to emergency facility **immediately.**
Leg pain following injury, but you can move leg.	Strained, inflamed, or torn tendon, ligament, or muscle. (See sprains and strains, page 44.)	Call doctor for immediate appointment.
Pain and fatigue in muscles of thighs, calves, feet, or hips when walking or exercising; stops with rest; mostly in older adults.	Peripheral vascular disease (see narrowed arteries, page 107).	Call doctor for immediate appointment.
Pain and burning sensation with redness, tenderness, and itching; hard, cordlike swelling beneath skin along length of a vein in leg (in phlebitis). Swelling, warmth, and redness throughout leg; bluish color in toes (in deep-vein thrombosis).	Phlebitis (also known as thrombophlebitis)—inflammation of a vein near surface of skin, usually a result of infection or injury and causing clotting. ● Deep-vein thrombosis—blood clots in deep veins.	Call doctor for immediate appointment. Phlebitis is usually not harmful, but deep-vein thrombosis can cause clots that break off and travel to lung. Varicose veins (see page 111) may increase risk of developing either condition.
In children: annoying but not severe ache or pain that comes and goes in leg muscles; usually felt at night, disappears by morning.	Growing pains—vague discomfort common in children aged 3 to 12.	Gently massage area. For pain, give acetaminophen with food at bedtime (never aspirin; see Reye's syndrome box, page 92). Call doctor for advice if pain persists and interferes with sleep.
Pain in front or side of lower leg that begins during or just after exercise.	Shinsplints—injury or inflammation of bone, tendon, or muscle in calf.	Rest, usually for 2–3 weeks. Use ice for inflammation, warm soaks for relief from discomfort. Switch from high-impact activities, such as running, to gentler activities, such as swimming or bicycling. Call doctor for advice if pain persists.

Leg Pain

SYMPTOMS	WHAT IT MIGHT BE	WHAT YOU CAN DO
Leg muscles tighten suddenly and painfully for a few minutes, then return to normal.	Leg cramps.	See muscle cramps, page 185.
Pain and sometimes swelling after vigorous athletic or other physical activity.	Overuse injury.	See overuse injuries, page 189.
Numbness, tingling, or shooting pain in buttocks or down back of one leg.	Protruded disk in spine that presses on sciatic nerve in leg, causing inflammation. • Other sciatic nerve injury.	See low back pain, page 182.
Aching or itching in legs, with prominent blue or purple veins; sometimes swelling in feet or ankles.	Varicose veins.	See varicose veins, page 111.

Muscle cramps are most common in the legs; they usually occur after exercise, particularly in the heat, or after spending a long time in an uncomfortable position. They may also result from an imbalance in minerals and fluids brought on by dehydration. Abdominal cramps may be caused by low back problems or menstruation. Diseases such as Parkinson's, untreated thyroid problems, or diabetes can also lead to cramps.

Muscle cramps are usually not serious, although heat cramps can be a sign of heat exhaustion or, if accompanied by dizziness or disorientation, impending heat stroke, which can be fatal. (See **heat stroke and heat exhaustion,** page 38.)

WHAT YOU CAN DO NOW

➤ Stretch. For leg muscles, face a wall and put your hands or forearms against it; then, keeping your feet flat on the floor, take steps backward until you are leaning against the wall from several feet away.
➤ Massage. Begin at the edges of the cramp and move in toward the center, squeezing the muscle gently.
➤ For a stubborn cramp, immerse the area in warm water while stretching and massaging the muscle.
➤ If you have heat cramps, get out of the sun and sip cool water or a sports drink.
➤ For menstrual cramps, take warm baths or put a hot-water bottle or heating pad on your abdomen.

WHEN TO CALL THE DOCTOR

Call 911 or go to an emergency facility **immediately:**
➤ If you get a severe, cramping pain in your chest, shoulders, or arms; this can signal a heart attack.
➤ If you have heat cramps accompanied by dizziness or disorientation; this can be a sign of heat stroke.
Call for advice and an appointment:
➤ If you suffer from long-term or frequent muscle cramps.

➤ Stay hydrated by drinking six to eight glasses of water every day.
➤ Do stretching exercises regularly, especially before bed.
➤ Warm up and stretch before exercising.
➤ To prevent heat cramps in hot weather, drink a small glass (about four ounces) of cool water before and after exercise and every 15 minutes during exercise. (Drinking lots of cold water at once may cause stomach upset.) If you use a sports beverage, drink one low in sugar.

Osteoporosis

SIGNS AND SYMPTOMS

■ A broken bone (sometimes the first symptom), commonly in the spine, hip, ribs, or wrist.
■ Becoming round-shouldered and stooped; loss of height (usually after the age of 70).
■ Severe backache.

O steoporosis simply means "porous bones." The human skeleton acts like a bank, accepting new mineral deposits that replace old bone until people reach their mid-thirties. From then on, it's easier to lose bone than to gain it. With increasing age, bones lose more calcium, becoming less dense and more brittle (see color illustrations, page 164).

Osteoporosis is most common in people over 70 and in women after menopause, when levels of bone-protecting estrogen drop. It usually progresses without symptoms until a fracture occurs—often in the spine and signaled by a severe backache. A person may then gradually lose height and become stooped as bones in the spinal column weaken and compress.

Major bone breaks may require surgery and recuperation in bed, which can lead to further weakness and additional ailments. In some cases, complications such as blood clots or pneumonia prove fatal.

Osteoporosis is preventable. If it has set in, it can be slowed down, although it cannot be cured. Hormone therapy for menopausal women has been shown to cut the number of spinal and hip fractures in half, but it may also increase the risk of breast cancer. (See **hormone replacement** box, page 229.) Your doctor may prescribe physical therapy and other medications that prevent bone loss or build new bone. Self-care, including gentle exercise and calcium supplements, also helps.

WHAT YOU CAN DO NOW

After diagnosis:
➤ For backache, take over-the-counter **pain relievers** (see box on page 301).
➤ Try regular, gentle exercise such as walking every day. But avoid spine-jarring activities such as high-impact aerobics.
➤ To prevent falls: Install handrails on stairs and grab bars in the bathroom. Cover slippery floors with carpet, rubber mats, or nonskid wax. Use bright lamps and night-lights.

WHEN TO CALL THE DOCTOR

➤ If you fracture a bone.
➤ If you have unexpected, persistent pain in your back, ribs, spine, or feet.
➤ If you have a backache or are developing a curved back ("dowager's hump").

HOW TO PREVENT IT

➤ Get enough exercise. Women past menopause who don't exercise are at higher risk than those who do. Weight-bearing exercise, such as walking and dancing, stimulates bone-building cells and helps keep osteoporosis from developing.
➤ Get enough calcium from your diet. Foods high in calcium include milk products, leafy green vegetables, tofu, and almonds. People at risk for osteoporosis (check with your doctor) should get 1,500 milligrams of calcium per day; others should get 1,000 mg per day.
➤ If you take over-the-counter calcium sup-

plements, be aware that they vary; calcium carbonate contains the most usable calcium (look for the amount of elemental calcium listed on the bottle). Also look at labels for phrases such as "Made to USP quality, purity, and potency standards" or "Laboratory tested to dissolve within 60 minutes." That means the calcium will be easily absorbed by your body. Take supplements with meals, no more than 500 mg at a time. Drink six to eight glasses of water each day to prevent constipation and decrease the slight risk of developing kidney stones. (If you have a history of kidney stones, consult your doctor about calcium supplements.)

➤ Try to gain a little weight if you're underweight; being too thin may decrease bone density and increase your risk.

➤ Ask your doctor about a bone density test; it's expensive, but it can show whether you have serious bone loss.

➤ Avoid smoking and alcohol use, which are associated with osteoporosis.

➤ Get some sun. The vitamin D in sunshine builds bones by increasing the body's calcium absorption.

➤ Try to drink enough milk—another good source of vitamin D; or ask your doctor if you should take vitamin D supplements.

FOR MORE HELP

Information line: National Osteoporosis Foundation, 800-223-9994, 24-hour line. Sends a free information packet.

Organization: Arthritis Foundation, P.O. Box 7669, Atlanta, GA 30357-0669. 404-872-7100, M–F 9–5 EST. Offers referrals to local chapters and a free brochure about osteoporosis.

Book: *The Osteoporosis Handbook,* by Sydney Lou Bonnick, M.D. Taylor Publishing, 1994, $19.95. Call 800-677-2800 to order.

Video: *Osteoporosis at Time of Diagnosis.* Clear, useful overview of causes and treatments, consisting of four reports—Understanding the Diagnosis, What Happens Next?, Treatment and Management, and Issues and Answers. Time Life Medical, 1996, $19.95.

Overuse Injuries

SIGNS AND SYMPTOMS

The tip-off to an overuse injury is pain that gets worse with activity. Often, it follows this progression:

■ At first, there is dull pain or discomfort and general fatigue (the normal effects of exertion).

■ Pain becomes sharper and more localized (it's felt mostly in one place, such as the knee, hip, or arm).

■ Pain lingers from one day to the next, and is often accompanied by swelling.

■ Pain or swelling becomes severe enough to interfere with the activity that caused it.

■ Pain or swelling interferes with the normal activities of daily living, such as walking or standing.

Overuse injuries result from using muscles, tendons, joints, or other body parts in the same way, over and over again, without enough rest—often in the strenuous, repeated motions of a sport. Runners in particular are subject to overuse injuries of the knees and feet; similarly, throwing a ball or swinging a tennis racket can be hard on the shoulders and elbows. But overuse injuries can be caused by any repeated motion, such as typing, as well as by infrequent activities, such as trimming the hedge for the first time in the spring.

Overuse injuries can take longer to heal than other injuries. Without rest, rehabilitation, and prevention, they may recur or develop into more serious problems, such as **arthritis** (see page 158).

WHAT YOU CAN DO NOW

➤ Stop or decrease the activity.

➤ Use the **RICE** treatment (see box on next page) on the affected area.

(continued)

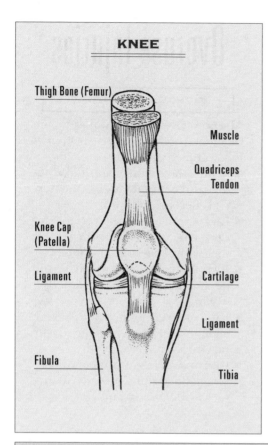

KNEE

Thigh Bone (Femur)

Muscle

Quadriceps
Tendon

Knee Cap
(Patella)

Ligament

Cartilage

Ligament

Fibula

Tibia

➤ When pain or swelling has eased, resume your normal activities gradually.

> **WHEN TO CALL THE DOCTOR**

➤ If a week of home care doesn't help.

> **HOW TO PREVENT IT**

➤ If you pursue a strenuous sport such as running, tennis, or swimming, allow at least 48 hours between hard workouts.

➤ Don't increase the duration or intensity of a sports activity too much at one time. For example, if you walk or run ten miles a week, increase your distance no more than about one mile each week.

➤ Know your body. Adjust your activities if you know you have a physical problem. For instance, people with flat feet (over-pronation) are more likely to get knee or foot injuries from running; they might want to try swimming or tennis instead.

➤ Get the right equipment. If you walk or run, for example, your shoes should be

---

FIRST AID FOR INJURIES: R•I•C•E

RICE stands for Rest, Ice, Compression, and Elevation. This is the best treatment for either an overuse injury or a sudden, acute injury, such as a sprain. Start it as soon as you notice symptoms. If begun promptly, it can save you days or weeks of discomfort and inactivity.

Rest: Try not to use the injured part until the pain and swelling go away (usually one to three days).

Ice: Apply ice within 15 minutes of injury, if possible, to reduce swelling and pain. Place a damp towel over the injured area and a plastic bag full of ice on top of it (a bag of frozen peas also works well). Hold the cold pack in place for 10 to 30 minutes, then leave it off for 30 to 45 minutes. Repeat this as often as possible. For most injuries, regular icing should continue for three days; for severe bruises, up to seven days. For chronic pain, continue whenever you have the symptoms.

Compression: Use an elastic bandage to apply gentle but firm pressure until the swelling goes down. Wrap the bandage in an upward spiral, starting several inches below the injured area. Apply even, moderate pressure to start, then wrap more loosely after you've passed the injured area. (To use ice and compression at the same time, wrap an elastic bandage over an ice pack.)

Elevation: For the first one to three days, keep the injured area raised above heart level whenever possible to help drain excess fluid from the area.

Note: For the first one to three days after an injury:
- Do not apply any heat (including hot showers and baths).
- Do not exercise the injured part.
- Do not massage the injury.
- Do not drink alcohol.

These can increase swelling.

Knee Pain

SYMPTOMS	WHAT IT MIGHT BE	WHAT YOU CAN DO
Pain and possibly a "pop" at moment of injury; swelling, stiffness, instability, difficulty walking.	Ligament sprain or rupture, and/or cartilage damage. (See sprains and strains, page 44, and illustration, opposite page.)	Call doctor for immediate appointment. Use RICE treatment for pain and swelling (see box, opposite page).
In adolescents: pain and swelling about 2 inches below kneecap; may cause limping or prevent running.	Osgood-Schlatter disease—temporary inflammation of tendon and bone.	Call doctor for advice and appointment. Use RICE treatment (see box, opposite page).
Pain, swelling, and stiffness in knee joint.	Arthritis (see page 158).	Call doctor for advice and appointment.
Tenderness, stiffness, and swelling above kneecap; pain when bending knee; possibly fever or redness.	Bursitis (see page 179).	Call doctor for advice and appointment.
Pain just below kneecap, especially when sitting or straightening leg; may be felt after running or jumping; knee pain and tightness that worsen with movement.	Patellar tendinitis, or "jumper's knee" (see tendinitis, page 194, and overuse injuries, page 189).	Call doctor for advice and appointment. Use RICE treatment for pain and swelling (see box, opposite page).

appropriate for your weight to help absorb the shock. (If you have foot problems, ask your doctor about orthotics, customized shoe inserts that can help prevent worsening of knee or foot troubles.)

➤ Consider changing your technique; you may want to learn a different swimming stroke if you're prone to shoulder or elbow problems, for instance.

➤ Warm up before exercise. Warm muscles, ligaments, and tendons are less likely to be injured.

➤ Dress appropriately. Layering clothing helps because it allows you to add and remove clothes as needed, keeping your muscles, ligaments, and tendons warm and flexible.

➤ Make sure your work site is comfortable (see **carpal tunnel syndrome,** page 180).

FOR MORE HELP

Book: *The Sports Medicine Bible,* by Lyle J. Micheli, M.D. Guidelines for the recreational athlete to help prevent and treat injuries. HarperPerennial, 1995, $20.

Foot and Ankle Pain

SYMPTOMS	WHAT IT MIGHT BE	WHAT YOU CAN DO
Pain in ankle or foot following injury; possibly swelling, bruising, or bleeding; inability to support weight.	Broken bone (see fractures and dislocations, page 35).	Call doctor for emergency advice. If not available, call 911 or go to emergency facility.
Pain and fatigue in feet, thighs, calves, or hips when active; discomfort stops with rest; most common in older adults.	Peripheral vascular disease (see narrowed arteries, page 107).	Call doctor for immediate appointment.
Pain, swelling, stiffness, and possibly redness in joints of ankles, feet, or toes.	Arthritis (see page 158).	Call doctor for advice and appointment.
Sharp pain or tenderness directly under heel; worsens when walking or running, often worse in morning.	Plantar fasciitis—inflammation of tissue that runs along heel and supports arch. Usually caused by stress on arch. Most common among runners (see overuse injuries, page 189).	Stay off foot as much as possible, take over-the-counter pain relievers to ease pain and inflammation, and use RICE treatment (see box, page 190). Ask doctor or physical therapist about exercises to stretch ligament.
Pain and tenderness in area of Achilles tendon in back of ankle, or in other tendons in ankle or foot; may restrict foot movement.	Tendinitis (see page 194).	Call doctor for advice and appointment.
Painful, hard lump on side of foot, at base of big toe (bunion). Toe clenched into painful, clawlike position (hammertoe).	Bunion or hammertoe.	See bunions and hammertoes, page 177.
Patch of thickened skin on foot; may be painful.	Corn or callus.	See corns and calluses, page 143.
Wart on sole of foot, making walking painful. Tight shoes may aggravate.	Plantar wart.	See warts, page 157.

Temporomandibular Disorder

SIGNS AND SYMPTOMS

- Pain in the chewing muscles or jaw joint on either side of the head.
- Recurring headaches or earaches.
- Noticeable clicking, popping, or grating sounds in the jaw joints when opening or closing the mouth.
- Pain that spreads to the face, neck, or shoulders.
- Difficulty opening the mouth because it feels locked or painful.

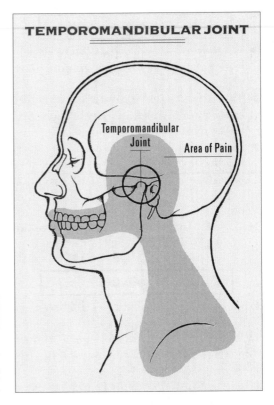

TEMPOROMANDIBULAR JOINT

Temporomandibular Joint

Area of Pain

Muscles, Bones, & Joints

Because we talk, chew, and yawn every day, the jaw is one of our busiest moving parts. And it is the flexible temporomandibular joints, which connect the lower jaw to a bone on each side of the head, that help the jawbone move smoothly (see illustration). Pain in or around these joints is known as temporomandibular disorder (TMD). Perhaps two-thirds of Americans have occasional bouts of such pain.

The causes of TMD are not well understood, but many factors have been linked to the condition, including strain on the jaw muscles from unconsciously clenching the teeth (see **tooth grinding,** page 81), degenerative changes such as arthritis, injury to the jaw, and even emotional stress. Poor posture (from thrusting the chin forward) may also contribute.

TMD usually resolves itself in a few days with rest and painkillers such as ibuprofen. When it is severe or chronic, treatments include physical therapy, anti-inflammatory drugs, tranquilizers to relieve muscle tension, and a splint or bite guard to redistribute tension. Surgery and injections are controversial last resorts.

WHAT YOU CAN DO NOW

- ➤ Take an anti-inflammatory pain reliever such as ibuprofen (see **pain relievers** box, page 301).
- ➤ Massage the muscles above and in front of your temples, as well as the large muscles along your jawline. Use small, circular motions.
- ➤ If your pain is severe, limit talking and chewing for a few days. Rest your jaw by eating soft or liquid foods.
- ➤ Apply a hot or cold pack, available in drugstores, or a damp, warm or cool towel for pain relief. Hold for a few minutes.
- ➤ Don't clench your teeth.

WHEN TO CALL THE DOCTOR

- ➤ If the pain of TMD interferes with eating or talking.
- ➤ If you grind or clench your teeth and think you may need a bite guard to protect them.

➤ Whenever you realize that you're clenching or grinding your teeth, remind yourself to stop.

➤ Take steps to decrease stress. Reducing stress through relaxation techniques may be the most effective treatment.

➤ If you are prone to jaw pain, stay away from chewy foods such as steak and bagels, and hard foods such as carrots and apples. Don't chew gum, pencils, or other objects.

➤ To lessen the strain on bones and muscles in the jaw, don't sleep on your stomach.

FOR MORE HELP

Organization: National Oral Health Information Clearinghouse, 301-402-7364, M–F 9–5:30 EST. Provides free brochures, packets, and fact sheets on oral health, including TMD.

Organization: American Dental Association, 211 E. Chicago Ave., Chicago, IL 60611. 312-440-2593, M–F 8:30–5 CST. Send a business-size, self-addressed, stamped envelope, and ask for the brochure on TMD. Also has brochures on other dental topics.

Tendinitis

SIGNS AND SYMPTOMS

■ Pain and tenderness around a joint, often worse with movement and in bed at night.
■ Muscle spasms.

Tendinitis is inflammation of a tendon—the tough, hardworking band of tissue that connects a muscle to a bone (see illustration, page 190). It's often caused by repetitive movements in sports or in assembly line or office work. (See **overuse injuries,** page 189, and **carpal tunnel syndrome,** page 180.) Other causes are injury, inadequate warm-up before exercise, calcium deposits in the tendon, and breakdown of the tendon because of aging.

Tendinitis is most common in shoulders ("golfer's shoulder"), the outside of elbows ("tennis elbow," see box on opposite page), the fingers ("trigger finger"), the wrist, and the back of the lower leg (Achilles tendinitis). Plantar fasciitis, common in runners, is an inflammation of tissue between the heel and the bottom of the toes. Although it's not tendinitis, it's prevented and treated the same way.

Most tendinitis heals with about two weeks of rest, but it can worsen and become chronic or disabling if the injured area isn't allowed to recuperate. Persistent tendinitis can be treated with medications to ease the inflammation or discomfort, plus physical therapy, ice packs, ultrasound treatments, and gentle exercise.

WHAT YOU CAN DO NOW

➤ Rest the area until pain and swelling ease.

➤ Use a splint if the cause is overuse, and if you can't rest the affected joint.

➤ Take anti-inflammatories such as aspirin or ibuprofen to relieve the pain and swelling (see **pain relievers** box, page 301).

➤ If your tendinitis comes on suddenly after an injury or heavy use, immediately put an ice pack on the area for 10 to 30 minutes at a time to relieve the swelling. Wait 30 to 45 minutes, and repeat. Repeat as often as possible. After two days, apply a towel soaked in hot water and wrung out or a heat pack (available in drugstores) to relieve the pain. (See **RICE** treatment box, page 190.)

➤ After a few days, start to exercise the injured area gently.

WHEN TO CALL THE DOCTOR

➤ If the area around the joint appears discolored or deformed.

➤ If pain and swelling continue for more than two weeks despite rest and over-the-counter pain relievers; these could be early signs of arthritis.

TENNIS ELBOW

In contrast to regular tendinitis, the symptoms of tennis elbow typically last from 6 to 12 weeks. Anyone who uses the arms and elbows repetitively in sports or on the job can get tennis elbow. It results when the forearm is frequently snapped, rolled, or aggressively twisted, and when people lift heavy objects with the elbow locked and the arm extended. In tennis, it can occur when the grip is incorrect.

The remedies for tennis elbow and ordinary tendinitis are the same. The best home care is rest and over-the-counter pain relievers, then gentle exercise. You can also try wearing a Velcro tennis-elbow strap, sold in sporting goods stores, to support muscles and tendons. Don't wear the strap for long periods, though, because it can reduce circulation.

Prevention of tendinitis and tennis elbow are similar. If tennis is the cause of your pain, try a more flexible tennis racket or one with a slightly larger grip; and ask a coach to help you modify your grip to ease the stress on your elbow.

If you have weak ankles, wear high-top athletic shoes.
- Don't grip tools, pens, or exercise equipment too tightly. Wrap utensils in felt or rubber to create larger grips.
- Switch to low-impact exercise, such as swimming or low-impact aerobics, if you think strenuous sports are to blame.

FOR MORE HELP

Organization: Arthritis Foundation, P.O. Box 7669, Atlanta, GA 30357-0669. 404-872-7100, M–F, 9–5. Offers information and a brochure about tendinitis. Local chapters maintain arthritis support groups.

Organization: American Chronic Pain Association, P.O. Box 850, Rocklin, CA 95677. 916-632-0922, 24-hour line. Ask for literature and information about support groups for people with chronic pain.

HOW TO PREVENT IT

- If you have symptoms, rest the joint to prevent the problem from getting worse.
- If you perform repetitive tasks during work—for instance, a lot of typing—ask your doctor to recommend an ergonomic specialist, who can suggest ways to change your workstation to ease the stress on tender tendons.
- Stretch before and after work. When you have to do the same movements over and over again, take a five- to ten-minute break every hour or so.
- Exercise regularly to maintain muscle and tendon strength, which will help prevent injuries.
- Always warm up before exercise or sports.
- Wear comfortable shoes with flexible soles and good heel control when you exercise.

Behavior & Emotions

◆

Alcohol Abuse and Alcoholism

Alcohol abuse:
- Temporary blackouts or memory loss after heavy drinking.
- Unusually irritable and aggressive behavior (sometimes).
- Use of increasing amounts of alcohol to relax, sleep, cheer up, deal with problems, or feel "normal."

Alcoholism (alcohol addiction):
Same symptoms as those above. Other symptoms can include:
- Headache, anxiety, insomnia, or nausea that develops when you stop drinking.
- Drinking in the morning.
- Depression and anxiety.
- Trouble maintaining family relationships and holding a job.
- Drinking alone regularly or drinking in secret; hiding bottles.
- Failed attempts to control drinking.
- Flushed skin and broken capillaries on the face.
- Trembling hands.
- Yellowish skin, which may indicate cirrhosis—a progressive disease of the liver.

Alcohol abuse causes more health problems in the United States than all illegal drugs combined, with an estimated 18 million adults suffering drinking-related problems. Besides disrupting a person's work, relationships, and social life, heavy drinking can damage organs in every system of the body—including the kidneys, liver, brain, heart, and intestines. It may increase the risk of many forms of cancer as well. Drinking when pregnant can severely damage the developing fetus. Alcohol is also estimated to play a role in half of all car-accident fatalities in the United States.

The line between alcohol abuse and alcoholism can be a gray one. But alcoholism is marked by a loss of control: The alcoholic continues to drink, even when it causes physical, psychological, or social harm. Most experts consider alcoholism a disease, not evidence of a character flaw. The causes are still not understood, but they seem to be a combination of many factors, including heredity. Some research suggests that a person's risk of becoming an alcoholic is three to four times greater if a parent is an alcoholic.

Treatment can begin only when an alcoholic admits that the problem exists and agrees to stop drinking and get help. Alcoholics with psychiatric problems or little social support or motivation tend to relapse within a few years of treatment. But among alcoholics with otherwise good health plus social support and motivation, the likeli-

Confusion

Everyone gets confused once in a while, but serious, repeated, or long-term confusion may signal a problem. Confusion is the inability to think clearly or make decisions; in severe cases, people may not know where they are or who they are. Confusion can come on suddenly or slowly. Depending on the cause—possibilities include physical or mental illness, injury, or exposure to a toxic substance—the condition can be serious and may require immediate medical attention.

SYMPTOMS	WHAT IT MIGHT BE	WHAT YOU CAN DO
Confusion; severe headache or agitation; drowsiness, sluggishness, possibly coma.	Poisoning from carbon monoxide fumes. Circumstances that indicate high levels of carbon monoxide include car running in garage, or old-fashioned gas or kerosene appliances in poorly ventilated room.	Get person into open air **immediately.** Check for pulse and breathing; if none, begin CPR (see page 14). Call 911 or go to emergency facility **immediately.**
Confusion or loss of consciousness, head wound or bruise, slurred speech.	Head injury causing concussion or internal bleeding. (See head, neck, and back injuries, page 37.)	Call 911 or go to emergency facility **immediately.**
Confusion, slurred speech, stumbling; shivering and numbness after exposure to cold air or water.	Hypothermia (see page 39).	Call 911 or go to emergency facility **immediately.**
Confusion, anxiety, or loss of consciousness; weak or rapid pulse; cold, clammy, pale, or bluish skin; rapid, shallow breathing.	Shock—vital organs are deprived of blood due to sudden illness or injury, or severe allergic reaction (see page 18).	Check for breathing and pulse; if none, begin CPR (see page 14). Call 911 or go to emergency facility **immediately.**
Sudden, temporary confusion; dizziness; loss of coordination; light-headedness; tingling; weakness or numbness, usually on one side of body; double vision or temporary blindness; speech difficulty; hearing loss; headache.	Transient ischemic attack (TIA)—interrupted blood flow to brain due to temporary blockage of artery. (See stroke, page 109.)	Call 911 or go to emergency facility **immediately.**

(continued)

Confusion *(continued)*

SYMPTOMS	WHAT IT MIGHT BE	WHAT YOU CAN DO
Confusion, fever over 100, chills, fatigue and/or weakness; possibly nausea and vomiting, loss of appetite, headache.	Bacterial or viral infection, such as pneumonia (see page 94), meningitis (see page 56), toxic shock syndrome (see page 236), or kidney infection.	Call doctor for emergency advice; if not available, call 911 or go to emergency facility.
Confusion, anxiety, dizziness, sweating, shakiness, hunger, headache, impaired vision, rapid heartbeat, numbness, lack of coordination.	Hypoglycemia—low blood sugar, especially in people who take insulin (see diabetes, page 269).	Diabetics should eat or drink something containing sugar; for others, sugarless foods. If symptoms persist, call doctor for advice and appointment. If seizures or loss of consciousness, call 911 or go to emergency facility **immediately.**
Confusion, sleepiness, loss of consciousness, muscle spasms, shortness of breath.	Chronic kidney disease.	Call doctor for immediate appointment.
Confusion, bruising or bleeding for no clear reason, jaundice.	Chronic liver disease.	Call doctor for immediate appointment.
Developing over time: confusion; faulty judgment and reasoning; inability to complete simple tasks; memory problems that worsen; tendency to lose things, and to wander and become lost.	Alzheimer's disease (see page 50).	Call doctor for advice and appointment.
Confusion; drowsiness; chronic breathing or sleep problems.	High levels of carbon dioxide in blood due to chronic lung disease, airway obstruction, or obesity.	Call doctor for advice and appointment.
Forgetfulness, poor concentration, irritability, anxiety, depression, falling asleep at inappropriate times.	Sleep deprivation or sleep apnea (see sleep disorders, page 277).	Call doctor for advice and appointment.

hood of recovery is good. As one expert puts it, "Alcoholism is the most treatable untreated disease in America."

Alcohol abuse:
➤ If you think you might have an alcohol problem, keep careful track of how much you drink over a specified period of time (a week or more), and don't fudge. Medical experts say women—who metabolize alcohol differently than do men—should have no more than one drink a day, and men no more than two. (A "drink" by this definition is one 12-ounce can of beer, one 5-ounce glass of wine, or 1.5 ounces of distilled spirits.) New research suggests that if you drink at all, for optimum health you should limit yourself to three or four drinks a week.
➤ Never have more than one drink in an hour. The liver cannot process more than an ounce of alcohol per hour.
➤ Don't drink on an empty stomach.
➤ Examine your attitude toward your drinking. If you notice yourself getting drunk despite your best intentions, hoarding alcohol, making statements that minimize how much you drink, or reacting angrily if someone confronts you about your drinking, seek professional help.
➤ Don't have any beer, wine, or other alcoholic drinks if you are pregnant, trying to get pregnant, or nursing.

Alcoholism:
➤ If you suspect that a partner or loved one is an alcoholic, talk to your physician or contact a reputable alcohol treatment program for advice on how to deal with him or her.
➤ If you consistently drink too much, acknowledge the problem and resolve to stop drinking on your own. If you have no success, call your doctor or an alcoholism treatment center for advice. In most cases, early treatment increases the chance of recovery.

➤ Join a self-help group. Alcoholics Anonymous (AA) is the best known, and it has groups throughout the country. If you are uncomfortable with AA's spiritual emphasis, you might want to explore alternative programs like Rational Recovery or Women for Sobriety. Family members may want to look into Al-Anon Family Groups, a support program for the parents, children, and spouses of alcoholics.
➤ Start exercising regularly. Exercise releases chemicals in the brain that provide a sense of well-being.

➤ If you have symptoms of alcohol abuse or alcoholism.
➤ If you drink regularly to intoxication and feel chronic or periodic depression.
➤ If you have tried to stop drinking and have experienced withdrawal symptoms such as headache, anxiety, insomnia, nausea, or, in rare cases, delirium tremens (confusion, shaking, and hallucinations).
➤ If you can't give up alcohol and you are pregnant or think you may be pregnant.

Alcohol abuse:
➤ Don't drink as an attempt to escape anxiety or depression.
➤ Substitute other, more healthful activities for social drinking if, during the day, you find yourself eagerly anticipating those beers or glasses of wine.

Alcoholism:
Most experts believe that staying away from alcohol completely is the key to recovery for those who have crossed the line into alcoholism. That might not be easy. The following steps can help prevent a relapse:
➤ Avoid places and events that you associate with alcohol, and don't spend time with friends when they are drinking heavily.
➤ Enlist the help of your family and friends. Tell them that you are trying not to drink, and let them know what they can do to support you.

- ➤ Replace your dependence on alcohol with other activities. Consider taking a class or volunteering your time.
- ➤ Get a medical checkup, and ask your doctor for advice about foods and vitamin supplements that can aid your physical recovery.
- ➤ If you have a relapse, don't use it as an excuse to give up all your gains. Think carefully about what led to the relapse and how to do things differently next time.

FOR MORE HELP

Organization: National Council on Alcoholism and Drug Dependence, 12 W. 21st St., New York, NY 10010. 800-622-2255, 24-hour line. Fax: 212-645-1690. Call to be referred to a local affiliate, which offers over-the-phone counseling and support.

Organization: Alcoholics Anonymous, P.O. Box 459, Grand Central Station, New York, NY 10163. 212-870-3400, M–F 8:30–4:45 EST. Call for the number of a local AA group, or look in the phone book under "Alcoholics Anonymous."

Organization: Al-Anon/Alateen Family Groups, P.O. Box 862, Midtown Station, New York, NY 10018-0862. 800-356-9996, M–F 9–6 EST. Al-Anon is a mutual-support program for families and friends of alcoholics. Alateen is a support program for teenagers and young people whose lives are affected by alcoholism.

Organization: Rational Recovery, P.O. Box 800, Lotus, CA 95651-0800. 916-621-4374, M–F 8–4 PST. A self-help program for people with alcohol or drug problems. Groups are available in 700 U.S. cities.

Organization: Women for Sobriety, P.O. Box 618, Quakertown, PA 18951. 215-536-8026, M–F 8:30–3 EST. Operates mutual-help groups that address the special needs of women with alcohol problems.

Video: *Alcoholism at Time of Diagnosis.* Clear, useful overview of causes and treatments, consisting of four reports—Understanding the Diagnosis, What Happens Next?, Treatment and Management, and Issues and Answers. Time Life Medical, 1996, $19.95.

Anorexia and Bulimia

SIGNS AND SYMPTOMS

Anorexia:
- ■ Eating very little food and insisting on dieting even while losing large amounts of weight.
- ■ Feeling convinced of being fat even when far below normal weight.
- ■ Compulsive exercising.
- ■ In women, loss of menstrual periods, or irregular periods.
- ■ In women, increase in facial and body hair.
- ■ Dry, sallow, or yellow skin.
- ■ Depression, moodiness, impatience, social withdrawal.
- ■ Constant use of over-the-counter diet pills or laxatives.

Bulimia:
- ■ Repeated periods of overeating, often followed by vomiting in secret.
- ■ Spending long periods of time in the bathroom, especially after meals, or other signs of frequent vomiting (such as bloodshot eyes) or laxative or diuretic use (dizziness).
- ■ Erosion of tooth enamel, gum infections, and cavities caused by stomach acids that enter the mouth during frequent vomiting.
- ■ Compulsive exercising.

As many as 8 million people in the United States are thought to have eating disorders: psychological illnesses in which the individual becomes obsessed with food and body image. Anorexia nervosa (self-starvation) and bulimia nervosa (binge eating and/or purging) are the most common eating disorders. Both are serious and possibly fatal if untreated, and they require immediate professional attention.

Anorexia nervosa is most common in young women, but it can affect anyone. The disorder often first appears as a seemingly normal concern about weight and dieting, which grows obsessive as the individual becomes locked into a vicious cycle of compulsive dieting and overexercise. The anorexic views him- or herself as fat even when emaciated. A person with bulimia, in contrast, goes on eating binges—sometimes consuming up to 20,000 calories at one sitting.

Anorexia and bulimia are closely linked: Approximately one-fourth of those with bulimia have also had anorexia. The cause of these disorders is still not understood, but it seems to involve low self-esteem, troubled family relationships, worries about physical changes during adolescence, and societal pressure to look thin, perhaps combined with a genetic predisposition.

Treatment may include monitoring physical and psychological health, and providing nutritional counseling, individual or family therapy, and support groups. Antidepressants can help with bulimia, even in those who aren't depressed. Hospitalization is sometimes necessary in serious cases or in those involving severe depression.

WHAT YOU CAN DO NOW

➤ Seek professional help from a doctor specializing in eating disorders as soon as possible. The longer an eating disorder goes untreated, the more difficult it is to reverse. Your family doctor may be able to refer you.

➤ Treat yourself or someone who has the disorder with love and understanding—be aware that this is a psychiatric illness.

➤ Avoid over-the-counter diet pills, laxatives, and diuretics. Overuse of diet pills can result in stroke; overuse of laxatives and diuretics, in heart failure.

WHEN TO CALL THE DOCTOR

➤ If you or someone close to you show symptoms of anorexia or bulimia, especially if the eating disorder involves depression and/or talk of suicide.

HOW TO PREVENT IT

➤ If you find yourself or a family member worrying obsessively about weight and appearance, see an eating disorders specialist for advice.

➤ Provide your children with examples of healthy attitudes toward food and body image, and handle issues of eating and weight with sensitivity. Don't make disparaging comments about your child's appearance.

➤ As a parent, be willing to admit your own mistakes and to accept those of your children. Since anorexia and bulimia are more common in families in which high achievement and the appearance of perfection are important, be careful to keep pressure to a minimum and refrain from demanding perfection.

FOR MORE HELP

Information line: National Association of Anorexia Nervosa and Associated Disorders, P.O. Box 7, Highland Park, IL 60035. 847-831-3438, M–F 9–5 CST. Specialists answer questions, send information on eating disorders, and refer callers to lists of experts and support groups.

Organization: National Eating Disorders Organization, Laureate Eating Disorders Program, 6655 S. Yale Ave., Tulsa, OK 74136-3329. 918-481-4044, 8–5 M–F CST. Provides educational materials and referrals to support groups.

Video: *Anorexia & Bulimia at Time of Diagnosis.* Clear, useful overview of causes and treatments, consisting of four reports—Understanding the Diagnosis, What Happens Next?, Treatment and Management, and Issues and Answers. Time Life Medical, 1996, $19.95.

Anxiety and Phobias

Generalized anxiety disorder:
Long-term, severe worry, tension, irritability, or depression, for no clear reason. Plus some of the following:

- Inability to relax, sleep, or concentrate on things.
- Fatigue.
- Headaches.
- Sweating or hot flashes.
- Tension, trembling, or twitching in the muscles.
- Being easily startled.

Phobias:

- Persistent, irrational fear of particular situations or objects, such as snakes, elevators, spiders, heights, blood, flying, or tunnels.
- Fear of social situations in which you think you will be humiliated or criticized.

Panic disorder:
Feelings of terror—"panic attacks"—that strike suddenly, sometimes in response to stressful situations, and typically last a couple of minutes. They are marked by:

- Racing or pounding heart, sometimes with chest pain.
- Shortness of breath.
- Dizziness, weakness, or faintness.
- Nausea.
- Tingling or numbness in the hands.
- Flushes or chills.
- Feelings of unreality or a sense of losing control.
- Fear of impending doom or dying.

Panic disorder is often accompanied by fear of situations that might bring on a panic attack and would be difficult to escape.

Obsessive-compulsive disorder:

- Continuous unwelcome thoughts, such as images of germs, dirt, or repugnant sexual acts; violent urges; or fear of harming people.
- Repeated actions and rituals performed in an effort to prevent or cast out obsessive thoughts. Examples include repeatedly washing the hands, counting things, and rearranging objects.

Post-traumatic stress disorder:

- Inability to escape memories and thoughts about horrifying past experiences involving war, violence, natural disasters, rape, or abuse.
- Flashbacks and nightmares.
- Difficulty sleeping.
- Irritability.
- Aggressive or violent feelings and behavior.
- Withdrawal, numbness, or loss of interest in things that used to be enjoyable.

Feeling anxious in certain circumstances is normal and healthy: It rouses you to action when faced with an actual threat. But too much anxiety disrupts daily life.

Anxiety disorders vary in severity from mild to immobilizing. Experts believe that life experiences may be partly responsible for the development of anxiety disorders, along with heredity. In some cases, medication can help; in others, psychotherapy may be useful.

➤ Be honest about how your anxiety is affecting you: Is it disrupting your life, keeping you from doing things you want to do?
➤ Educate yourself about the problem by reading up-to-date books and studies and by getting information from mental health organizations.
➤ Find a good therapist to talk to. Ask your friends or primary care doctor for a referral—preferably to someone experienced in treating anxiety disorders; then go to a session to see if you feel comfortable with the therapist's approach.
➤ Get some daily exercise, such as brisk walking or a sport you enjoy. Research

shows that people who exercise regularly are less likely to be depressed or overly tense than those who don't.

➤ Cut down on alcohol and caffeine; too much caffeine often causes anxiety and may trigger panic attacks. Avoid street drugs such as cocaine.

➤ Simplify your life by making your schedule less hectic; spend less time on activities you don't find relaxing.

➤ Do deep breathing and relaxation exercises, especially when your anxiety level starts to rise. Learn yoga or meditation.

WHEN TO CALL THE DOCTOR

➤ If you feel uncontrollably anxious and can't function normally.

➤ If, along with your anxiety, you have lost weight and your eyes seem to bulge; you may have a **thyroid problem** (see page 279) or other physical ailment.

FOR MORE HELP

Information line: Panic Disorder Information, 800-647-2642, M–F 8:30AM–9PM EST. Sends information on panic disorder.

Organization: National Empowerment Center, 800-POWER-2U (769-3728), M–F 8:30–4 EST. Mental health consumers' group offers referrals to support groups and drop-in centers as well as print and audio information on various topics.

Organization: National Mental Health Association, 800-969-6642, M–F 9–5 EST (messages requesting information taken 24 hours a day). Sends free pamphlets on anxiety and other mental health problems, and makes referrals to services and support groups nationwide.

Organization: "Vet Centers" of the Department of Veterans Affairs. Counseling centers for Vietnam veterans and other vets with post-traumatic stress disorder are located in many cities. Check your phone book or call local information for the number of the one nearest you.

Video: *Stress & Anxiety at Time of Diagnosis.* Clear, useful overview of causes and treatments, consisting of four reports—Understanding the Diagnosis, What Happens Next?, Treatment and Management, and Issues and Answers. Time Life Medical, 1996, $19.95.

Attention Deficit Disorder

SIGNS AND SYMPTOMS

■ Frequent inability to pay attention.
■ Difficulty focusing on work.
■ Strong pattern of making careless mistakes or having difficulty following instructions.
■ Impulsiveness.
■ Talking too much and interrupting others frequently.
■ In some cases, hyperactivity—fidgeting and running about in otherwise quiet situations.

Attention deficit disorder (ADD) is one of the most frequently diagnosed behavioral disorders and—because some experts believe it is widely overdiagnosed—one of the most controversial. Genuine ADD seems to run in families, although environmental factors can also play a role in causing it. If a woman smokes, uses drugs or alcohol, or is exposed to lead during pregnancy, it can affect the fetus and produce symptoms of ADD later in childhood; exposure of young children to lead can do the same.

The symptoms should be seen as a problem only if they interfere with a person's ability to function in more than one setting—at school and at home, or at work and at play. Many children are labeled with attention deficit disorder when their behavior is actually quite normal for their age or situation.

Furthermore, symptoms of ADD can be triggered by problems other than ADD: Learning disabilities, physical or sexual abuse, tension, depression, stress, and family violence can all cause children to act in ways that resemble its symptoms.

ADD is most commonly diagnosed in children (mostly boys), though adults can also have it. When people with symptoms of ADD are also hyperactive, the disorder is called attention deficit hyperactivity disorder (ADHD).

People with ADD do not lack intelligence; rather, they have difficulty focusing their attention, and as a result, their performance suffers. Life can be very frustrating for children with ADD: They have problems at school, they become known as troublemakers or slow learners, they get angry easily, they see themselves as bad or stupid.

Since there is no known cure for ADD, the normal treatment is to try to manage it with medication, chiefly the stimulant methylphenidate (brand name Ritalin). While some children are helped by this drug and other stimulants, many experts think they are prescribed too often. Antidepressants may also be prescribed for some children.

Although children with ADD were once thought to outgrow it, many doctors now believe that most will continue to have some symptoms as adults, only in different forms. Adults may be highly disorganized, given to uncontrollable temper outbursts, and feel unable to cope with the stresses of life; they may have difficulty in personal relationships and problems with drug or alcohol abuse.

WHAT YOU CAN DO NOW

➤ If you suspect that your child may have ADD, find a skilled specialist you trust and get a thorough evaluation. Child psychiatrists, pediatricians, neurologists, and psychologists are among the professionals who work with ADD. Your family doctor may be able to refer you.

After diagnosis:
➤ Consider a second opinion if a doctor says your child has ADD—particularly if methylphenidate or another drug is prescribed or if the doctor does not specialize in childhood psychiatric disorders.
➤ Know your child: Learn about his or her patterns and habits, strengths and weaknesses. Some children with ADD do best with lots of planned activity and minimal distractions, while others need lots of

activity and do poorly if their environment is too controlled.
➤ Educate yourself and your child about the disorder.
➤ Try not to punish your child for behavior he or she can't control.
➤ Locate a support group for people with ADD and get involved.

WHEN TO CALL A MENTAL HEALTH PROFESSIONAL

➤ If you or your child show symptoms of ADD that interfere significantly with daily life and work or school.

FOR MORE HELP

Organization: Children and Adults with Attention Deficit Disorder (CHADD), 800-233-4050, 24-hour recording. Leave your name and address to receive information on ADD and a list of local support groups.

Organization: National ADD Association, 800-487-2282, 24-hour recording. Leave your name and address to receive a list of local ADD support groups. Sponsors conferences and educational programs on ADD for parents.

Book: *The Misunderstood Child,* by Larry Silver, M.D. A guide for parents of children with learning disabilities and ADD. McGraw Hill, 1995, $9.95.

Depression

SIGNS AND SYMPTOMS

■ Feelings of sadness or pessimism that don't go away.
■ Feelings of guilt, worthlessness, hopelessness, or despair.
■ Loss of interest and pleasure in work, relationships, food, sex, or other aspects of life.
■ Fatigue and lack of energy.
■ Sleep problems such as insomnia, oversleeping, or repeatedly waking before dawn.

- Difficulty concentrating, remembering, making decisions, and completing simple tasks; a feeling of moving in slow motion.
- Unusual weight gain or loss.
- Frequently occurring thoughts of suicide or death.
- Nagging physical ailments—such as headaches or stomach pain—that don't get better with treatment.

A lmost everyone occasionally feels blue or unmotivated, or finds it hard to concentrate. Feeling down is normal—up to a point. When people are so unhappy that their ability to work, enjoy life, or simply function is disrupted, they are said to be suffering from depression.

The causes—and treatments—for the various forms of depression are hotly debated, but clearly genetics, environment, brain chemistry, and life experiences all play parts. Depression can strike at any age, including childhood, though severe depression most often affects adults. Women are twice as likely as men to be diagnosed with depression, for reasons that are unclear.

Depression can take different forms. Feelings such as unhappiness, pessimism, or self-pity in response to painful events or situations are sometimes called **depressive reactions.** These feelings, which are normal, can be quite severe but usually go away in a short time without treatment.

There's also a form of chronic, low-level depression (called **dysthymia**). People with this condition are not severely depressed or suicidal, but they generally have little enthusiasm for life and feel discouraged about the future. Some suffer from fatigue, insomnia, and low self-esteem, and they tend to heap blame on themselves, often relentlessly. They have a hard time making decisions or shaking their negative mood, and they can sometimes succumb to major depression.

People who suffer from **major depression** feel so miserable that they have a difficult time functioning day to day. They are often inconsolable and are troubled by guilt, insomnia, fatigue, overwhelming sadness, and feelings of emptiness and worthlessness. They may be suicidal or obsessed with death.

In very rare cases, they may lose touch with reality and have delusions and hallucinations. Their depression—which may have been triggered by a significant loss and can last for months afterward—may eventually lift, only to return later. Research suggests that such depression may sometimes be linked to family history or an imbalance in the brain chemicals that influence mood and behavior.

When depression develops with the onset of fall or winter and then fades in the spring or summer, the condition is called **seasonal affective disorder** (SAD). People with SAD are troubled by the lack of natural light and often go through major mood shifts between the seasons.

Mood swings are even more extreme for people with **manic depression,** also known as **bipolar affective disorder.** They go from being intensely energetic or extremely elated (though they may also be irritable, unfocused, and paranoid) to periods of lethargy, misery, and despair.

WHAT YOU CAN DO NOW

➤ Get professional help. Your family doctor should be able to refer you to a counselor experienced in dealing with depression.
➤ Try a support group. Some people are helped by peer-led groups, including those geared toward individuals who suffered traumas in childhood (such as adult children of alcoholics and survivors of abuse) or who have had significant losses (see **grief,** page 209). What's important is to get support from people who will treat you with respect and understanding.
➤ Educate yourself about depression. There is a lot of information available through consumer self-help and professional organizations. Many self-help groups distribute information and communicate on-line.

WHEN TO CALL A MENTAL HEALTH PROFESSIONAL

➤ If you, your child, or someone close to you has suicidal thoughts or depression that doesn't seem to lift. (Check your phone book: Many cities have suicide hotlines for emergencies.)

➤ If depression is seriously disrupting your work, school, or relationships. Psychologists, psychiatrists, social workers, and peer counselors all work with people suffering from depression. They often take radically different approaches to treatment, including individual psychotherapy ("talk therapy") and antidepressant medication.

HOW TO PREVENT IT

➤ Try not to isolate yourself.
➤ When you're feeling blue, find a friend or someone with whom you're comfortable and talk about what's bothering you.
➤ Stay active. Research shows that regular exercise can improve your mood.
➤ Be sure to get enough sleep.
➤ Eat balanced meals.

FOR MORE HELP

Organization: National Mental Health Association, 800-969-6642, M–F 9–5 EST (messages requesting information taken 24 hours a day). Sends free pamphlets on depression and other mental illnesses, and makes referrals to services and support groups nationwide.

Organization: National Empowerment Center, 800-POWER-2U (769-3728), M–F 8–4 EST. Mental health consumers' group offers referrals to support groups and drop-in centers as well as print and audio information on various topics.

Video: *Depression at Time of Diagnosis.* Clear, useful overview of causes and treatments, consisting of four reports—Understanding the Diagnosis, What Happens Next?, Treatment and Management, and Issues and Answers. Time Life Medical, 1996, $19.95.

Drug Abuse

SIGNS AND SYMPTOMS

■ Changes in appearance and/or behavior that threaten relationships and work performance.
■ Irritability or abrupt changes in mood or attitude.
■ Restlessness, sometimes alternating with extreme lethargy.
■ Unexplained absences.
■ Unexplained money problems.
■ Blackouts and memory lapses.
■ Drug cravings, inability to stop using, lying about drug use, preoccupation with obtaining the drug and using it.

The use of drugs to obtain pleasure, relieve pain, or alter reality is common in our society—as it has been in most cultures throughout history. But drug use can also lead to abuse and sometimes to addiction.

Drug abuse is the use of a substance—legal or illegal—frequently enough or in large enough quantities to cause the user physical, mental, emotional, or social harm. Addiction is loss of control over drug use.

Experts still don't understand why some people are able to use drugs occasionally while others get hooked almost right away. It is generally agreed today that drug addiction is a disease, not a sign of weak character, and should be treated as such.

Abuse of illegal drugs can be risky and even fatal (see **street drugs** chart, page 208). But abuse of legal drugs is also an extraordinary problem. Twenty-one million Americans have abused prescription drugs, such as painkillers, sleeping pills, and tranquilizers, at least once in their lives. Alcohol and tobacco alone claim more lives than all illegal drugs combined. Death from automobile and other accidents as a result of drinking is a particular risk.

Like alcoholics, drug abusers can be hard to treat because they often deny their addiction—even when it threatens to destroy their lives. Once a person acknowledges his or her drug problem, treatment will depend on the type and severity of the addiction. Successful recovery programs aim to establish social support, enhance self-esteem, and teach ways to avoid situations that can trigger relapse. Most people who enter such programs recover successfully.

WHAT YOU CAN DO NOW

➤ If you believe you have a drug problem and have tried to stop using but could not, call a drug treatment program or professional right away. Remember that it's difficult to overcome drug abuse on your own and that help is available.
➤ If you detect any combination of the listed symptoms in a family member or friend (particularly a child or an adolescent) and suspect drug abuse, call your doctor or one of the organizations listed here for referrals to professionals or clinics that specialize in drug treatment.

WHEN TO CALL THE DOCTOR

Call for an immediate appointment:
➤ If you are pregnant (or think that you might be pregnant) and have been abusing drugs.
➤ If someone (especially a child or an adolescent) shows symptoms of drug abuse.

HOW TO PREVENT IT

Preventing relapse often requires significant changes in habits and lifestyle. Depending on the severity of the drug problem, recovery (the stage that follows withdrawal) can be extremely difficult. Still, there are steps you can take to make it easier to remain clean:
➤ Seek the support of family members, friends, and colleagues.
➤ Join a support group such as Narcotics Anonymous or Cocaine Anonymous.
➤ Avoid places and situations that you associate with drug use. Try to make new friends who don't use drugs, and stay away from friends when they are using drugs.
➤ Be careful not to substitute another kind of addictive behavior—such as gambling, smoking, or overeating—for your former addiction.
➤ Make sure that your diet is healthy and that you get regular exercise; physical activity stimulates your body to release chemicals that make you feel good.
➤ Remember, recovery doesn't happen overnight. If you have a relapse, don't use it as an excuse to go back to your old habits. Think carefully about what led to the incident, and plan how to avoid the same reaction next time.

FOR MORE HELP

Hotline: National Drug Information Treatment and Referral Hotline of the Center for Substance Abuse Treatment, 800-662-4357, M–F 24-hour line. Information specialists refer callers to treatment programs for drug and/or alcohol problems.

Hotline: Phoenix House, 800-COCAINE (262-2463), 24-hour line. Gives names and phone numbers of local treatment programs.

Hotline: Cocaine Anonymous National Hotline, 800-347-8998, 24-hour line. A self-help/mutual support program patterned on the Alcoholics Anonymous 12-step approach. Call for referrals to local meetings.

Information line: National Council on Alcoholism and Drug Dependence Hope Line, 800-622-2255, 24-hour line. Provides fact sheets and other materials. State and local affiliates offer treatment referrals to individuals and families.

Organization: National Clearinghouse for Alcohol and Drug Information, P.O. Box 2345, Rockville, MD 20847-2345. 800-729-6686 in Maryland, 301-468-2600 elsewhere, M–F 8--7 EST. Provides alcohol and drug abuse information.

Organization: Narcotics Anonymous, P.O. Box 9999, Van Nuys, CA 91409. 818-773-9999, M–F 8–5 PST. A self-help/mutual support program patterned on the Alcoholics Anonymous 12-step approach. Call for referrals to local meetings.

Street Drugs: Symptoms and Risks

TYPE OF DRUG	SYMPTOMS OF USE	RISKS
Amphetamines (speed, uppers).	Restlessness; unusual talkativeness; decreased appetite with weight loss; dilated pupils; insomnia; trembling; dry mouth; angry, paranoid, or violent behavior.	Stroke or heart failure; increased risk of violence.
Opiates, including heroin (smack) and opium.	Fatigue, euphoria, weight loss, sweating, poor appetite, needle marks on arms (sometimes), sniffling and runny nose (if snorted).	Overdose can lead to coma and death; if injected, greater risk of HIV infection and hepatitis from contaminated needles.
Cocaine (coke); called crack or rock when smoked.	Decreased appetite; mood swings; unusual talkativeness; dilated pupils; apparent intoxication; sniffling, runny nose, and nosebleeds (if snorted); weight loss; paranoia; disconnected speech.	Holes in cartilage separating nostrils (if snorted); seizures and coma; death by cardiac arrest or respiratory failure; suicidal behavior after prolonged use.
Inhalants, including nitrous oxide (laughing gas), amyl nitrite (poppers), butyl nitrate (rush), chlorohydrocarbons (aerosol sprays), and hydrocarbons (glue, paint thinner).	Nausea, coughing, nosebleeds, fatigue, lack of coordination, violent behavior.	Suffocation; with glue or paint thinner, permanent damage to brain and nervous system; increased risk of violence.
Sedatives (downers), including tranquilizers and barbiturates.	Lethargy, confused speech, lack of balance, impaired judgment and motor ability.	Overdose; combined with alcohol, can lead to coma and death.
Hallucinogens, including LSD (acid), mescaline, and PCP (angel dust).	Seeing things that aren't there, nausea, sweating and trembling, mood disorders, increased heart rate, paranoia, violent behavior (PCP).	PCP in large doses can lead to convulsions, coma, and increased risk of violence. LSD can cause panic or loss of control.

Street Drugs: Symptoms and Risks

TYPE OF DRUG	SYMPTOMS OF USE	RISKS
Designer drugs, including synthetic heroin (China white), MPTP, and MDMA (ecstasy).	Euphoria, tremors, impaired speech, nausea, sweating.	Ecstasy may cause paranoia and depression. Synthetic heroin can lead to Parkinson's-like symptoms, including tremors, paralysis, and impaired speech or permanent brain damage.
Cannabis, including marijuana and hashish (pot, grass, hash).	Mood swings, increased appetite, red eyes, slowed time sense and reflexes, anxiety, lethargy, alienation (sometimes).	Not physically addictive, but may cause psychological dependence and damage to lungs from smoking.

Grief

SIGNS AND SYMPTOMS

Grief is a natural process that people go through when they suffer a deep loss. The reactions or symptoms it produces vary greatly from one person to another. They may include:

- Extreme depression and fatigue.
- Sudden shifts in emotions—being numb and robotlike one minute and crying uncontrollably the next.
- Feelings of helplessness, confusion, and despair.
- Significant changes in sleeping patterns, such as trouble falling asleep, waking up repeatedly at night, or wanting to sleep all the time.
- Physical pain or discomfort.
- Either loss of appetite or compulsive overeating.
- Absentmindedness; such difficulty making decisions or concentrating that even simple acts, like reading a newspaper, seem nearly impossible.
- Self-destructive behavior, including such actions as driving recklessly or abusing drugs or alcohol.

Few things can be as emotionally wrenching and as hard to recover from as the death of a loved one. But other losses can also leave people stunned with grief; these include divorce, miscarriage, the end of a friendship or serious relationship, and a disabling illness or accident.

Grieving often happens in stages. The first stage is frequently marked by a combination of numbness, shock, and denial. You may feel as though you're in a trance and unable to make decisions. Many people feel so drained or so badly neglect their own physical needs (such as eating or sleeping) that they get sick. Others try to deal with the shock by pretending it's not so bad: "Don't worry about me. I'm fine."

After the shock passes, you may go through phases of intense emotion. When someone close to you has died, these may include anger (at the unfairness of the death), fear (that you or other loved ones will also die), guilt (for having survived, or for something you think you failed to do for the person who died), depression, and helplessness or aimlessness.

What's important is not to block your grief. Experts advise allowing yourself (and others) to feel numb, sad, angry, or depressed. Then, at your own pace, move on with your life. "Grief is not a sign of weakness," is a favorite saying of the Theos Foundation, which organizes support groups for widowed people. "Allow grief to have its way for a while; then, gradually and gently, you can release yourself from its grip."

WHAT YOU CAN DO NOW

➤ Don't hide your grief from friends; if you express your needs, they will be more available to help.
➤ Find a support group. Call one of the organizations listed, or get a referral from a local hospital, psychologist, or place of worship. Being with others who are going through the same process can help. (Many groups also work with people who have a loved one in the process of dying.)
➤ If there is a death or other traumatic event in your family, your children need to grieve, too, and may need your encouragement. Grief groups for children exist but may be hard to find. For young children, individual counseling may be more appropriate.
➤ Put off making major decisions—whether to move from your home, what to do with your loved one's possessions—while you're in the midst of grieving.
➤ Don't leave important things unsaid or undone before someone dies. Seeking the person out and making sure you've resolved everything possible can spare you much grief and guilt later.
➤ If you know someone who is grieving, don't be afraid to make contact and talk with him or her.

WHEN TO CALL THE DOCTOR

➤ If you feel physically ill and think you need professional help. Ailments caused by grief are real and can be serious.
➤ If symptoms of depression last longer than two months, or if you feel suicidal.

FOR MORE HELP

Information line: Theos Foundation, 412-471-7779, M–Th 9–4 EST. National organization for widows and widowers that will connect callers with local support groups and send out information on the grieving process.

Information line: Compassionate Friends, 708-990-0010, M–F 9–4 CST. Refers bereaved parents and siblings to local support groups, and sends brochures related to various kinds of death.

Information line: Kara, 415-321-5859, M–F 9–5 PST. Connects children and adolescents who have lost a parent or sibling with support groups, and sends brochures on various topics.

Information line: Pregnancy and Infant Loss Center, 612-473-9372, M–F 9–4 CST. Provides referrals to bereaved parents coping with miscarriage, stillbirth, and infant death.

Smoking and Illness

SIGNS AND SYMPTOMS

■ Shortness of breath, wheezing.
■ General fatigue.
■ Persistent or hacking cough.
■ Poor sense of smell and taste.
■ Bad breath.
■ Poor circulation (cold hands and feet are a sign).
■ Frequent bouts of respiratory illnesses such as bronchitis.
■ Premature wrinkling of skin.

Cigarette smoking is the leading cause of preventable illness and death in the United States. It kills more Americans every year than do alcohol, cocaine, heroin, homicides, airplane and automobile accidents, and AIDS combined—more than 120,000 a year from lung cancer and about 180,000 from heart disease. (See **lung cancer,** page 93, **congestive heart failure,** page 102, **chronic bronchitis and emphysema,** page 88, and **high blood pressure,** page 105.)

Smoking harms more than just the person who lights up: Secondhand smoke (other people's tobacco smoke) may kill as many as 50,000 Americans a year. Smoking by parents can aggravate asthma in children and increase their risk of colds, ear infections, and sudden infant death syndrome. Smoking during pregnancy increases the risk of miscarriage, premature delivery, and fetal death.

Nicotine is an extremely addictive drug, which is why so many people continue smoking despite the known risks. Nevertheless, if you're a smoker, there are things you can do to make quitting easier—and to help yourself stay away from cigarettes for good.

WHAT YOU CAN DO NOW

The best and only advice is to quit smoking. The benefits of quitting kick in right from the start. Within 20 minutes after your last puff, your blood pressure—which rises when you smoke—returns to normal. Within 8 to 48 hours, the excess carbon monoxide in your blood drops to normal. One year after that, your risk of heart disease will be half that of a smoker's. Fifteen years after giving up cigarettes, your risk of heart disease will be the same as that of someone who has never smoked. You'll also reduce your risk of getting many types of cancer.

Tips for making quitting easier:
➤ Get as much support as you can. Some people find that it helps to quit with a friend or relative, or to join a "quitting support group." Your doctor may be able to refer you.
➤ If you are a heavy smoker, consult your doctor about using nicotine gum or skin patches (available by prescription only). These aids are meant to reduce the physical urge for a cigarette. Never smoke while using the gum or patches, though, or you'll risk a dangerous nicotine overdose.
➤ Exercise regularly. Daily walks or bike rides help your body overcome its need for nicotine as a stimulant.
➤ Recognize "triggers"—situations and places that make you want to smoke—and avoid them, if possible. Substitute other activities when you're tempted to light up.
➤ Consider acupuncture, meditation, guided imagery, hypnotherapy, and biofeedback. All of these can be useful.

➤ Drink lots of water and have low-calorie snacks available during the first weeks when you have an urge to put something in your mouth.

What to expect when you quit:
The good news is that you decided to quit smoking. The bad news? You may experience at least one of these withdrawal symptoms: headache, nausea, constipation or diarrhea, fatigue, drowsiness, loss of concentration, and insomnia. You may also feel more irritable, anxious, or depressed than usual, or have a bigger appetite or an increased desire for sweets.

These reactions occur because your body is scrambling to adjust to the sudden absence of nicotine. But don't be alarmed—and don't rush off to buy a pack of cigarettes. Withdrawal symptoms are only temporary, and once they pass, you'll feel better than you've felt in years.

WHEN TO CALL THE DOCTOR

Call for an immediate appointment:
➤ If you notice a persistent cough, wheezing, breathlessness, and chest pains.
Call for advice and an appointment:
➤ If you are a tobacco user and become concerned about your health for any reason. Smokers are more susceptible than nonsmokers to many major illnesses.

FOR MORE HELP

Information line: Smoking, Tobacco and Health Information Line, Centers for Disease Control and Prevention, 800-232-1311, 24-hour recording. Distributes free information about smoking.

Organization: American Lung Association, 1740 Broadway, New York, NY 10019. 800-586-4872, M–F 9–5 your time. Has more than 100 offices around the country, some of which offer support groups. Offers educational programs and literature.

Organization: American Cancer Society, 1599 Clifton Rd., Atlanta, GA 30329-4251. 800-227-2345, M–F 9–5 your time. Provides literature about smoking and refers callers to local chapters.

Organization: Smokenders, 4455 E. Camelback Rd., #D-150, Phoenix, AZ 85018. 800-828-4357, M–F 8–4:30 MST. A private organization with a program that provides techniques that can help people quit smoking.

Stress

Stress is the reaction of our bodies and minds to anything that upsets their regular balance. Stressful events physically trigger the release of stress hormones—including adrenaline—that provide a quick supply of oxygen and energy. But these hormone surges, if sparked again and again, can deplete the body's resources and result in problems such as ulcers, high blood pressure, and loss of appetite. Ongoing stress also puts you at risk of migraine headaches, depression, chronic fatigue, adult-onset diabetes, and digestive ailments.

Chronic stress can lead to hopelessness and depression. At the same time, your body's immune system is disrupted, increasing your vulnerability to disease.

Stress is typically caused by external events and situations that are painful or overwhelming and that leave you feeling out of control: burnout on the job, financial problems, grief, or divorce. Minor stresses range from arguments to traffic jams. Even a positive experience, such as marriage, a job promotion, or a new baby, can trigger stress. Internal causes include illness, loneliness, physical pain, emotional conflict, perfectionism, and the drive to excel.

WHAT YOU CAN DO NOW

- Do things that relax you; take walks or long, hot baths.
- Do some stretching exercises.
- Do the following deep-breathing exercise: Sit or lie in a comfortable position, and count how many breaths you take in one minute. Then, breathing deeply and slowly, try to take half as many breaths in the same time period. Continue for five minutes. Stop if you feel dizzy or faint.
- Call a friend or family member you feel you can talk to easily.

WHEN TO CALL THE DOCTOR

- If you believe that your condition is due to anxiety, depression, or psychological factors more severe than routine stress. (See **depression,** page 204, and **anxiety and phobias,** page 202.)
- If you have symptoms of stress combined with any of the following: unusual sleep patterns, mood swings, loss of sex drive, persistent crying jags, a sense of exhaustion or great difficulty associated with minor tasks, movement that is unusually agitated or slow, or a change in menstrual cycles (in women). You may have a form of clinical depression.
- If your symptoms of stress are especially long-lasting and bothersome.

HOW TO PREVENT IT

- Try to figure out what is causing the stress in your life and where changes can be made. Set reasonable goals for yourself and be forthright with other people about what you can and can't do.
- Let go of perfectionism. If you are juggling too many things, let a ball or two

drop. Your house doesn't have to be spotless, for example, and you don't always have to be the last one to leave the office. Practice giving yourself a break.

➤ Get regular exercise. Vigorous aerobic exercise can reduce the level of stress hormones and release the endorphins that bring a sense of well-being. Exercise for 30 minutes at least three times a week.

➤ Learn relaxation techniques such as deep breathing, stretching exercises, yoga, visualization, or meditation.

➤ Spend time outdoors. According to some research, contact with nature may help reduce stress.

➤ Take a true vacation, leaving your work behind. A real break should be slow-paced and pressure-free.

➤ If your stress is severe and long-term, consider enrolling in a stress-management program, either through your local hospital or with a private therapist.

FOR MORE HELP

Organization: American Institute of Stress, 124 Park Ave., Yonkers, NY 10703. 800-24-RELAX, M–F 9–5 EST. Offers a monthly newsletter and an information packet.

Book: *Women's Burnout: How to Spot It, How to Reverse It, and How to Prevent It,* by Herbert J. Freudenberger, Ph.D. Penguin Paperbacks, 1985, $9.95.

Book: *Why Zebras Don't Get Ulcers,* by Robert M. Sapolsky. W.H. Freeman, 1994, $14.95.

Video: *Stress & Anxiety at Time of Diagnosis.* Clear, useful overview of causes and treatments, consisting of four reports—Understanding the Diagnosis, What Happens Next?, Treatment and Management, and Issues and Answers. Time Life Medical, 1996, $19.95.

Sexual Health

◆

AIDS

SIGNS AND SYMPTOMS

- Swollen lymph nodes, especially at the back of the neck, or in the armpits or groin.
- Sore throat.
- Fatigue and overall sick feeling.
- Fevers, chills, and night sweats.
- Increasingly frequent colds, cold sores, fungal infections in the mouth, or yeast infections.
- Weight loss, coughing, and breathing problems.
- Frequent diarrhea or constipation.
- Skin sores, especially the purple lesions of Kaposi's sarcoma.
- Confusion, memory loss, and personality changes.

First reported in 1981, AIDS, or acquired immunodeficiency syndrome, is now a worldwide epidemic. It's caused by the human immunodeficiency virus (HIV), which is found in blood, semen, and vaginal fluids, and sometimes in saliva and breast milk. The illness is most commonly spread by sexual contact or by sharing unsterilized, intravenous needles. It can be passed from an infected woman to her infant during childbirth or breast-feeding. AIDS cannot be spread by casual contact such as hugging, using the same towel, or sharing a drinking glass.

HIV, which destroys the white blood cells that fight off infections, first produces symptoms, such as fatigue and swollen glands, similar to those of mononucleosis. A person may then have no other symptoms for months, or even years, until so many white blood cells have been destroyed that he or she develops an infection such as **pneumonia** (see page 94) or **tuberculosis** (see page 100), or a cancer such as Kaposi's sarcoma.

Although AIDS has no cure, new kinds of medicines that attack the virus and slow the development of complications have helped infected people live longer, healthier lives. The spread of the disease is easy to prevent.

WHAT YOU CAN DO NOW

➤ If your sexual partner is infected with the virus or if you have symptoms, get an HIV antibody test immediately. The sooner you know whether you are infected, the better the chance of delaying the illness. You should also be retested in three to six months; antibodies to the virus may take that long to develop.

After diagnosis:

➤ Practice **safe sex** (see box, page 217); you can catch other HIV strains or spread the infection, even if you have no symptoms.

WHEN TO CALL THE DOCTOR

➤ If you have HIV or AIDS, and your symptoms worsen or you develop a new one.

(continued)

Sexually Transmitted Diseases

Every sexually transmitted disease (STD) listed here except syphilis may produce no symptoms at first. When symptoms do develop, they may be easily confused with those of other diseases. If you are infected but have no noticeable symptoms, you can still pass an STD on to your partner. Note, too, that any STD that involves open sores or skin irritation, either on the inside or outside of the genitals, puts you at greater risk of HIV infection. That's why, if you have sex with more than one person, periodic testing and checkups are extremely important, as is **safe sex** (see box, page 217).

SYMPTOMS	WHAT IT MIGHT BE	WHAT YOU CAN DO
1–3 weeks after infection: watery mucus from penis or vagina, burning feeling with urination, mild lower abdominal pain.	Chlamydia—bacterial disease. Can result in pelvic inflammatory disease in women (see page 230) or sterility. In newborns exposed during childbirth, can cause pneumonia and eye infections.	Call doctor for immediate appointment. You and partner(s) should be treated with antibiotics.
2–10 days after infection: itching or burning pain in genital area, then red bumps in or on genitals that may turn into blisters or open sores; these disappear within 3 weeks. Attacks that occur later (with same symptoms) heal faster.	Genital herpes—viral infection spread through sex or, rarely, by hands that have herpes blisters or sores. Most contagious when symptoms are present. Can be transferred from mother to baby during childbirth.	Call doctor for immediate appointment. Medications lessen length and severity of outbreaks. Avoid sex until sores heal. **For more help:** ASHA Resource Center, 800-230-6039, M–F 9–7 EST. National Herpes Hotline: 919-361-8488, M–F 9–7 EST.
Small, red, flat, round, itchy bumps inside vagina or on outer genital area or around anus; can also appear in mouth of someone who has had oral contact with genitals of infected person.	Genital warts—viral infection. Some strains may increase risk of cervical or penile cancer. After warts are removed, virus remains and can cause future outbreaks.	Call doctor for immediate appointment. Treatment can include medication or laser surgery. Avoid over-the-counter wart preparations, which are too harsh for genital area. Women who've had warts should get Pap smear every 6 months to check for cervical cancer.

(continued)

Sexually Transmitted Diseases *(continued)*

SYMPTOMS	WHAT IT MIGHT BE	WHAT YOU CAN DO
2–10 days after infection: thick, yellowish discharge from vagina or penis; burning and itching with urination; possibly discharge from rectum. In later stages in women: abdominal pain, bleeding between periods.	Gonorrhea—bacterial infection. Left untreated, may spread to joints, tendons, or heart. May also cause pelvic inflammatory disease in women (see page 230). Infants exposed during birth can become blind.	Call doctor for immediate appointment. Treatment consists of antibiotics and pain relievers. Abstain from sex until doctor says it's safe. Your partner(s) should be tested and treated even if they have no symptoms.
10 days to 3 months after infection: painless open sores on or in genitals, rectal area, or mouth; enlarged lymph nodes in area of sores. If untreated, in second stage (3 weeks to several months later): mild fever, rash, patchy hair loss, and sore throat, which may recur. In third stage (5 to 30 years later): loss of balance, paralysis, dementia, numbness in legs, and blindness (rarely).	Syphilis—bacterial infection. Can damage brain, nervous system, and heart; can be fatal. Highly contagious in first two stages but not in third stage. Infected mothers may pass to infants during childbirth.	Call doctor for immediate appointment. Antibiotics can cure syphilis, although in later stages some damage cannot be reversed. Avoid sex during treatment. Your partner(s) should be tested and treated.
In women, 4–20 days after infection: heavy, greenish-yellow or gray discharge from vagina; discomfort during intercourse; vaginal odor; painful urination.	Trichomoniasis—infection caused by parasite. May increase risk of premature or underweight newborns.	Call doctor for immediate appointment. You and your partner(s) will be treated with antibiotics. A man may have no symptoms but can infect others if not treated. Abstain from sex until treatment is finished.

FOR MORE HELP

Hotline: National STD Hotline of the Centers for Disease Control and Prevention, 800-227-8922, M–F 8AM–11PM EST. Staffers answer questions about sexually transmitted diseases and refer callers to doctors and testing locations.

Organization: American Social Health Association, 800-972-8500, 24-hour line. Provides pamphlets on sexual health and information on support programs.

Organization: National Institute of Allergy and Infectious Diseases, Office of Communications, Bldg. 31, Rm. 7A-50, 9000 Rockville Pike, Bethesda, MD 20892. Write for free STD packet.

HOW TO PREVENT IT

➤ Practice **safe sex** (see box above).
➤ Don't inject drugs. If you do use intravenous drugs, don't share needles.
➤ Avoid contact with other people's blood.
➤ If you continue to engage in high-risk sexual behavior, you and your partner(s) should be tested every 6 to 12 months.

FOR MORE HELP

Hotline: National HIV/AIDS Hotline, Centers for Disease Control and Prevention. English: 800-342-AIDS, seven days a week, 24-hour line. Spanish: 800-344-7432, seven days a week, 8AM–2AM EST. Staffers answer questions about AIDS, refer callers to experts on health, legal, and financial issues. Calls are confidential.

Organization: National AIDS Clearinghouse, Centers for Disease Control and Prevention, P.O. Box 6003, Rockville, MD 20849-6003. 800-458-5231 (English and Spanish), M–F 9–7 EST. Provides free publications and referrals.

Contraception Health Risks

C hoosing which kind of contraception to use takes careful consideration. How effective is a certain method in preventing pregnancy? How well does it protect against HIV and other sexually transmitted diseases? How easy is the method to use, and how willing is each partner to use it? How much does it cost?

One of the most important things to think about is the health risk.

Birth control pills: With today's lower-estrogen birth control pills, serious side effects are rare in women under 30. The Pill does pose significant risks, however, including the possibility of blood clots in the veins, heart attack, and stroke, as well as higher rates of breast cancer and cervical cancer. Discuss the risks with your doctor, especially:

➤ If you have a family history of high blood pressure, blood clots, or diabetes, or if you have had these conditions yourself.
➤ If you have a personal or family history of breast cancer, uterine cancer, or uterine fibroids.
➤ If you smoke, especially if you're over 35.

If you are in any of these risk categories, ask your doctor about the mini-Pill, which doesn't contain estrogen and has fewer side effects. Although it is less effective in preventing pregnancy and sometimes causes irregular bleeding, it is believed to be safer.

If you take either type of birth control pill, be sure to get a Pap smear annually to check for cervical cancer.

Implanted or injected hormones: In addition to being taken in pill form, hormones can be injected or implanted under the skin on a woman's arm. Side effects can include:

➤ Bleeding or spotting between periods, heavy or prolonged bleeding, or no bleeding at all for several months.
➤ Headache, dizziness, or nausea.

Sexual Health

➤ Weight gain or change in appetite.
➤ Nervousness.

There is also a slight risk of infection in the skin area where hormones are implanted.

You should not use hormonal implants or injections if you might already be pregnant or if you have ever had unexplained vaginal bleeding, breast cancer, liver disease, or blood clots in your legs, lungs, or eyes.

Also, certain conditions may worsen the side effects or raise your risk of serious complications. Talk to your doctor if you (or anyone in your family) have ever had:
➤ Breast nodules or fibrocystic breasts (see **breast pain or lumps** chart, page 231), bleeding from the nipples, or an abnormal mammogram.
➤ High blood pressure, high cholesterol levels, or diabetes.
➤ Kidney, heart, or gallbladder disease.
➤ Irregular or very light menstrual periods.
➤ Migraines or frequent headaches.
➤ Asthma or epilepsy.
➤ A history of depression.

Condoms: This method of contraception—including the female condom, which fits inside the vagina—has few health risks or side effects. It is also the only form of contraception that offers protection against HIV, the virus that causes AIDS.

However, some people have allergic reactions to latex. Lambskin or other nonlatex condoms can be used instead, but be aware that they may not protect you against HIV, because the virus may pass through the condom material.

Diaphragm, cervical cap, and spermicide: When used correctly, diaphragms and cervical caps pose few serious health risks. Some women who use diaphragms have urinary tract infections, which sometimes can be remedied by being fitted with a smaller size diaphragm.

Very rarely, the spermicide used with a diaphragm or cervical cap (or used by itself) causes an allergic reaction in either partner, resulting in itching and redness in the genital area. Try switching to another brand or another type (cream, jelly, or foam).

Careless use of a diaphragm or cervical cap might increase your risk of **toxic shock syndrome** (see page 236). Never leave a diaphragm in your body for more than 24 hours (or for more than six to eight hours during your period), and never leave a cervical cap in place for more than 48 hours.

Intrauterine device (IUD): A copper or plastic T-shaped device is inserted into the uterus by a doctor or other trained health professional. Its presence can cause cramping pain and heavy menstrual bleeding. IUDs are not recommended for women who already have heavy or painful periods. They are also risky for women who have a sexually transmitted disease or who have more than one sex partner, which increases the chance of exposure to such diseases.

The most dangerous conditions associated with using an IUD are pelvic infections (see **pelvic inflammatory disease,** page 230) and ectopic pregnancy (pregnancy outside the uterus).

Call your doctor for an immediate appointment if you are using an IUD and:
➤ You think you might be pregnant.
➤ You have pain in the pelvic area.
➤ You have fever with no apparent cause.
➤ You have foul-smelling vaginal discharge.

Tubal sterilization: A surgical procedure to close off the fallopian tubes (see color illustration, page 175) is a common means of permanent birth control for women. Although it's a simple operation, there is some risk of complications, such as infection or a reaction to the anesthesia.

Vasectomy: Men who want permanent birth control can choose to have a minor surgical procedure in which the tubes through which the sperm travel from the testicles into the penis (see color illustration, page 175) are tied off. The operation doesn't affect sexual performance. Doctors often recommend vasectomy for couples because it's easier, cheaper, and safer than tubal sterilization. Possible complications include excessive bleeding and infection.

FOR MORE HELP

Organization: Planned Parenthood, 800-230-PLAN, 24-hour line. Automatically connects you to your local chapter, which has information on contraception.

Organization: Office of Population Affairs

Clearinghouse, P.O. Box 30686, Bethesda, MD 20824-0686. 301-654-6190, M–F 9–5 EST. Call or write for information on contraception.

Diminished Sexual Desire

SIGNS AND SYMPTOMS

- Lack of interest in sex for more than two months.
- Avoidance of sex, a low level of sexual activity in couples (less often than every other week), or anxiety about sex.
- Sometimes impotence, premature ejaculation, pain during intercourse, or inability to have an orgasm.

A temporary loss of sexual desire is quite normal; people of all ages go through peaks and declines in sexual interest. Diminished desire is the most common complaint at sex therapy clinics. The problem is usually caused by psychological factors: depression, anger, boredom, conflict in a relationship, stress, fear of pregnancy, or memories of sexual abuse. It can also result from alcohol abuse or the use of some prescription medicines, such as antidepressants or tranquilizers, or sometimes antihistamines. Less often, the cause may be a hormonal imbalance or a disease such as diabetes.

A marriage counselor or sex therapist can often help if the problem is related to emotional or psychological issues. Reducing stress or treating any underlying health problems may also help.

WHAT YOU CAN DO NOW

- ➤ Experiment with your sex life—have sex in different locations, in different positions, and at different times of day.
- ➤ Talk to your partner about what arouses you sexually.

- ➤ Try reading erotic materials, watching erotic videos, or indulging in sexual fantasy, if these appeal to you.
- ➤ If you are feeling anxious about your ability to perform sexually, discuss these feelings with your partner.

WHEN TO CALL THE DOCTOR

- ➤ If you develop problems such as impotence or pain during intercourse.
- ➤ If diminished sexual desire is causing problems in your relationship.
- ➤ If you don't respond to self-help measures; you may have an illness.
- ➤ If you think a medication is the cause.
- ➤ If you are depressed.

HOW TO PREVENT IT

- ➤ Take steps to reduce **stress** (see page 212).
- ➤ Exercise regularly and eat healthfully; get plenty of sleep.
- ➤ Devote time to your relationship. Set aside time to go out on "dates," or create romantic evenings at home.
- ➤ Try to solve problems in your relationship before they build up.

FOR MORE HELP

Information line: American Association of Marriage and Family Therapists, 800-374-2638, 24-hour recording. Provides referrals to relationship counselors.

Organization: Sexuality Information and Education Council of the United States, 130 W. 42nd St., Suite 350, New York, NY 10036. 212-819-9770, M–F 12–5 EST. Provides referrals to clinics and hospitals dealing with sexual dysfunction, and sends literature about sexual dysfunction (15 cents per page).

Organization: American Association of Sex Educators, Counselors, and Therapists, 435 N. Michigan Ave., Suite 1717, Chicago, IL 60611-4067. 312-644-0828, M–F 9–5 CST. Provides referrals to sex therapists ($5 fee).

Men's Health

Erection Problems

- Frequent difficulty getting and keeping an erection adequate for sexual intercourse.

Erection problems are more common than many people think—although what is considered a "problem" may be a personal judgment. Most men have trouble getting an erection now and then, and it may happen more often as they age. But if you are frequently unable to get erections and this bothers you, talk to your doctor about it.

The mechanics of an erection are complex, and many things can interfere with it. The most common are physical problems, including **diabetes** (see page 269); narrowed or blocked arteries that reduce blood flow to the penis (see **narrowed arteries,** page 107); injury; drinking too much alcohol (see **alcohol abuse and alcoholism,** page 196); and prescription drugs, including some used for high blood pressure and depression. Psychological stresses, such as depression, worry, guilt, or "performance anxiety," can also cause difficulties.

Although erection problems may be embarrassing or upsetting, they can usually be treated successfully.

WHAT YOU CAN DO NOW

- ➤ During lovemaking, relax and take your time. Talk to your partner about what arouses you sexually.
- ➤ Try reading erotic materials, watching erotic videos, or indulging in sexual fantasy, if these things appeal to you.
- ➤ If you are anxious about your ability to perform sexually, discuss the feelings with your partner (but not during lovemaking).

WHEN TO CALL THE DOCTOR

- ➤ If erection problems regularly interfere with your ability to have sexual intercourse or are causing difficulties in your relationship with your partner.
- ➤ If you're taking drugs that might be causing the problem.
- ➤ If physical causes have been ruled out, ask for a referral to a qualified counselor or therapist to help you identify and address any psychological issues.

HOW TO PREVENT IT

- ➤ If you drink alcohol, have no more than two 12-ounce cans of beer, two 5-ounce glasses of wine, or two 1.5-ounce drinks of hard liquor a day.
- ➤ If you smoke, quit.
- ➤ Exercise regularly and eat healthfully (see **staying healthy,** pages 284 and 286).
- ➤ Take steps to reduce your stress; try deep breathing, meditation, or yoga.
- ➤ Ask your doctor about the Kegel pelvic

Testicle Problems

SYMPTOMS	WHAT IT MIGHT BE	WHAT YOU CAN DO
Excruciating pain and tenderness in either testicle; may spread to lower abdomen. Scrotum may be swollen, unusually firm, and red. Sometimes faintness and nausea.	Testicular torsion—twisting of testicle and of tube between prostate and testicle, cutting off blood supply.	Call doctor for immediate appointment. Can cause permanent damage if not treated promptly.
Firm, usually painless lump or knobby swelling on one testicle. Testicle may feel heavy or hard, sometimes painful.	Testicular cancer. Usually strikes men between 15 and 34. Rarely fatal.	If you notice symptoms, call doctor for immediate appointment. To screen yourself, do a self-exam once a month after warm bath or shower: hold testicle and gently roll it between fingers and thumb.
Pain and swelling around testicle; comes on gradually, becomes severe. Swollen area is hot and tender; swelling may spread to scrotum.	Epididymitis—inflammation of coiled tube (epididymis) that connects to each testicle. Has various causes, including prostate infections and sexually transmitted diseases.	Call doctor for immediate appointment. Bed rest and ice packs may help. Antibiotics usually cure it; sex partners (male or female) may also need treatment.
Soft, painless swelling in scrotum.	Hydrocele—excess fluid that builds up in sac surrounding each testicle.	Treatment of small hydroceles is usually unnecessary. If painful or very large, call doctor for advice and appointment.
Swollen veins in scrotum, almost always on left side. Usually no pain. Swelling lessens when you lie down.	Varicocele—varicose or enlarged veins in scrotum. Very common and usually harmless. In 20% of cases, can cause infertility.	Call doctor for advice.
Pain and tenderness in testicles or scrotum; not severe, may come and go.	Orchialgia—discomfort in testicles; no known cause, may be viral.	To ease pain, take pain relievers and warm baths. Call doctor for advice if pain lasts more than a week.

Men's Health

muscle exercises; these may work well for men with narrowed arteries or other circulation problems.

FOR MORE HELP

Organization: American Foundation for Urologic Disease, 300 W. Pratt St., Suite 401, Baltimore, MD 21201. 410-727-2908, M–F 8:30–5 EST. Ask for the brochure on erection problems.

Organization: National Kidney and Urologic Diseases Information Clearinghouse, Box NKUDIC, 3 Information Way, Bethesda, MD 20892-3580. Write for information on erection problems.

Prostate Problems

SIGNS AND SYMPTOMS

General symptoms:
- Frequent, sometimes painful, or urgent need to urinate; urine might be bloody.
- Consistently weak stream of urine, dribbling.
- Incontinence (sometimes).

Enlarged prostate:
- Occasional feeling of incomplete bladder emptying.

Prostate cancer:
Often no symptoms in early stages, occasionally followed by the symptoms described above. In later stages:
- Pain in the pelvis or lower back, or sometimes in other areas.

Prostatitis:
- Pain in the area between the scrotum and anus.
- Painful ejaculation, blood in the semen or urine.
- Fever and chills (acute prostatitis).
- Pain in the lower back.

The prostate is a walnut-size gland that sits at the base of the tube (the urethra) that runs between a man's bladder and the end of his penis. (See color illustration, page 175.) It produces some of the fluid that carries sperm.

Enlarged prostate: In most men, the prostate gland grows larger with age; in fact, 75 percent of men over 50 have some enlargement. An enlarged prostate gland can squeeze the urethra and obstruct urine flow. This benign enlarged prostate isn't cancer, it doesn't lead to cancer, nor does it need to be treated unless difficult or frequent urination becomes too bothersome. Then it can be treated by surgery or medication.

Prostate cancer: The growth of malignant cells into a tumor in the prostate is the most common cancer in American men. It can exist for many years without symptoms, until the tumor grows large enough to affect urination and produce symptoms.

Prostate cancer progresses slowly and can usually be treated effectively when caught early enough. If untreated, it may spread to other organs or bone. Treatment can include surgery, radiation, or hormone therapy.

Prostatitis: This condition is marked by an inflammation of the prostate. One form is caused by bacteria, which can move to the prostate from the urinary system. In acute cases, an abscess may form that has to be drained surgically. In chronic cases, the infection causes lasting discomfort but rarely a fever. Sometimes its only symptom is repeated bladder infections. The second, noninfectious form of prostatitis has no known cause and does not respond to antibiotics.

WHAT YOU CAN DO NOW

➤ If you are getting up frequently to urinate at night, avoid caffeine and alcohol, and reduce fluid intake before bed.

➤ Warm baths may help relieve pain and other symptoms.

➤ Take the prostate quiz (see box on opposite page). Go over the results with your doctor.

WHEN TO CALL THE DOCTOR

➤ If you develop the symptoms listed.

DO YOU HAVE A PROSTATE PROBLEM?

Urinary problems are key signals of an enlarged prostate gland. The American Urological Association's Symptom Score Index, aimed at spotting such problems, was developed as a way for men to initially evaluate their condition. It does not detect prostate cancer.

Circle your response to each question. A total score of 7 or below indicates no problem or no more than a mild problem; 8 to 19 is moderate; 20 to 35 is severe. Note: The AUA recommends that your doctor interpret the results of this test.

In the last month, how often have you:	Never	Less than one time in five	Less than half the time	About half the time	More than half the time	Almost always
Had a sensation of not having emptied your bladder completely after you finished urinating?	0	1	2	3	4	5
Had to urinate again less than two hours after you last urinated?	0	1	2	3	4	5
Found your flow stopped and started again several times when you urinated?	0	1	2	3	4	5
Found it difficult to postpone urination?	0	1	2	3	4	5
Had a weak urinary stream?	0	1	2	3	4	5
Had to push or strain to begin urination?	0	1	2	3	4	5
In the last month, about how many times a night did you:	**None**	**One**	**Two**	**Three**	**Four**	**Five or more**
Get up to urinate from the time you went to bed until the time you got up in the morning?	0	1	2	3	4	5

Adapted with permission of the *Journal of Urology*

HOW TO PREVENT IT

Enlarged prostate:
➤ There is no known way to prevent this condition.

Prostate cancer:
➤ Know your family history (see **staying healthy,** page 302): If your father or brother had prostate cancer, your risk is much higher than if they didn't. This makes following the next steps even more important.

➤ Cut down on animal fat in your diet; men who eat a lot of fat may increase their risk.

PENIS PROBLEMS

Many problems can affect the penis. Fortunately, most of them are rare.

An erection that won't go away (priapism): If untreated, this can cause permanent damage. If an erection does not subside after four hours, call your doctor for emergency advice. If your doctor isn't available, call 911 or go to an emergency facility. This rare and painful problem occurs when blood cannot drain from the penis. It may result from penile injections (including those intended to produce erections), diseases such as leukemia or sickle-cell anemia, side effects of some medications, or injury. It is not connected to sexual arousal.

A small, pimplelike sore: Usually on the head of the penis, a sore that lasts more than one or two weeks can be a sign of penis cancer or of a **sexually transmitted disease** (see chart on page 215). In later stages, cancer symptoms may include bleeding or unusual discharge, pain with urination, and enlarged lymph nodes in the groin. Penis cancer is most common in uncircumcised men. Call your doctor for an immediate appointment if you detect any unusual sore or growth.

Blisters: Either one or several, on or around the penis, can mean a herpes infection. An outbreak can be itchy, painful, or both, and needs a doctor's care.

A bend in the penis (Peyronie's disease): This condition occurs during an erection and can be painful. It may be caused by scar tissue in the penis—usually from an injury—that does not stretch or expand enough. The problem usually takes care of itself without treatment, but in rare cases, surgery may be necessary.

Soreness and inflammation of the tip of the penis (balanitis): This can be caused by infection or by irritation from clothing, condoms, or spermicides. It's most common in men who are uncircumcised. Call your doctor for advice and an appointment.

Tight foreskin (phimosis): Sometimes the foreskin in uncircumcised boys or men is too tight to retract easily; this may make erections painful. Phimosis can also be caused by an infection under the foreskin. Uncircumcised men and diabetics have a higher chance of developing such infections. Call your doctor for advice and an appointment.

➤ Men over 50 should have an annual rectal exam to check for lumps on the gland. Some doctors also recommend a blood test (called a prostate specific antigen, or PSA, test) that can detect prostate cancer.

➤ African-Americans and men with a family history of prostate cancer should begin their annual tests at age 40.

Prostatitis:

➤ Treat any urinary tract infection before it can spread.

FOR MORE HELP

Organization: American Foundation for Urologic Disease, 300 W. Pratt St., Suite 401, Baltimore, MD 21201. 410-727-2908, M–F 8:30–5 EST. Information specialists make referrals to prostate cancer support groups and send material on prostate problems.

Book: *The Prostate Book: Sound Advice on Symptoms and Treatment,* by Stephen N. Rous, M.D. A handy guide to the male genital and urinary anatomy and prostate conditions. W. W. Norton, 1995, $22.95 hardcover, $12 paperback.

Videos: *Prostate Cancer at Time of Diagnosis* and *Prostate Disorders at Time of Diagnosis.* Clear, useful overviews of causes and treatments, each consisting of four reports—Understanding the Diagnosis, What Happens Next?, Treatment and Management, and Issues and Answers. Time Life Medical, 1996, $19.95 each.

Women's Health

Menopause

- Hot flashes or flushes—a sudden sensation of heating up, usually on the face, neck, and chest. May include profuse sweating and night sweats that disrupt sleep.
- Irregular periods. Menstrual flow may be very heavy or very light and, eventually, periods cease.
- Irritability, mood swings, and difficulty concentrating.
- Vaginal dryness.
- Pain during intercourse.

Around the time a woman reaches her mid-forties or early fifties, her ovaries stop producing eggs and her periods end. Perimenopause refers to the natural changes that occur in a woman's body three to five years before her final period, menopause to the time when menstruation ceases, and postmenopause to the months or even years afterward. The changes are caused by a decrease in the production of the hormones estrogen and progesterone.

During menopause—which is also called the "change of life"—many women don't notice any difference except the end of their menstrual periods, while others have only slight emotional or physical discomfort.

About 25 percent will experience the more bothersome symptoms, such as profuse sweating, which can occur on and off for several weeks to several years.

In some women, menopause can be the start of long-term health problems. The decrease in estrogen can cause bone loss (see **osteoporosis,** page 188), which may result in broken bones. It can also raise cholesterol levels in the blood and lead to cardiovascular disease. You may wish to discuss hormone replacements with your doctor to help prevent these problems (see box on page 229).

Although menopause can include positive changes—such as freedom from concerns about pregnancy—the physical and emotional changes can also lead to stress. Exercise, reaching out to friends and family, and making changes in your lifestyle to reduce stress can help.

WHAT YOU CAN DO NOW

- Wear absorbent cotton clothes if you are having night sweats or hot flashes.
- Dress in layers so you can cool down quickly. Use a fan, and drink plenty of water—at least eight glasses a day.
- For vaginal dryness, use a lubricant. If you and your partner use condoms, use a water-soluble lubricant, not petroleum jelly.
- Ask if your local hospital has a menopause support group, or talk to your family and friends about the changes you are going through.

(continued)

Menstrual Irregularities

All women should have regular pelvic exams—as often as once a year if they are sexually active—so that any abnormalities can be detected and treated early. Be sure to tell your doctor about any changes in your menstrual cycle.

SYMPTOMS	WHAT IT MIGHT BE	WHAT YOU CAN DO
Missed menstrual periods or unusually heavy, painful periods; cramps, pain, or sense of pressure in lower abdomen; vaginal spotting or bleeding.	Ectopic pregnancy—pregnancy outside uterus, usually in fallopian tube. (See color illustration, page 175.)	Call doctor for immediate appointment. If bleeding or abdominal pain is severe, call 911 or go to emergency facility **immediately.**
Unusually heavy or painful periods, especially toward the end; pain in lower abdomen, vagina, or lower back that may begin just before period and worsen just after; pain during intercourse; blood in urine or stool while menstruating; nausea and vomiting just before period begins.	Endometriosis—disorder in which tissue that normally lines uterus appears outside uterus and becomes attached to other reproductive or abdominal organs.	If experiencing symptoms for first time or if pain is severe, call doctor for immediate appointment.
Unusually heavy, irregular, or missed menstrual periods; pain in lower abdomen or back; foul-smelling vaginal discharge; pain during intercourse; fever and sometimes chills.	Pelvic inflammatory disease (see page 230)—infection of reproductive organs, often caused by sexually transmitted diseases (see chart on page 215).	Call doctor for immediate appointment.
Compared to your usual pattern: changes in heaviness of flow, length of periods, or time between periods; aches or pain in abdomen; sensation of fullness, swelling, or pressure in abdomen; frequent urination.	Noncancerous ovarian cyst. ● Noncancerous ovarian tumor. ● Ovarian cancer.	Call doctor for immediate appointment. It's important to diagnose condition as soon as possible.
Unusually heavy or painful menstrual period that begins a week or more late.	Early pregnancy and miscarriage.	If you think you may be pregnant and you are bleeding, call doctor for advice and appointment.

(continued)

Menstrual Irregularities *(continued)*

SYMPTOMS	WHAT IT MIGHT BE	WHAT YOU CAN DO
No menstrual period for several months.	Amenorrhea (absence of menstruation), which can be caused by emotional distress, hormone imbalance, dieting or eating disorders (see anorexia and bulimia, page 200), or strenuous athletic training. ● Pregnancy (see page 232). ●Breast-feeding. ● Menopause (see page 226). ● Abnormality of reproductive organs. ●Use of certain drugs. ●Discontinuing use of birth control pills.	Call doctor for advice and appointment. **Note:** If a girl is over 16 and has never had a menstrual period, schedule appointment with doctor.
Unusually heavy periods; bleeding between periods; pain or discomfort in lower back or abdomen; frequent urination; constipation; possibly sudden, sharp pain in lower abdomen.	Uterine fibroid tumors—common, noncancerous masses in uterus. Sometimes tumor becomes twisted, cutting off its blood supply and causing severe pain.	Call doctor for advice and appointment. Write down dates you are bleeding and how many pads or tampons you use each day.
Unusually heavy or painful menstrual periods while using IUD or after you stop taking birth control pills.	Common side effect of IUDs. ● Hormonal changes caused by going off the Pill. (See contraception health risks, page 217.)	Call doctor for advice about your birth control method.
Bleeding or spotting during pregnancy.	Common occurrence, but may signal problem.	Call doctor for advice.
Unusually heavy menstrual period soon after childbirth.	Normal occurrence.	If you have more than two heavy periods after giving birth, call doctor for advice.
Menstrual flow that is always heavy; periods that last more than seven days; large clots of blood.	Probably no underlying disorder, but heavy bleeding can result in anemia (see page 264).	If bleeding is extremely heavy (you use more than one pad or tampon in an hour), call doctor for advice.

➤ Keep using birth control even when periods became irregular and for a year or two after they cease, as pregnancy can result if an egg is released, even if you're not menstruating regularly. If you are on birth control pills, you may continue to have periods even after menopause. If you are near 50 and taking the Pill, ask your doctor about a blood check, called an FSH test, that can determine whether it's safe to stop.

➤ Try to reduce stress. Exercise regularly, eat balanced meals, avoid caffeine, and take naps during the day if night sweats are interrupting your sleep.

➤ Reduce your risk of heart disease by making efforts to lose weight if you are overweight, by quitting smoking (see **smoking and illness,** page 210), and by switching to a low-fat diet.

➤ Take calcium supplements daily, and do weight-bearing exercise (such as walking, dancing, or lifting light weights) to guard against osteoporosis.

WHEN TO CALL THE DOCTOR

➤ If you experience long-term heavy bleeding, or any bleeding one year after your period stops. This could be a sign of uterine cancer.

➤ If you have any symptoms that seriously disrupt your sleep, work, or daily activities.

FOR MORE HELP

Organization: National Institute on Aging, Information Center, P.O. Box 8057, Gaithersburg, MD 20898. 800-222-2225, M–F 8:30–5 EST. Provides fact sheets on menopause and estrogen therapy.

Organization: National Women's Health Resource Center, 202-293-6045, M–F 9–5 EST. Ask to be sent a copy of the newsletter *National Women's Health Report,* which includes information about menopause ($2). Staffers also refer callers to women's centers and support groups.

Video: *Menopause at Time of Diagnosis.* Clear, useful overview of causes and treatments, consisting of four reports—Understanding the Diagnosis, What Happens Next?, Treatment and Management, and Issues and Answers. Time Life Medical, 1996, $19.95.

IS HORMONE REPLACEMENT RIGHT FOR YOU?

Once a woman enters menopause, she'll face a decision about hormone replacement therapy. Studies have shown that estrogen—the major ingredient in hormone therapy—is highly effective in preventing bone loss and fractures, and in reducing the risk of heart disease. Hormone therapy also helps combat the temporary symptoms of menopause.

Doctors commonly prescribe a combination of estrogen and progestin for women who have not had a hysterectomy. This therapy protects women against endometrial cancer, which taking estrogen alone does not. Combined hormone therapy has also been shown to raise levels of HDL ("good") cholesterol and lower levels of LDL ("bad") cholesterol, and

to help prevent bone fractures in women who already have osteoporosis.

After menopause, women may take hormones for the rest of their lives to protect against osteoporosis and heart disease. Questions remain about this therapy. Some studies have shown that it may increase the risk of breast cancer if continued for more than five years. Others suggest that the increased risk is due to aging. If you are considering hormone replacement therapy, be sure to discuss all the risks with your doctor.

For women seeking relief from vaginal dryness or discomfort, estrogen vaginal creams are also available. Women who use these regularly must take progestin to reduce their risk of endometrial cancer.

Pelvic Inflammatory Disease

SIGNS AND SYMPTOMS

Often the infection has no symptoms. Sometimes it can cause:

- Mild to severe aching in the lower abdomen, sometimes accompanied by backache.
- Pain during intercourse.
- Fever, sometimes with chills.
- Absent or irregular menstrual periods, or unusually heavy bleeding.
- Heavy or foul-smelling discharge from the vagina.
- Frequent urination accompanied by burning pain.
- Nausea and vomiting.

Pelvic inflammatory disease (PID) is an infection of the female reproductive organs, including the ovaries, the fallopian tubes, the cervix, and the uterus. (See color illustration, page 175.) Untreated, it can result in life-threatening complications, such as blood poisoning, infection of the abdominal cavity, or ectopic pregnancy (in which a fertilized egg settles outside the uterus). It can also cause infertility.

PID is often caused by the bacteria that produce gonorrhea and chlamydia (see **sexually transmitted diseases** chart, page 215). It may also be brought on by other bacteria that get into the upper genital region through sexual intercourse, abortion, miscarriage, childbirth, or hysterectomy.

Sexually active teenagers, women with more than one sexual partner, and those with a partner who has sex with others are most likely to get PID. Some experts believe that frequent douching may also increase the risk by pushing bacteria farther up into the reproductive system. Birth control pills, however, hinder the passage of bacteria and may slightly lower the chance of getting PID or may keep it from becoming more severe.

The infection can be successfully treated with antibiotics, but it frequently comes back and may become chronic. When antibiotics don't help, a doctor may have to operate to remove or repair infected tissue.

WHAT YOU CAN DO NOW

After diagnosis:
- Take all of your medication, even if symptoms have disappeared.
- If gonorrhea or chlamydia caused your infection, make sure your partner is treated. Otherwise, he may reinfect you or infect others.
- Don't have sex until all symptoms have disappeared.
- Get plenty of bed rest.
- If needed, take an over-the-counter pain reliever such as ibuprofen.

WHEN TO CALL THE DOCTOR

- If you have symptoms of PID.

HOW TO PREVENT IT

- Practice **safe sex** (see box on page 217) to protect yourself from sexually transmitted diseases.
- Have regular medical checkups if you are sexually active.
- To prevent infection after surgery or minor gynecological procedures, don't douche or have intercourse for a week.

FOR MORE HELP

Hotline: National STD Hotline, Centers for Disease Control and Prevention, 800-227-8922, M–F 8AM–11PM EST. Staffers answer questions about sexually transmitted diseases and refer callers to testing locations.

Organization: American College of Obstetricians and Gynecologists, Resource Center, 409 12th St. NW, Washington, DC 20024-2188. Send a business-size, self-addressed, stamped envelope; ask for the brochure on pelvic inflammatory disease and the patient education order form, which lists all women's health brochures.

Breast Pain or Lumps

Breasts change with puberty, with your menstrual cycle, and with pregnancy, and they continue to change with age. Starting at puberty, women should examine their breasts every month, so that they become familiar with their structure and can detect any masses or lumps. (See **breast self-exam** box, page 233.) Most changes in breasts are perfectly normal and no cause for concern. Some conditions, however, require medical attention.

SYMPTOMS	WHAT IT MIGHT BE	WHAT YOU CAN DO
Lump (usually painless) in breast or underarm area; flattening or indentation on breast; change in contour, texture, size, or symmetry of breast; change in nipple (such as indrawn or dimpled look, itching or burning sensation, or discharge that may be dark or bloody).	Noncancerous cyst. • Noncancerous tumor. • Breast cancer (if breast is painful, could signal advanced stage).	Call doctor for immediate appointment. Most lumps are not cancerous, but it is very important to have an exam. Biopsy may be necessary to diagnose or rule out breast cancer.
After having recently given birth: pain and tenderness in breast, hard or swollen breast, fever, area with redness and pain.	Infection of breast (mastitis), caused by bacteria. Redness and pain can indicate an abscess.	Call doctor for advice and appointment. Continue normal breast-feeding. If abscess develops, use breast pump on infected side and continue feeding on uninfected side. If you have a fever, rest in bed and drink plenty of fluids.
Pain, tenderness, or swelling in breasts; missed period; fatigue; nausea.	Pregnancy (see page 232).	Call doctor for advice and make appointment for pregnancy test. Wear support bra to ease discomfort.
Less than 5 days after having given birth: tenderness, hardness, or swelling in breast. Discomfort can also occur when breast-feeding mother cannot keep to usual feeding schedule.	Engorgement with milk.	Nurse more often, or try applying warm compresses to reduce discomfort. Call doctor for advice if symptoms persist.
In women who are breast-feeding: sore nipple or sharp pain in nipple while nursing.	Irritated or cracked nipples, common during first few weeks of breast-feeding.	Gently wash nipples after nursing and apply pure vitamin E oil. With fever, call doctor for advice.

(continued)

Breast Pain or Lumps *(continued)*

SYMPTOMS	WHAT IT MIGHT BE	WHAT YOU CAN DO
Lumpy or swollen breasts; pain or discomfort, especially week before menstrual period.	Fibrocystic breasts. More than half of all women develop this harmless condition, usually between ages of 25 and 50.	Call doctor for advice if you notice lumps for first time; if you notice a new lump; or if a lump becomes larger, harder, or more painful. Limit intake of caffeine. Wear support bra to ease discomfort.
Pain or tenderness in breasts before menstrual period.	Premenstrual syndrome. ● Irregular periods.	See premenstrual syndrome, page 235, and menstrual irregularities chart, page 227.
Breast pain while taking estrogen medication.	Drug side effect.	Call doctor for advice.

For more help: You can buy the videos *Breast Lumps at Time of Diagnosis* and *Breast Cancer at Time of Diagnosis*. Each provides a clear, useful overview of causes and treatments, consisting of four reports—Understanding the Diagnosis, What Happens Next?, Treatment and Management, and Issues and Answers. Time Life Medical, 1996, $19.95 each.

Pregnancy

If you plan to have children, the best time to start focusing on your health is before you become pregnant. The first few weeks of your pregnancy can be crucial for the rapidly developing fetus; poor nutrition or harmful substances in your body—such as alcohol, medications, or cigarette smoke—can interfere with fetal growth.

Good health habits and good prenatal care help assure a healthy baby and also help you cope with the stress that comes with pregnancy, childbirth, and parenthood. If you are planning a pregnancy, you may want to schedule a visit with your health care provider to discuss your diet, lifestyle, past pregnancies, medical history, and any medications you are taking.

WHAT YOU CAN DO NOW

Diet, Rest, and Exercise

During your pregnancy, it is important to get plenty of rest and exercise, maintain a well-balanced diet, and avoid substances that can harm the fetus. Follow your health care provider's advice as well as these guidelines:

➤ Get enough calories, protein, iron, calcium, and folic acid in your diet. (Ask your health care provider about any specific changes you should make and which foods are good sources of the nutrients you need.)

➤ Take any vitamin and mineral supplements that have been prescribed for you, but no more than the amount your health care provider recommends. Too much of some vitamins and minerals can be dangerous. (For example, some recent research showed that women who took more than 10,000 IU of vitamin A per day were more likely to have babies with major heart defects and other problems.)

(continued)

HOW TO DO A BREAST SELF-EXAM

Regularly doing a breast self-exam is one of the best ways to find a cancerous tumor when it is small, before the cancer has a chance to spread. Examine yourself at the same time every month, two to three days after your period. (Remember, self-examination is not a substitute for regular breast exams by a doctor.)

❶ Stand in front of a mirror with your arms at your sides. Look for anything unusual on your breasts: dimples, scaly patches, puckers, or discharge coming from a nipple.

❷ Check for changes in the shape or contour of your breasts. Watch in the mirror as you lift your hands behind your head, clasp your hands, and press them against the back of your head.

❸ Check again with your hands on your hips and your elbows pulled forward.

❹ Squeeze your nipples gently to check for discharge.

❺ With one arm raised, use the fingertips of your other hand to feel your breast for any lumps under the skin. Start in your armpit and move towards your breast, pressing your fingers in small areas, about the size of a quarter. (Try this in the shower; your fingers will slide more easily over soapy skin.)

Use a definite pattern—a spiral, line, or wedge. Be sure you cover the entire breast, including upper chest and underarm. Repeat on other side.

Spiral: Start at the outer edges of the breast and slowly work your way around the breast in smaller and smaller circles.

Line: Start under your arm and slowly move toward and across the breast.

Wedge: Start at the outer edge of the breast and move slowly toward the middle, then back to the edge. Repeat until you have covered the whole breast.

❻ Repeat step 5 lying on your back, with one arm over your head and a pillow under your shoulder. Use one of the patterns above to check each breast.

If you find a lump, unusual firmness, a change in shape, or any discharge from a nipple, call your doctor for an immediate appointment.

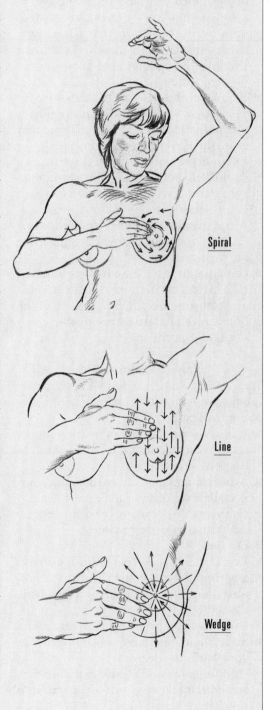

Spiral

Line

Wedge

- Avoid the substances that are known to cause birth defects, miscarriages, or other harm to the fetus: alcohol, tobacco, illegal drugs, and any drugs that are not prescribed or approved by your doctor, including over-the-counter medications such as aspirin or cold medicines. (Some of these, including alcohol, should also be avoided when you are trying to get pregnant or when you are breast-feeding a baby. Consult your health care provider.) Doctors also recommend that you cut down on caffeine.
- Be aware of potential hazards in your workplace, such as radiation or heavy metals like lead and mercury. If you can't avoid them, consider changing jobs.
- Exercise regularly (at least three times a week). Brisk walking, jogging, swimming, yoga, and low-impact aerobics are all good forms of exercise during pregnancy. Avoid strenuous exercise, though, especially in hot weather. Wear a supportive bra to protect your breasts.
- Get enough rest. Go to bed earlier, and take breaks throughout the day to relax and put your feet up. Share more of the housework or child care with your partner, family, or friends.

Staying Comfortable

Try the following remedies for some of the common discomforts of pregnancy:

Abdominal pain:
- Use a hot-water bottle or heating pad to relieve pain or cramps from stretched abdominal muscles.
- Avoid changing positions too quickly, especially when turning at the waist.
- Call your doctor for advice if your abdominal pain persists or gets worse.

Backache:
- Don't take over-the-counter drugs such as aspirin and ibuprofen. Instead, use a hot-water bottle or a heating pad to relieve discomfort.
- Don't stand for long periods of time.
- Sit in chairs that have good support for your back, or use a small pillow behind your lower back. Try to sit with your back straight and keep your feet elevated, if possible.

PREGNANCY DANGER SIGNS

Call your doctor for an immediate appointment if you notice any of the following during your pregnancy:
- Vaginal spotting or bleeding. This is common, but it sometimes signals a miscarriage or another serious complication.
- Fever over 100 degrees; chills; backache; and frequent, burning urination or blood in the urine; you may have a kidney infection.
- Sudden weight gain over a few days, swelling of the hands and face, severe headache, and blurred vision; you may have preeclampsia, a form of high blood pressure. If untreated, it can be very dangerous.
- After the fetus has begun to move: less fetal movement or none at all for more than a day; the fetus may be in trouble.

- Use a firm mattress. Sleep on your side, and put a pillow between your knees for support.
- Wear low-heeled, supportive shoes or shoe inserts designed specifically for pregnant women. Avoid high heels.
- Try a pregnancy girdle or an elastic sling to support your abdomen.

Breast discomfort:
- Wear a bra that gives you proper support. If your breasts leak small amounts of fluid, use nursing pads in your bra.

Constipation: See page 115.

Headache:
- Make sure you get enough rest.
- Eat small, frequent meals, and drink at least eight glasses of water a day.
- Practice yoga or meditation to relieve day-to-day stress.
- Take a warm bath with a cold pack on your forehead.
- Don't take aspirin or any other over-the-counter pain relievers.
- Call your doctor for advice if your headache is persistent or severe, or if it is accompanied by nausea or blurry vision.

Heartburn: See page 121.

Hemorrhoids:

➤ See page 122.

➤ Don't use over-the-counter hemorrhoid treatments unless your health care provider recommends them.

Nausea and vomiting (morning sickness):

➤ Eat crackers or plain toast as soon as you wake up in the morning. Sit on your bed for a few minutes before getting up.

➤ Try to eat often so you never have an empty stomach. Snack throughout the day rather than eating three full meals. (The best snacks are high-protein foods such as nuts, yogurt, granola, and peanut butter on apple slices or celery.) Have a snack at bedtime and whenever you get up during the night.

➤ Drink plenty of water and other liquids, but avoid milk, citrus juices, coffee, tea, and caffeinated sodas.

➤ Try papaya juice or almonds; both are known to ease morning sickness. Also try fresh ginger—either put a small piece on your tongue or make a tea by grating and steeping ginger in boiling water.

➤ Call your doctor for advice if you have severe nausea and vomiting; rapid heartbeat; pale, dry skin; or signs of dehydration (dry mouth, sticky saliva, dizziness, decreased urination, sometimes thirst).

Urinary tract infections:

➤ Call your doctor for advice and an appointment if you have pain when you urinate, or if you think you have a bladder or other urinary tract infection (see **painful urination,** page 134).

➤ Use a hot-water bottle or heating pad on your lower abdomen to relieve discomfort.

➤ Drink lots of water (at least eight to ten glasses a day).

➤ Drink several glasses of cranberry juice a day to help prevent urinary tract infections from developing.

Varicose veins and swelling in the legs:

➤ Sit or lie down and put your legs up, above hip level whenever possible.

➤ Make moderate exercise part of your daily routine; walking or swimming are especially good activities.

➤ Don't stand or sit for long periods.

FOR MORE HELP

Organization: Healthy Mothers, Healthy Babies Coalition, 800-673-8444, ext. 2458, M–F 9–5 EST. Offers information on prenatal and baby health education programs. Call to ask for referrals to local health education groups.

Book: *The Complete Book of Pregnancy and Childbirth,* by Sheila Kitzinger. A comprehensive resource. Alfred A. Knopf, 1989, $22.50.

Video: *Pregnancy at Time of Diagnosis.* Clear, useful overview, consisting of four reports—Understanding the Diagnosis, What Happens Next?, Treatment and Management, and Issues and Answers. Time Life Medical, 1996, $19.95.

Premenstrual Syndrome

SIGNS AND SYMPTOMS

■ Bloating and weight gain.
■ Breast swelling or tenderness.
■ Headaches.
■ Dizziness.
■ Fatigue.
■ Decrease or increase in sex drive.
■ Outbreaks of acne.
■ Mood swings, increased irritability, nervousness, or depression.
■ Food cravings.
■ Diarrhea or constipation.

Premenstrual syndrome, known as PMS, is marked by a range of physical and emotional changes that begin one to two weeks before a woman's period and generally stop when her period starts. Symptoms vary greatly from one woman to the next. Some feel just a little low on energy, while a small number get so depressed or tense that they can barely function. Although few experience the extremes, most women notice at least one of the listed symptoms.

No one knows for sure what causes PMS. It may result from a hormonal imbalance, monthly changes in brain chemicals, or poor nutrition.

<hr>

WHAT YOU CAN DO NOW

➤ Avoid salt, sugar, caffeine, and dairy products the week before your period.
➤ Avoid alcohol the week before your period. It can worsen headaches, fatigue, and depression.
➤ Eat smaller, more frequent meals to help maintain a steady level of blood sugar and to avoid big drops in energy.
➤ Get some exercise every day.
➤ Get more sleep the week before your period; take long, warm baths to relax.

WHEN TO CALL THE DOCTOR

➤ If you've followed the advice above, but your symptoms still interfere with your normal activities or relationships, make an appointment with your doctor to discuss medications or other treatment.

HOW TO PREVENT IT

Although there are no specific ways to prevent PMS, following these guidelines can help prevent the symptoms from interfering with your life:

➤ Eat meals that include lots of complex carbohydrates (pasta, potatoes, bread).
➤ Exercise daily.
➤ Try to reduce stress. Learn to practice yoga or meditation.
➤ If you smoke, quit.

FOR MORE HELP

Book: *All About Eve: The Complete Guide to Women's Health and Well-Being*, by Tracy Chutorian Semler. Contains a comprehensive chapter on PMS. HarperCollins, 1995, $16.

Toxic Shock Syndrome

SIGNS AND SYMPTOMS

Call 911 or go to an emergency facility **immediately** if you have:
■ Sudden, high fever (higher than 102 degrees).
■ Watery diarrhea.
■ Vomiting.
■ A rash resembling a sunburn, often on the palms of the hands or the soles of the feet.
■ Headache, dizziness, or confusion.
■ Weakness or fainting.

Toxic shock syndrome is a dangerous condition that comes on suddenly. It is caused by common bacteria (*Staphylococcus aureus*) that multiply rapidly and release toxins into the bloodstream.

Toxic shock occurs primarily among menstruating women who use tampons—especially superabsorbent tampons. When a tampon is left in place for a long time, it can trap the bacteria and give them a better chance to grow. Toxic shock has also been linked to the use of contraceptive sponges and—very rarely—to diaphragms and cervical caps.

The disease can also affect children, men, and women beyond childbearing age who are exposed to the bacteria while recovering from surgery, a burn, or an open wound.

Toxic shock syndrome requires emergency care. In most cases, people are hospitalized and given intravenous antibiotics to kill the bacteria. If untreated, the condition can cause liver or kidney failure, severe shock, and—in rare cases—death. Most patients, however, recover fully if they are treated quickly.

WHAT YOU CAN DO NOW

➤ If you have symptoms of toxic shock syndrome and you have a tampon, a menstrual sponge, a contraceptive sponge, a diaphragm, or a cervical cap inside you, remove it immediately.

WHEN TO CALL THE DOCTOR

Call 911 or go to an emergency facility **immediately:**
➤ If you have symptoms of toxic shock syndrome—especially if you are menstruating and have been using tampons.
Call for an immediate appointment:
➤ If you have already been diagnosed with toxic shock syndrome and you develop new symptoms. Drugs used to treat the illness may produce side effects.

HOW TO PREVENT IT

➤ Minimize your use of tampons. If you don't want to stop using them, wear tampons made of cotton, which pose the least risk, and alternate tampons with sanitary pads. If you've ever had toxic shock syndrome, avoid using tampons altogether.
➤ Don't use superabsorbent tampons. Use the least absorbent tampon that will control your menstrual flow.
➤ Change tampons frequently during the day—at least every four to six hours.
➤ Avoid using tampons or menstrual sponges overnight.
➤ If you use a diaphragm or cervical cap, remember to remove it within the time recommended in the directions. Never leave a diaphragm in for more than 24 hours or a cervical cap in for more than 48 hours.
➤ Wash your diaphragm or cervical cap in warm, soapy water after each use; rinse and dry it thoroughly with a clean towel.
➤ Wash your hands thoroughly before you insert a tampon or any other device.
➤ Always clean and disinfect cuts or scrapes anywhere on your body. If a wound appears to be infected, get medical help.

FOR MORE HELP

Organization: National Women's Health Network, 202-628-7814, M–F 9–5 EST. Staffers will answer questions on toxic shock syndrome and send an information packet ($8 nonmembers).

Vaginal Problems

SIGNS AND SYMPTOMS

Yeast infection:
■ Redness, itching, and sometimes burning during urination.
■ Pain during intercourse.
■ White, cheesy, odorless discharge (sometimes).
Bacterial vaginosis:
■ Watery, grayish white or yellow discharge with a fishy odor.
■ Mild burning or irritation.
Contact dermatitis:
■ Redness and itching of the vulva (the outer genital area).

The term *vaginitis* covers several conditions in which a woman's outer genital area becomes irritated.

A **yeast infection,** the most common of these, is caused by the overgrowth of a fungus normally found in the vagina. It can be brought on by pregnancy, diabetes, use of antibiotics, and sometimes use of oral contraceptives. Hot weather and clothing made of synthetic materials such as polyester (which doesn't allow air to reach your skin) can also contribute; some experts believe that feminine hygiene products cause it to develop as well. If you get frequent yeast infections, your doctor can prescribe an oral antifungal medication.

Bacterial vaginosis occurs when bacteria normally found in the vagina multiply out of control or when bacteria normally found in the rectum spread to the vagina. Women who are in poor health, lack good hygiene, or wear clothing made of material that does not allow air to reach their skin are more likely to get vaginosis.

Contact dermatitis may be caused by chemical irritation from the use of latex condoms, spermicides, or diaphragms; feminine hygiene sprays; colored or scented toilet tissue; soaps, detergents, or fabric softeners; and deodorant tampons or sanitary pads.

Persistent cases of contact dermatitis can be treated with a prescription ointment.

Yeast infection or bacterial vaginosis:
➤ Dry the vulva area thoroughly, especially after urinating or showering.
➤ For a yeast infection, try an over-the-counter antifungal suppository cream containing miconazole or clotrimazole.
➤ If urinating causes burning, urinate through a plastic cup with the bottom cut out, pressed against your vulva, to keep urine from touching sensitive skin; or use a squirt bottle to spray warm water over the vulva while urinating.
➤ To prevent a recurrence, take all your medications until they run out, even after symptoms disappear.

Contact dermatitis:
➤ Apply a cool compress or try hydrocortisone cream on irritated skin.
➤ Rinse your underwear a second time with plain water after it has been washed with detergent. Avoid fabric softeners.

WHEN TO CALL THE DOCTOR

Call for an immediate appointment:
➤ If you have bleeding between menstrual periods or after menopause; a firm, raised lesion or bump on the vulva or inside the vagina; or persistent vaginal pain and itching. These may be signs of cancer of the vagina or vulva.
➤ If you have vaginal discharge that is yellow or green and foul-smelling. This may signal a **sexually transmitted disease** (see chart on page 215).

Call for advice and an appointment:
➤ If you have symptoms of bacterial vaginosis; your doctor can treat the infection with an oral antibiotic.
➤ If you have any vaginal symptoms for the first time, or if they recur more than twice a year.
➤ If symptoms don't go away after prescribed or home treatment, or are severe.

HOW TO PREVENT IT

➤ Avoid spreading bacteria from the rectum to the vagina by wiping from front to back after a bowel movement.
➤ Avoid scented toilet paper and perfumed soaps, feminine hygiene sprays, douches, and scented or deodorant tampons.
➤ Thoroughly clean diaphragms, cervical caps, and spermicidal applicators after each use.
➤ Don't wear tight pants, panties or panty hose without a cotton crotch, or other fabrics and clothing that can trap moisture.
➤ If you are taking antibiotics, ask your doctor if you should apply an antifungal cream to the vulva to prevent a yeast infection.
➤ Examine your vulva monthly for changes.
➤ Have a pelvic exam and Pap smear at least once a year. Get an exam and a Pap smear every six months if you've had genital warts that your doctor has told you are cancer-related, if you know your mother took the drug DES (diethylstilbestrol), if you've had a hysterectomy or radiation therapy, or if you are sexually active with more than one partner. You may be at higher risk for vaginal cancer or sexually transmitted diseases.

FOR MORE HELP

Organization: National Women's Health Network, 202-628-7814, M–F 9–5 EST. Staffer will answer questions on vaginitis and yeast infections and send information packet ($6 members, $8 nonmembers).

Organization: American College of Obstetricians and Gynecologists Resource Center, 409 12th St. SW, Washington, DC 20024. Send a business-size, self-addressed, stamped envelope, and request the pamphlet on vaginitis. You can also ask for the patient education order form, which lists all brochures.

Book: *Every Woman's Body: Everything You Need to Know to Make Informed Choices About Your Health,* by Diana Korte. Fawcett Columbine, 1994, $15.

Children's Health

◆

Bed-Wetting

SIGNS AND SYMPTOMS

Occasional bed-wetting is normal. It may be a problem:

- If your child is six or older and seldom stays dry overnight.
- If you, your spouse, or your child are concerned.

Bed-wetting is common, even well beyond the period of toilet training. About one child in ten continues to wet the bed past the age of five. Boys are more prone to bed-wetting than girls, and it tends to run in families. Some children who wet the bed simply have small bladders, or their nerves and muscles haven't matured enough to control their bladders all night. Less often, a child may not have enough of a hormone that helps the kidneys hold urine. Most children outgrow these problems by adolescence.

If your child has been dry during the night for a while and then starts wetting the bed, this could be a sign of something more serious, such as diabetes or a bladder infection. It may also be a reaction to a stressful recent event, such as the birth of a sibling.

WHAT YOU CAN DO NOW

➤ Remind your child to use the bathroom just before bed each night.

➤ Limit the amount your child drinks before bedtime.

➤ Don't give your child drinks, such as colas and teas, that contain caffeine; caffeinated drinks produce more urine.

➤ Wake your child to use the toilet again before you go to bed, if he or she has been sleeping for more than an hour.

➤ Praise your child whenever he or she stays dry. (Never scold a child for bed-wetting; you may make the problem worse.)

WHEN TO CALL THE DOCTOR

Call for an immediate appointment:

➤ If your child has painful urination, bloody or very cloudy urine, abdominal pain, or a very narrow urine stream; this could signal a bladder infection.

Call for advice and an appointment:

➤ If either you or your child feel frustrated and want more help.

HOW TO PREVENT IT

➤ Try bladder training: Once a day, encourage your child to hold his or her urine for a few minutes past the first sensation of a full bladder. Practice for three months to give the technique a chance to work.

FOR MORE HELP

Information line: National Kidney Foundation Information Center, 800-622-9010, M–F 8:30–5 EST. Staffers answer questions and send literature on bed-wetting.

Children's Rashes

SYMPTOMS	WHAT IT MIGHT BE	WHAT YOU CAN DO
Rash of itchy, red welts with pale centers, anywhere on body.	Hives (see page 149).	If child begins wheezing or has trouble swallowing, call 911 or go to emergency facility **immediately.** Otherwise, call doctor for advice and appointment.
Purple rash, pale skin, general fatigue, headache, aching limbs, swollen glands, vulnerability to infection, mouth sores.	Childhood leukemia.	Call doctor for immediate appointment.
First symptoms: sore throat, slight fever; 2 weeks later: painless, purple, spotted rash on ankles, elbows, shins, or buttocks.	Allergic purpura—a reaction that causes bleeding under the skin, forming a rash.	Call doctor for immediate appointment.
First symptoms: low fever, swollen glands; 2–3 days later: slightly raised, red rash on face that spreads to rest of body.	German measles (rubella) (see page 250).	Call doctor for immediate appointment. Keep child away from pregnant women (virus that causes this illness can damage fetus).
First symptoms: fever as high as 105, cough, runny nose, pinkeye, general sick feeling; 1–2 days later: rash of small, red bumps starts on face and neck, then spreads to rest of body.	Measles (see page 254).	Call doctor for immediate appointment.
First symptoms: sore throat, fever of 101–104, headache; 1–2 days later: red, sandpaperlike rash begins on face and groin, spreads to torso, arms, and legs; may itch.	Scarlet fever (see page 258).	Call doctor for immediate appointment.
Whitish patches in mouth and throat, or red patches in genital area.	Yeast infection (see fungal infections, page 147).	Call doctor for immediate appointment.

(continued)

Children's Rashes *(continued)*

SYMPTOMS	WHAT IT MIGHT BE	WHAT YOU CAN DO
Blisters in mouth; blistering rash on hands, feet, and sometimes buttocks; fever up to 102; sore throat; loss of appetite.	Hand, foot, and mouth disease (see page 251).	Call doctor for immediate appointment if child develops extreme difficulty swallowing.
Small, red, itchy spots that turn into clear, fluid-filled blisters; slight fever. Rash starts on face and torso.	Chicken pox (see page 243).	Call doctor for advice and appointment. Ease itching with oatmeal baths or calamine lotion.
Bright red rash starts on cheeks, then spreads to other areas of body, may itch; fever as high as 102; sometimes sore throat, headache, or fatigue.	Fifth disease (see page 249).	Call doctor for advice and appointment. Keep child away from pregnant women (virus that causes this illness can damage fetus).
First symptoms: fever as high as 105; mild cough, runny nose; 3–6 days later: red, spreading rash that disappears in few days to few hours.	Roseola (see page 257).	Call doctor for advice and appointment. If child's fever reaches 102 or higher, call doctor immediately.
Round, scaly, itchy rash that appears mainly on scalp, feet, or around nails; creates bald patches on scalp.	Ringworm—a contagious fungal infection.	Call doctor for advice and appointment.
Dry, scaly skin; itchy, red bumps; depending on severity, rash may cover small area or most of body; common on knees and elbows.	Eczema (see page 146).	If spreading, call doctor for advice and appointment. Soothe mild cases with moisturizing cream; avoid lotions with preservatives, oils, or perfume.
Rash of small blisters, generally on face, legs, or arms; blisters usually break and weep, forming honey-colored crust.	Impetigo (see page 252).	Keep rash and surrounding area clean with soap and water. If rash persists or gets worse, call doctor for advice and appointment.

Children's Rashes

SYMPTOMS	WHAT IT MIGHT BE	WHAT YOU CAN DO
Light red rash in spots or large blotches; occurs in hot weather.	Heat rash.	Remove unnecessary clothing. Call doctor for immediate appointment if rash lasts 24 hours or if other symptoms appear.
Dry scales that turn into yellow, greasy patches; may be uncomfortable or itchy. Located on scalp (in cradle cap); or in creases of neck, behind ears, in armpits, on face, or in diaper area (in seborrheic dermatitis).	Cradle cap. ● Seborrheic dermatitis (see dermatitis, page 144).	Shampoo frequently with baby shampoo. If condition persists, call doctor for advice and appointment.
Bright red, tight, and/or irritated skin in diaper area; rash that may consist of small bumps.	Diaper rash (see page 247).	Change wet diapers frequently, and immediately after bowel movement. If no improvement in 1 week, call doctor for appointment.

Chicken Pox

SIGNS AND SYMPTOMS

■ An itchy rash that usually appears on the face and torso. It starts out as small, red spots; these turn into clear, fluid-filled blisters. In the final stage of the rash, the blisters burst and scab over. The rash typically lasts seven to ten days.

Occasionally:

■ Painful blisters in the mouth or vagina, or around the eyes.

■ A low fever.

Chicken pox is a highly contagious childhood disease that affects about three-fourths of children before the age of 15. After someone gets the virus, the rash and other symptoms usually don't appear for one to three weeks, so infected people can spread the disease before they know they have it.

Chicken pox is not a serious illness, and a vaccine is now available that will help prevent it. Chicken pox can be uncomfortable, but there are many simple things you can do to ease your child's discomfort. It's important to try to relieve the itchiness, since a lot of scratching can cause infections and scars, although infection can be treated with antibiotic ointment or an oral medication.

WHAT YOU CAN DO NOW

➤ Give acetaminophen for pain. (Never give aspirin to a child under 12 who has chicken pox, flu, or any other illness you suspect of being caused by a virus, such as a bad respiratory infection; see box on **Reye's syndrome,** page 92.)

➤ If your child wears diapers, leave them off as much as possible to let the blisters dry.

➤ Make sure your child gets plenty of rest and lots to drink.

To relieve itching:

➤ Apply calamine lotion to the rash, and try

RECOMMENDED CHILDREN'S IMMUNIZATIONS

During your child's early years, doctor checkups include immunizations. They provide protection against a range of major diseases, from polio to diphtheria. At one point, these diseases were widespread and deadly. Most states require children to get their shots before starting school. If a child is sick or has had a serious reaction to a previous vaccination, to neomycin, or to eggs, tell your doctor before any new vaccination.

Serious reactions are rare, but ask about symptoms to watch for.

CHILD'S AGE	VACCINE(S)	CHILD'S RECORD
Birth	Hep B (hepatitis B)	
2 months	Hep B	
	DTP (diphtheria, tetanus/lockjaw, pertussis/whooping cough)	
	OPV (oral polio vaccine)	
	Hib (Haemophilus B conjugate). Immunizes children against *Haemophilus influenzae* type b, which can cause meningitis. (DTP and Hib can be given in one injection.)	
4 months	DTP	
	Hib	
	OPV	
6 months	Hep B	
	DTP	
	Hib (may not need, depending on vaccines at 2 and 4 months)	
	OPV	
12–15 months	DTP or DTaP (diphtheria, tetanus, and acellular pertussis). DTaP is used only for children 15 months or older; it has fewer side effects than DTP.	
	Hib	
	MMR (measles, mumps, rubella/German measles)	
	VZV (varicella zoster virus). Immunizes against chicken pox.	
4–6 years	DTP or DTaP	
	MMR (may be given at 11–12 years instead)	
	OPV	
	Td (tetanus and diphtheria). May be required for school; then every 10 years for rest of life.	
11–12 years	Hep B (if not given when infant) VZV (if not given at 12–15 months and child hasn't had chicken pox)	

This chart is based on recommendations by the American Academy of Pediatrics and the Centers for Disease Control and Prevention. These recommendations are subject to change, so be sure to ask your pediatrician for the most current schedule.

adding a handful of oatmeal, baking soda, or an over-the-counter anti-itch bath powder to your child's bath water.

To help prevent skin infections:

➤ Keep your child's skin, clothes, and bed linens clean.

➤ To prevent scratching, trim your child's fingernails and/or cover his or her hands with socks or mittens.

| WHEN TO CALL THE DOCTOR |

Call 911 or go to an emergency facility **immediately:**

➤ If chicken pox is accompanied by persistent drowsiness, double vision, extreme sensitivity to light, eye pain, speech impairment, loss of hearing, a stiff neck or back, or a severe cough; these may be symptoms of acute encephalitis, an inflammation of the brain. (See **meningitis and encephalitis,** page 56.)

➤ If breathing becomes difficult; this may be a symptom of **pneumonia** (see page 94), a possible complication (sometimes in adults, rarely in children).

Call for advice and an appointment:

➤ If areas of your child's rash look increasingly red, swollen, or tender, or produce a yellow discharge.

➤ If chicken pox is accompanied by a fever over 102 for three to four days, a symptom of possible strep infection.

| HOW TO PREVENT IT |

➤ A chicken pox vaccine is available for all children over 13 months, and it can be combined with other routine immunizations. For children under 13 years old, a single injection should provide immunity to the disease. Anyone over 13 needs two shots, four to eight weeks apart.

| FOR MORE HELP |

Organization: American Academy of Pediatrics, P.O. Box 927, Elk Grove Village, IL 60009-0927. Include a business-size, self-addressed, stamped envelope with your request for information on chicken pox.

Further resources: See box on page 262.

Colic

| SIGNS AND SYMPTOMS |

In an otherwise healthy infant, three months or younger:

■ Crying that goes on for three hours or more at a time, despite efforts to comfort the baby. Crying is often worse in the evening and continues into the night.

When gas pain is the cause:

■ Baby extends legs or pulls them up to the abdomen.

■ Baby passes gas.

I f your baby is acting colicky, he or she is in good company. About 20 percent of infants have colic. Often it has no apparent cause, but sometimes it can be the result of gas pains from sensitivity to certain foods in the nursing mother's diet or to the type of milk in the baby's formula.

Although colic is harmless, it can be very tiring for parents. This phase of your baby's life may seem endless, but most colicky babies grow out of it by about the time they are three months of age. Sometimes, however, colicky behavior may signal an illness, such as a hernia or an ear infection.

| WHAT YOU CAN DO NOW |

➤ If gas pain seems to be the problem, place your baby stomach-down on your lap and gently massage the baby's back.

➤ Walk with your baby in a body carrier, rock him or her in your arms or in a swing, or take him or her for a car ride. Rhythmic motion often soothes babies.

➤ Try putting the baby near the sound of a clothes dryer or a vacuum cleaner. Some babies are calmed by "white noise" or rhythmic sounds.

➤ Wrap your baby snugly in a blanket for security and warmth.

➤ Ask a friend or neighbor for help when you feel yourself getting frustrated from trying to soothe your colicky child.

Children's Health

➤ If your baby has not had colic before and is now acting colicky. Your doctor will want to rule out any illness.
➤ If the colic gets worse.
➤ If your baby is older than three months and is still colicky.
➤ If your colicky baby is not hungry and is not gaining weight.

HOW TO PREVENT IT

➤ If you're nursing, notice whether your baby is colicky after you eat certain foods, so that you can avoid them. Frequent offenders include cabbage, onions, garlic, broccoli, and turnips, and the caffeine in coffee, tea, chocolate, and cocoa.
➤ For a colicky bottle-fed baby, switch to formula without cow's milk.
➤ Always burp your baby after a feeding.
➤ Try feeding your infant smaller amounts more frequently.

FOR MORE HELP

For a list of resources on children's health, see box on page 262.

Croup

SIGNS AND SYMPTOMS

■ Loud, barking, seal-like cough.
■ Difficulty breathing.
■ Shrill wheezing or grunting noise while breathing.
■ Hoarseness.
■ Sometimes fever (can be as high as 104 degrees).

Children who have croup find it hard to breathe because their airways have become inflamed and narrowed. Croup usually starts as a respiratory infection caused by a virus that is easily passed between young-sters. Some children are particularly prone to croup and may get it every time they have a respiratory illness, most commonly between October and March.

Children between the ages of six months and three years are most likely to get croup. Those over five tend not to develop it because their airways have grown larger, so swelling is less likely to interfere with breathing. Boys are more prone to croup than girls.

Croup usually clears up in about six days; meanwhile, you can ease your child's discomfort with simple at-home measures. But in rare cases, your child's airways may swell so much that breathing becomes nearly impossible. If so, hospitalization may be needed.

WHAT YOU CAN DO NOW

➤ Have your child breathe moist air, either from a bowl filled with steaming water, a cool-mist humidifier, or a hot shower. Your child's breathing should ease after about 15 to 20 minutes.
➤ Take your child outside for a few minutes—dressed warmly if it's cold out. Breathing cold, moist air, especially at night, may make breathing easier. Going for a drive with the car windows open can also help.
➤ Sit your child up straight to ease breathing. For a baby, use an infant seat.
➤ Stay calm, and try to keep your child calm, too. Crying makes the symptoms worse.

WHEN TO CALL THE DOCTOR

Call for emergency advice (if not available, call 911 or go to an emergency facility):
➤ If your child starts to make loud, high-pitched wheezing noises while inhaling.
➤ If your child struggles to get a breath or can't speak for lack of breath.
➤ If your child has difficulty swallowing.
Call for an immediate appointment:
➤ If your child breathes quickly and noisily.
➤ If your child's temperature is 102 degrees or higher.

HOW TO PREVENT IT

➤ Get prompt treatment for any child with a respiratory infection.

➤ Make sure your children wash their hands often to reduce the chance of spreading infections.

FOR MORE HELP

For a list of resources on children's health, see box on page 262.

Diaper Rash

SIGNS AND SYMPTOMS

■ Redness or small bumps on a baby's buttocks, genitals, lower abdomen, thigh folds, or anyplace that has contact with wet or soiled diapers.

■ In the same areas, tight, papery skin or shiny, bright red skin.

■ Strong ammonia odor (sometimes).

Most babies will get diaper rash at least once. Those who are between eight and ten months old, or who are just starting to eat solid foods, are especially likely to get it. Formula-fed babies are more disposed to develop diaper rash than are breast-fed babies.

Most diaper rash is caused by too much contact with moisture, urine, or feces. Lotions or soaps used directly on the baby's skin, and detergents used to launder cloth diapers, can also cause rashes.

If home care doesn't get rid of diaper rash in two or three days, your baby may have a fungal or bacterial infection. Babies on antibiotics are especially prone to fungal rashes.

WHAT YOU CAN DO NOW

➤ Keep your baby's bottom as clean and dry as possible.

➤ Use a blow-dryer set on low to blow warm, dry air on your baby's bottom.

➤ After washing and drying your baby, apply an over-the-counter zinc oxide ointment to the inflamed area. Baby powder is generally ineffective.

WHEN TO CALL THE DOCTOR

➤ If you see no improvement after three days of home treatment.

➤ If your baby's rash affects more than the diaper area.

➤ If the diaper area is covered with red or pus-filled blisters, which then crust over; this may be **impetigo** (see page 252).

➤ If a baby boy's foreskin becomes very red and inflamed.

HOW TO PREVENT IT

➤ Change soiled or wet diapers as soon as you can.

➤ Expose your baby's bottom to the air as much as possible.

➤ Make sure air can circulate inside your baby's diaper. You might want to avoid plastic pants or disposable diapers with tight gathers around the tummy or legs.

➤ If you launder cloth diapers yourself, use a mild laundry soap, and avoid fabric softeners, which can irritate skin. Put the diapers through several rinse cycles to remove all traces of detergent. Add two tablespoons of vinegar to the rinse water; this helps fight bacteria.

FOR MORE HELP

Organization: American Academy of Pediatrics, P.O. Box 927, Elk Grove Village, IL 60009-0927. Include a business-size, self-addressed, stamped envelope with your request for information on diaper rash.
Further resources: See box on page 262.

Diarrhea in Children

See **diarrhea,** page 116.

Ear Infections in Children

See **ear infections,** page 71.

Fever in Children

SIGNS AND SYMPTOMS

- A temperature of 100 degrees or higher (taken orally).
- Hot forehead.
- Flushed face.
- Sweating.
- Crying, irritability, or little appetite.

A fever of 100 degrees or higher is often the first signal that your child may be sick. Although 98.6 degrees is considered normal, body temperature varies with age, activity, and the time of day (it's usually lower in the morning and higher in the late afternoon). A temperature of 97 to 99 is usually no reason to worry.

But a fever can be a sign of a childhood ailment, including viral or bacterial illnesses. In a baby or young child, fever can lead to a **seizure** (see box).

Childhood illnesses marked by fever include chicken pox; croup; ear infection; German measles; hand, foot, and mouth disease; measles; mumps; rheumatic fever; strep throat; and whooping cough.

WHAT YOU CAN DO NOW

- ➤ Check your child's temperature with a thermometer. For a child up to the age of five, use a rectal thermometer.
- ➤ Make sure your child is not overdressed or in a place that's too hot. Remove extra clothing, and, if possible, cool the room.
- ➤ Watch your child's behavior. If a child is eating and sleeping well and is playful, there's probably no serious problem. But complaints of feeling sick or tired, lack of appetite, and crying for no clear reason are likely signs of illness.
- ➤ Have your child drink plenty of cool fluids to help lower body temperature and prevent dehydration.
- ➤ Give your child acetaminophen to help lower the fever. (Never give aspirin to a child under 12 who has a fever, chicken pox, flu, or any other illness you suspect of being caused by a virus, such as a bad respiratory infection; see box on **Reye's syndrome,** page 92.) Consult your pediatrician before giving medication to an in-

FEVER SEIZURES

Watching a feverish child have a convulsion (febrile seizure) is a terrifying experience. These seizures are not uncommon in children from six months to five years old whose temperatures have risen quickly. Despite the violence of a convulsion, it is rarely harmful and usually has no lasting effects.

The signs of seizure include shaking or jerking of the arms and legs, a fixed stare or the eyes rolling back, drooling, heavy breathing, and the skin turning blue, especially on the face. A seizure can last for less than a minute, more than five minutes, or, rarely, up to 20 minutes.

Take immediate action to prevent injury. Lay your child on a flat surface on his or her stomach or side, away from any sharp or hard objects. Turn your child's head to the side so that vomit or saliva can drain. If your child does vomit, clean out the mouth with your finger. Try to reduce his or her temperature by taking off clothing and sponging the body with lukewarm water.

If the seizure lasts for more than a few minutes or is severe, call 911 or go to an emergency facility **immediately.** Even if a seizure is brief or mild, call your doctor for an immediate appointment to rule out a serious condition, such as **meningitis** (see page 56).

fant under three months old.

➤ To lower body temperature, sponge your child with lukewarm water, especially if he or she has had a history of convulsions or is vomiting.

WHEN TO CALL THE DOCTOR

Call for an immediate appointment:

➤ If your baby (three months old or under) has a fever of 100.4 or higher, or if a child over three months old has a fever of 102 or higher.

➤ If your child has a temperature that climbs as high as 105 degrees after spending time on a hot beach or in a closed car or other hot place. This is not a fever but a dangerous condition called **heat stroke** (see page 38).

Call for advice and an appointment:

➤ If your child has other symptoms, such as vomiting, diarrhea, difficulty breathing, or a stiff neck; or if he or she cries persistently and is confused or delirious.

➤ If your child has a fever that lasts more than three days.

HOW TO PREVENT IT

There is no way to prevent most fevers. To avoid fevers caused by overheating:

➤ Don't overdress your child, and never leave your child alone in a closed car.

➤ Encourage your child to drink lots of water, rest in the shade, and wear a hat when playing in hot sun.

➤ Keep your child's room at a comfortable temperature. Use a fan if the room is hot or stuffy, and never put a crib next to a radiator, heater, or heating vent.

FOR MORE HELP

For a list of resources on children's health, see box on page 262.

Fifth Disease

SIGNS AND SYMPTOMS

■ A rash that begins as bright red patches on the cheeks. Over the next few days, it becomes pink, slightly raised, and lacy-looking, and spreads to the buttocks, torso, arms, and thighs. Physical activity or bathing may worsen the rash.

■ Fever, as high as 102 degrees.

■ Coldlike symptoms, including sore throat, headache, reddish eyes, and fatigue (sometimes).

■ Itchiness (sometimes).

Fifth disease, a viral childhood illness, is so named because it is among the five common infections—along with measles, German measles (rubella), roseola, and scarlet fever—that cause a rash and fever, and that are contagious. Children between the ages of 5 and 14 are most likely to get fifth disease, and outbreaks occur most often in the spring and early summer.

Once the virus has taken hold, the rash may take up to 14 days to appear. Meanwhile, your child, who may have the symptoms of a cold, can spread the disease to other children through the air. Your child is contagious before the rash is present, but not while he or she has the rash or after it disappears.

Fifth disease is mild; most children feel fine even while they have the rash, and the illness usually clears up in about ten days. The virus (named parvovirus) can, however, cause arthritis in older children and adults, and serious complications in children and adolescents who have sickle-cell anemia.

WHAT YOU CAN DO NOW

➤ If your child feels sick, encourage bed rest and give plenty of water and other fluids.

➤ If the rash is itchy, apply an over-the-counter cream, such as calamine lotion.

➤ For minor aches or pains, or discomfort from fever, you can give your child acetaminophen. (Never give aspirin to a child under 12 who has fifth disease, chicken pox, flu, or any other illness you suspect of being caused by a virus, such as a bad respiratory infection; see box on **Reye's syndrome,** page 92.)

➤ Keep your child away from pregnant women, because fifth disease can harm a developing fetus.

WHEN TO CALL THE DOCTOR

Call for advice and an appointment:
➤ If your child develops any kind of rash. Fifth disease isn't serious, but it has symptoms that can appear similar to those of more serious illnesses.
➤ If your child develops new symptoms or a fever of 102 degrees or higher.

HOW TO PREVENT IT

➤ Make sure your children wash their hands often to reduce the chance of spreading infections.

FOR MORE HELP

For a list of resources on children's health, see box on page 262.

German Measles (Rubella)

SIGNS AND SYMPTOMS

■ Fever of 102 degrees or lower.
■ Swollen glands, usually in the neck.
■ By the second or third day, a rash appears, generally starting on the face and spreading to the chest and back, then the legs and arms. Rash can appear as tiny red or pink spots or irregular blotches, and usually lasts only a few days.
■ Painful, aching joints, especially in adolescents.

German measles, also known as rubella, is a mild viral illness that, along with chicken pox and mumps, used to be one of the milestones of early childhood. Today, thanks to the availability of a vaccine, German measles is far less common than it was a decade ago.

The virus is spread through the air when an infected person coughs or sneezes. A child with rubella may feel no worse than he or she would with a simple cold; rubella usually clears up on its own five to seven days after the first symptoms appear.

The infection presents a serious threat, however, in early pregnancy. A pregnant woman who gets German measles has more than a 50 percent chance of having a child with birth defects. These can include blindness, deafness, mental retardation, and congenital heart defects.

WHAT YOU CAN DO NOW

➤ Keep your child quiet and comfortable, and provide lots of liquids.
➤ Give your child acetaminophen for discomfort. (Never give aspirin to a child under 12 who has German measles, chicken pox, flu, or any other illness you suspect of being caused by a virus, such as a bad respiratory infection; see box on **Reye's syndrome,** page 92.)
➤ Keep your infected child away from other children, pregnant women, and any susceptible adults. A person with rubella is contagious two days before and up to one week after the rash appears.

WHEN TO CALL THE DOCTOR

➤ If you suspect that your child has rubella.
➤ If your child has rubella or had it recently, and develops symptoms such as lethargy, a stiff neck, or severe headache. This could signal **meningitis** (see page 56), a very rare complication.
➤ If you are pregnant and have not been immunized against measles.
➤ If you are pregnant, have been immunized in the past, and may have been exposed to rubella. You need to find out whether you are still immune.

HOW TO PREVENT IT

➤ Make sure your children get the MMR (measles, mumps, and rubella) vaccine, a routine part of early childhood immunizations. (See **children's immunization** chart, page 244.)

➤ If you're a woman and you weren't immunized in childhood, you've never had German measles, and you're considering having children, get the rubella vaccine at least three months before you get pregnant. The vaccine should never be given during pregnancy.

FOR MORE HELP

For a list of resources on children's health, see box on page 262.

Hand, Foot, and Mouth Disease

SIGNS AND SYMPTOMS

■ Small, raw, cankerlike sores on the tongue and insides of the cheeks that make the mouth painful.

■ An itchy rash with red spots, bumps, and/or small blisters on the hands and feet, between the fingers and toes, and sometimes appearing on the buttocks.

■ Low fever (up to 102 degrees).

■ Tiredness.

Like many childhood illnesses, hand, foot, and mouth disease is caused by a virus. Commonly spread by the feces-to-mouth route, the virus can also be inhaled. Once it takes hold, symptoms usually show up in three to six days.

Outbreaks of hand, foot, and mouth disease occur most often in the summer and fall, when the virus grows most easily. The disease is not dangerous and usually clears up by itself within a week. There's no specific treatment, but you can ease your child's discomfort at home.

WHAT YOU CAN DO NOW

➤ Avoid citrus fruits, spicy foods, and other foods that might irritate your child's sore mouth. Try serving nutritious liquids, such as chicken or vegetable broth, and soft foods, such as mashed banana, if solid foods are too painful to chew.

➤ Be sure your child drinks plenty of fluids.

➤ If the rash is itchy, apply an over-the-counter anti-itch cream.

➤ To help relieve pain or reduce your child's fever, give acetaminophen. (Never give aspirin to a child under 12 who has hand, foot, and mouth disease, chicken pox, flu, or any other illness you suspect of being caused by a virus, such as a bad respiratory infection; see box on **Reye's syndrome,** page 92.)

WHEN TO CALL THE DOCTOR

Call for an immediate appointment:

➤ If your child complains of extreme difficulty swallowing.

Call for advice and an appointment:

➤ Whenever your child gets a rash. Hand, foot, and mouth disease is not serious, but it can be confused with a rash that is. (See **children's rashes** chart, page 241.)

HOW TO PREVENT IT

➤ Make sure children wash their hands after using the toilet.

➤ See that children don't share glasses, silverware, or toys that have been in other children's mouths.

➤ Choose a babysitter or day care center with high standards of cleanliness. Frequent hand washing, especially after diaper changes, is important.

FOR MORE HELP

For a list of resources on children's health, see box on page 262.

Impetigo

SIGNS AND SYMPTOMS

- Small patches of red or pus-filled blisters, typically on the face, legs, or arms (but they can show up anywhere); blisters range from the size of a matchstick head to a quarter.
- Once blisters pop: golden-colored, sticky crust.
- Itching.

Impetigo is a bacterial skin infection most common in children because they're prone to scrapes, skinned knees, and other minor skin injuries that give bacteria a place to thrive. It also occurs more often in children with colds or runny noses because the skin around the mouth and nose becomes raw. With poor hygiene, impetigo is very contagious and spreads quickly from one place on the body to another, and from one person to another through touching or even using the same towels.

The bacteria that cause it are harmless until they enter the body through a cut, insect bite, or other break in the skin. Impetigo occurs most often in the summer, particularly in hot, humid climates. It's also common in hospitals, day care centers, schools, and other crowded places.

Impetigo is uncomfortable and looks unattractive, but it's easily treated.

WHAT YOU CAN DO NOW

- Gently wash away the crusty discharge with warm water and soap.
- Apply an over-the-counter antibiotic ointment to help clear up a minor case.
- To avoid infecting other people, warn them not to touch your child's towel, washcloth, and unwashed clothing. Change linens daily; wash them in hot water and detergent, and add bleach.
- To limit the spread of the infection, encourage your child not to touch or scratch the blisters.
- To discourage the bacteria from growing, expose the affected area to air rather than bandaging it.
- Give your child lukewarm baths. (Heat increases itching.) Use an antibacterial soap.
- Dress your child in long-sleeved shirts and long pants to go to school or day care until the crusts are gone and the skin clears, which generally takes seven to ten days. This will lower the chance of spreading the infection to others.

WHEN TO CALL THE DOCTOR

Call for an immediate appointment:
- If your child's urine turns red or dark brown; this signals a related, rare kidney ailment that might be dangerous.

Call for advice and an appointment:
- If the impetigo covers a large area or keeps spreading after three days. The doctor may prescribe antibiotic cream or oral antibiotics to fight the infection.
- If your child develops a fever of more than 100 degrees or has a blister larger than one inch wide; this could indicate a deeper skin infection.

HOW TO PREVENT IT

- Wash all cuts, scrapes, and wounds with antibacterial soap and water to avoid infection. Keep them clean and dry while they heal.
- Encourage cleanliness. Make sure children wash their hands regularly with soap and keep their nails trimmed. Remind them not to scratch insect bites, scabs, or other skin irritations.
- Never have children share towels, washcloths, or bedding .
- Guard against **diaper rash** (see page 247) to protect your baby from the infection.

FOR MORE HELP

For a list of resources on children's health, see box on page 262.

Lead Poisoning

SIGNS AND SYMPTOMS

Most children with low levels of lead poisoning show no clear symptoms. Sometimes, however, they will have:

- Constipation.
- Vomiting.
- Loss of appetite.
- Fatigue.
- Learning disabilities and/or behavior problems.

Severe lead poisoning:

- Stomach pain.
- Headaches.
- Loss of physical coordination.
- Loss of recently acquired developmental skills.

One in 11 American children has an elevated level of lead in his or her blood. Lead poisoning isn't a problem only for inner-city families trapped in deteriorating housing; many children of middle- and upper-income families living in older houses (especially ones being renovated or redecorated) are also at risk.

Almost three-quarters of the houses built before 1980 have lead paint either inside or outside. Lead-based paint and paint dust are responsible for most childhood lead exposure today. Lead may also be present in the water from your faucet, in the dishes in your cabinets, and in your backyard soil.

Children between the ages of six months and six years are at highest risk. They are more likely than older children and adults to put objects in their mouths and to play in places where the lead particles that collect in dirt, dust, and peeling paint are concentrated most. Lead can harm a developing fetus as well, so pregnant women should also avoid exposure.

Severe lead poisoning can cause mental retardation, intestinal problems, hearing loss, anemia, and even death. At low but chronic levels, lead that reaches a child's bloodstream can result in learning disabilities, behavior problems, and reduced IQ.

The Centers for Disease Control and Prevention (CDC) recommends that children have their blood tested for lead by the time they are one year old.

WHAT YOU CAN DO NOW

➤ Ask your pediatrician to give your child a blood test for lead; this is the only way to know the level in your child's blood.
➤ If test results show an elevated lead level—10 micrograms per deciliter or more, according to the CDC—talk to your doctor about ways you can protect your child from further exposure. Also, call your local health department; many now have lead poisoning prevention programs.
➤ In severe cases (45 to more than 69 micrograms per deciliter), a treatment that increases the body's ability to eliminate lead (chelation therapy) can be given.

WHEN TO CALL THE DOCTOR

➤ If you believe your child has been exposed to lead; for example, if your house paint is old and peeling or if your house has recently been renovated.

HOW TO PREVENT IT

Consider having the paint, water, and soil in and around your home tested; you may then need to rid your home of lead hazards. Other steps to take:

➤ Especially if your house was built before 1980, keep it as clean and dust-free as possible. Pay attention to areas where dust tends to gather, such as windowsills and baseboards. Damp-mop floors frequently, and damp-dust surfaces.
➤ If your house was built before 1980 and you plan to repaint or renovate it, ask your local health department for a list of companies whose workers take precautions against lead hazards. If possible, children and pregnant women should move out of the house during renovation. If this is not possible, they should take extra precau-

tions to avoid being exposed to lead.

➤ Unless a lead test shows that your tap water is safe, use bottled water or a water filter that removes lead from the water (get the maker's certification that it does). Use only cold water from the tap for drinking, cooking, or preparing baby formula.

➤ Wash children's toys, pacifiers, and bottle nipples frequently.

➤ Wash your hands before preparing food, and wash your child's face and hands before meals.

➤ Feed your child balanced meals that include plenty of calcium and iron-rich foods; these can reduce lead absorption.

➤ Never purchase, store, or heat foods in cans manufactured in another country; these may contain lead.

➤ Have painted toys and glazed dishes that were made outside of the United States tested for lead, or dispose of them. Never use imported dishware to store foods.

➤ If you work with lead in your job, remove your work clothes and shower before going home.

FOR MORE HELP

Information line: National Safety Council's National Lead Information Center, 800-LEAD-FYI, 24-hour taped message that provides information and referrals. 800-424-LEAD, M–F 8:30–5:30 EST. An information specialist answers questions.

Organization: Lead Poisoning Prevention Branch, Centers for Disease Control and Prevention, 4770 Buford Hwy. NE, Bldg. 101, Mail Stop F42, Atlanta, GA 30341. 404-488-7330, M–F 8:30–5 EST. Provides information on lead hazards.

Organization: Alliance to End Childhood Lead Poisoning, 227 Massachusetts Ave. NE, # 200, Washington, DC 20002. 202-543-1147, M–F 9–5:30 EST. Provides publications and referrals.

Book: *Lead Is a Silent Hazard,* by Richard Stapleton. Walker and Company, 1994, $11.95.

Measles

SIGNS AND SYMPTOMS

First two to three days:
■ Fever (as high as 105 degrees).
■ Coldlike symptoms that include a runny nose; dry cough; swollen glands; red, watery eyes that are sensitive to light; loss of appetite; and aching muscles.

A day or two later:
■ In the mouth, painless, small, gray or white bumps, like grains of salt, surrounded by red rings.

In another day or so:
■ Red bumps that start on the face and neck, and then spread down the abdomen and back to the arms and legs.

Measles is a very contagious viral illness. After exposure, one to two weeks pass before the first, coldlike symptoms show up. During this period, the disease is most contagious, although it can be spread until the fever and rash are completely gone, after about five to eight more days. Infected children usually pass measles to others (including nonimmune adults and children) via coughing or sneezing.

Today, however, few children in the United States get measles, thanks to an effective vaccine. Two doses of the vaccine usually provide lasting immunity (as does having had the disease).

There's no specific treatment for measles, but you can take steps to ease your child's discomfort. Typically there are few complications, but, rarely, measles can develop into a serious problem, such as a middle **ear infection** (see page 71) or **pneumonia** (see page 94), which can usually be treated with antibiotics. Very rarely, measles can trigger **encephalitis** (see page 56), an inflammation of the brain.

Mumps

WHAT YOU CAN DO NOW

➤ Give your child lots of fluids to drink.
➤ Encourage your child to rest in bed as much as possible.
➤ Use a cool-mist humidifier in your child's bedroom.
➤ If your child's eyes are sensitive to light, darken the bedroom.
➤ If your child has minor aches or pains, or if fever is causing discomfort, you can give acetaminophen. (Never give aspirin to a child under 12 who has measles, chicken pox, flu, or any other illness you suspect of being caused by a virus, such as a bad respiratory infection; see box on **Reye's syndrome,** page 92.)
➤ Keep your child away from anyone who is not immune to measles.

WHEN TO CALL THE DOCTOR

Call 911 or go to an emergency facility **immediately:**
➤ If your child has a headache, is sensitive to bright light, and feels so drowsy that he or she is difficult to awaken. These can be warning signs of encephalitis.

Call for an immediate appointment:
➤ If your child has a feeling of fullness in the ear, which may be accompanied by pain.
➤ If your child is short of breath while resting; he or she may also have chills, sweating, and chest pain.
➤ If your child develops any kind of a rash. Other infectious diseases can have symptoms that resemble measles.
➤ If your child develops a fever of 102 degrees or higher (100 degrees or higher for infants six months or younger).

HOW TO PREVENT IT

➤ Make sure that your child gets immunizations against measles, mumps, and rubella (MMR). (See **children's immunization** chart, page 244.)

FOR MORE HELP

For a list of resources on children's health, see box on page 262.

SIGNS AND SYMPTOMS

■ Low fever (100 to 101 degrees).
■ Headache.
■ Loss of appetite.
■ Fatigue.
■ Swollen, inflamed neck glands below the ear near the jawbone, on one or both sides of the face.
■ Earache (sometimes).
■ Nausea and vomiting (sometimes).
■ In adults (sometimes): swelling in one or both testes in men; swelling of ovaries in women.

Mumps is a viral infection that is most common in children between the ages of 2 and 12, but unvaccinated adults who have never had mumps can get it, too. The virus is spread through the air when an infected person coughs or sneezes; it is only mildly contagious. Generally mumps is uncomfortable but not serious, and symptoms should disappear within seven to ten days.

Infected adults are more likely to have an especially painful symptom: inflamed testes in men and inflamed ovaries in women. The symptom should pass within four days. There is a slight risk of sterility, however, so check with your doctor if you have concerns.

Once a person has had mumps, she or he usually won't get it again because immunity develops after infection.

WHAT YOU CAN DO NOW

➤ Call your pediatrician for advice and to confirm the diagnosis.
➤ Be sure your child gets lots of rest as long as he or she has a fever.
➤ Provide plenty of liquids and a diet of soft foods, such as soups, cooked vegetables, and fruits. But don't offer sour fruits and juices, which can irritate swollen glands.
➤ To ease discomfort, apply ice packs (a bag of frozen peas wrapped in a washcloth

makes a good one), warm cloths, or heating pads to swollen areas.

➤ Your physician may recommend acetaminophen or ibuprofen to ease pain and reduce fever. (Never give aspirin to a child under 12 who has mumps, chicken pox, flu, or any other illness you suspect of being caused by a virus, such as a bad respiratory infection; see box on **Reye's syndrome,** page 92.)

WHEN TO CALL THE DOCTOR

Call for emergency advice (if not available, call 911 or go to an emergency facility):

➤ If your child has the symptoms of mumps and a severe headache, neck pain, listlessness, or unusual behavior; this could indicate **meningitis** (see page 56).

Call for an immediate appointment:

➤ If your child has mumps and feels severe abdominal pain or vomits; this could signal an inflamed pancreas.

Call for advice:

➤ If you suspect your child has mumps.

HOW TO PREVENT IT

➤ The MMR (measles, mumps, and rubella) vaccine, available through your pediatrician, will help prevent mumps (see **children's immunization** chart, page 244). The injection is usually given at 12 months, with a booster at 12 years.

➤ To prevent other children from catching mumps from your child, keep him or her home from school or day care for seven to ten days after the swelling appears.

FOR MORE HELP

For a list of resources on children's health, see box on page 262.

Rheumatic Fever

SIGNS AND SYMPTOMS

■ Early stage: sometimes a sore throat (usually one to six weeks before other symptoms appear), possibly with swollen glands in the neck.
■ Fever of 100 degrees or higher.
■ Very sore, swollen joints.
■ Fatigue and breathlessness.
■ Loss of appetite.
■ Pale skin.
■ Rash on chest, back, and abdomen (sometimes).

Rheumatic fever is a rare but potentially dangerous complication of an infection with streptococcus bacteria, usually **strep throat** (see page 258). It's most common in children between the ages of 5 and 15, although adults can also get it.

Rheumatic fever occurs as part of the body's immune response to a strep infection. Antibodies created to destroy the bacteria instead attack the joints or, in some cases, the valves of the heart. Symptoms of rheumatic fever usually appear one to six weeks after a strep infection.

If diagnosed and treated promptly with antibiotics, rheumatic fever poses little threat and passes within two to 12 weeks. If the heart has been affected, symptoms may persist for as long as six months. Any damage to the heart valves may not appear until years later.

WHAT YOU CAN DO NOW

➤ Have your child rest in bed and drink plenty of liquids.
➤ Once the diagnosis is confirmed, your doctor may advise aspirin for joint pain.

WHEN TO CALL THE DOCTOR

➤ If a child or an adult has recently had a strep infection and then shows symptoms of rheumatic fever.

➤ If a child or an adult has a fever, sore throat, and swollen glands that persist for 48 hours or more; these symptoms could signal a strep infection.

➤ If new, unexplained symptoms appear after treatment has begun; this could be a reaction to a prescribed drug.

| HOW TO PREVENT IT |

➤ Seek prompt diagnosis and treatment of a strep infection.

| FOR MORE HELP |

For a list of resources on children's health, see box on page 262.

Roseola

| SIGNS AND SYMPTOMS |

Early symptoms:
- Sudden high fever (102 to as high as 105 degrees).
- Decreased appetite.
- Mild diarrhea.
- Slight cough.
- Runny nose.
- Mild irritability, drowsiness.
- Swollen glands (rarely).

In severe cases:
- Convulsions

Later symptoms:
- Temperature returns to normal after three to six days; at the same time, a spotty, red, slightly raised rash appears on the torso.
- Rash may spread to the arms, neck, legs, and face; it disappears in a few hours to a few days.

Roseola is sometimes called the "baby measles" because it occurs most often between the ages of six months and two years. It often frightens parents because of its alarming symptoms: the high fever followed by the abrupt bloom of a rash. In fact,

this common viral infection poses little risk, although there are sometimes complications such as convulsions from the high fever (see box, page 248). These feverish convulsions are usually harmless, but they should be reported to your pediatrician right away.

From the first appearance of symptoms, the illness usually passes within a week; as soon as the rash disappears, the child is no longer contagious and can return to school and normal activities.

| WHAT YOU CAN DO NOW |

➤ Give your child plenty of liquids.
➤ Have your child rest as long as he or she has a fever.
➤ Give a feverish child sponge baths with lukewarm water.
➤ Ask your doctor if you should give acetaminophen to reduce fever. (Never give aspirin to a child under 12 who has roseola, chicken pox, flu, or any other illness you suspect of being caused by a virus, such as a bad respiratory infection; see box on **Reye's syndrome,** page 92.)

| WHEN TO CALL THE DOCTOR |

Call for an immediate appointment:
➤ If your child has a temperature of 102 degrees or higher.
➤ If your child has convulsions.

| HOW TO PREVENT IT |

➤ To prevent the virus from spreading, don't let a child with roseola play with other children until the rash clears up.
➤ Make sure all family members wash their hands frequently, especially before touching food and after using the bathroom.

| FOR MORE HELP |

For a list of resources on children's health, see box on page 262.

Scarlet Fever

Symptoms can vary, but in most cases the illness develops as follows:

- First day: fever from 101 to 104 degrees; red and sore throat; fuzzy tongue; white coating on tonsils; headache; swollen neck glands; vomiting (sometimes).
- By the second day: bright red rash that breaks out on face (except right around mouth) and in groin area.
- By third day: rash, which feels like fine sandpaper to the touch and may itch, spreads to rest of body. Temperature falls, and tongue turns bright red.
- By sixth day: rash fades and skin and tongue may peel, exposing raw, tender skin.

Scarlet fever, a contagious childhood infection, is caused by streptococcus bacteria. It occurs most often in children between the ages of two and ten. It is basically a **strep throat** (see page 258) with a rash produced by the bacteria.

Scarlet fever can have serious complications if it goes untreated. It can lead to abscesses on the tonsils or, rarely, **rheumatic fever** (see page 256), which may develop two to three weeks after the rash appears.

After treatment with antibiotics for ten days, or one shot of penicillin, the fever, sore throat, and headache usually disappear, although the rash may linger. Prompt treatment usually results in full recovery.

WHAT YOU CAN DO NOW

- Make sure your child gets plenty of rest and drinks lots of liquids. Provide soft foods that won't irritate a raw throat.
- Your doctor may recommend acetaminophen to reduce fever and relieve pain. (Never give aspirin to a child under 12 who has an illness such as chicken pox, flu, or any other illness you suspect of being caused by a virus, such as a bad respiratory infection; see box on **Reye's syndrome,** page 92.)

WHEN TO CALL THE DOCTOR

Call for an immediate appointment:
- If your child has a temperature of 102 degrees or higher.
- If your child has a sore throat with a rash, or if he or she has other symptoms of strep throat or scarlet fever.

Call for advice:
- If your child doesn't get better with treatment at home.

HOW TO PREVENT IT

- Get prompt diagnosis and treatment for strep throat or other strep infections.
- Keep your child away from anyone who has been diagnosed with a strep infection.
- Once scarlet fever is diagnosed, make sure other family members are tested for strep if they develop a sore throat, with or without a rash.

FOR MORE HELP

For a list of resources on children's health, see box on page 262.

Strep Throat

SIGNS AND SYMPTOMS

Infants:
- Low fever (100 to 101 degrees).
- Thick mucus from nose.

Children ages one to three:
- Mild sore throat.
- Swollen glands in throat.
- Low fever (100 to 101 degrees).
- Irritability.
- Loss of appetite.

Older children and adults:
- Sudden, severe sore throat.
- Swollen glands in throat.
- High fever (102 degrees or higher).
- White coating on tonsils.

The streptococcus bacteria that cause strep throat are spread by physical contact or through the air when an infected person coughs or sneezes. Strep throat is most common in 5- to 15-year-olds and can affect adults; it is rare in children under 3.

If strep throat goes untreated, it can lead to **rheumatic fever** (see page 256), kidney problems, and other complications. Unfortunately, strep symptoms are easily mistaken for signs of cold or flu; so if your child has a sore throat that lasts 48 hours or longer, you should call your doctor. A throat culture or strep test can determine whether it's strep.

Prompt treatment with antibiotics (usually penicillin or erythromycin) usually eases symptoms within a day or so.

WHAT YOU CAN DO NOW

- Your child should rest, drink liquids, and eat foods that won't irritate a raw throat.
- Give your child acetaminophen for pain relief. (Never give aspirin to a child under 12 who has chicken pox, flu, or any other illness you suspect of being caused by a virus, such as a bad respiratory infection; see box on **Reye's syndrome,** page 92.)
- For children age three and older, gargling with warm salt water can ease discomfort.
- If antibiotics are prescribed, take them all, even after symptoms have disappeared.

WHEN TO CALL THE DOCTOR

- If a child or an adult has the symptoms listed or a sore throat that lasts 48 hours or longer.

HOW TO PREVENT IT

- Wash your and your child's hands and face with soap and warm water frequently, especially after being in public places.
- Stay away from people who are coughing and sneezing.
- To prevent your sick child from infecting others, wait until he or she has been on antibiotics for 48 hours before a return to school or day care.

FOR MORE HELP

For a list of resources on children's health, see box on page 262.

Teething

SIGNS AND SYMPTOMS

- Increased fussiness, nighttime crying, and clingy behavior.
- Excessive drooling.
- Chewing on fingers, teething rings, and other objects.
- Swollen, red, and inflamed gums.
- Increased desire for nursing or bottle-feeding, or child may refuse breast or bottle because sucking action hurts sore gums.
- Poor appetite.

Few parents forget the emergence of their children's first teeth, and in most cases, the memories are as painful as they are sweet. As new teeth push their way through tender gums, children experience various degrees of discomfort and distress. Your normally sunny toddler, who appears otherwise healthy, may suddenly be crabby and restless all night long.

Teeth appear at different ages in different children. In general, the front teeth appear during the child's first year, and the first and second molars appear between the ages of one and three.

For most children, the front teeth cause less discomfort, though some children fuss with the appearance of each tooth. The first and second molars, which cause more obvious pain, often disrupt eating and sleeping routines. The discomfort is likely to last a few days with each new tooth.

WHAT YOU CAN DO NOW

➤ When your child seems uncomfortable, rub his or her gums with a clean finger. A chilled (but not frozen) washcloth or teething ring can ease soreness and provide something to chew on.

CARING FOR THOSE FIRST TEETH

Here are some simple steps you can take to protect your baby's new teeth and ensure healthful habits later on:

■ When the first teeth appear, make toothbrushing part of your child's daily routine. Use either a child's toothbrush with small, soft bristles or a gauze pad. Gently rub the teeth bottom to top, front and back.

■ Never put your baby to bed with a bottle. Juice and milk contain sugars that if left in the mouth for long periods can lead to tooth decay.

■ Try to limit the amount of sweets your child eats.

■ Begin regular visits to the dentist when all 20 baby teeth have appeared (around age three).

For more help:

■ American Academy of Pediatric Dentistry, 211 E. Chicago Ave., Suite 700, Chicago, IL 70611. Send a business-size, self-addressed, stamped envelope for "The Pediatric Dentist" pamphlet.

■ American Academy of Pediatrics, P.O. Box 927, Dept. C, Elk Grove Village, IL 60009-0927. Send a business-size, self-addressed, stamped envelope for the brochure "A Guide to Your Children's Dental Health."

➤ Wrap an ice cube in a soft cloth, and rub it gently on your child's gums to reduce inflammation. Keep moving the ice over the gums to avoid damaging tissue.

➤ Comfort and distract your child with holding, cuddling, and rocking.

➤ If discomfort persists, consult your doctor about using acetaminophen. (Never give aspirin to a child under 12 who has chicken pox, flu, or any other illness you suspect of being caused by a virus, such as a bad respiratory infection; see box on **Reye's syndrome,** page 92.)

➤ The drooling that accompanies teething can cause a rash on the face, neck, and upper chest. Using a protective infant cream can help. Change wet clothing often, or use bibs.

➤ Never rub brandy or any other alcoholic drink on your child's gums (no matter what you might have heard). Alcohol, even in small amounts, is bad for children.

WHEN TO CALL THE DOCTOR

➤ If your child runs a fever that lasts more than 48 hours or is higher than 100 degrees, has diarrhea, or is lethargic; these symptoms may indicate a condition more serious than teething.

➤ If your child has cold symptoms, a persistent fever, trouble eating or sleeping, or grabs at the side of his or her face; this could signal an ear infection.

➤ If your child has no teeth by 12 months of age. This could indicate a harmless, inherited tendency to late teething, but it might mean a condition that causes delayed bone development.

FOR MORE HELP

For a list of resources on children's health, see box on page 262.

Vomiting in Children

See **nausea and vomiting,** page 127.

Whooping Cough

First stage (lasts one to two weeks):
- Runny nose and sneezing.
- Dry cough.
- Low fever (100 to 101 degrees).

Second stage (lasts two to ten weeks):
- Severe, frequent coughing spasms, sometimes followed by a whooping sound when breathing in (as air is forced over the swollen voice box). Babies may have repeated coughing fits without making the whooping sound.
- Red or blue face during coughing episodes. If your child turns blue or stops breathing, call 911 and give CPR **immediately.** (See page 14 for **CPR** instructions.)
- Vomiting may follow coughing fits.

Third stage (which may last for several months):
- Cough that gradually becomes less frequent and severe.

Whooping cough, also called pertussis, is one of the most serious of the classic childhood diseases. This highly contagious bacterial infection affects the respiratory tract and is spread through the air by coughing or sneezing. If untreated, the illness can cause pneumonia and permanent lung damage.

Thanks to widespread immunization, whooping cough is now relatively rare in the United States. It is most common in children, but teenagers and adults can also get it (even if they've been immunized), though their symptoms are less severe.

Antibiotics can prevent more serious symptoms if given during the first stage of the illness. During the second stage, antibiotics can only make the infection less contagious. For infants, hospitalization may sometimes be necessary.

WHAT YOU CAN DO NOW

After diagnosis:
- Keep your child comfortable, and give plenty of liquids to drink. Frequent small meals may reduce likelihood of vomiting.
- To keep a baby from inhaling mucus while coughing, place the baby on his or her stomach with the head turned to the side. Children may be able to breathe more easily when coughing if they sit up and lean forward.
- Do not give your child a cough suppressant, as it may prevent the clearing of mucus from blocked airways.
- Give acetaminophen for pain relief. (Never give aspirin to a child under 12 who has chicken pox, flu, or any other illness you suspect of being caused by a virus, such as a bad respiratory infection; see box on **Reye's syndrome,** page 92.)

WHEN TO CALL THE DOCTOR

Call 911 and give CPR **immediately:**
- If your child turns blue or stops breathing during or after coughing. See page 14 for **CPR** instructions.

Call for an immediate appointment:
- If your child's cough becomes more severe and frequent, or if he or she has been exposed to someone with whooping cough, even if your child has been immunized.

HOW TO PREVENT IT

- Starting at the age of two months, a child should be immunized against whooping cough (see **children's immunization** chart, page 244). The vaccine is about 80 percent effective after three doses.
- Your doctor may recommend preventive antibiotics for family members or schoolmates of a child who has whooping cough, even for those who have been immunized.
- Avoid exposing your child to anyone who has whooping cough.

FOR MORE HELP

For a list of resources on children's health, see box on page 262.

Children's Health

Sensible Advice on Discipline

As a parent, you want more than anything else to keep your child healthy and safe—both physically and emotionally. One of the most important ways to do this is to provide loving discipline that helps your child grow and learn in an atmosphere of support and respect.

At home, you teach by example. No parent is perfect, of course; everyone flies off the handle or makes mistakes now and then. But if you treat your child with respect, honesty, and understanding—particularly when you have to discipline—your child will likely develop the self-esteem to give those qualities back to the world. Equally important, he or she will learn self-discipline.

Here are some guidelines:

➤ **Set clear, reasonable limits.** Mean what you say. If you make a rule for your child— say, going to bed at 8:30—you must be prepared to follow through and enforce it. It's natural for kids to test limits, but children won't feel secure unless the limits are firm and consistent. You can be flexible about house rules and let your child make an argument for a new policy—but not when emotions are high. Talk the next day instead.

➤ **Remember to praise.** Encourage behavior you like with hugs, smiles, and other signs of approval. (Don't reward behavior you dislike, though; giving a whining child candy might encourage more of the same.) If you have to criticize, try to add a positive comment for balance. For example, you might thank your children for putting your clothes back in the closet after playing dress-up, but remind them that they shouldn't pull out the clothes without your permission.

➤ **Keep the rules simple.** Save "don't" for important rules, and try not to use it for everyday annoyances: Unless your child is in danger, "Wait for me" is probably better than "Don't run."

➤ **Put love first.** Always make clear that you don't think your child is a bad person, and that you're talking about his or her *behavior*. Your children need to know that you love them even when you are upset with them. You can cut down on misbehavior by letting your child know that he or she is loved. Many parents care deeply about their children but are unable to show that love. One way is simply to listen to your child with complete attention, rather than mumbling "Mm-hmmm" while thinking about something else.

➤ **Explain yourself.** When your child is old enough to understand, explain why you have set certain rules—particularly if he or she challenges you on them. Young children, however, do not need a lengthy explanation.

➤ **Admit it when you are wrong.** Your children will respect you for it, and you'll set a good example for them. The best apology is one that is short and simple.

➤ **Never hit your child.** Today health professionals agree that hitting children harms them emotionally as well as physically, fosters rage and self-hate, and often does lasting damage to their self-esteem and sense of worth. An ineffective discipline, it usually leaves a child resentful rather than sorry.

Psychologists also point out that hitting children teaches them that might makes right; and that children whose parents hit them often grow up to be violent, abusive, or self-destructive adults themselves. If you are so angry that you feel you're about to hit your child, leave the room or call Parents Anonymous (see **children's health resources**, opposite page).

➤ **Know what's happening at school.** If your child goes to a school that uses physical punishment, talk to the superintendent, the principal, and the teachers, and write a letter saying you do not want your child paddled or otherwise physically punished. Insist on it.

➤ **Never shake an infant.** Parents or caregivers who feel near the end of their rope when trying to calm a crying baby should take a time-out. Put the baby in the crib and go into another room for a few minutes—or call someone for emotional support. Frustrated, desperate parents sometimes shake a baby who won't stop crying—not realizing that, because babies' necks are so weak and their brains so fragile, shaking them can cause serious injuries, including blindness, seizures, and brain damage, even death.

➤ **Don't say cruel things.** Verbal abuse can be as damaging as physical abuse. Avoid lashing out in a moment of anger, telling your children that they're lazy or stupid, or that you wish they had never been born: They might believe you.

Likewise, avoid sarcasm, name-calling, or other disrespectful asides; treat your children as you would like to be treated yourself. Rather than blaming, communicate your displeasure in a nonjudgmental way by saying how your child's behavior makes you feel. Instead of saying, "You never think of anybody but yourself," tell your child, "I don't want to clean up after you"; or say, "I can't stand all this squabbling," instead of, "You're impossible!"

➤ **Build trust.** Keep your promises and be honest with your child. Try to avoid mixed messages. If you are upset, say so; don't pretend you're not. Children can read your body language and will feel insecure if your words don't match it.

➤ **Keep a cool head with teenagers.** They, too, need consistent limits, but remember that rebellion is normal and healthy at their age. Try to listen rather than lecture, and don't take things personally or get too emotional during confrontations. (To get to the deeper issues troubling your teenager, try asking repeatedly, "What else is on your mind?" or "Anything else?" during conflicts.) No matter how distant or disdainful teenagers may seem, they still want and need your love and support.

General Problems

◆

Anemia

General symptoms:
- Weakness and fatigue.
- Pasty skin; paleness of gums, nail beds, and eyelid linings.
- Shortness of breath, dizziness, and fainting.
- Headaches and difficulty concentrating.

Iron deficiency anemia:
General symptoms, plus:
- Brittle nails.
- Black or bloody stools from intestinal bleeding.

Folic acid deficiency anemia:
General symptoms, plus:
- Sore mouth and tongue.
- Loss of appetite.
- Swollen abdomen.
- Nausea and diarrhea.

Vitamin B12 deficiency anemia:
General symptoms, plus:
- Sore mouth and tongue.
- Problems with walking and balance.
- Tingling in hands and feet.
- Memory loss and confusion.

If you are anemic, your blood has trouble carrying oxygen to your tissues and carrying away the carbon dioxide. Anemia occurs either because you don't have enough red blood cells or because your red blood cells lack a protein that allows them to carry oxygen. There are several kinds of anemia:

Women who have heavy menstrual flow, or who are pregnant or nursing, may get **iron deficiency anemia.** It can usually be remedied by taking iron supplements. If, however, your anemia stems from chronic **diarrhea** (see page 116), which robs your body of iron, or conditions that cause blood loss, such as **ulcers** (see page 130) or stomach or **colon cancer** (see page 112), the underlying problem needs to be treated.

Lack of folic acid, a vitamin necessary for making red blood cells, can cause **folic acid deficiency anemia.** Adolescents, pregnant women, smokers, alcoholics, and people who don't eat healthfully are at risk.

Vitamin B12 deficiency anemia (the most common type is called pernicious anemia) may permanently affect the brain, spinal cord, and mental capacities. In the United States, B12 anemia is rarely caused by a lack of B12 in the diet. Instead, it's usually caused by an inability to absorb the vitamin from food—a problem that can be inherited.

A form of anemia not caused by diet is **aplastic anemia** (see box on page 267).

WHAT YOU CAN DO NOW

If you think you have anemia, talk to your doctor. **Note:** Don't take over-the-counter iron supplements; ask your doctor first. Too much iron can cause symptoms similar to anemia and may worsen your condition.

(continued)

Fever

The average body temperature is 98.6 degrees, but some people have higher normal levels; temperatures also tend to rise as the day goes on. In adults, a fever is a temperature of 100 or above. A temperature of 100.4 in infants under three months, 102 in children, and 104 in adults is reason to call your doctor for advice. Most of us try to detect a fever by feeling the forehead, but that is misleading. Use a thermometer—after shaking it down and rinsing it with cool water—and leave it under the tongue for three minutes.

SYMPTOMS	WHAT IT MIGHT BE	WHAT YOU CAN DO
Fever after several hours in a hot place, no sweating, rapid heartbeat, confusion, loss of consciousness.	Heat stroke (see page 38).	Call 911 or go to emergency facility **immediately.**
Fever with severe headache, pain when bending over, nausea, vomiting, sensitivity to light, drowsiness, confusion, red or purple rash.	Meningitis (see page 56).	Call 911 or go to emergency facility **immediately.**
Fever and stiff jaw, muscle spasms and pain, sweating, difficulty swallowing.	Tetanus (sometimes called lockjaw)—bacterial infection from a wound.	Call 911 or go to emergency facility **immediately.**
Sudden, high fever; vomiting and diarrhea; red rash; fatigue; headache, confusion, and dizziness.	Toxic shock syndrome (see page 236).	Call 911 or go to emergency facility **immediately.**
In children: fever, sudden convulsions; possibly turning blue in face.	Fever seizure (see fever in children, page 248).	If seizure is severe or lasts more than a few minutes, call 911 or go to emergency facility **immediately.** Otherwise, lay child on side or stomach, away from sharp objects. Usually harmless.
Rapid onset of fever, chills, pounding heart, confusion, signs of infection.	Blood poisoning (see box on page 29).	Call doctor for emergency advice; if not available, call 911 or go to emergency facility.
Low fever, pain in lower-right area of abdomen, nausea and vomiting.	Appendicitis (see page 20).	Call doctor for immediate appointment. Don't eat or take laxatives before diagnosis; surgery may be required.

(continued)

Fever (continued)

SYMPTOMS	WHAT IT MIGHT BE	WHAT YOU CAN DO
Low fever at first, higher 1–3 weeks later; pain in lower pelvis; foul-smelling vaginal discharge; painful urination.	Pelvic inflammatory disease (see page 230).	Call doctor for immediate appointment.
Fever and cough with or without sputum; chest pain, shortness of breath, abdominal pain.	Pneumonia (see page 94).	Call doctor for immediate appointment.
Sudden onset of fever and sore throat with white coating on tonsils; bright red rash about 24 hours later.	Scarlet fever (see page 258).	Call doctor for immediate appointment.
Night sweats, swollen lymph nodes, recurring infections, weight loss, fatigue, diarrhea, sores.	AIDS (see page 214).	Call doctor for advice and appointment for testing.
Low fever, nausea or loss of appetite, yellowish skin or eyes (jaundice), dark urine, light-colored stools, fatigue.	Hepatitis (see page 270).	Call doctor for advice and appointment.
Fever lasting weeks or months, bad sore throat, fatigue, swollen lymph glands.	Mononucleosis—viral illness spread by close contact such as kissing; attacks respiratory system, liver, spleen, and lymph glands; usually in teenagers and young adults.	Call doctor for advice and appointment. Recovery takes 10 days to 6 months. Resume normal level of activity gradually.
Low fever, heavy night sweats, weight loss, chest pain, coughing—sometimes with bloody sputum.	Tuberculosis (see page 100).	Call doctor for advice and appointment.
Fever over 103, chills, headache, fatigue, runny nose, dry cough, sore throat, muscle aches.	Flu (see page 91).	Call doctor for advice. In children, fever of 102 or higher may be dangerous.
In children: fever with earache, rash or swelling, blisters, noisy breathing, dry cough, runny nose, red eyes.	Any of several childhood diseases (see children's health chapter, page 240).	See fever in children, page 248.

APLASTIC ANEMIA

Aplastic anemia is a rare, potentially fatal disease that isn't related to your diet. In this illness, the bone marrow stops producing red blood cells. The symptoms include weakness; fatigue; ulcers in the throat, mouth, and rectum; and unusual bleeding or bruising. If you have any combination of these symptoms, call your doctor to make an immediate appointment.

Aplastic anemia can be caused by medications used in the treatment of some cancers or other diseases, or by exposure to toxins such as arsenic, benzene, and radiation. Once the damage is done, this form of anemia can sometimes be cured with a bone marrow transplant.

For more help: Aplastic Anemia Foundation of America, 800-747-2820, M–F 9–5 EST. Counselors offer information, brochures, and a resource directory; they will also connect callers to "phone buddies" who also have aplastic anemia.

WHEN TO CALL THE DOCTOR

Call 911 or go to an emergency facility **immediately:**
➤ If you have been taking iron supplements and you have these symptoms: vomiting, bloody diarrhea, fever, lethargy, and/or seizures. You may have iron overload, which can be fatal.

Call for advice and an appointment:
➤ If you have symptoms of anemia.
➤ If you are being treated for a nutritional anemia and don't get better in two weeks.

HOW TO PREVENT IT

To get enough iron:
➤ Eat plenty of iron-rich foods, including potatoes, broccoli, raisins, dried beans, oatmeal, and blackstrap molasses.
➤ Include lean red meat, liver, and shellfish in your diet.

➤ Don't drink coffee or tea with meals. They contain a substance that makes it hard for your body to absorb iron.

To get enough folic acid:
➤ Eat plenty of citrus fruits (oranges, grapefruit), dried beans, and green vegetables.
➤ Include liver, eggs, and milk in your diet.
➤ If you drink alcoholic beverages, drink moderately (no more than two 1.5-ounce drinks of hard liquor, two 12-ounce cans of beer, or two 5-ounce glasses of wine a day for men, one for women). Alcohol can interfere with the absorption of folic acid.
➤ If you're pregnant or nursing, or if you have very heavy periods, discuss your diet with your doctor.

To get enough vitamin B12:
➤ Include meat, chicken, fish, and/or dairy products in your diet; B12 is also added to some cereals.

FOR MORE HELP

Information line: National Heart, Lung, and Blood Institute Information Center, 301-251-1222, M–F 8:30–5 EST. Staffers answer questions and send literature.

Chronic Fatigue Syndrome

SIGNS AND SYMPTOMS

■ Fatigue that is not a result of exertion and that interferes with your daily activities, is not relieved by rest, and continues for six months or longer.
■ More than 24 hours of weakness and fatigue following moderate exercise (sometimes fatigue occurs one or two days later).
■ Sore throat.
■ Low fever (temperature up to 101 degrees) or chills.
■ Painful lymph nodes.

(continued)

- Headaches that feel different from those you had in the past.
- Pains that spread to various joints without causing redness or swelling.
- Temporary blind spots and sensitivity to light.
- Difficulty thinking or concentrating, forgetfulness, irritability, and confusion.
- Difficulty sleeping.

Little is known about chronic fatigue syndrome (CFS); its causes are unclear, and it is diagnosed by ruling out other diseases. CFS strikes people of all ages, races, and sexes, although 75 percent of those who have been diagnosed are women. There's no evidence that it's contagious.

The pain, fatigue, and difficulty thinking that mark the condition often keep people out of work or school. This can lead to depression. The symptoms sometimes ease up or go away on their own after a number of months or years, but often they come and go indefinitely. Treatment emphasizes plenty of rest, a healthful diet, and gentle exercise. Medications such as antidepressants and over-the-counter pain relievers can help lessen specific symptoms.

HOW TO PREVENT IT

There is no known way to prevent chronic fatigue syndrome.

WHAT YOU CAN DO NOW

➤ Take over-the-counter painkillers, such as ibuprofen, for muscle aches and headaches.
➤ Stay physically active, but not to the point of becoming overtired.
➤ Join a support group for those with chronic pain or depression.

WHEN TO CALL THE DOCTOR

➤ If you have persistent fatigue and other symptoms of CFS.

FIBROMYALGIA

Fibromyalgia, which can accompany chronic fatigue syndrome and is sometimes confused with it, typically causes pain and fatigue in muscles, tendons, and ligaments, though not in joints. Unlike chronic fatigue syndrome, however, fibromyalgia can be identified by a medical test.

Fibromyalgia tends to affect women between the ages of 20 and 50. It may be present constantly or run in three- or four-day cycles. Typically, it is accompanied by sleep problems. The symptoms are treated with antidepressants, painkillers, and muscle relaxants. Regular exercise may also relieve discomfort.

For more help: Fibromyalgia Network, 800-853-2929, M–F 8–5 PST. Call for an information packet, a list of doctors, information about support groups in your area, and a newsletter.

➤ If you feel new symptoms after you have been diagnosed.

FOR MORE HELP

Information line: Centers for Disease Control and Prevention, 404-332-4555, 24-hour line. Provides information on current research and recommended treatments for chronic fatigue syndrome, by phone recording or fax.

Information line: Chronic Fatigue and Immune Dysfunction Syndrome Association of America, 800-442-3437, 24-hour line. Provides information, a newsletter, conferences for patients, and a listing of local support groups; also raises money for medical research.

Information line: American Chronic Pain Association, 916-632-0922, 24-hour line. Ask for literature and information about support groups run by and for those with chronic pain.

Diabetes

SIGNS AND SYMPTOMS

- Increased and excessive thirst.
- Frequent urination—sometimes almost hourly.
- Unexplained weight loss.
- Blurred vision.
- Persistent fatigue.
- In women: frequent yeast and bladder infections, sometimes missed menstrual periods.

Diabetes mellitus affects about 16 million Americans, yet perhaps only half of them know they have it. Often those with the most common type of diabetes, which tends to show up in older adults, confuse their symptoms with aging or being overweight. As a result, they don't get the treatment they need. Untreated diabetes can cause serious problems, including an increased risk of stroke and heart attack, blindness, kidney trouble, nerve damage, and amputation of limbs due to circulatory problems.

There are two types of diabetes. The varity called Type I diabetes usually starts in childhood. It occurs when the pancreas stops making insulin, which converts glucose (sugar) into energy for use by the muscles. People who have Type I diabetes generally require daily insulin injections.

About 90 percent of diabetics have Type II diabetes, which results when the muscles become resistant to insulin, even though the body may be producing enough. These people usually don't require insulin injections.

The risk of getting Type II diabetes rises with age (it's also called adult-onset diabetes). If you have a relative with Type II diabetes, you're at greater risk. Obesity, lack of exercise, and a high-fat diet also increase the risk. While neither type of diabetes can be cured, both can be managed well with a combination of drugs, exercise, a healthful diet, and monitoring of blood sugar levels.

WHAT YOU CAN DO NOW

➤ If you know you have diabetes, follow your doctor's advice about diet, exercise, and monitoring your blood sugar levels.

WHEN TO CALL THE DOCTOR

Call 911 or go to an emergency facility **immediately:**

➤ If you feel weak and nauseous, excessively thirsty, are urinating very frequently, and have abdominal pain, rapid breathing, and noticeably sweet-smelling breath. You may have ketoacidosis—a life-threatening condition (in Type I only).
➤ If you experience extreme thirst, lethargy, weakness, and mental confusion; you may have dangerously high blood sugar levels that could lead to coma.
➤ If a person known to have diabetes loses consciousness.

Call for an immediate appointment:

➤ If you or your child develop symptoms of diabetes.
➤ If you have diabetes and you get the flu; flu and some other illnesses can make your blood sugar levels go out of control.

DANGER IN THE MEDICINE CABINET

Some medicines can affect blood sugar levels, which diabetics need to monitor closely. For example:

➤ Aspirin can lower blood sugar if taken in large amounts.
➤ Phenylephrine, epinephrine, and ephedrine—which are contained in some asthma medicines, cold remedies, and even herbal teas—can raise blood sugar and blood pressure levels.
➤ Fish oil, which some people take to lower their cholesterol levels, may raise blood sugar levels.
➤ Caffeine, found in coffee, sodas, appetite suppressants, some headache remedies, "pep" pills, and diuretics, may also raise blood sugar levels.

There is no way to prevent Type I diabetes. To prevent Type II diabetes:
➤ Keep your weight within the healthy range for your age, height, and build.
➤ Exercise regularly. This is very important in preventing diabetes or managing it once it occurs.
➤ If you are over 40, and overweight, or have a family history of diabetes, get screened for diabetes every one to three years.

FOR MORE HELP

Organization: American Diabetes Association, 800-342-2383, M–F 8:30–5 EST. Offers information on diabetes management, educational materials, and referrals to local affiliates.

Organization: Juvenile Diabetes Foundation, 800-533-2873, M–F 9–5 EST. Offers referrals to local chapters that have free educational materials, a list of support groups, and names of local physicians.

Video: *Diabetes at Time of Diagnosis.* Clear, useful overview of causes and treatments, consisting of four reports—Understanding the Diagnosis, What Happens Next?, Treatment and Management, and Issues and Answers. Time Life Medical, 1996, $19.95.

Hepatitis

SIGNS AND SYMPTOMS

First symptoms are flulike:
■ Fever.
■ Fatigue.
■ Nausea and vomiting.
■ Loss of appetite.
■ Abdominal pain.
Other, less common symptoms:
■ Dark urine.
■ Pale, clay-colored stools.
■ Jaundice—yellow eyes and skin.
Note: Some forms of hepatitis produce no symptoms.

Hepatitis, an inflammation of the liver, is neither a rare disease nor a single disease. There are five kinds of viral hepatitis: Hepatitis A (one in three Americans has been infected with this), plus varieties that are labeled B, C, D, and E. There are forms of nonviral hepatitis as well, brought on by long-term alcohol or drug use, immune system disorders, or exposure to chemicals.

Viral hepatitis is contagious; it's spread through direct human contact or through contaminated water or food. Hepatitis B and C, common in young adults, are spread through unprotected sex and dirty needles.

A liver inflamed with hepatitis has trouble regulating bile for digestion and screening poisons from the bloodstream. The yellow eyes and skin characteristic of jaundice, which is sometimes a symptom of hepatitis, result from bile buildup in the blood.

Nearly everyone with hepatitis A recovers in a month or two with rest and plenty of liquids. Most of those with B and C recover as well. However, many with C and some with B develop cirrhosis (liver damage), and some with B, C, or D develop chronic hepatitis; they have no symptoms, but they may still spread the infection.

WHAT YOU CAN DO NOW

➤ If you have symptoms of hepatitis, don't drink alcohol. It increases the risk of liver damage.
➤ Stay home and get lots of rest. You don't have to stay in bed, but you should lie down if you feel tired.
➤ Drink at least eight glasses of water a day.

WHEN TO CALL THE DOCTOR

➤ If you have two or more of the first symptoms listed or any of the less common symptoms, especially if you have been exposed to someone with hepatitis.
➤ If you are recovering from hepatitis and you start to have symptoms again.

HOW TO PREVENT IT

➤ Get vaccinated for hepatitis A if you are going to a foreign country where it's widespread or if you have been exposed to someone with it. (The vaccine becomes effective two to four weeks after you get it.)

➤ The hepatitis B vaccine is recommended for health professionals, people with multiple sexual partners, and those living with anyone who has emigrated from areas of Asia where hepatitis B is common.

➤ When traveling abroad, drink boiled water, don't eat unpeeled or uncooked fruits and vegetables, carry your own utensils, and wash your hands often with soap.

➤ Practice **safe sex** (see box on page 217).

➤ If you drink alcohol, drink in moderation (no more than two 1.5-ounce drinks of hard liquor, two 12-ounce cans of beer, or two 5-ounce glasses of wine a day for men, one for women).

➤ Don't use intravenous drugs.

➤ Make sure sterilized needles are used for acupuncture, piercing, or tattooing.

➤ People infected with A or E should not prepare or touch other people's food; their bedding should be washed regularly.

FOR MORE HELP

Hotline: National STD Hotline, Centers for Disease Control and Prevention, 800-227-8922, M–F 8AM–11PM EST. Ask for information on hepatitis and referrals to clinics for testing.

Information line: American Liver Foundation, 800-223-0179, M–Th 9–7, F 9–5 EST. Offers advice and brochures on hepatitis.

THE FIVE KINDS OF HEPATITIS

Type of hepatitis	How transmitted	People at risk	Incidence in United States	Risks	Vaccine available
A	Food, water, feces, family contact.	Children in day care, travelers.	32% of acute hepatitis cases.	None.	Yes.
B	Intravenous drug use, sex, blood, family contact.	Intravenous drug users, people with multiple sexual partners.	43% of acute hepatitis cases.	May become chronic; increases risk of liver cancer.	Yes.
C	Intravenous drug use, blood.	Intravenous drug users.	21% of acute hepatitis cases.	High risk of chronic liver disease.	No.
D	Found only in people with B.	Same as B.	Not common.	May become chronic.	B vaccine prevents D as well.
E	Food, feces, water— common in India and Africa.	Travelers.	Very rare.	Unusually high death rate for women who are pregnant.	No.

Sudden Weight Gain or Loss

Your weight changes slightly from day to day even when you eat normally. Dieting or overeating can, of course, cause more significant weight changes. But not all changes result from gains or losses of fat; you might lose several pounds of fluid in a single day from sweating if you're doing strenuous work. Hormonal changes in women during the menstrual cycle, or eating a lot of salty food, can result in fluid retention (often signaled by puffy hands and ankles) and gains of several pounds in a short time. But unexplained weight gain or loss can be a sign of an underlying disease—such as those listed here. If you gain or lose more than 10 to 15 pounds in a month for no apparent reason, call your doctor for advice and an appointment.

WEIGHT GAIN

SYMPTOMS	WHAT IT MIGHT BE	WHAT YOU CAN DO
Rapid weight gain with swelling in legs, ankles, and midsection; fatigue; yellowish skin; easy bruising and bleeding; impotence; dark urine; black or bloody stools; blood in vomit.	Cirrhosis—liver damage. May be caused by alcohol abuse, hepatitis, or some hereditary diseases.	If you vomit blood, call 911 or go to emergency facility **immediately.** Otherwise, call doctor for immediate appointment.
Rapid weight gain with swelling in legs, ankles, and midsection; shortness of breath; fatigue; heart palpitations; frequent urination; loss of appetite.	Congestive heart failure (see page 102). ● Kidney disease.	If you have severe chest pain or shortness of breath, call 911 or go to emergency facility **immediately.** Otherwise, call doctor for immediate appointment.
Gradual weight gain, with swollen face, fat collecting on torso and upper back; fatigue; acne; reddish skin; insomnia. In men: impotence, breast growth. In women: facial hair, interrupted menstruation.	Cushing's syndrome— adrenal glands produce too much of hormone that affects connective tissue. Usually caused by taking corticosteroids for rheumatoid arthritis, asthma, or other illnesses.	Call doctor for advice and appointment.
Gradual weight gain, fatigue, dry skin, goiter (swelling in neck).	Underactive thyroid gland (see thyroid problems, page 279).	Call doctor for advice and appointment.

Sudden Weight Gain or Loss

WEIGHT LOSS		
SYMPTOMS	WHAT IT MIGHT BE	WHAT YOU CAN DO
Weight loss, fatigue, vomiting, diarrhea, brownish skin, hair loss, feeling cold, dramatic mood changes (confusion, aggression, or depression).	Addison's disease—adrenal glands produce too little of hormones that regulate metabolism and responses to stress. Very rare.	Call doctor for immediate appointment.
Rapid weight loss despite increased appetite, anxiety, sweating, rapid heartbeat, goiter (swelling in neck).	Overactive thyroid gland (see thyroid problems, page 279).	Call doctor for immediate appointment.
Gradual weight loss, fatigue, recurring infections, night sweats, coughing and breathing problems, rashes and purplish patches on skin (sometimes).	HIV infection. ● AIDS (see page 214).	Call doctor for advice and appointment for testing.
Weight loss with changes or lumps in skin, abnormal bleeding, digestive problems, changes in bowel or bladder habits.	Cancer—abnormal, uncontrolled growth of cells. Symptoms vary with type of cancer.	Call doctor for advice and appointment.
Rapid weight loss, fatigue, extreme thirst, frequent urination, infections in vagina.	Diabetes (see page 269).	Call doctor for advice and appointment.
Weight loss and diarrhea; fatigue; gas and stomach pains; large, unusually foul-smelling stools.	Malabsorption—intestines fail to absorb one or more nutrients from food.	Call doctor for advice and appointment if symptoms last longer than a few days.
Extreme weight loss from not eating, compulsive exercising, interrupted menstruation, increase in facial hair, depression (in anorexia). Extreme weight loss from binge eating followed by vomiting (in bulimia).	Eating disorder.	See anorexia and bulimia, page 200.

General Problems

Infections

General:
- Fever higher than 100 degrees (oral thermometer reading) and/or chills and sweating.
- Headache.
- Muscle aches or soreness.
- Fatigue.
- Swollen lymph nodes (sometimes).

Intestinal infection:
- Diarrhea.
- Nausea and vomiting.
- Abdominal cramps or gas pains.
- Dehydration.

Respiratory infection:
- Coughing and sneezing.
- Sinus or chest pain, sore throat, congestion, and excess mucus.
- Watery eyes.

Bladder infection:
- Painful, burning, and frequent urination.
- Bloody urine.

Infection of the mouth, ears, or eyes:
- Localized pain or irritation.
- Swelling, tenderness, and/or unusual redness.

Joint infection:
- Tenderness, redness, or pain and inflammation in the joints, often in only one part of the body.

Our bodies are at constant war against disease-causing organisms, which enter through the air, food and water, broken skin, or sexual contact. Whether a germ is a bacterium, virus, or fungus, it tries to survive and reproduce once it's inside your body. Viruses invade living cells and multiply. They may temporarily weaken the body's defenses against more serious bacterial infections.

You feel sick in part because of your body's immune response. When your body senses an attack, your immune system releases antibodies and white blood cells to fight off the invaders. The white blood cells produce chemical triggers that cause the fevers that often accompany infection. Some germs release toxins and steal nutrients from healthy cells; this assault also makes you feel sick.

In most cases, all your immune system needs to fight infection is for you to rest and maintain a healthy diet. For more stubborn infections, germ-destroying medications will help. After some infections, such as chicken pox or measles, your immune system is able to "remember" contact with a particular virus or bacterium, so it can suppress repeat bombardments. This is what gives you immunity. Vaccines can also offer immunity to specific infections.

For infections in children, see **children's health** chapter, page 240. For infected wounds or cuts, see **cuts, scrapes, and wounds,** page 27.

WHAT YOU CAN DO NOW

➤ If you are younger than 65 and otherwise in good health, let a low fever run its course. A low fever—under 104 degrees (oral thermometer reading) in adults, 102 in children, and 100.4 in infants under three months—is usually not dangerous and may actually speed recovery from the infection.

➤ Give your body a chance to recover. Rest, drink lots of water, and eat healthfully. Avoid alcohol and smoking.

WHEN TO CALL THE DOCTOR

➤ If your temperature rises to 104 or higher, or goes over 101 with joint pain; if a child's rises to 102 or higher; or an infant's to 100.4 or higher.

➤ If you develop symptoms of severe infection, such as problems speaking, seeing, swallowing, or breathing, or if you have difficulty moving.

➤ If your skin has been broken by a human or animal bite.

➤ If you have symptoms such as diarrhea, vomiting, or a sore throat, that persist or worsen after one or two days.

HOW TO PREVENT IT

➤ Keep your immune system in good working order:
  ● Eat healthfully; drink plenty of fluids.
  ● Exercise regularly.
  ● Get enough sleep.
  ● Don't smoke or use drugs.
  ● If you drink alcohol, do so moderately (no more than two 1.5-ounce drinks of hard liquor, two 12-ounce cans of beer, or two 5-ounce glasses of wine a day for men, one for women).
  ● Take steps to reduce stress in your life; stress weakens the immune system. Try meditation, yoga, or deep breathing.
➤ Get a flu shot before each flu season.
➤ Ask your doctor about immunization against pneumonia .
➤ Have your children vaccinated against childhood diseases (see **children's immunization** chart, page 244).
➤ Wash your hands frequently, and avoid putting your fingers in your mouth or rubbing your eyes.
➤ Be sure that meat is cooked fully and that food is prepared in a clean place. Do not share silverware.
➤ Practice **safe sex** (see box on page 217).
➤ Menstruating women should change tampons at least every six hours to avoid incubating harmful bacteria. (See **toxic shock syndrome,** page 236.)
➤ Keep an eye out for changes in your body—from inflammation around nicks and cuts to a runny nose or genital discharge. Attend to symptoms promptly.

Lupus

SIGNS AND SYMPTOMS

■ Butterfly-shaped rash across the nose and cheeks.
■ Aching, swollen joints.
■ Fever over 100 degrees.
■ Persistent fatigue.
■ Sores in the nose, mouth, or throat.
■ Unusual bleeding or bruising.
■ Numbness in the fingers and toes.
■ Swollen abdomen and swollen ankles (sometimes).
■ Dark urine.
■ Chest pain when breathing deeply.
■ Sensitivity to sunlight that results in a rash after time spent in the sun.
■ Mental or personality changes, including depression.

Lupus is a chronic disease in which the immune system mistakes proteins in the body's tissues for foreign invaders. This internal war—which may go into long remissions between flare-ups—causes swelling and pain, especially in the joints. It may also inflame the kidneys, skin, and lining of the lungs, heart, and brain, and it may damage white blood cells. In severe, untreated cases, lupus can lead to kidney failure. The disease is often accompanied by depression.

Why the body attacks itself in this way is unknown. It is known that lupus can be triggered by infections, ultraviolet or fluorescent light, and certain drugs, such as some used to treat arrhythmias or hypertension.

Lupus usually strikes those between the ages of 35 and 45, and women almost ten times more often than men. It's most common among African-Americans, Asians, and Native Americans. It also runs in families.

The long-term outlook for people with lupus has improved in recent years. Now 80 to 90 percent can expect to live normally with early treatment, including medications to ease symptoms, as well as changes in diet, exercise, and mental outlook.

General Problems

➤ Get lots of rest if you're feeling tired. Take naps when you're having a flare-up.
➤ When the disease is in remission and you feel well, start a regular exercise program. Swimming is one good way for people with lupus to keep their muscles in shape.
➤ Put warm compresses on achy joints.
➤ For discomfort, take aspirin or ibuprofen (with meals to avoid stomach upset).
➤ Avoid the sun during the middle of the day. Thirty minutes before leaving home each day, apply a sunscreen with an SPF of at least 15. Sun exposure alone can cause a flare-up in some people.
➤ Eat healthfully—stick to a diet that's low in fat and salt, high in complex carbohydrates and calcium.
➤ Protect your hands from cold or irritation by wearing gloves.
➤ Avoid alcohol, tobacco, and caffeine.

WHEN TO CALL THE DOCTOR

Call for emergency advice (if not available, call 911 or go to an emergency facility):
➤ If you are experiencing the symptoms of kidney disease: frequent urination; swollen ankles; shortness of breath; nausea and vomiting; pain in your chest and bones; itching, bruising, or bleeding; mental confusion; loss of consciousness.
Call for advice and an appointment:
➤ If you have symptoms of lupus.
➤ If you have been diagnosed with lupus and your symptoms get worse or change.

FOR MORE HELP

Information line: National Institute of Arthritis and Musculoskeletal and Skin Diseases Information Clearinghouse, 301-495-4484, M–F 8:30–5 EST. Request a packet of recent articles on lupus.
Information line: Lupus Foundation of America, 800-558-0121, 24-hour line. Offers a packet with brochures on lupus and a listing of Lupus Foundation chapters that have support groups in your area.

Lyme Disease

SIGNS AND SYMPTOMS

■ A bull's-eye rash, often with a pale center, that develops where a tick bite occurred two days to a month before. The rash may last two to four weeks or longer. (Some people, however, don't remember having a rash.)
■ Within a month, headache, fatigue, fever, chills, sore throat, and aching muscles and joints.
■ After several weeks or months, paralysis of the face, stiff neck, sensitivity to light, irregular heartbeat, and fainting.
■ Joint pain and swelling.

Lyme disease is a bacterial infection transmitted by tick bites. It afflicts more than 10,000 people each year.

The ticks pick up the bacteria from mice, deer, and other animals. The tick, often as small as a poppy seed, must remain attached to a person for 36 to 48 hours to transmit the bacteria, which can invade the skin, nervous system, heart, and joints.

Lyme disease can be difficult to diagnose. It has vague symptoms that seem like those of other illnesses, and the blood test is not always reliable. If untreated, the infection can lead to long-lasting illness, including neurological problems, a type of arthritis, and heart troubles such as irregular heartbeats.

The good news is that the illness is preventable, responds well to treatment in the early stages, and sometimes goes away by itself. Lyme disease is treated with antibiotics, and if arthritis develops, with corticosteroids for joint pain and inflammation.

WHAT YOU CAN DO NOW

If you find a tick on your skin:
➤ Remove it immediately with tweezers: Grasp it as close to the skin as possible; pull gently and steadily to remove the en-

tire tick. Avoid squeezing or twisting the tick's body, since this may spread bacteria into your skin or blood (see **tick bites, page 46**).

➤ Drop the tick in rubbing alcohol to preserve it for analysis.

➤ After removal, disinfect the bite with alcohol; wash your hands in soap and water.

➤ Don't use any of these ineffective techniques to dislodge a tick: kerosene, petroleum jelly, or a lighted cigarette or match.

WHEN TO CALL THE DOCTOR

➤ If you've been in tick country or you've been bitten by a tick, and you have symptoms of Lyme disease.

➤ If your symptoms return after treatment.

HOW TO PREVENT IT

➤ Wear light-colored clothing when you're in grassy or wooded areas to make ticks easier to spot. Wear shoes (not sandals), long pants, and long-sleeved shirts. Tuck your pants into your socks.

➤ Spray an insect repellent containing DEET on clothing. Use sparingly on skin.

➤ Check your skin, hair, and clothing for ticks after an outing.

➤ Fit your pet with a tick-repellent collar.

➤ Clear away brush near your home that might attract ticks. Stack your firewood away from the house (woodpiles attract mice and the ticks they carry).

FOR MORE HELP

Information line: American Lyme Disease Foundation, 800-876-5963, 24-hour recording. 914-277-6970, M–F 9–5 EST. Provides a nationwide physician referral list and free brochures on Lyme disease and controlling ticks.

Organization: Arthritis Foundation, P.O. Box 7669, Atlanta, GA 30357. 404-872-7100, M–F 9–5 EST. Offers a free brochure on Lyme disease, and provides services through local arthritis support groups.

Sleep Disorders

SIGNS AND SYMPTOMS

Insomnia:
■ Trouble falling asleep.
■ Early waking.
■ Daytime sleepiness.
■ Poor concentration.

Obstructive sleep apnea:
■ Loud bursts of snoring and snorting while sleeping on back.
■ Morning headaches.
■ Daytime sleepiness with difficulty concentrating.
■ Personality changes, such as unusual irritability.

Narcolepsy:
■ Falling asleep suddenly and uncontrollably in the daytime for periods of five minutes to over an hour.
■ Sudden loss of muscle control triggered by strong emotion or fatigue.
■ Vivid hallucinations when falling asleep or waking up.
■ Fatigue.

Sleep disorders, which range from mild insomnia caused by jet lag to severe, health-threatening cases of sleep apnea, affect as many as 70 million Americans. Short-term **insomnia** is usually caused by stress or emotional upset. Long-term sleeplessness may be a sign of a medical problem, such as **thyroid problems,** (see page 279), **chronic bronchitis or emphysema** (see page 88), **Parkinson's disease** (see page 57), **Alzheimer's disease** (see page 50), **alcohol abuse** (see page 196), or **drug abuse** (see page 206). Treating the underlying condition and creating restful bedtime routines often help.

Obstructive sleep apnea is most common among overweight men. It occurs when the muscles in the throat allow the airway to sag, briefly closing off the flow of air and jerking the sleeper out of restful sleep. This usually happens when the sleeper is on his back. The process continues all night long; those with this condition don't get enough deep sleep and feel exhausted during the day. Obstructive sleep apnea can eventually cause serious health problems, including heart disease. People who are sleep-deprived may become depressed or have other personality changes. One remedy for the condition is a special breathing device, prescribed by a doctor, that keeps the airway open during sleep.

People with **narcolepsy** may fall deeply asleep just about anywhere, anytime, throughout the day. This condition is not well understood, but it seems to run in families. It can be treated with prescription stimulants and antidepressants.

WHAT YOU CAN DO NOW

Insomnia:
➤ Establish a calming bedtime routine: Drink warm milk, listen to soothing music, or read a book.
➤ Use your bed only for sleep or sex, not for working or watching TV.

Obstructive sleep apnea:
➤ Sew a tennis ball into the back of your pajamas to keep from sleeping on your back.

Narcolepsy:
➤ Schedule one or more daytime naps at regular times.

WHEN TO CALL THE DOCTOR

➤ If you have symptoms of obstructive sleep apnea or narcolepsy, particularly if you are sleepy all the time.
➤ If you have had insomnia for more than two weeks.

HOW TO PREVENT IT

➤ Avoid caffeinated drinks for at least six hours before bedtime.
➤ Don't drink alcohol or smoke for at least two hours before bedtime.
➤ Exercise regularly, but not within three hours of bedtime.
➤ If you are overweight, take steps to lose the extra pounds.

➤ Rise each morning at the same time, no matter when you went to bed.
➤ If you can't get to sleep, get up, drink a glass of milk, and read and relax for a while until you feel sleepy.

FOR MORE HELP

Organization: National Sleep Foundation, 1367 Connecticut Ave. NW, Dept. SCM, Washington, DC 20036. Write for free brochures on sleep and sleep disorders.

Organization: Narcolepsy Network, P.O. Box 1365, FDR Station, New York, NY 10150. 513-891-3522, M–F 9–5 EST. Request a brochure and a newsletter.

Video: *Insomnia at Time of Diagnosis*. Clear, useful overview of causes and treatments, consisting of four reports—Understanding the Diagnosis, What Happens Next?, Treatment and Management, and Issues and Answers. Time Life Medical, 1996, $19.95.

CATCHING UP TO JET LAG

Jet lag happens when you change time zones rapidly. Your sleeping patterns are out of sync with the local time, leaving you drowsy and disoriented.

If you will be staying more than two days at your destination, you can avoid many of the symptoms. (It's difficult to adjust on trips of two days or less.) Here's what to do:

■ If you arrive in the daytime, spend some time outdoors after your arrival. The sunlight helps reset your biological clock.
■ Avoid alcohol, caffeine, rich and sweet foods, and lively conversation before bed. The stimulation can keep you awake.
■ Bring earplugs and a blindfold to block out unfamiliar noises and lights when sleeping.
■ Wake up at the appropriate local time, even if you don't have to.

Thyroid Problems

General Problems

SIGNS AND SYMPTOMS

Hyperthyroidism:
- Weight loss despite an increase in appetite.
- Trembling hands.
- More rapid heart rate, rise in blood pressure, nervousness, and excessive perspiration.
- Bulging, watery eyes.
- More frequent bowel movements.
- Lighter and less frequent menstrual periods.
- Sometimes a goiter—swelling in the front of the neck.

Hypothyroidism:
- Lethargy, slower mental processes.
- Unexplained weight gain.
- Increased sensitivity to cold, with tingling or numbness in hands.
- Dry, thick, flaky skin and hair loss.
- Constipation.
- Heavier, longer menstrual periods.
- Sometimes a goiter—swelling in the front of the neck.

Thyroiditis:
- Mild to severe pain in the front of the neck.
- Pain when you swallow or when you turn your head.
- Fever.

Your thyroid gland makes hormones that regulate how fast your body absorbs food and turns it into energy.

People with **hyperthyroidism** have an overactive thyroid, which produces an oversupply of the hormones. As a result, their physical processes speed up dramatically. Graves' disease, the most common form, is sometimes brought on by severe stress. Hyperthyroidism is five times more likely to strike women than men, and it is most common in those between 20 and 40 years old.

People with **hypothyroidism** produce too little of the hormones. Most people with this condition—mainly women over 50—don't know they have it. Hypothyroidism can be caused by some medications or it can follow treatment for hyperthyroidism.

In **thyroiditis,** the body's own immune system attacks the thyroid, causing it to produce too much or too little of the hormones. Thyroiditis can follow a viral illness or pregnancy.

Most of these conditions can give rise to a goiter, which is a swollen thyroid gland. The goiter goes away with treatment.

Most thyroid problems can be handled successfully. Some hyperthyroidism is treated with medications, but in other cases hormone production is cut back either with radioactive iodine or by surgically removing part of the gland. Hypothyroidism is treated with hormone supplements. Thyroiditis often goes away on its own or after treatment with medications, including hormones.

WHEN TO CALL THE DOCTOR

➤ If you feel nervous, tremble (especially your hands), lose weight, and have a rapid pulse. You could have an overactive thyroid gland.
➤ If you feel increasingly cold, drowsy, and low on energy, and you gain weight. You could have an underactive thyroid gland.
➤ If you have symptoms of thyroiditis.

FOR MORE HELP

Information line: Thyroid Foundation of America, 800-832-8321, M–F 8:30–4 EST. Call for information about thyroid problems and referrals to local doctors. Members receive a newsletter.

Book: *Your Thyroid: A Home Reference,* by Lawrence C. Wood, M.D., et al. A guide to thyroid problems, causes, and treatments. Ballantine Books, 1995, $5.99.

Video: *Thyroid Disorders at Time of Diagnosis.* Clear, useful overview of causes and treatments, consisting of four reports—Understanding the Diagnosis, What Happens Next?, Treatment and Management, and Issues and Answers. Time Life Medical, 1996, $19.95.

Staying Healthy

◆

Doing all the things you're supposed to do to stay healthy isn't easy. How many of us actually get 30 minutes of aerobic exercise five days a week, every week? Who wants to pass up every ice cream sundae that comes along?

One reason it's hard to follow all the rules for staying healthy is that so many of them take a while—sometimes a long while—to show medically significant results. But there's more to life than avoiding heart attacks, diabetes, and other serious diseases. There is also living well.

This section of the *Self-Care Advisor* gives you the blueprint:

Eight Ways to Feel Your Best lays out a clear, comprehensive plan of action for lifelong good health, based on authoritative, up-to-date scientific research.

Helping Your Doctor Help You offers tactics for making sure that you and your doctor are full partners in your health care.

Your Personal Health Record demonstrates how to set up a family health tree and keep track of things you should know, from ailments that run in the family to lists of self-tests, regular checkups, and immunizations.

Medicines: Playing It Safe shows, at a glance, medications that you shouldn't mix, as well as foods to avoid when you're taking certain medicines.

You'll probably see a number of things you're already doing. And whatever else you choose to add from this feast of expert advice will only improve your chances of feeling your best.

Eight Ways to Feel Your Best

········◆········

Living life to its fullest means more than treating medical problems quickly and intelligently. It means staying healthy, fit, and vital in the first place. What does that take? For all its extraordinary complexity, the human body requires surprisingly little special care. Of course there are some obvious don'ts: Don't live on potato chips. Don't drink and drive. Don't let the plugged-in hair dryer drop into the tub while you bathe. But the foundation for feeling your best is in what you do every day—what you eat, how much you move, how you deal with stress. Researchers may always argue about the details—butter or margarine? mammograms starting at 40 or 50?—but in truth, the basics of a healthy lifestyle are known, uncontroversial, and uncomplicated. If you follow these eight proven steps, you will not only enhance your prospects of a long and fulfilling life, you'll add spring to your step right now.

1. **Get some exercise.**
2. **Maintain a healthy weight.**
3. **Eat well.**
4. **Put out the smoke.**

5. **Be careful out there.**
6. **Stay involved.**
7. **Relax.**
8. **Take care of your teeth.**

Get Some Exercise

Our bodies were made to move—to walk and run, to climb and carry. Movement and physical effort build our bones and muscles and keep us feeling our best. Among the demonstrated rewards of exercise:

More energy and a stronger heart. Increasing your heart rate improves the body's ability to deliver oxygen to cells—the aerobic power that not only determines how much pep you have day to day but also cuts your risk of heart disease.

A stronger immune system. In one study, sedentary women who began a program of brisk walking 45 minutes a day, five days a week, cut their risk of colds and flu in half. In another, women who had exercised through their twenties and thirties, four hours week-

ly, reduced their risk of getting breast cancer by 60 percent.

Less stress. More than a hundred studies have shown that regular doses of rhythmic exercise—walking, running, or swimming, for example—cut anxiety. And after ten weeks of regular workouts, studies show, the calmer feeling starts to last from one day to the next.

Greater strength. Any kind of physical activity can maintain muscle mass. Weight-bearing exercise such as walking, running, or weight lifting can help preserve bone mass. One study found that men and women in their eighties *doubled* their muscular strength after ten weeks of workouts. Many got better at climbing stairs, and a few even discarded their walkers for canes.

Weight control. The more calories you burn with exercise, the fewer you store as fat. And as you replace fat with new muscle, you can ratchet up the number of calories your body burns while you're sitting around. (Muscle tissue burns more calories to maintain itself than does fat tissue.)

A sharper mind. A lifetime of physical activity preserves blood supply to the brain and also boosts the brain chemicals involved in learning and remembering. Active older people score better on tests of thinking ability than inactive older people.

But exactly how much exercise, and what *kinds*, offer these glowing benefits? If you're out of shape, even little bits of activity—neighborhood strolls, weeding in the garden, taking the stairs rather than the elevator—can lower your disease risk. The chart below can help you figure out how to build such life-lengthening spurts into your day-to-day life.

For rewards beyond a longer life, however, you'll need to do more. (See the next page for a fuller description of how much exercise you need to get specific benefits.) Start with a program of at least three 20-minute aerobic workouts a week, in which you work hard enough to get your heart beating faster and feel your breathing quicken. Brisk walking, jogging, bicycling, swimming, or using a stair-climbing machine are good choices. For added stress-reducing benefits, try repeating a calming word, phrase, or even a prayer as you go.

Finally, twice-a-week strength training sessions might be the most effective exercise of all, researchers say, because by building new muscle, you develop the balance, endurance, and confidence you need to keep active into old age. Work all the major muscle groups—back, chest, shoulders, arms, hips, thighs, and abdomen—either by using the weight machines available at most gyms or by lifting hand and ankle weights at home. Do two sets of 10 to 12 repetitions. To decide how much to lift, first determine the maximum possible weight you can lift once, then cut that amount in half.

HOW TO EXTEND YOUR LIFE—WITHOUT WORKOUTS

You know the slightly winded sensation you get when you're rushing to catch a train or rubbing out a spot on the rug? That feeling means you're exercising, experts say—in numerical terms, burning 4.5 or more calories a minute if you weigh about 130 pounds or 6 calories a minute if you weigh about 180. (The heavier you are, the more calories an activity burns.)

Burn an average of 200 a day doing such incidental exercise and you'll cut your risk of disease and live longer—without ever going near the gym. Most household tasks won't qualify. Changing bed linens or putting on makeup, for instance, burns but 2.5 calories a minute; doing the dishes, just 2.3. Walking around the office (3.5) won't cut it either. The operative word is *vigorous*. When you vacuum, it won't count unless you're a whirling dervish. When you walk the dog, make sure the dog is trotting after *you*.

Here are the calories burned by 20 everyday activities.

Calories Burned (10 minutes)*	Women	Men
Walking fast	45	60
Painting	45	60
Weeding	45	60
Passionate sex	45	60
Washing car	45	60
Playing tag with a child	50	67
Cleaning gutters	50	67
Mowing lawn	55	73
Square-dancing	55	73
Scrubbing floors	55	73
Hiking off-trail	60	80
Biking to work	60	80
Shoveling snow	60	80
Moving furniture	60	80
Walking upstairs	70	93
Cross-country skiing	80	106
Backpacking	80	106
Carrying a two-year-old upstairs	80	106
Running to catch a plane	115	153
Running upstairs	150	200

Figures are for a 132-pound woman and a 176-pound man.

Exercise: What You Get for What You Do

How much exercise do you need? It all depends on what you want. To cut the risk of heart disease, stroke, diabetes, and even cancer, you barely need to work up a sweat. But if you want to do more—for instance, trim a few pounds and tighten up your torso—get ready to push harder. Here's what the latest studies say exercise has to offer—and what it takes to get there.

A Longer Life

Every hour you're active, the experts say, adds one and a half hours to your life. But to ward off most of the major killers and possibly osteoporosis, you don't have to kill yourself.

What it takes: Move around enough during each day to burn at least 200 calories—all told, a total of about 30 minutes—in any combination of walking, gardening, climbing stairs, playing with the kids, lifting groceries, or formal exercise. Don't worry about intensity; what matters in doing Exercise Lite is making it a regular part of your daily life.

What to expect: Nothing immediate. The payoff—reduced risk of heart attack and many chronic diseases—doesn't come until later in life. Don't expect to see unwanted pounds melt away quickly. Over time you may slim down, but it will happen gradually.

Better Health Now

When you commit to regular workouts, you start getting more immediate benefits—a boost in energy, a more robust immune system, a more relaxed outlook, healthier blood pressure, and lower cholesterol levels.

What it takes: Burning calories isn't enough; to notice quick health gains, you need to get your heart thumping hard enough so you're winded for at least 20 minutes at a stretch three times a week. Brisk walking, aerobics classes, running, swimming, or any other aerobic exercise all qualify.

What to expect: Fewer colds and bouts of flu. A better ratio of good to bad cholesterol. For people with borderline hypertension, an average drop in blood pressure of ten points. Most important, you'll feel better—more optimistic and less stressed.

Ready-for-Anything Fitness

More vigorous exercise will help maintain strength and cardiovascular vitality well into old age.

What it takes: 20 to 60 minutes of walking, running, swimming, biking, or other aerobic activity three to five times a week. You need to drive your heart rate up to at least 60 percent of its maximum. Add to that a twice-weekly program of floor exercises, weight lifting, or other resistance exercises, plus stretching or yoga, to put your arms, abdomen, and legs through their paces.

What to expect: Greater strength, balance, flexibility, and endurance. Improved athletic performance with fewer injuries and less soreness. The beginnings of a better body. And, for those who stay this fit throughout their lives, a slower decline in the immune system, which could further help ward off infection and even cancer.

A Sleeker Physique

An effective weight-loss program must include both exercise and healthy eating. But if the formula sounds simple—cut the calories you take in, and increase the calories you burn—in truth, it's extremely hard to do.

What it takes: Set a goal of 60 minutes total of brisk walking, running, swimming, biking, or other aerobic exercise five days a week. The more calories you burn, the better; so go for activities you can stick with. Then, to tighten muscles, put your body through a full round of floor exercises, weight lifting, or other resistance work three times a week.

What to expect: Exercise builds muscle, which is denser and heavier than fat, so some exercisers actually gain weight at first. But by adding muscle, and speeding up your metabolism in the process, you'll lose inches on your waist before you shed pounds. Keep at it, eat right, and weight loss will follow.

② Maintain a Healthy Weight

In the past two decades, the body weight carried around by the average American has climbed by eight pounds, and at least one of every four Americans is overweight. (For how you're doing, see the box on the next page.) Hauling around that extra weight does more than keep us from being as active as we want to be. It also can kill us. Excess fat brings higher rates of heart disease, high blood pressure, stroke, diabetes, gallbladder disease, and some cancers.

But how do you determine *your* best healthy weight? And what's the best way to *stay* at that weight for life? Here's what the experts recommend.

Be realistic. Many dieters fail because they shoot for a fantasy weight that's just about impossible to maintain. To determine a realistic weight-loss goal, ask yourself: What is the least you've weighed as an adult, for at least one year? What weight were you able to maintain during previous diets without feeling a lot of hunger pangs? Those weights are good places to start when you set your goal for weight loss. And remember: Losing just 5 to 10 percent of your current weight will make you feel and look better.

Start by exercising. In one study, 90 percent of people who lost weight and kept it off were regular exercisers. A brisk half-hour walk burns about 150 calories—roughly as much as you'd get in a scoop of ice cream. Exercise is particularly important when you're dieting, since cutting back on calories tends to decrease muscle mass; the exercise will help you *increase* it.

Cut calories. Consuming even a few more calories a day than you burn can make you gain weight over time. So by taking in fewer calories—and also burning more with exercise—you can't help dropping some weight. The best way to cut calories, oddly, is to eat *more* of some kinds of food—such as fresh fruit, vegetables, and grains, which are nutritious yet carry less than half the calories in similar quantities of fatty foods. An example: Half a cup of tomato sauce weighs in at 35 calories, but exactly the same amount of cheese sauce, which is high in fat, packs 230 calories. See page 287 for additional tips on how to choose tasty, nutritious, slimming foods over fattening ones.

Don't deprive yourself. Instead of giving up foods you love, just eat less of them. Treat yourself to one cookie instead of four—and savor every bite.

Give yourself time. Any program that promises fast and dramatic weight loss is almost certain to fail. When you set out to lose weight, think in terms of a year or more. The more gradually you lose weight, the more likely you'll keep it off. And remember: The

---

HOW TO KEEP YOURSELF FROM QUITTING

Starting an exercise program is easy. Staying with it is the challenge. Here's what fitness experts recommend:

Slow down. Beginning exercisers usually walk, run, or swim too hard at first (or, with strength training, they heft too much weight) and then quit after a few workouts because they dread the pain. Sure, you should feel tired after a workout; but an hour later you should feel invigorated. If not, you're doing too much, too soon.

Find a partner. Exercising with someone doubles the chance that you'll stick with it.

Write up a contract. Set realistic goals for yourself and write them down. Tell friends and family members so they can encourage and support you.

Chart your progress. Keep an exercise log and reward yourself along the way when you meet specific goals, such as pedaling that extra mile or lifting twice a week for a month straight.

Be patient. The first three to six months on a new exercise regimen are the hardest. If you make it to six months, researchers report, odds are good you'll still be working out a year later.

healthful changes in your exercise and eating habits will make you look and feel better in ways that don't show up on the bathroom scale. So stick with them even if the pounds are slow to budge.

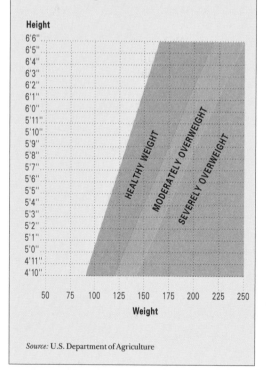

IS YOUR WEIGHT HEALTHY?

The weight chart below will help give you an idea of where you stand. But don't take it as the final word because you should also consider:

Your fitness level. If you land in the moderately overweight category, your weight is less likely to be a health risk—if you're in good physical condition.

Your family history. Overweight individuals with a family history of heart disease, high blood pressure, or diabetes should consider weight loss a top priority.

Your body type. People with "pear" shapes (fat in the thighs, hips, and buttocks) seem to be at far lower risk of weight-related disease than those with "apple" shapes (fat around the abdomen), so they can worry less about being moderately overweight.

Height

6'6" 6'5" 6'4" 6'3" 6'2" 6'1" 6'0" 5'11" 5'10" 5'9" 5'8" 5'7" 5'6" 5'5" 5'4" 5'3" 5'2" 5'1" 5'0" 4'11" 4'10"

HEALTHY WEIGHT MODERATELY OVERWEIGHT SEVERELY OVERWEIGHT

50   75   100   125   150   175   200   225   250

Weight

Source: U.S. Department of Agriculture

Eat Well: Tips for Creating Healthy Meals

The only way to keep your health, Mark Twain once quipped, is to "eat what you don't want, drink what you don't like, and do what you'd druther not." For once, Twain was wrong, because the hallmark of healthful eating is actually good taste and variety. Indeed, even the best diets have room for sweets, meats, and other treats, when you:

Emphasize fruits, vegetables, and grains. High in fiber, loaded with vitamins, low in fat and sodium, plant-based foods fill you up with nutrients without loading you down with fat and cholesterol. The fiber in fruits, vegetables, and grains helps speed toxins out of the body. Plants also contain a wealth of active compounds, called phytochemicals—*phyto* for plant—that boost the body's cancer-fighting defenses. The more of these foods you eat, the healthier you'll be.

Cut back on saturated fat. All of us know that we should eat less fat—especially the big culprit, the saturated kind found in fatty meats, whole milk, ice cream, and cheese. Saturated fat raises cholesterol levels and increases heart disease risk. Reach for nonfat or low-fat milk, and also help yourself to smaller portions of beef, veal, lamb, pork, and ham. On your pasta, try a light tomato sauce instead of a heavy cream sauce. Instead of a rich dessert, reach for a piece of fruit.

Go easy on smoked, salt-cured, and charbroiled foods. All contain high levels of nitrates, which have been linked to several forms of cancer. Enjoy them only occasionally, if at all.

If you drink, go easy. Alcohol in moderation—one drink a day for women, two a day for men—may have some health benefits. As a group, moderate drinkers have less risk of heart disease and seem to live longer than nondrinkers. If you don't drink now, however, that news is no reason to start. You'd benefit far more by eating less saturated fat than by adding alcohol.

What's one drink? A bottle of beer (12 ounces), a glass of wine (5 ounces), or a jigger of liquor (1.5 ounces).

The Mediterranean Diet

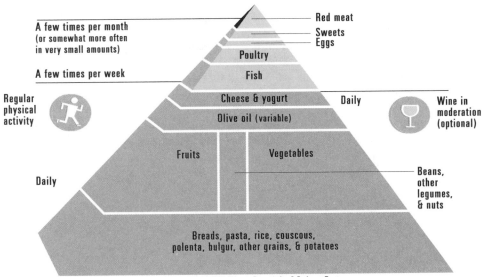

A few times per month
(or somewhat more often
in very small amounts) — Red meat, Sweets, Eggs

A few times per week — Poultry, Fish

Regular physical activity — Cheese & yogurt / Olive oil (variable) — Daily — Wine in moderation (optional)

Daily — Fruits / Vegetables — Beans, other legumes, & nuts

Breads, pasta, rice, couscous, polenta, bulgur, other grains, & potatoes

Copyright © 1994 Oldways Preservation & Exchange Trust

Eat this way. As for the ideal mix of foods, a current alternative favored by nutritionists over the well-known government version is the Traditional Healthy Mediterranean Diet Pyramid, developed in 1994 by researchers at the Harvard School of Public Health and endorsed by the Oldways Preservation & Exchange Trust. Based on the traditional eating habits of southern Italy and Greece—places where chronic disease rates have historically been low and life expectancy has been high—it emphasizes generous helpings of bread and grains, fresh fruits and vegetables, beans and potatoes every day, along with small portions of cheese or yogurt. Modest amounts of fish and poultry are another regular feature. Red meat is only an occasional treat.

THE LOWDOWN ON LOW FAT

Cutting back on fat doesn't mean going hungry. The swap chart below offers some low-fat alternatives to common foods. (Portions are average serving sizes.)

INSTEAD OF	fat grams	GO FOR	fat grams
Corn muffin	5	English muffin and jam	1
Granola	12	Nonfat yogurt sprinkled with granola	2
Bacon and eggs	37	Pancakes with syrup	6
Tuna salad sandwich	16	Turkey breast sandwich with mustard	7
Cheeseburger	30	Bagel with lox and low-fat cream cheese	10
French fries	20	Oven-fried potatoes	8
Cream-of-chicken soup	18	Chicken noodle soup	6
Potato chips	18	Pretzels	2
Bean dip	4	Salsa	0
Alfredo sauce	10	Tomato sauce	1
Sautéed vegetables	14	Steamed vegetables	0
Ranch-style dressing	18	Vinaigrette	8
Ice cream	18	Sorbet	0
Apple pie	16	Four fig bars	4

Copyright © 1996 *Health* magazine

The Nutrition Top Ten

Here's a handy chart to fill you in on the richest food sources of vitamins C, A, and E, folic acid, calcium, iron, and fiber. This chart simply lists the top ten foods for each item. Granted, no one sitting down for a meal eats 3½ ounces—nearly a quarter pound—of Parmesan cheese (highest in calcium) or parsley (rich in vitamin C, vitamin A, and iron). But as you consider the health benefits of each food on the lists, keep this point in mind: A little goes a long way. The RDA (recommended dietary allowance) figure shows you the minimum to aim for daily.

VITAMIN C
RDA: 60 milligrams
mg per 3½ ounces

Red bell peppers	190
Parsley	133
Kiwifruit	98
Broccoli	93
Green bell peppers	89
Brussels sprouts	62
Edible-pod peas	60
Strawberries	57
Red cabbage	57
Oranges	53

VITAMIN A
RDA: 4,000–5,000 international units
IU per 3½ ounces

Carrots	28,129
Pumpkin, canned	22,056
Sweet potatoes	20,063
Red chile pepper	10,750
Apricots, dried	7,240
Spinach	6,715
Red bell peppers	5,700
Parsley	5,200
Watercress	4,700
Squash, winter	4,060

VITAMIN E
RDA: 12–15 international units
IU per 3½ ounces

Wheat germ oil	178
Sunflower seeds	74
Vegetable oils	12–73
Almonds	41
Margarine	19
Wheat germ	17
Peanuts, dry-roasted	11
Peanut butter	9
Butter	3
Asparagus	3

FOLIC ACID
RDA: 180–200 micrograms
mcg per 3½ ounces

Fortified breakfast cereal	353
Wheat germ, toasted	352
Spinach	194
Lentils, cooked	181
Pinto beans, cooked	172
Peanuts, dry-roasted	145
Romaine lettuce	136
Peanut butter	92
Hummus (garbanzo puree)	65
Peas	59

CALCIUM
RDA: 800 milligrams
mg per 3½ ounces

Parmesan cheese	1,376
Mozzarella cheese, part skim	646
Ricotta cheese, part skim	272
Almonds	266
Tofu	250
Salmon, canned, with bones	213
Plain low-fat yogurt	183
Collard greens	156
Orange juice with added calcium	131
Skim milk	123

IRON
RDA: 10–15 milligrams
mg per 3½ ounces

Clams	14–28
Fortified breakfast cereal	12–28
Tofu, firm	10
Liver	7
Oysters	4–12
Cashews, dry-roasted	6
Parsley	6
Apricots, dried	5
Lean beef	4
Spinach	3

FIBER
Suggested daily total: 20–35 grams
g per 3½ ounces

High-fiber breakfast cereal	35–46
Bran flakes	18
Rye crisp crackers	16
Popcorn, air-popped	15
Wheat germ, toasted	13
Granola	11
High-fiber bread	11
Pinto beans, cooked	10
Mixed nuts	9
Whole-wheat bread	9

TOP TEN MOST NUTRITIOUS VEGETABLES

Broccoli
Spinach
Brussels sprouts
Lima beans
Peas
Asparagus
Artichokes
Cauliflower
Sweet potatoes
Carrots

RDA=recommended dietary allowance

Sources: U.S. Department of Agriculture *Handbook 8;*
The Vitamin E Fact Book

Some heavily fortified breakfast cereals, designed to provide most or all of the RDAs, have been omitted from this ranking.

Put Out the Smoke

Smoking is bad for your health. Period. Cigarettes are the nation's top cause of preventable death—they kill over 350,000 people a year and cause serious health problems to millions more. The bottom line: If you don't smoke, don't start. If you do, quit.

Since nicotine is one of the most addictive drugs around, many people find they have to try several times before they give up smoking for good. Even if you've tried and failed, don't give up. There are many successful strategies for kicking the perilous habit, from nicotine patches to support groups. And the body quickly mends itself once you do quit. Within two days of quitting, carbon monoxide levels in the blood return to normal. Within three months, lung function improves by as much as 30 percent.

For more information and a list of resources that can help you kick this deadly habit, see **smoking and illness,** page 210.

Be Careful Out There

Accidents are the top reason Americans land in the emergency room. In fact, for people under the age of 45, accident—not disease—is the leading cause of death. More than half of all these deaths involve motor vehicles or firearms. Guns kill more than 38,000 Americans a year and wound hundreds of thousands more—a number that continues to climb. Half a million people a year are hurt riding bicycles. Nearly 20 million a year have an accident at home that sends them to a doctor or limits their activity for at least half a day. Too many each year get sunburns, which can lead to skin cancer.

To increase safety on the road:
➤ Always wear seat belts in the car.
➤ Use child safety seats for kids under four.
➤ Wear a helmet when you ride a bike (look for one meeting the ANSI or Snell standard) or motorcycle (U.S. Department of Transportation—DOT—standard).
➤ Never drink and drive—or ride with any-

ESSENTIAL ADVICE ON VITAMINS AND MINERALS

Pills can't replace a healthy diet. But if you don't always eat as well as you should, vitamin and mineral supplements can help ensure that you get all the nutrients you need. A few buying tips:

Skip fancy high-potency combinations loaded with vitamin C and E. Instead, choose a basic formula that provides the recommended dietary allowance (RDA) of a broad range of vitamins.

If you want an extra dose of vitamins C and E, buy them separately. For vitamin C, a 250- to 500-milligram pill once a day is a safe choice. For vitamin E, choose a supplement that contains 100 to 400 international units (IU)—a lot more than the RDA.

Folic acid reduces the risk of neurological birth defects, so pregnant women should eat foods rich in it, including leafy green vegetables, beans, cereals, and whole-grain breads. For added protection,

many doctors recommend taking a 400-microgram supplement before and during pregnancy.

Calcium, which is plentiful in milk, yogurt, and leafy green vegetables, may protect against osteoporosis. If you don't feel you're getting enough in your food, consider a supplement. Choose one that contains vitamin D if you don't eat dairy products. Take no more than 1,500 mg a day, since too much calcium can cause nausea and constipation, and may lead to kidney stones. Antacids with calcium, available at drugstores, are inexpensive sources.

For iron, the RDA of around 15 mg for women and 10 mg for men is generally plenty. Pregnant women—especially those who eat little red meat—are often advised to take 30- to 60-mg supplements. But don't go higher than that; doses above 100 mg can cause heart and liver problems.

SUN LOVERS: ARE YOU IN THE DARK?

Close to one million Americans will be diagnosed with skin cancer this year (see color illustration, page 166). The next step isn't pretty. At best, the cut-away tumor will leave a scar. At worst, it'll turn out to be melanoma, which kills 7,000 people a year. And researchers believe that most skin cancers could be avoided if we just did more to protect our skin from sunlight. Did you know, for instance, that men get lip cancer far more often than women, suggesting that even ordinary lipstick protects the lips as effectively as light-duty sunscreen? Still, what amounts to true protection? Do your sunscreen habits measure up? Take this quiz: Are these statements true or false?

❶ **A light tan is perfectly fine, as long as I don't get a sunburn.** T F

❷ **A T-shirt will protect my shoulders from sun damage.** T F

❸ **I'm safe driving around with my windows rolled up.** T F

❹ **I'm more likely to get too much sun when I'm swimming than when I'm sunbathing.** T F

❺ **Growing my hair long is the best way to protect my ears and scalp.** T F

❻ **For maximum blockage, I should put on sunscreen before I go outside.** T F

❼ **The higher my sunscreen's sun protection factor (SPF) rating, the better protected I am.** T F

---

1. False. Some perpetually tan people—those who work outside for at least 40 hours a week—do have lower rates of melanoma, apparently because tan skin protects against the sunburns linked to the cancer. But if you don't work as a park ranger, you raise your odds for getting skin cancer each time you burn or tan. That's because the damage that causes most cancers adds up; ultraviolet light causes cells in the epidermis to reproduce faster, at the same time suppressing the body's immune response to this growth. After decades, the result can be a reddish patch, shiny bump, or open sore—a tumor.

2. True. A bold-colored T-shirt might have a sun protection factor, or SPF, of 15. That means someone who normally burns in 15 minutes is protected for 15 times as long—about 4 hours—before starting to color. But one study did find that wearing a very light-colored or loosely knit shirt let through too much light. Hold a layer of fabric up to a window. If you can see outlines through it, consider changing your shirt.

3. True. Glass windows block the most damaging ultraviolet rays, UVB. But if your car has a sunroof, you're being exposed to UVA rays, which shine straight through horizontal panes of glass.

4. False. Whether you're playing in the water or lounging on a beach chair, the exposure to the sun is the same. But you should use a waterproof sunblock and reapply it after your dip.

5. False. A full head of hair—it doesn't matter which color—does shield against tumors on the scalp and ears. (Cancer on the tops of the ears is a special risk for anyone with short hair). But the best defense isn't hair, which can leave many parts of your head exposed. It's a wide-brimmed hat.

6. False. For full protection, put on sunscreen 30 minutes before leaving the house. That's how long it takes for sunscreen to bond to the outer layer of your skin.

7. True. For most people, SPF 15 lotion or moisturizer adequately blocks the sun. But watch your skin. If you see signs of sunburn despite being covered with SPF 15, switch to a stronger sunscreen—say, SPF 30—to get full protection. And don't put too little on. It takes two tablespoons to cover the average body, but in one study beachgoers put on a third that much.

one who has been drinking.

➤ Keep a flashlight in the car for emergencies and for walking through unlighted parking areas after dark.

To accident-proof your home or office:

➤ Install smoke detectors.

➤ Keep a fire extinguisher handy near the kitchen.

➤ Establish escape routes in case of fire.

➤ Buy antiscald devices for showerheads or faucets, or keep your water heater set at 120 degrees or lower to protect children from scalding.

➤ Store drugs and toxic chemicals out of the reach of children.

➤ Post poison control and other emergency numbers near the phone.

To prevent falls:

➤ Have a sturdy stepladder handy for reaching high shelves.

➤ Install nonslip pads and mats in shower and bathtub areas.

➤ Secure carpet and stair treads.

➤ Don't use unsecured throw rugs.

➤ Be sure stairways are well lighted.

➤ Use night-lights in bathrooms and halls.

➤ Never leave objects on stairs.

To protect yourself outdoors:

➤ Wear a sunscreen with an SPF of at least 15 and a wide-brimmed hat every day to block ultraviolet rays.

➤ Use bug spray with 10 to 15 percent DEET to keep ticks and mosquitoes at bay.

Stay Involved

How would you describe the healthiest person you know? Probably as someone who is alert and curious. Excited about new possibilities. Good at love and friendship. Passionate about life's simple pleasures. Well, researchers couldn't agree more with that description. They've found that healthy people tend to stay enthusiastic about life as they age. Their recommendations:

Be an optimist. Studies suggest that people who usually look on the bright side remain healthier than pessimists. An opti-

---

SHOULD YOU REACH OUT?

There's no magic recipe for social support that works for everyone. A self-sufficient loner might need just one close confidant, while a people person may feel lost without an army of friends. This quiz was adapted from one given by Carnegie Mellon psychologist Sheldon Cohen to gauge whether a person has the right mix of connections to stay healthy. Circle the statements as true or false for you.

❶ **If I needed a loan of $100, there is someone I could get it from.** T F

❷ **There is someone who takes pride in my accomplishments.** T F

❸ **I often meet or talk with family or friends.** T F

❹ **Most people I know think highly of me.** T F

❺ **If I needed an early morning ride to the airport, there's no one I would feel comfortable asking to take me.** T F

❻ **I feel there is no one with whom I can share my most private worries and fears.** T F

❼ **Most of my friends are more successful at making changes in their lives than I am.** T F

❽ **I would have a hard time finding someone to go with me on a day trip to the beach or country.** T F

For your score, add your number of true answers to questions 1 to 4 to the false answers you gave to questions 5 through 8.

If that score is 4 or above, you have enough support to protect your health, even if your safety net has a few holes. During tough times people need connections to draw on or the confidence to ask for help; you've got one or both.

If your score is 3 or below, you may need to reach out. If you're not a group person, make an effort to become close to a trusted relative, friend, or neighbor. Or, if intimacy isn't your strength, join a social or religious group or sign up for a class.

IS STRESS PUTTING YOUR HEALTH AT RISK?

Each of us reacts differently to life's little challenges. Faced with a long line at the bank, most of us will get heated up for a few seconds before we shrug and move on. But for others—the one in five of us whom researchers call hot reactors—such incidents are an assault on good health. That's why rating your stress requires you both to tally your life's stressors (part one) and to figure out whether you are particularly susceptible to stress (part two).

Part One
The Stress in Your Life

How often are the following stressful situations a part of your daily life?

1 Never   2 Rarely   3 Sometimes
4 Often   5 All the time

I work long hours 1 2 3 4 5

There are signs my job
isn't secure 1 2 3 4 5

Doing a good job goes
unnoticed 1 2 3 4 5

It takes all my energy just to
make it through the day 1 2 3 4 5

There are severe
arguments at home 1 2 3 4 5

A family member is
seriously ill 1 2 3 4 5

I'm having problems
with child care 1 2 3 4 5

I don't have enough
time for fun. 1 2 3 4 5

I'm on a diet 1 2 3 4 5

My family and friends count
on me to solve their problems . . 1 2 3 4 5

I'm expected to keep up a
certain standard of living 1 2 3 4 5

My neighborhood is
crowded or dangerous. 1 2 3 4 5

My home is a mess 1 2 3 4 5

I can't pay my bills on time 1 2 3 4 5

I'm not saving money 1 2 3 4 5

Your total score . . . .

Below 38: You have a lower-stress life.
38 and above: You have a high-stress life.

Part Two
Your Stress Susceptibility

Try to imagine how you would react in these hypothetical situations.

You've been waiting 20 minutes for a table in a crowded restaurant, and the host seats a party that arrived after you. You feel your anger rise as your face gets hot and your heart beats faster. **T F**

Your sister calls out of the blue and starts to tell you how much you mean to her. Uncomfortable, you change the subject without expressing what you feel. **T F**

You come home to find the kitchen looking like a disaster area and your spouse lounging in front of the TV. You tense up and can't seem to shake your anger. **T F**

Faced with a public speaking event, you get keyed up and lose sleep for a day or more, worrying about how you'll do. **T F**

On Thursday your repair shop promises to fix your car in time for a weekend trip. As the hours go by, you become increasingly worried that something will go wrong and your trip will be ruined. **T F**

Two or Fewer True: You're a cool reactor, someone who tends to roll with the punches when a situation is out of your control.

Three or More True: Sorry, you're a hot reactor, someone who responds to mildly stressful situations with a "fight-or-flight" adrenaline rush that drives up blood pressure and can lead to heart rhythm disturbances, accelerated clotting, and damaged blood vessel linings. Some hot reactors can seem cool as a cucumber on the outside, but inside their bodies are silently killing them.

mistic attitude may even boost the body's immune defenses.

Join a group. Community, church, and social organizations provide a good way to meet new friends. Even after people retire, those who remain active in volunteer work or church and social organizations stay healthier and sharper mentally than those who shut themselves in and quit being active.

Challenge yourself. The more we challenge our bodies and minds, the more vital they remain. Studies show that the act of learning something new actually increases the connections between brain cells and makes the brain more robust.

Cherish your friends and loved ones. In one study, unmarried people who didn't feel they had anyone to share their innermost feelings with were three times more likely to die over the next five years than those who had someone close to talk to. Indeed, social isolation can be as hazardous to health as smoking or having high cholesterol levels.

Stay active. A lifetime of physical activity helps preserve blood supply to the brain, because it keeps the cardiovascular system in top shape. Exercise also seems to boost brain chemicals involved in learning and remembering. The bottom line: Active and fit older people not only live longer, they also have faster physical reaction times and score better on tests of thinking ability than do inactive older people.

Relax

These days, most of us lead busy, crowded lives. And most of the time we cope smoothly with the pressures we face. But sometimes life's strains and disappointments become too much and our bodies react. Blood pressure rises, heart rate quickens, and the stress hormone adrenaline surges through the bloodstream. Stress can contribute to everything from colds, headaches, and back pain to allergies, asthma, arthritis, infertility, insomnia, depression, and heart disease.

Luckily, mastering a few tricks can help reduce stress and lower the risk of health

---

What Your Scores Mean

Combine the results from parts one and two to get your total stress rating.

Lower-Stress Life   Cool Reactor

Whatever your problems, stress isn't one of them. Even when stressful events do occur—and they will—your health probably won't suffer.

Lower-Stress Life   Hot Reactor

You're not under stress—at least for now. Though you tend to overreact to problems, you've wisely managed your life to avoid the big stressors. Before you honk at the guy who cuts you off in rush hour traffic, remember that getting angry can destroy thousands of heart muscle cells within minutes.

High-Stress Life   Cool Reactor

You're under stress, but only you know if it's hurting. Even if you normally thrive with a full plate of challenges, now you might be biting off more than you can chew. Note any increase in headaches, backaches, or insomnia; that's your body telling you to lighten your load. If your job is the main source of stress, think about reducing your hours. If that's not possible, find a way to make your job more enjoyable, and stress will become manageable.

High-Stress Life   Hot Reactor

You're in the danger zone. Make an extra effort to exercise, get enough sleep, and keep your family and friends close. Unfortunately, even being physically fit does little to protect you if your body is in perpetual stress mode. To survive, you may need to make major changes—walking away from a life-destroying job or relationship, perhaps—and you may need to develop a whole new approach to life's hourly obstacles. Such effort will be rewarded. In one experiment, 77 percent of hot reactors were able to cool down—lower their blood pressure and cholesterol levels—by training themselves to stay calm.

HOW WELL DO YOU KNOW YOUR TEETH?

Of course we're supposed to brush every day. But how many of us know why? Take this test to find out if you're truly treating your teeth well.

1 **You can catch gum disease from**
a. kissing
b. sharing a toothbrush
c. both
d. neither

2 **Toothbrushing prevents**
a. detached gums
b. root decay
c. stained teeth
d. none of the above

3 **You're least likely to get cavities from eating**
a. raisins
b. pure sugar
c. an English muffin

4 **Who's especially susceptible to getting gum disease?**
a. pregnant women
b. menopausal women
c. teetotalers

5 **If you can't brush your teeth after a meal, what's the best thing to do?**
a. eat a banana
b. chew gum
c. use a toothpick

6 **The minimum time for a thorough toothbrushing is**
a. one minute
b. three minutes
c. four minutes

7 **Which will relieve toothache pain fastest?**
a. aspirin
b. clove oil
c. salt water

Answers

1. c By age 35, three in four Americans have at least the beginnings of gum disease, an irritation and infection below the gum line caused by certain bacteria in dental plaque. But occasionally bacteria transmitted via the saliva of someone with gum disease can bring on the condition in someone who doesn't even have plaque. So if your partner isn't taking care of his or her teeth, take the problem seriously. Your own gums may be at risk.

2. d Toothbrushing removes plaque and prevents cavities above the gum line, but not below. When plaque isn't cleaned out, the gums fall away, allowing germs to get at your roots and even at the bone anchoring the teeth. Gum disease is the nation's leading cause of tooth loss. To prevent it, you have to floss regularly.

3. b Sugary foods, including candy and chocolate, are cleared from the mouth more quickly than starchy foods. Raisins are a special case because they stick between teeth so tenaciously.

4. a Nearly all pregnant women get some signs of gum disease because hormones associated with pregnancy increase swelling, bleeding, and tiny infections in the gums. There's an old saw: Lose a tooth for every child. To keep it from coming true, brush after every meal, floss daily, and see a dentist at the beginning of your pregnancy.

5. b Chewing gum stimulates copious secretions of saliva, and saliva's chemicals neutralize tooth-decaying acids. Pop in a piece when you finish a meal. Sugarless gum works much better than regular, and gum containing xylitol works best of all, reducing tooth decay by as much as 85 percent. (The sweetener keeps bacteria from multiplying.) This gum is sold mostly in health food stores.

6. b To make this task seem less daunting, try dividing your mouth into ten sections. (Include a section each for the roof of your mouth, your tongue, and the insides of your right and left cheeks, all places where bacteria congregate.) Then count to 20 alligators as you brush each section. The average American spends about 30 seconds brushing.

7. b If your dentist can't see you right away for a painful cavity or infection, saturate a cotton ball in oil of clove (sold at many pharmacies) and put it on the aching tooth. The anesthetic oil should ease the pain in a couple of seconds.

problems. In one study, medical students who used simple relaxation techniques during exam time were much less likely to show a slump in their immune systems than other students. Here are several simple ways to calm frazzled nerves:

Take a 15-minute breather. When things get hectic, go for a walk, listen to a favorite song, browse through a magazine, or soak in a hot bath. Any enjoyable distraction from the day's pressures can calm you down.

Practice relaxation techniques, such as deep breathing, meditation, or simply sitting quietly with your eyes closed. All have been shown to reverse the physical symptoms of stress. Studies have even shown that regular meditation decreases levels of lactate, a chemical associated with muscular tension. Meditation also makes the body less responsive to adrenaline—exactly what the leading blood-pressure-lowering drugs do.

Use your imagination. Positive mental images can have a powerfully calming effect on the body. If you feel your stress level spiking, close your eyes and take five minutes to picture yourself in a quiet, peaceful, pleasant setting—say, you and a friend on a clean, sunny beach lapped by gentle waves, or a green mountainside meadow.

Move around. Doing a favorite form of exercise—one that leaves you slightly winded—will ease your anxiety and help you feel more in control of your life.

Laugh it off. Laughter really *is* one of the best medicines. A good laugh relaxes muscles and stimulates the production of stress-reducing brain chemicals. Read a book that makes you laugh, or sit down to watch a favorite comedy show or film. Another good bet: Get together with friends for some light-hearted conversation.

Take Care of Your Teeth

Cavities used to be the big deal in dental care. The new frontier is gum disease—a bacterial infection that works below the gum line to ravage the bone and ligaments holding your teeth in place. Lose enough of that important foundation, the experts warn, and you could also lose your teeth. So, as they say, "Clean only the teeth you want to keep." Specifically:

Brush *and* floss at least twice a day, in the morning and before bed. It doesn't matter whether you floss first or brush first—just be thorough. The nighttime cleaning amounts to a preemptive strike—knocking down the bacterial army before you lie there all night asleep, letting the fluids in your mouth stagnate. The morning cleaning knocks them down again when their numbers have peaked.

Dentists want you to have your teeth cleaned professionally at least once every six months to keep ahead of any damage that might creep in despite your best efforts.

If you can follow all eight steps, great. If you can't, try seven, or six. The point is not just to live longer, though you very well might. The real reward is feeling better and enjoying life.

Staying Healthy

Helping Your Doctor Help You

◆

To get the most from your health professionals, you'll need to meet them halfway. Here's how. ❀ **Learn how to stay well.** It may seem obvious, but the better you take care of yourself, the less likely you'll get sick in the first place—and the more quickly you'll get well if you do get sick. ❀ **Know as much as you can.** Learn about your body and how it works. If you start feeling sick, pay close attention to your symptoms. If you have an illness, study up on it. When it comes to your health, knowledge really is power. ❀ **Be active on your own behalf.** When you visit the doctor, take an interest, ask questions, and pay attention. Here are ten ways to help your doctor help you, plus tips on how to collect the information you'll need.

1 **Talk first about what worries you most.** Don't save your biggest concern for last—or you may not have time to ask about it.

2 **Be specific.** Saying, "I feel hot and I've had a sharp pain in the right side of my abdomen since last night," is more helpful than saying, "I feel rotten." Bring up all the changes you've noticed, even if you don't think they're important. (See **when you're sick** box, page 300.)

3 **Tell the truth.** It's important to be completely honest about what you eat, how much you exercise, and whether you smoke or use drugs or alcohol.

You should also let your doctor know about any nonmedical or family remedies you've been using—going to a chiropractor or an acupuncturist, for instance, or taking megadoses of vitamins. Even if you feel shy talking about sexual practices or problems, be sure to mention them; your doctor may need the information.

Remember to bring up any special stresses you may be under, such as the recent death of a loved one or working a double shift—and even good news, such as getting married.

4 **Ask questions.** Some doctors welcome questions from patients more than others do. But many say they are actually surprised by how few questions patients ask, considering that their health is at stake.

Clear up everything you don't understand during your visit. If you don't quite grasp an explanation, ask your doctor to show you a diagram or even draw a picture. Ask for brochures and other sources of information.

Depending on your illness, ask what you can do to keep the problem from recurring.

If your doctor can't answer all your questions in one visit, ask for time to talk at the next appointment, or ask when to call, if you can get the answer by phone. But if a question is crucial, ask—politely but firmly—for an answer before you leave.

5 **Ask for translations.** If your doctor speaks in medical terms you don't understand, ask for a simpler explanation. If information comes at you too quickly, ask the doctor to slow down. To make sure you understand, say, "Now let me see if I've got that straight," and repeat the explanations and instructions.

6 **Find out more about referrals and tests.** If your doctor suggests a referral, ask why (and also check to see if the doctor is on your health plan). If a test is suggested, make sure you understand:

Why it's necessary.
How accurate and reliable it is.
How you should prepare for it.
Whether it's painful.
How the results will affect treatment.
When and how you'll get the results.
Whether it's covered by your health plan.
Whether you need prior authorization.
How much it will cost you.

After a diagnosis of something serious, you might face difficult choices about treatment to follow. Ask your doctor to explain all your options. Make sure you understand the risks and benefits of each choice—as well as the pros and cons of doing nothing. You can also ask about other sources of information, or about getting a second opinion.

Once you are fully informed, you and your doctor can work together to pick the best course. Before deciding, though, give yourself time to think about these important issues:

How much pain am I willing to endure?
How much risk am I willing to take?
How much cost am I willing to bear?

7 **Speak up.** If you want medication to relieve your symptoms, say so. If you're worried you can't afford a prescribed drug and wonder if a generic substitute might be cheaper, ask. If you're afraid you might have heart problems and wonder if you should be tested, say so. If you don't speak up, you may walk away frustrated— and still worried. If you need reassurance and you're open about it, your doctor might be able to help you regain peace of mind. But remember: You have to say what's bothering you. Doctors are often rushed, and medical schools don't teach mind reading.

8 **If you can't follow doctor's orders, say so.** There may be times when you just don't think you can do what your doctor advises—whether it's getting more sleep, cutting out fried foods, exercising every day, or taking a certain drug. Maybe your schedule's too irregular or you're just plain forgetful. But don't walk out feeling discouraged, thinking you'll just ignore it all. Instead, explain the situation to your doctor, who may have ideas about simplifying treatment or working it into your daily schedule.

Don't be afraid to negotiate. For instance, if your doctor recommends a drug or treatment that has side effects that you would find difficult to accept, try saying, "I'd find that hard to live with. Is there another option I could try?"

9 **Bring along your own ideas.** If you read or hear about a treatment or medication that you'd like to try, bring the information along. Ask your doctor if it could work for you. That way you can make informed decisions about your own care.

10 **Don't leave what you've learned at the office.** It's tough to recall everything a doctor tells you, especially if you are feeling nervous.

Before you leave the office, know what you should do once you get home. Be sure you have prescriptions for medicines you need, and be sure you know how you should take them, how you should handle any side effects, and what changes to make in your diet or activities. Ask your doctor to write down the important points. Find out whom to call and when to call if you run into any problems. Ask if a follow-up visit is needed. Again, you may want to take notes.

If for any reason you know you will find it difficult to understand or remember what your doctor tells you, consider taking along a tape recorder, or asking a trusted friend or relative to come with you to take notes and help clarify information.

Staying Healthy

Reminders for Recovery

Even if your doctor pinpoints your problem and comes up with an effective treatment, you won't get all the benefits unless you're willing to do your share of the work. Here are some ways to speed recovery:

Find out how long your recovery should take. If you know what to expect—how long it will take before you can go back to your walking routine, for example—you'll have a better idea about when to check in with the doctor. If you're taking longer to heal than expected, call your doctor and say so.

Stay in touch. Call for an immediate appointment if your illness takes a turn for the worse, or if you develop new symptoms.

Take all medication exactly as prescribed—even if you start to feel better. This is especially true for antibiotics, which kill bacteria. If you stop taking antibiotics too early, your infection may linger because some germs have survived. Be sure to call your doctor immediately to report any unexpected or extreme side effects. (See **medicines: playing it safe**, page 306.)

Find a care partner. If you are sick and feeling overwhelmed, ask for help. A dependable friend, neighbor, or relative might serve as a volunteer care partner, helping you stay on top of your medication schedule, driving you to the doctor's office, and offering emotional support. If you're facing a long or difficult illness, loneliness can be one of your worst enemies. Surround yourself with people who are optimistic and helpful. Ask your doctor if there is a support group for people who share your condition.

Consider your health to be a long-term project. Getting well and staying well isn't just a matter of taking some medication for a while and then neglecting yourself. It's best to make good self-care an important part of your life—for the rest of your life.

For More Help

There's a wealth of information waiting for anyone who wants to seek it out. For a specific condition, see the For More Help listing at the end of most entries in this book. Here are some other sources:

Your own health maintenance organization or hospital. Many HMOs offer re-

GETTING READY FOR A REGULAR VISIT

Routine visits can help you and your doctor catch any problems early, perhaps before you notice symptoms. If caught in time, many conditions can be treated successfully. Your doctor will recommend a regular schedule of exams based on your particular needs.

Before you go, make a list. Know ahead of time what you'd like to talk about—both general concerns and specific questions. Putting your thoughts on paper can help you focus; list anything that's been worrying you and any questions you want to ask. Here's a way to organize your thoughts:

My major concerns: Doctor's comments and advice:

1 _____

2 _____

3 _____

My minor concerns:

1 _____

2 _____

3 _____

Things to talk about on the next visit:

_____

_____

Write down your own health history. If you're visiting for the first time, your doctor will need some important information about you, including chronic conditions you may have, such as asthma or high blood pressure; and any serious illnesses or injuries you've had in the past, including hospitalizations, surgeries, and accidents.

Know your family health history. Your doctor will want some health background on your parents, siblings, and grandparents, such as chronic illnesses and causes of death, because some tendencies run in families—heart disease and cancer, for example, or unusual longevity. Your doctor will write down your medical history on his or her own form, but you can help out by being prepared. (See **your family health tree,** page 303.)

Brown-bag all your medications, both prescription and over-the-counter drugs. Your doctor needs to know about all the drugs you're taking, including those prescribed by other physicians. It's a good idea to round up all the containers and take them with you to your appointment. That way your doctor can protect you from taking too much medication or mixing drugs in a harmful way (see **drug combinations to avoid** chart, page 307). Remember to include any vitamin supplements and all your other nonprescription items, such as allergy medications, cold medicine, and the like.

Staying Healthy

source centers stocked with pamphlets, books, and videotapes on various health subjects—from coping with Alzheimer's disease to losing weight. Many HMOs also have health educators, as well as support groups, lectures, and classes (ranging from Lamaze sessions for expectant parents to programs for smokers who want to quit). If your HMO doesn't offer a resource center, check with a local hospital to see if it has a library that patients and the interested public can use.

Many hospitals also offer classes, seminars, and support groups.

Libraries and computer networks. Both public and university libraries have health sections. Some libraries also have a computer database, such as Infotrac or MEDLINE, which can help you track down medical information.

The National Network of Libraries of Medicine can help you find a medical library in your area. Call 800-338-7657, M–F 8–5 your time.

The Planetree Health Resource Centers is an outstanding network of consumer health libraries. For the location of the center nearest you and for information about its services, call the national offices at 415-956-4215, M–F 9–5 PST.

The National Institutes of Health offers public information on allergies and infectious diseases (including AIDS), mental health, aging, cancer, diabetes, and digestive diseases. For information on specific topics, call the NIH Office of Communications, at 301-496-4000, 24-hour line.

The National Health Information Center is a free referral service; if you have specific health or medical questions, the people there can direct you to national organizations. You can also order publications from the NHIC list for a fee. Call 800-336-4797, M–F 9–5 EST.

Support groups. National organizations often have local support groups. Two major ones, the American Cancer Society and the American Heart Association, list local chapters in the telephone directory. If you don't find a listing, call the national office of the **American Cancer Society** at 800-227-2345, M–F 8–5 your time; or the **American Heart Association** at 800-242-8721, M–F 8:30–5 your time.

For referral to AIDS support groups, call the **National HIV and AIDS Hotline** at 800-342-AIDS, 24-hour line.

WHEN YOU'RE SICK

When you go to the doctor for a specific purpose, give as much information as you can. Try to cover these things, in particular:

➤ Every change you've noticed since you started feeling sick.

➤ When the symptoms began.

➤ The time of day they occur.

➤ Whether you've had them before.

➤ What makes them better or worse.

➤ If you've done anything unusual lately, such as camping out or playing softball for the first time in five years, that might be affecting how you feel.

➤ If you have eaten anything unusual recently or if you have started taking any new over-the-counter or prescription medications.

➤ If any unusual events have occurred recently in your family, such as the sudden death of a relative, or anything else you can think of that might have a bearing on your illness.

➤ Any mood changes or changes in your sleep patterns.

➤ Activities that seem to make you feel better or worse.

PAIN RELIEVERS: THE BIG THREE

The three most common over-the-counter pain relievers are acetaminophen, aspirin, and ibuprofen. All can relieve pain and reduce fever. None should be taken by pregnant women without consulting a doctor. (Also, anyone who is taking any other medicine should see the **drug combinations to avoid** chart, page 307, before taking any of these pain relievers.) All are available as generics, identical to name brands. Here are some pros and cons of each:

Acetaminophen (common brand name, Tylenol): Effective for pain relief but not inflammation. It's easier on the stomach than aspirin or ibuprofen, and it's the only one of the three that does not significantly prolong bleeding.

People who are having teeth pulled or other medical procedures that cause bleeding—as well as people with ulcers, frequent nosebleeds, or other bleeding problems—should take acetaminophen for pain relief. It's also the safest alternative for children because it isn't associated with **Reye's syndrome** (see box on page 92). Taking larger-than-recommended doses for several weeks can cause liver damage; daily use for several months may damage the kidneys. Combining larger-than-recommended doses with heavy alcohol consumption can also be dangerous.

Aspirin (common brand names, Bayer, Bufferin, Anacin): Effective for relief of mild to moderate pain such as headaches, toothaches, backaches, and muscle aches. It reduces inflammation but only at maximum daily doses, and it reduces the clotting capacity of blood, thereby prolonging bleeding, more than ibuprofen or acetaminophen does. Aspirin can cause or worsen ulcers, so people with ulcers or other bleeding problems should not take it. Aspirin can trigger asthma attacks in 5 to 10 percent of people with asthma. It can also cause stomach upset or heartburn. Taking aspirin after a meal and following it with a glass of milk or water may lessen irritation; enteric-coated or buffered tablets are even less upsetting.

Never give aspirin to a child under 12 who has chicken pox, flu, or any other illness you suspect of being caused by a virus, such as a bad respiratory infection, because aspirin has been linked with Reye's syndrome.

Ibuprofen (common brand names, Advil, Motrin, Nuprin): Effective for pain relief and inflammation; especially good for menstrual cramps and arthritis. It prolongs bleeding less than aspirin does, but ibuprofen can cause bleeding in people with ulcers if taken for more than two weeks. Taking it with food or milk can reduce stomach irritation. Ibuprofen may cause fluid retention, and continuous use for several months can cause kidney problems. It can bring on asthma attacks in people with asthma who are also sensitive to aspirin. Ibuprofen in liquid form has recently been approved for children.

Your Personal Health Record

♦

You can improve your chances of staying well by learning everything possible about your family's health history and by doing regular self-exams, getting regular checkups, and keeping your shots up to date. It's much less expensive to prevent an illness than to treat it, with far less physical and emotional strain. And remember: The earlier an illness is detected, the easier it is to treat. Here are some ways to keep track of your own health.

A Family Tree

One way to get a clear look at your family's health history is to make a family health tree—a genogram.

A genogram shows at a glance the names of family members, how they are related, their dates of birth, their health problems, and the dates and causes of their deaths. Creating a genogram allows you to see patterns in your family's health history. It's a tool you and your doctor can use to judge your risks for some of the more than 3,000 ailments believed to run in families—including heart disease, cancer, diabetes, Alzheimer's disease, thyroid disease, certain birth defects, alcoholism, depression, and schizophrenia.

Illnesses that have occurred in family members before the age of 55 may particularly interest you and your doctor—because you may be able to avoid them. If you know your risks, you can often decrease them by changing your health habits or by spotting a condition early so it can be treated.

➤ To make your own genogram, start with yourself and work back through time. (Use circles for women, squares for men.)

➤ Write in your name, date of birth, and any serious health conditions, illnesses, or operations you've had.
➤ To the side of your own information, add the names of your biological sisters and brothers, with notes about their health conditions.
➤ Add your parents and any aunts or uncles on the two branches above you—and above them, your four grandparents, each with date of birth and a list of any known ailments.
➤ For people who have died, include the date of death and the cause of death, if you know it. For example:

Jane Smith: b. 4-1-1890, d. 6-14-1960. Tuberculosis, angina, high blood pressure. Died of stroke.

You may need to call some of your relatives or check family records to get all the information you need. Then, update the genogram every year or so, and keep it with your other health records.

The sample on the next page can help you get started. Copy the form, and make a chart for yourself. If you have children, make a chart for their other parent; then combine that chart with yours to make a chart for your children. If your family is large, you will need to extend the chart.

Your Family Health Tree

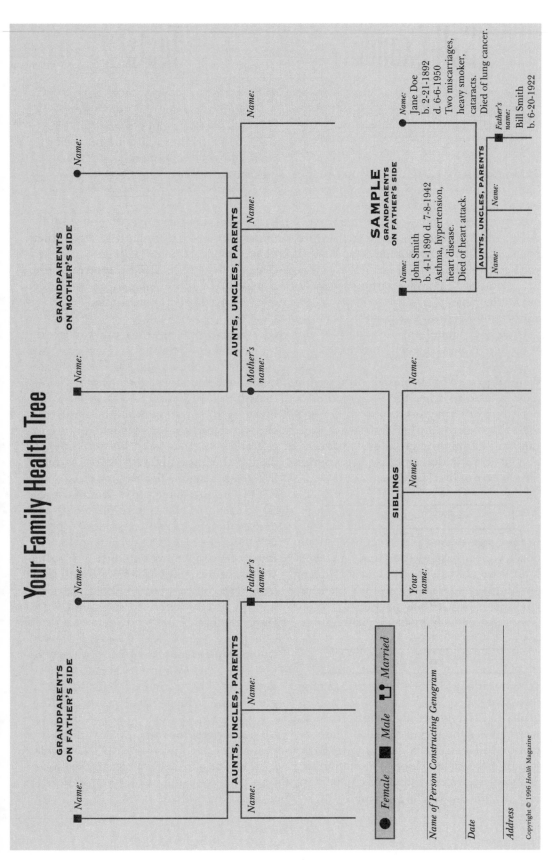

GRANDPARENTS ON FATHER'S SIDE

Name:

Name:

AUNTS, UNCLES, PARENTS

Name:

Name:

Father's name:

GRANDPARENTS ON MOTHER'S SIDE

Name:

Name:

AUNTS, UNCLES, PARENTS

Name:

Name:

Mother's name:

SIBLINGS

Name:

Name:

Your name:

● Female ▪ Male ♞ Married

Name of Person Constructing Genogram

Date

Address

Copyright © 1996 *Health* Magazine

SAMPLE
GRANDPARENTS ON FATHER'S SIDE

Name:
John Smith
b. 4-1-1890 d. 7-8-1942
Asthma, hypertension,
heart disease.
Died of heart attack.

Name:
Jane Doe
b. 2-21-1892
d. 6-6-1950
Two miscarriages,
heavy smoker,
cataracts.
Died of lung cancer.

AUNTS, UNCLES, PARENTS

Name:

Name:

Father's name:
Bill Smith
b. 6-20-1922

Staying Healthy

Self-Exams

Most doctors advise that you do the following health checks yourself:

Skin checkup (yearly, unless you're especially susceptible because of extra-fair skin or lots of moles; then also make regular appointments with your doctor). Keep an eye out for unusual scaliness, oozing, bleeding, or changes in freckles or moles, especially if you have fair skin or if you spend a lot of time in the sun. (See color illustrations of cancerous moles, page 167.) At least once a year, examine yourself fully. Use a mirror (or ask a partner) to examine hard-to-see parts of your body. Report any changes to your doctor.

Weighing in. Maintaining a healthy weight is essential to good health. (See page 286 for healthy weight ranges.) If your clothes start to feel too tight or too loose, step on a scale. Any unusual weight gain or loss should be reported to your doctor. (Also see **sudden weight gain or loss** chart, page 272.)

FOR WOMEN

Breast self-exam (once a month). If you check your breasts at the same time every month, you have a good chance of finding any lump that may need a doctor's attention. For instructions, see box, page 233. Tell your doctor immediately about any changes.

FOR MEN

Testicular exam (once a month). Though testicular cancer amounts to only 1 percent of all cancers, it is the leading cancer among men between the ages of 20 and 35. Early detection can lead to a complete cure. Every month, roll each testicle between your thumb and forefinger, feeling for lumps. Report any unusual lump or swelling to your doctor.

Tests

The following simple tests require a visit to a doctor or clinic. Depending on your age and physical condition, your doctor may recommend that you have checkups more often or less often.

Blood pressure (once a year for most adults; more often if your doctor advises it). Normal blood pressure is around 120 over 80. If yours is higher than that (see **high blood pressure,** page 105), your doctor may recommend exercise, changes in diet, or medication.

Cholesterol (at least once every five years for most adults). High levels of cholesterol in your blood increase your risk of heart disease and stroke. One form of cholesterol—low-density lipoproteins, or LDL—has been nicknamed "bad cholesterol" because it can clog your arteries. There is also "good cholesterol"—high-density lipoproteins, or HDL—which actually helps remove bad cholesterol (see **staying healthy,** page 286).

One blood test measures overall cholesterol. A reading of less than 200 (milligrams per deciliter) is usually considered normal. A reading of 200 to 240 is considered borderline. A reading above 240 means a higher chance of heart disease. People with high overall readings are usually advised to get a lipoprotein analysis, which will give LDL and HDL readings.

Colon: digital rectal exam (once a year after age 40). A doctor inserts a rubber-gloved finger into the rectum to check for rectal growths and, in men, signs of prostate cancer.

Colon: sigmoidoscopy (every three to five years after age 50). By guiding a flexible, lighted tube into the rectum and lower intestine, a doctor can look for colon cancer or precancerous polyps.

Fecal occult blood test (once a year after age 50). The stool sample is checked for traces of blood, which might indicate cancer.

Dental checkup (every six months to a year for an exam and cleaning). If you go regularly, your dentist will be able to spot tooth decay or signs of gum disease early enough for effective treatment. Regular professional cleaning can help prevent gum disease.

FOR WOMEN

Breast exam by a doctor (every three years for women in their 20s and 30s, every year after age 40). Even if you do monthly breast exams yourself, it's a good idea to have regular exams by your doctor as an extra precaution.

Pap smear and pelvic exam (once a year for women 18 and over, and for younger women who are sexually active). Cells gently scraped from the cervix can show changes that signal cancer.

Mammogram (once a year for women 50 and over; some doctors recommend 40 and over—especially if there is a family history of breast cancer). An X-ray of the breast can spot cancer in its early stages by detecting lumps too small to feel with your hand.

FOR MEN

PSA blood test for prostate cancer (some doctors recommend once a year for men 50 and over). The prostate-specific antigen test (PSA) can pick up early signs of prostate cancer, the most common cancer in American men. The test is controversial: It is not always reliable, and authorities disagree about its usefulness. Ask your doctor for advice.

Immunizations

Immunizations are a shot of prevention against many serious illnesses, including polio, hepatitis, diphtheria, tetanus, and whooping cough.

They work by exposing the body to a killed or weakened form of a virus or other infectious agent, provoking the immune system to strengthen its defenses. Most doctors recommend the following:

ADULTS

Tetanus-diphtheria (Td) booster. Once every 10 years for adults from age 19 to 64.

Influenza (Hib) vaccine. Yearly for people age 65 and over and for those at high risk for flu, including adults with diabetes, kidney disease, cancer, chronic heart and respiratory conditions, or anemia; people with weakened immune systems; and adults who work with people at risk.

Pneumococcal vaccine. Once in a lifetime (or more, depending on your doctor's advice) for adults at high risk of pneumonia—including those age 65 and over, those who have had organ transplants, and those with diabetes, alcoholism, cirrhosis (liver damage), congestive heart failure, kidney failure, chronic pulmonary disease, or weakened immune systems.

Hepatitis B vaccine. A single series, once in a lifetime, for those at high risk—including health care workers, people who have contact with dirty needles, hemophiliacs who have frequent blood transfusions, and intravenous drug users (see **hepatitis,** page 270).

CHILDREN AND TEENAGERS

See **recommended children's immunizations** chart, page 244.

Medicines: Playing It Safe

◆

If you're like most Americans, you've taken prescription drugs, and you've probably taken more than one kind of drug at the same time. You probably also take drugs now and then that you can buy without a prescription in supermarkets and drugstores— pain relievers, for instance, or allergy medicines. Yet many drugs, whether over-the-counter or prescription, can have serious side effects when they bump up against each other. Other drugs are dangerous when combined with alcohol, some vitamins or minerals, nicotine, caffeine, or certain foods. In addition, some drugs cancel out each other's usefulness if taken together. (Older people are at higher risk of harmful drug combinations because they often take more than one prescription medicine at a time.)

Medication Safety Tips

To protect yourself, follow these suggestions:

➤ Tell *each* doctor you see about all the medications you are taking—both prescription and over-the-counter drugs.

➤ Mention any vitamin and nutritional supplements as well, and whether you drink alcohol or smoke tobacco.

➤ If you're taking a number of medications, bring the containers with you to show the doctor; have them recorded in your file.

➤ Be sure you thoroughly understand all your doctor's directions about a drug, and always read the label and follow the instructions exactly.

➤ Also ask your doctor:

• What time should I take the medication? Should I take it with food or an hour or two before or after eating?

• Should I avoid any foods, prescription medicines, or over-the-counter drugs while taking this? Should I avoid vitamins or other supplements? Is it safe to drink alcohol while I'm taking it? What about caffeine, tobacco, or exposure to sunlight? Is it safe to drive?

• What side effects, if any, can there be?

• What should I do if they occur?

➤ Remember that your pharmacist, too, is an excellent source of information. Fill all your prescriptions at the same pharmacy, so that your pharmacist will have a computerized record of your medications and can alert you to potential problems.

➤ Always take the full course of medication prescribed for you, but call your doctor immediately if you notice any new or unusual symptoms, such as confusion, depression, insomnia, or memory loss. Dizziness as you get up, vomiting, diarrhea, constipation, or abdominal pain may also be side effects of certain drugs.

➤ Store medications as the label directs; some, for example, should be refrigerated.

➤ Don't share medications.

➤ Don't buy a medicine if the protective packaging is broken or looks as though it has been tampered with.

➤ Always take medications in good lighting—never in the dark—so that you can see what you're swallowing or applying.

➤ Throw out leftover medicine if the package date shows it has expired. That makes it less likely that you—or someone else— will take it by mistake.

Drug Combinations to Avoid

This chart lists some potentially dangerous combinations involving common prescription and over-the-counter medicines. Some react badly with each other; others shouldn't be combined with alcohol or certain foods and vitamins. This is by no means a complete list of all harmful drug combinations. (To learn about others, see **for more help,** page 309.) Nor is the chart intended as a substitute for medical advice. Be sure to tell each of your health care providers about every prescription medicine and over-the-counter drug you're taking, and never start or stop taking any medication without talking to your doctor first.

IF YOU'RE TAKING	DON'T MIX WITH	WHAT CAN HAPPEN	RECOMMENDATION
Antibiotic— ciprofloxacin (Cipro).	Antacids (Mylanta, Maalox, others).	Decreased effect of antibiotic.	Don't combine these medications without your doctor's approval.
Antibiotics— ciprofloxacin (Cipro), erythromycin, others.	Theophylline (Theo-Dur, Slo-bid, Bronk-aid, others), used to treat asthma.	Excessive levels of theophylline in blood. Symptoms include nausea, vomiting, palpitations, seizures.	Make sure your doctor knows you are taking both. Ask for advice about monitoring theophylline levels in your blood.
Antibiotics—metronidazole (Flagyl, Femizole, others).	Alcohol (beer, wine, hard liquor).	Low blood pressure, vomiting, confusion; rapid heartbeat.	Don't combine these drugs with alcohol.
Antibiotics— quinolones, including ciprofloxacin (Cipro) and norfloxacin (Noroxin).	Iron—including supplements and iron-laden tonics.	The antibiotic may not be as effective if combined with iron.	Check with your doctor and pharmacist before combining this antibiotic with iron.
Antibiotics—tetracycline, quinolone antibiotics (Cipro, Noroxin, others).	Calcium (dairy products) and calcium found in antacids (Mylanta, Maalox, Tums, others).	Drastically reduced absorption of tetracycline or quinolones, lessening their effectiveness.	Wait two hours after eating dairy products to take medication. Do not take antacids with these medications without your doctor's approval, and then take the antacids only 6 hours before or 4 hours after taking the antibiotic.
Anticoagulants (oral)—including warfarin (Panwarfin, Coumadin, others), used to help prevent blood clots.	Aspirin.	Abnormal bleeding, particularly in stomach. Symptoms include black stools, blood in urine.	Avoid aspirin when taking oral anticoagulants unless told otherwise by doctor.
Anticoagulants— (oral)—including warfarin (Panwarfin, Coumadin, others).	Vitamin K–rich foods and drinks (broccoli, cabbage, green tea, lentils, soybeans, spinach, others).	Reduced effectiveness of anticoagulant.	Check with your doctor about combining drug with foods rich in vitamin K.

(continued)

Drug Combinations to Avoid *(continued)*

IF YOU'RE TAKING	DON'T MIX WITH	WHAT CAN HAPPEN	RECOMMENDATION
Antidepressants— selective serotonin re-uptake inhibitors, such as Fluoxetine (Prozac), sertraline (Zoloft), paroxetine (Paxil).	Monoamine oxidase (MAO) inhibitors (Marplan, Nardil, Parnate, others), used to treat depression.	Confusion, muscle twitches, sweating, shivering, agitation; in very rare cases, can be fatal.	Don't take these antidepressants with an MAO inhibitor, or for 2 weeks after discontinuing an MAO. Wait 5 weeks after going off these drugs to start an MAO.
Antidepressants— monoamine oxidase (MAO) inhibitors (Marplan, Nardil, Parnate, others).	Over-the-counter cold medicines, decongestants, or diet pills containing phenylpropanolamine (Allerest, Dexatrim, others); phenylephrine (Dristan Decongestant, others); and pseudoephedrine (Sudafed, others).	Rapid heartbeat; light-headedness; headache; sudden, dangerous elevation in blood pressure; could lead to a fatal stroke.	Don't take these cold medicines with an MAO inhibitor, or for 2 weeks after discontinuing an MAO.
Antidepressants— MAO inhibitors (Marplan, Nardil, Parnate, others).	Alcoholic drinks containing tyramine (including red wines). Also foods containing tyramine (aged cheeses; liver; yeast concentrates; broad beans; salted, smoked, or pickled fish; others).	Dramatic rise in blood pressure, dizziness, nausea; in rare cases, bleeding around brain and death.	Avoid alcoholic drinks and foods rich in tyramine if you're taking an MAO inhibitor.
Antidepressants— tricyclic medications (Elavil, Sinequan, others).	Antidepressants— MAO inhibitors (Marplan, Nardil, Parnate, others).	Confusion, fever, dizziness, seizures, overexcitement, coma.	These drugs should be combined only if specifically prescribed to be taken together.
Antihistamines— terfenadine (Seldane) and astemizole (Hismanal). Nonsedating antihistamines, used to treat allergies.	Antifungal drugs— ketoconazole (Nizoral) and itraconazole (Sporanox); and certain antibiotics—including erythromycin (EryPed, others).	Mixing these drugs can cause dangerous, possibly lethal changes in liver function. Symptoms include irregular heartbeat, chest pain, shortness of breath.	Don't combine these medications.
Calcium channel blockers—(Plendil, Procardia, Adalat, others). Used to treat high blood pressure and angina.	Grapefruit juice (contains flavonoids, including naringenin).	Possibly hazardous increase in the level of medication in blood. Symptoms include headaches and light-headedness.	Do not take these medications with grapefruit juice.
Gastrointestinal drugs—cimetidine (Tagamet), used to treat ulcers and heartburn.	Anticoagulants (oral)—including dicumarol and warfarin (Panwarfin, Coumadin, others).	Increased anticoagulant effect. Symptoms include coughing up or vomiting blood, black or bloody stools.	Don't combine these medications.

Drug Combinations to Avoid

IF YOU'RE TAKING	DON'T MIX WITH	WHAT CAN HAPPEN	RECOMMENDATION
Gastrointestinal drugs—cisapride (Propulsid).	Antifungal drugs—including miconazole (Monistat); and certain antibiotics, including erythromycin.	Irregular heartbeat, heart attack.	Don't combine these medications.
Heart medication—digoxin (Lanoxin).	Antacids (Mylanta, Maalox).	Decreased absorption of heart drug, reducing its effectiveness.	Don't combine these medications.
Heart medication—digoxin (Lanoxin).	Natural licorice (glycyrrhizin), found in some imported candy, cough drops, other products.	Irregular heartbeat; in rare cases, heart attack.	Don't combine products containing natural licorice with this drug.
Hormonal drugs—estrogen-containing oral contraceptives (Demulen, Ortho Novum, others).	Tobacco (smoking any brand of cigarettes).	Increased risk of stroke, heart attack, blood clots.	Never smoke if you take birth control pills.
Hormonal drugs—estrogen-containing oral contraceptives (Demulen, Ortho Novum, others).	Antibiotics (amoxicillin, ampicillin, oxacillin, penicillin, rifampin, tetracycline, others).	Rifampin can reduce effectiveness of oral contraceptives; other antibiotics may also increase risk of pregnancy.	Talk to your doctor about using a different form of birth control while on antibiotics.
Pain reliever—aspirin.	Alcohol (beer, wine, hard liquor).	Irritation of stomach lining; greater risk of ulcers and bleeding.	Consult your doctor about combining these drugs.
Pain relievers—acetaminophen (Tylenol, Panadol, others).	Alcohol (beer, wine, hard liquor).	Possibility of liver damage.	Consult your doctor about combining these drugs.
Pain relievers—ibuprofen (Advil, Motrin, others).	Alcohol (beer, wine, hard liquor).	Irritation of stomach lining; increased risk of stomach ulcers and bleeding.	Consult your doctor about combining these drugs.
Tranquilizers and sleeping pills—benzodiazepines, including diazepam (Valium), chlordiazepoxide (Librium), others.	Alcohol (beer, wine, hard liquor).	With excessive amounts, dizziness, severe drowsiness, impaired reactions (such as diminished driving skills), coma.	Don't combine these drugs with alcohol.

FOR MORE HELP

Organization: United States Pharmacopeia, 12601 Twinbrook Pkwy., Rockville, MD 20852. 301-881-0666, M–F 7:30–5. Call to order free booklets on understanding your medications, using medicines properly, recognizing drug tampering, and preventing medication errors.

Book: *The Customer's Guide to Drug Interactions,* by Jeffrey R. Schein and Philip Hansten, Pharm. D., Collier Books, 1993, $15.

Book: *The People's Guide to Deadly Drug Interactions,* by Joe Graedon and Teresa Graedon, Ph.D., St. Martin's Press, 1995, $25.95.

Staying Healthy

Index

◆

Please note: Page numbers in **bold** refer to the main discussion of the topic or to summary charts. Specific drug names mentioned in the text can be found under the heading *Drugs*.

Benign paroxysmal positional
vertigo, 55
Biceps muscle, color
illustration, 173
Bile, 119
Binge eating/purging
(bulimia), **200**
Bipolar affective disorder, 205
Birth control pills, 106, 110,
217, 228
Bites
animal, **19**
bee and wasp, **18**, **20**
mosquito, 56
scorpion, **44**
snake, **43**
spider, **44**
tick, **46**, 276
Black widow spider bite, **44**
Blackheads, 138
Blackouts, 206
Bladder
color illustration, 174
training, for children, 240
Bladder problems
cancer, 133
infection, 133, 134, **274**
loss of control, 136, 159,
182, 183
See also Urinary system
problems
Bleeding
causing shock, **18–19**
emergency care, **28**
excessive menstrual,
227–228
first aid for, **27**, **29**
from ear, **30**, 69, 70
gums, 76, 78, 81, 295
internal, **19**
into brain, 109, 110
nose, **40**, 106, 208
pressure points to stop, **28**
rectal, 112, 122, **128–129**
that won't stop, **28**
Blepharitis, 62
Blind spots, with fatigue,
generalized pain, 268
Blindness, sudden or
temporary, 61, 197
Blinking, infrequent, 57
Blisters, **141**, 154
blistering rash on hands,
feet, 242
fever blisters (cold sores), **79**
genital, 215
itchy spots that turn into,
242

on lips or mouth, 79, 242
penile, 224
rash of, on face, legs, arms,
242
shingles, **154**
weeping, with honey-
colored crust, 242, 252
Bloating, 112, 114, 115, 120, 126
premenstrual, 235
Blood clot
aspirin and, 110, 301
color illustration, 169
deep vein, 186
to brain, 109, 110
to lung, 83
Blood infection (septicemia),
54
Blood loss, severe, causing
shock, **18–19**
Blood poisoning, **29**, 265
Blood pressure
high. *See* High blood
pressure, 103, **105**
tests of, understanding the
numbers, 105, 304
Blood sugar
low (hypoglycemia), 55, 198
medications affecting, **269**
Bloodshot eyes. *See* Eye
problems
Bloody nose, **40**, 106, 208
Bloody stools, 112, 114, 122,
125, 130, 227, 264
Bluish fingernails, 87, 94
Bluish skin, 14, 41, 83, 94, 197,
265
Blurred vision, 54, 61, 62, 269
with sudden dizziness, 54
See also Vision problems
Boils, 70, **142**
Bone spurs, 158
color illustration, 163
Bones (skeletal system), color
illustration, 164, 165, 171,
172
Boredom, 212
Botulism, 35, 98, 129
Bowel movements
black, 264, 272
bloody, 112, 114, 122, 125,
130, 227, 264
bright red blood in, 122
changes in, 112
constipation. *See*
Constipation
diarrhea. *See* Diarrhea
hard, 115

home remedy for
stimulating, 116
increase in frequency of,
279
light or clay-colored stools,
266, 270
long, thin, "pencil," 112
loose, watery, 116, 117
painful, 122
rectal bleeding chart,
128–129
unusually fowl-smelling,
273
unusually thin, 114, 118
Brachial artery, color
illustration, 170
Brain, color illustration, 172
Brain diseases
Alzheimer's disease, **50**
encephalitis, **56**
hemorrhage, 51
meningitis, **56**
Parkinson's disease, **57**
tuberculosis, **100**
tumor, 50, 51, 54, 58
Breast
cancer, 231
changes in, with pregnancy,
231, 232
fibrocystic disease, 232
lumps or swelling, 232
nipple discharge, 231
pain or lumps chart,
231–232
self-exam, **233**, 304, 305
swelling, 235
Breastbone (sternum), color
illustration, 171
Breath, bad, **76**, 77, 80, 210
Breathing problems
allergies, **85**
anaphylactic shock, **18**, 83
asthma, 83, **86**
blood clot, 83
bronchial tubes, color
illustration, 168
bronchitis, **82**, 83, **88**
chart, **83–84**
colds, **90**
collapsed lung, 83
dry cough, 83, 84, 266
emergency care, **14–18**
emphysema, 83, 88
flu, 91
gasping for breath, 83
heart attack, **38**, 83
humidifiers and, **89**
lung cancer, 83, **93**

mucus-producing cough, 83
pleurisy, 84, 103
pneumonia, 83, **94**
rapid, shallow, 83, 197
rescue breathing techniques, **15–17**
shortness of breath, 83
sinusitis, **95**
tuberculosis, 83, **100**
wheezing, 83
with bloody mucus, phlegm, 83
with bluish skin, 83, 197
with crushing chest pain, 83
with drowsiness, confusion, 198
with fatigue, 83
with fever, 84
with headache, 84
with itching and hives, 83
with lack of appetite, 83
with loss of consciousness, 83
with confusion, 83, 197
with moist skin, cold hands, feet, 83
with nausea, 83
with panic, 83
with rapid pulse, 83
with sharp chest pain, 83, 84
with stomach cramps, 83
with sweating, nausea, 83
with swollen eyes, lips, tongue, 83
with tightening of chest or throat, 83
with vomiting, 83
with weakness, 84
with weight gain or loss, 272, 273
with weight loss, 83
See also Coughs; Lung problems
Bronchial tubes, color illustration, 168
Bronchitis
acute, **82**
chronic, 83, **88**
Brown recluse spider bite, **44**
Bruises, **35**
first aid for, **21**
Bruising, easy, 272
Bruxism (tooth grinding), 78, **81**
Bulge, in abdomen or groin, 123

Bulging eyes, 279
Bulimia, **200**, 273
Bull's-eye rash, 140, 276
Bunions, **177**, 192
Burns
blisters from, 142
chemical, **22**
emergency care, **22**
Burping. *See* Belching
Bursitis, 178, **179**, 191
Buttocks
acne on, 138
lumps, rashes, 140, 147, 158
pain, numbness, or tingling in, 182, 183, 187
Buzzing in ears, 68, 69, 70, 73
tinnitus, **74**

Caffeine
blood sugar and, 269
heart palpitations and, 102, **108**
pregnancy and, 234
tinnitus and, 75
withdrawal headache, 52
Calcium, 109
recommended dietary allowance, **288**
supplements, 188
Calcium channel blockers. *See* Drug combinations to avoid chart, **307–309**
Calf muscle, color illustration, 173
Calluses, **143**
Calories
burned, during daily activities, **283**
healthy meals and, 286–288
Cancer
bladder, 133
breast, 231
cervical, 215
colon, **112**
esophagus, 98
kidney, 133
lung, 83, **93**
oral, 77, 79, 98
penile, 215
pneumonia and, 94
prostate, 222, 305

rectal, **112**
skin, **155**
color illustration, 166–167
stomach, 98
testicular, 221
throat, 71
weight loss and, 273
Cancer prevention
breast, 233
cervical, 305
colon, 112, 304
general, 282–295
lung, 93, 210
prostate, 222
skin, 155, 304
testicular, 304
See also Health and fitness basics
Canker sores, **78**
Cannabis, 209
Carbon monoxide poisoning, 197
Carcinoma
basal cell, **155**, 167
of skin, color illustration, 167
squamous cell, **155**, 167
Cardiac arrest, emergency care, **14–17**
Cardiopulmonary resuscitation (CPR)
for adults, **14–15**
for children ages one to eight, **17**
for infants up to age one, **16**
Carotid artery, color illustration, 170
Carpal tunnel syndrome (CTS), **180**
Carpals (wrist bones), color illustration, 171
Cartilage, color illustration, 163
Cataracts, **60**, 62
surgery, color illustration, 161
Cavities (dental). *See* Dental care; Mouth and tooth problems
Cerebellum, color illustration, 172
Cerebral embolism, 110
Cerebral hemorrhage, 110
Cerebral thrombosis, 109
Cerebrum, color illustration, 172

Index

Disciplining children,
guidelines for, 262–263
Disk (spinal) problems
bulging disk, color
illustration, 162
color illustration, 162
neck pain and, **159**
protruded, 183, 187
torn disk, color illustration,
162
See also Spine
Disks, spinal. *See* Disk (spinal)
problems
Dislocations, 178
emergency care, **35**
Diverticulitis, 114, **118**, 128
Dizziness, **68**, 109, 139, 202
after head injury, 54, 55
chart, **54–55**
premenstrual, 235
sudden, severe, with loss of
balance or hearing, 55
sudden, with headache,
weakness, or numbness,
54
with cramps; cool, clammy
skin, 54
with double vision, 51
with ear or hearing
problems, 55, 69, 70
with fatigue, weakness or
numbness on one side,
54
with fever over 104, no
sweating, 54
with fever, rash, 236
with headache, 51, 54, 55
with hunger, shakiness,
confusion, 198
with intense hunger,
shaking, irritability,
anxiety, 55
with loss of balance, 55
with memory loss, 51
with moving of head,
nausea and vomiting, 55
with neck pain and
stiffness, 55
with pasty skin, fainting,
264
with personality changes, 51
with sudden, temporary
confusion, 197
with vomiting, sudden high
fever, 54

with weakness, fatigue, pale
skin, shortness of
breath, 55
Doctor visits
communication during,
296–297
getting ready for, 299–300
information resources, 300
Dog bite, emergency care, **19**
Double vision, **61**, **62**, 198, 202
with dizziness, headache,
seizures, confusion,
memory loss, 54
with headache upon
waking, 51
with sudden, temporary
confusion, 197
See also Vision problems
Dowager's hump, 165, 188
color illustration, 165
Drinking problem, **196**, 206,
212
Drowning, emergency care, **30**
Drowsiness, **41**, 198, 265
daytime, 277
Drug abuse, **206**
street drugs chart, **208–209**
Drug allergies, 85
emergency care, **18**
See also Drug combinations
to avoid chart, **307–309**
Drug combinations to avoid
chart, **307–309**
Drug cravings, 206
Drugs
acetaminophen, **301**
aspirin, **301**
benzoyl peroxide, 138
capsaicin cream, 154, 160
corticosteroids, 60, 87, 138,
142, 272
cortisone, 142
DES, 238
diethylstilbestrol, 238
ephedrine, 269
epinephrine, 18, 269
generic, 59
hydrocortisone cream, 145,
146
ibuprofen, **301**
iron supplements, 264
levodopa, 57
lindane, 152
lithium, 138
methotrexate, 153
methylphenidate, 204
methylsalicylate, 160

phenylephrine, 269
phenylpropanolamine, 85
pseudoephedrine, 85
pyrethrin shampoos, 151
quinine, 75
Ritalin, 204
salicylic acid, 138, 157
selegiline, 57
street, 206, 208–209
See also Drug combinations
to avoid chart, **307–309**;
Medications
Dry cough. *See* Coughs
Dry mouth, 51, 78
DTP vaccine, **244**
Ductus epididymis, color
illustration, 175
Ductus (vas) deferens, color
illustration, 175
Duodenum, color illustration,
174
Dust mite allergies, 85, 86
Dysentery, 114, 128
Dysthymia, 205

Ear, illustration of, 72
Ear and hearing problems
age-related hearing loss, 70
airplane ears, **68**
background noise
problems, 70, 74
benign paroxysmal
positional vertigo, 55
bleeding from ear, **30**, 69, 70
blocked or full feeling in
ear, 55
caused by drug side effects,
75
chart, **69–71**
difficulty understanding
speech, 70
earache, pain. *See* Earache
eardrum rupture, **30**, 69, 75
earwax buildup, 70, **73**, 74,
75
emergency care, **30**
flaky skin around ear, 70
foreign object/insect in ear,
30
from throat cancer, 71
from tonsillitis, 71

Index

in blisters, 141
in ear, 70
in eye, 62
in groin area, 147
penis, 215
rashes chart
adults, **139–140**
children, **241–243**
rectal, 122
rectal (chart), **128–129**
skin, 146
vaginal, 215, 237
with blisters, 252
with dry, red, thickened
patches of skin, 144
with raised, red or pink
swellings on skin, 149
with red bumps, cough,
fever, sore throat, 84
with urination, 216
with worsening at night,
140, 150
See also Rashes
IUD (intrauterine device),
218, 228

Jaundice, 119, 120, 266, 270
Jaw pain, 77, 95, 100
temporomandibular
disorder (TMD), 52, 70,
81, **193**
tooth abscess and, 80
tooth grinding and, 78, 81
with earache, 70, 193
with stiffness, fever, muscle
spasms, difficulty
swallowing, 265
Jet lag, **278**
Jock itch (tinea cruris), 147
Joint, color illustration, 163
Joint pain, 158, 179, 274, 277
after tick bite, 276
with butterfly-shaped rash
across nose, cheeks, 139,
275
with swelling, redness, 158
without redness or swelling,
268
worsened with movement,
158

Joint problems
arthritis, **158**
color illustration, 163
infection, **274**
swelling, 158, 178, 179, 182,
189, 191, 194
Jugular vein, color
illustration, 170
Jumper's knee, 191

Kegel exercises, 220
Kidney disease, 97, 100, 105,
198, 272
cancer, 133
illustration, 134
stones, 113, **132**, 133
See also Urinary system
problems
Kidneys, color illustration, 174
Knee
dry, scaly skin on, 242
illustration, 190
kneecap (patella), color
illustration, 171
Knee pain
chart, **191**
severe, sudden, with joint
swelling, 158
Kneecap (patella), color
illustration, 171

Labyrynthitis, 55, 69
Lactose intolerance, 114
Large intestine, color
illustration, 174
Laryngitis, 84, 98
Larynx, color illustration, 172
Larynx infections
epiglottitis, 97
laryngitis, 84, 98
Latex allergies, 218
Latissimus dorsi muscle, color
illustration, 173
Lead poisoning, **253**
Legs
abrupt weakness or
numbness in, 45

bone, color illustration, 165
fractures, emergency care,
36
narrowed arteries in, 107
pain chart, **186–187**
sudden, sharp pains in,
when resting, 107
swollen, 111
varicose veins, 111
See also Back problems
Lens of eye, color illustration,
161
Lethargy, 206, 208, 209, 279
Leukemia, childhood, 241
Levadopa, 57
Lice, 140, **150**
Life extension activity. *See*
Health and fitness basics
Lifestyle, healthy, basic steps
of, 282–295
Ligament sprain or rupture,
191
Light sensitivity, 60, 61, 254,
265, 268, 276
with headache, 51, 52, 56,
159
Lightheadedness. *See*
Dizziness
Lindane, in lice/scabies
treatments, 152
Lips
bluish, 94
canker sores, **78**
cold sores, **79**
swelling on, 149
Liver, color illustration, 174
Liver disease, 198
cirrhosis, 272
hepatitis, 266, **270**
Lockjaw (tetanus), 265
vaccine, **244**, 305
Longevity. *See* Health and
fitness basics
Loose bodies, color
illustration, 163
Loss of appetite. *See* Appetite
loss
Loss of balance, 208
with ear or hearing
problems, 69
with sore mouth and
tongue, 264
with sudden, severe
dizziness, 55

Index

Index

Sores
    canker, **78**
    cold (fever blisters), **79**
    genital, 215, 216
    purple, 214, 273
    that won't heal, 155
    varicose veins, **111**
Spastic colon, **126**
Speech problems, 208, 209
    abrupt difficulty speaking
        or understanding, 45
    slurred, 197
    with hearing loss, 70
    with sudden dizziness, 54
    with sudden, severe
        headache, 51
    with sudden, temporary
        confusion, 197
Speed, 208
Spermicide, **218**
Sphenoidal sinus, color
    illustration, 172
Sphincter muscle tears, 128,
    129
Spider bite, emergency care,
    44
Spider veins, 111
Spinal cord
    color illustration, 162
    injury, 159
Spine
    color illustrations, 162,
        164–165, 171, 172
    curve of, illustration, 184
    nerves in, color illustration,
        162
    spinal cord injury, 159
    stenosis of, 183
    tumors of, 183
    See also Back problems;
        Disk (spinal) problems
Spleen, color illustration, 174
Splints, emergency, **36**
Spondylitis, ankylosing, 183
Spondylosis, cervical, 159, 178
Sprains, **44**, 183
    knee, **191**
    leg, **186**
Squamous cell carcinoma, **155**
    color illustration, 167
Squamous cells, skin, color
    illustration, 166
Starvation, self (anorexia
    nervosa), **200**
Stasis dermatitis, **144**
Stenosis, spinal, 183
Sterility, 215

Sterilization, tubal, **218**
Sternum (breastbone), color
    illustration, 171
Stiffness in the morning, 158
Stings. *See* Insect bites and
    stings
Stomach, color illustration, 174
Stomach medicines. *See* Drug
    combinations to avoid
    chart, **307–309**
Stomach problems
    abdominal pain chart,
        113–114
    cancer, 98
    food allergies, 85
    heartburn, 98, 104, **121**
    inflammation, **130**
    reflux, 104, **121**
    stomach flu, 113, 127, 130
    ulcer, 104, 113, 114, **130**
    See also Digestive system
        problems
Stools. *See* Bowel movements
Strains, **44**, 160, 179, 183
    back, 183
    leg, 186
Strangulated hernia, 128
Street drugs chart, **208–209**
Strep throat, 97, **258**
    See also Scarlet fever, 241,
        258, 266
Stress, **212**
    how to reduce, 293, 295
    rating your level of,
        292–293
Stress incontinence, **136**
Stroke, 54, 61, **109**
    cerebral hemorrhage and,
        110
    emergency care, **45**
    headache and, 51
    heat. *See* Heat stroke
    phenylpropanolamine
        and, 85
Styes, 62, **66**
Subconjunctival hemorrhage,
    62
Subdural hematoma, 54
Subdural hemorrhage, 54
Sudden sleep, daytime, **277**
Suicidal thoughts, 205
Sun sensitivity, resulting in
    rash, 275
Sunburn, **45**, 155
    rash that resembles, 236
Sunglasses, 60, 63
Sunscreen, 156, **290**

Swallowing difficulty, 77, 98, **98**
    with stiff jaw, fever, muscle
        spasms, 265
Sweat glands, color
    illustration, 166
Sweating, 202, 274
    excessive, 226, 273, 279
    excessive, with cramps,
        dizziness, 54
    in children, 248
    lack of, with fever over 104,
        hot, dry skin, 54
    night, 101, 214, 226, 266,
        273
    with confusion, anxiety,
        dizziness, 198
    with fever and stiff jaw, 265
Swelling
    leg, 186
    neck, 159, 255, 256, 258,
        272, 273, 274, 278, 279
    of face, ankles, with no
        urine passing, 133
    of joints, 158, 178, 179, 182,
        189, 191, 194
    shoulder, 178
Swimmer's ear, 70, **73**
Swollen lymph nodes. *See*
    Lymph nodes
Syndromes
    carpal tunnel, **180**
    chronic fatigue, **267**
    Cushing's, 272
    irritable bowel, 114, **126**
    Ménière's, 55, 69, 75
    premenstrual, 232, **235**
    Reye's, **92**
    toxic shock, 54, 139, 198,
        236, 265
Synovial fluid, color
    illustration, 163
Syphilis, 216
Systolic blood pressure, 105

Tailbone (coccyx), color
    illustration, 171
Talking excessively, 203, 208
Tar shampoo, 145
Tarsals (ankle bones), color
    illustration, 171
Taste, unpleasant, in mouth,
    76, 77, 78, 80

Index

Uric acid, 158
Urinary bladder, color
  illustration, 174
Urinary problems, dark urine,
  270
Urinary system problems
  bladder infection (cystitis),
    133, **134**
  blood in urine, 133, 222,
    227, 274
  burning feeling with
    urination, 215, 230
  chart, **133**
  cloudy urine, 113, 132
  dark urine, 117, 132
  frequent urge to urinate,
    133, 222
  frequent urination,
    excessive thirst, 133
  incontinence, **136**, 222
  interruption of stream
    during urination, 132
  kidney stones, 113, **132**, 134
  painful urination, **134**
  passing no or little urine,
    133
  urinary tract infection, **134**,
    136
  weight gain, and swelling of
    ankles and face, 133
  See also Kidney disease
Urination
  burning feeling with, 216,
    274
  dark urine, 266, 272, 275
  frequent, 102, 113, 222,
    223, 227, 228, 230, 267,
    272, 273, 274
  itchiness with, 216
  painful, 113, **134**, 216, 222,
    274
  weak stream, dribbling,
    222, **223**
  with vaginal itching, 236
Uterine fibroid tumors, 228
Uterus, color illustration, 175
Uveitis/iritis, 61

Vaccinations. *See*
  Immunizations
Vagina
  burning feeling with
    urination, 215
  burning or irritation, 237
  color illustration, 175
  fishy odor, with discharge,
    237
  foul odor from, 216, 227
  foul-smelling discharge
    from, 227, 230
  greenish, yellow or gray
    discharge, 216
  red, flat, itchy bumps, 215
  thick, yellowish discharge,
    216
  watery, grayish white or
    yellow discharge, 237
  white, cheesy, odorless
    discharge, 237
Vaginal problems, 133, **237**
  vaginosis, 237
  with menstruation, 227
Vaporizers
  for bronchitis, 82
  for sore throat, 97
  See also Humidifiers
Varicella zoster virus vaccine,
  244
Varicocele, 221
Varicose veins, **111**, 187
Vascular disease, peripheral,
  107
Vasectomy, **218**
Vegetables, ten most
  nutritious, **288**
Veins
  deep-vein thrombosis, 186
  itching around, 111
  swollen, blue or purple, 111
  varicose, **111**, 187
Vena cava, color illustration,
  170
Vertebra in spine, color
  illustration, 162
Vertigo, 55
Violent or aggressive feelings,
  behavior, 202, 208
Viral infections, **274**
Vision problems
  blind spots, temporary, 268
  blindness (sudden), 61, 197

blurred vision, 54, 61, 62,
  269
chart, **61–62**
dark, empty area in visual
  field, 61
dimmed, distorted vision,
  61
double vision, 51, 54, 61, 62,
  197, 198, 202
flashes of light, 61
floating dark shapes, 61
halos around lights, 61, 65
hazy vision, 60, 62
light sensitivity, 51, 52, 56,
  60, 61, 159, 254, 265,
  268, 276
peripheral vision loss, 61
rainbow halos around
  lights, 65
straight lines look wavy, 61
sudden changes in, 61
sudden loss of, often in one
  eye, 45
teary, aching, 61
triple vision, 60
white area in pupil, 62
with eye pain, 51, 52, 61, 62
with eye redness, 61
with headache, 51, 52, 61,
  62
with nausea and vomiting,
  61
See also Eye problems
Vitamins
  B12 deficiency anemia, **264**
  recommended dietary
    allowance, **288**
  vitamin C, 90
Vocal cords
  color illustration, 172
  strained, 84
Voice box infection. *See*
  Laryngitis, 84, 98
Vomiting and nausea, **127**
  blood in vomit, 272
  with confusion, fever, 198
  with dizziness, 54, 55
  with ear and hearing
    problems, 69
  with headache, 51, 52
  with menstruation, 227
  with rash, 236
  with red rash, fever, 265
Vulva, color illustration, 175
VZV (varicella zoster virus)
  vaccine, **244**

Index

The Self-Care Advisor

Editor
John Poppy

Art Director
Charli Ornett

Managing Editor
Karin Evans

Senior Editors
Diana Hembree, Eric Olsen,
Colleen Paretty

Consulting Editor
Susan West

Administrative Editor
Cassandra Wrightson

Writers
Barbara Boughton, Jeanie
Puleston Fleming, Sarah Henry,
Peter Jaret, Katherine Kam,
Susan LaCroix, Lisa Margonelli,
Constance Matthiessen,
Clark Norton, Mary Purpura,
Laurie Udesky, Rob Waters

Copy Editors
Antonia Moore, Catharine
Norton, O'Brien Young

Researchers
Laird Harrison, Carol Levine,
Joy Rothke, Jessica Shattuck

Indexer
Karen Hollister

Associate Art Director
Kimberle Nogay

Designers
Cici Kinsman, Marsha Levine,
Mario Reyes, Emma Rybakova,
Glen Shannon, Jerald Volpe

Photo Editor
Mary Schoenthaler

Production Director
Linda K. Smith

Production Coordinator
Michael A. Nealy

Medical Illustration

Many of the color images on pages 161–176 are taken from 3-D digital computer
animation and graphics in the Time Life Medical *At Time of Diagnosis* video programs.

Executive Art Director
Jane Hurd

Art Director
Neil Lavey

Illustrators
Donna DeSmet, Brian Evans,
Maura Flynn, Craig Foster,
Neil Hardy, Rong-Zeng Li

Graphics Producers
Matthew Canton, Amy Lisewski

Graphics Coordinator
Kristin Ellington

Senior 3-D Artist
Jay Nilsen

3-D Artists
Jose Cepeda, T. Gates Councilor,
Michael Gay, Jeff Hoppler,
Kattie Konno, Craig J. Kovacs,
Grant Niesner, Bhavesh Patel,
Rudy Poot, Eric Ryder, Ying Tan

3-D Design Consultant
Rena Debortoli

Produced in association with
Sonalysts Studios
Waterford, Connecticut

Black-and-White Illustration

Neil Hardy: pages 65, 72, 119, 124, 134, 184, 190, 193.
Jeffrey Smith: pages 15, 16, 17, 25, 26, 27, 28, 33, 36, 96, 181, 233.

Color Photographs, page 167: Moles A, B, and D: Custom Medical Stock Photo. Mole C: Biophoto Associates/Photo Researchers, Inc.

Cover Photographs: Father and daughter: Janeart/Image Bank. Couple: Anthony Edgeworth/Stock Market. Mother and son: Mugshots/Stock Market. Apple: Karen Capucilli. Child: Stephanie Rausser. Family: Brian Smith. Hands: Paul Clancy/Graphistock. Laughing woman: Michael Johnson. Runner: Michael Kevin Daly. Swimmer: Michael Douglas/The Image Works.

Time Inc Health

President and CEO
Eric W. Schrier

General Manager
Martha Lorini

Editor
Barbara Paulsen

Executive Editor
Sheridan Warrick

Time-Life Books

**President and CEO,
Time Life Inc.**
George Artandi

President, Time-Life Books
John D. Hall

Project Editor
Time-Life Medical Advisor
Robert Somerville

Administrative Editor
Time-Life Medical Advisor
Judith W. Shanks

Time Life Medical
Patient Education Media, Inc.

President and CEO
J. Keith Green

Medical Director
C. Everett Koop, M.D.

Deputy Medical Director
Florence Comite, M.D.

**President and COO,
Consumer Products Division**
James B. Arnold

**Vice President,
Product Development**
Nan-Kirsten Weinstock Forté

Time Life Medical is a trademark of Time Warner Inc. *At Time of Diagnosis* and *Because no prescription is more valuable than knowledge* are trademarks of Patient Education Media, Inc. All rights reserved.

Acknowledgments

This book would not be as helpful and accurate as it is without the assistance of health professionals in every part of the United States—men and women who answered hundreds of questions, offered guidance and resources, and repeatedly displayed their commitment to improving information about health care. We owe them our sincerest thanks.

Emergency & First Aid

Sheldon Clark, M.D.
R. Scott Jacobs, M.D.

Head & Nervous System

Seymour Diamond, M.D.
Robert G. Feldman, M.D.
R. Michael Gallagher, D.O.
Howard Gruetzner, M.Ed.
W. Michael Scheld, M.D.
Mark Spitz, M.D.
Cathi Thomas, R.N., M.S.

Eyes

Ronald M. Burde, M.D.
Monica L. Monica, M.D., Ph.D.

Ears

Richard Goode, M.D.
Michael Seidman, M.D.

Mouth

Bruce Bagley, M.D.
Donald Collins, D.D.S., M.P.H.
Jon Richter, D.M.D., Ph.D.
Thomas Weida, M.D.

Nose, Throat, Lungs, & Chest

Stephen Astor, M.D.
Robert Breiman, M.D.
James Cook, M.D.
Donald Donovan, M.D.
Dominick Iacuzio, Ph.D.
Clayton Kersting, M.D.
Barry Make, M.D.
Harold Nelson, M.D.
Carol Reid, M.D.
Nathan Schultz, M.D.

Heart & Circulation

Rodman D. Starke, M.D.
Katharine Weiser, M.D.

Stomach, Abdomen, & Digestive System

Quan-Yang Duh, M.D.
Johannes Koch, M.D.
Peter McNally, D.O.
Stephen Pardys, M.D.
Theodore R. Schrock, M.D.
Marvin Schuster, M.D.

Skin, Scalp, & Nails

Deborah Allen, M.D.
William Epstein, M.D.
Glenn B. Gastwirth, D.P.M.
Robert Jackson, M.D.
Mark Lebwohl, M.D.
Jerome Z. Litt, M.D.
Alan R. Shalita, M.D.
Stephen Tyring, M.D., Ph.D.

Muscles, Bones, & Joints

Daniel Benson, M.D.
Stanley Bigos, M.D.
Doyt Conn, M.D.
Scott Dye, M.D.
James Garrick, M.D.
David Kell, M.D.
Nancy Liu, M.D.
John Rugh, Ph.D.
Cody Wasner, M.D.

Behavior & Emotions

Robert Bailey, M.D.
Herbert Freudenberger, Ph.D.
Nancy Kennedy, Dr. P.H.
Vivian Hanson Meehan, R.N., B.A., D.Sc.
Robert Sapolsky, Ph.D.
Rick Seymour, M.A.
Joe Takamine, M.D.
Scott Thomas, Ph.D.

Sexual, Men's, & Women's Health

Stanley Althof, Ph.D.
Sondra Lynne Carter, M.D.
Stuart Howards, M.D.
Tom F. Lue, M.D.
Joseph E. Oesterling, M.D.
Michael Spence, M.D., M.P.H.
Paul Stumpf, M.D.

Children's Health

David Batts
Armando Correa, M.D.
Robert Prentice, M.D.
S. Norman Sherry, M.D.
Donald Shifrin, M.D.

General Problems

Grover Bagby, Jr., M.D.
Kathleen Bliese, M.D.
Alan Blum, M.D.
Robert Katz, M.D.
Rick Kellerman, M.D.
Emmanuel Mignot, M.D., Ph.D.

Helping Your Doctor Help You

Pamela Stitzlein Davies, R.N., M.S.
Rachel Naomi Remen, M.D.
John Stoeckle, M.D.
David Stutz, M.D.
Mary Wade

Your Personal Health Record

Bruce Gollub, M.D.
Stirling Puck, M.D.
Robert Rakel, M.D.
Ssu Weng, M.D.

Medicines: Playing It Safe

Ron Finley, R.Ph.
Frederic J. Zucchero, M.A., R.Ph.

◆

If I'd known I was going to live this long,
I'd have taken better care of myself.

~James Herbert (Eubie) Blake, age 100